THE ARCHITECTURE OF FUNDAMENTAL RIGHTS IN THE EUROPEAN UNION

This book analyses the new architecture for the protection of fundamental rights in the European Union after the entry into force of the Lisbon Treaty. As a starting point, it identifies how the EU has gained a prominent role in promoting and protecting fundamental rights at European level despite the absence of an unlimited mandate to address fundamental rights violations. This new setting affects the traditional relationship between the EU, the ECHR system and the Member States and, in the absence of EU accession to the ECHR, enhances the risk of tensions and conflicts between the case law of the CJEU and the ECtHR. Examples of these tensions and conflicts are explored in the Area of Freedom, Security and Justice, which is one of the most fundamental rights-sensitive areas of EU law and one of the busiest areas of activity for the CJEU. The book offers new insights into existing rules on the resolution of conflicts between EU and ECHR law before mapping out techniques actually used by domestic courts to avoid or address such conflicts.

Volume 107 in the Series Modern Studies in European Law

Modern Studies in European Law
Recent titles in this series:

Critical Reflections on Constitutional Democracy in the European Union
Edited by Sacha Garben and Inge Govaere

Constitutional Law of the EU's Common Foreign and Security Policy: Competence and Institutions in External Relations
Graham Butler

The Juridification of Individual Sanctions and the Politics of EU Law
Eva Nanopoulos

Sixty Years of European Integration and Global Power Shifts: Perceptions, Interactions and Lessons
Edited by Julien Chaisse

Fundamental Rights and Mutual Recognition in the Area of Freedom, Security and Justice: A Role for Proportionality?
Ermioni Xanthopoulou

Law and Judicial Dialogue on the Return of Irregular Migrants from the European Union
Edited by Madalina Moraru, Galina Cornelisse and Philippe De Bruycker

Framing Convergence with the Global Legal Order: The EU and the World
Edited by Elaine Fahey

EU Citizenship at the Edges of Freedom of Movement
Katarina Hyltén-Cavallius

The Internal Market 2.0
Edited by Sacha Garben and Inge Govaere

New Directions in European Private Law
Edited by Mateja Durovic and Takis Tridimas

Standing to Enforce European Union Law before National Courts
Hilde Ellingsen

The Relative Authority of Judicial and Extra-Judicial Review: The EU Courts, the Boards of Appeal and the Ombudsman
Michal Krajewski

Responsive Human Rights: Vulnerability and the ECtHR
Corina Heri

For the complete list of titles in this series, see
www.bloomsbury.com/uk/series/modern-studies-in-european-law/

The Architecture of Fundamental Rights in the European Union

Šejla Imamović

•HART•
OXFORD • LONDON • NEW YORK • NEW DELHI • SYDNEY

HART PUBLISHING

Bloomsbury Publishing Plc

Kemp House, Chawley Park, Cumnor Hill, Oxford, OX2 9PH, UK

1385 Broadway, New York, NY 10018, USA

29 Earlsfort Terrace, Dublin 2, Ireland

HART PUBLISHING, the Hart/Stag logo, BLOOMSBURY and the Diana logo are trademarks of Bloomsbury Publishing Plc

First published in Great Britain 2022

A catalogue record for this book is available from the British Library.

Library of Congress Cataloging-in-Publication data

Names: Imamović, Šejla, author.

Title: The architecture of fundamental rights in the European Union / Šejla Imamović.

Description: Oxford ; New York : Hart, 2021. | Series: Modern studies in European Law ; volume 107 | Based on author's thesis (doctoral - Universiteit Maastricht, 2018) issued under title: Resolving conflicts in European fundamental rights protection : national and European courts' perspectives. | Includes bibliographical references and index.

Identifiers: LCCN 2021042173 (print) | LCCN 2021042174 (ebook) | ISBN 9781509940585 (hardback) | ISBN 9781509955503 (paperback) | ISBN 9781509940608 (pdf) | ISBN 9781509940592 (Epub)

Subjects: LCSH: Civil rights—European Union countries.

Classification: LCC KJE5132 .I43 2021 (print) | LCC KJE5132 (ebook) | DDC 341.4/8094—dc23/eng/20211005

LC record available at https://lccn.loc.gov/2021042173

LC ebook record available at https://lccn.loc.gov/2021042174

ISBN: HB: 978-1-50994-058-5
ePDF: 978-1-50994-060-8
ePub: 978-1-50994-059-2

Typeset by Compuscript Ltd, Shannon
www.bloomsbury.com

To find out more about our authors and books visit www.hartpublishing.co.uk. Here you will find extracts, author information, details of forthcoming events and the option to sign up for our newsletters.

FOREWORD

GRÁINNE DE BÚRCA

This book deals with a number of intersecting topics of European and EU law which are of perennial interest. The first is the complex multilevel system of human rights law in the EU, and the second is the relationship between national courts, the European Court of Justice and the European Court of Human Rights.

The book combines these subjects by examining the legal situation in which Member State courts are placed when they are faced with conflicting rulings of the Court of Justice and the Court of Human Rights on the same set of issues, often in the fields of asylum and criminal law. Whereas in earlier times, the risk of conflicting rulings by the two European courts on specific human rights used to be mainly a hypothetical posed by scholars, and an unlikely occurrence in practice given the primary focus of the CJEU on market integration while the ECtHR dealt with human rights, that position has changed significantly over the past decade or more. This is partly due to the legal status of the EU Charter of Fundamental Rights since the Lisbon Treaty, but also due to the ever- widening fields of application of EU law, and particularly to the ways in which the basic rights of individuals are affected by measures adopted within the EU's Area of Freedom Security and Justice and other policy fields. National courts are not infrequently called on to decide on a trans- border custody dispute, or on whether a suspect should be surrendered under a European arrest warrant, or an asylum seeker returned to another member state, and in such cases there are provisions of EU law, including the Charter of Fundamental Rights, as well as provisions of the ECHR which are highly relevant.

The author examines a selection of national court cases in which domestic courts had to decide how to proceed in the face of apparently different rulings on the same issue from the two European courts. She describes a range of different approaches or solutions that national courts have tended to adopt, and suggests that the preferred approach in a situation of conflict is for the national court to make a reference to the Luxembourg court for a ruling on the issue, and to engage actively with the CJEU as to how the provision in question should be interpreted. The book contains discussion of the problem of 'international treaty conflicts' for national courts more generally, and describes the approach of various European constitutional systems, but gives particular attention to the difficulty for national courts of an apparent conflict between what EU law would prescribe and what the ECHR would require. The author examines the problem from the perspective of each of four systems: national law, EU law, the ECHR, and finally international law. She concludes that insofar as there is a conflict over a specific right that cannot be 'harmoniously interpreted' as between EHCR and EU law in accordance with Article 52(3) of the EU Charter, the provision of the ECHR and the interpretation of the European Court of Human Rights should prevail over EU law where it gives stronger protection to the right in question.

This book is a clear and lucid account of the complex relationships between three legal orders in Europe from the perspective of national, EU, ECHR and international law, and provides interesting illustrations of the dilemmas facing national courts when there are conflicts between these three, as well as suggesting the best approach to the dilemma from the author's perspective. It should be of real interest to students, scholars and teachers of EU and European human rights law.

ACKNOWLEDGEMENTS

This book is founded on my doctoral thesis defended a few years ago at Maastricht University. I was blessed with brilliant supervisors, Professor Monica Claes and Professor Petra Foubert, whose commitment and unwavering support have been invaluable. I am deeply grateful for their mentorship in the context of this project and beyond.

I am also greatly indebted to Professor Bruno de Witte, for generously sharing his knowledge with me throughout this project and acting as my advisor during my research stay at EUI in Florence. I feel very fortunate to have had the opportunity to work with him and his impact on my work is reflected in different chapters of this book.

In addition, this book has benefited immensely from comments from Professor Elise Muir, Professor Leonard Besselink, Professor Aida Torres Pérez, Professor Aalt Willem Heringa, Professor Janneke Gerards, Professor Jan Theunis, Professor Anne Pieter van der Mei, and Professor Gráinne de Búrca. Their work continues to be a great source of inspiration.

I owe special thanks to my friends and colleagues, for always being ready to share their thoughts on issues I struggled with during my research. Among many, I wish to thank Maja Brkan, Vigjilenca Abazi, Matteo Bonelli, Pauline Melin, Kim Berg, Marie-Therese Gold, Jana Trifunović, Thu Nguyen, Petra Gyöngyi, Karolina Podstawa, Sarah Schoenmaekers, Natassa Athanasiadou, Elin Börjedal, Annalisa Volpato, Mariolina Eliantonio, Giulia Gentile, Jasper Krommendijk, Laura de Deyne, Caroline Habets, Yelena Gordeeva, Sead Kadić and Maria Fanou. I am also thankful to my students for our nice discussions on different aspects of this book.

Warm thanks are also due to Hart Publishing, for the excellent support and for making this publication possible.

Last but not least, I am grateful to my family for their support and encouragement throughout this journey and to my husband and best friend, Denis, for always being there.

Maastricht, August 2021

CONTENTS

Foreword v
Acknowledgements vii
Table of Cases xiii
Table of Legislation xxi
Table of Institutional Documents xxiii

Introduction **1**
I. Aims and Scope of this Book 1
II. Structure and Outline of Chapters 8

PART I
THE NEW EUROPEAN FUNDAMENTAL
RIGHTS ARCHITECTURE

1. The Development of EU Fundamental Rights Law **15**
I. Introduction 15
II. The Creation of the European Community and the Silence on Human Rights 16
III. Fundamental Rights as General Principles of EU Law 19
IV. Fundamental Rights Protection in Post-Lisbon Europe 23
V. Some Reflections on the Role and Place of Fundamental Rights in EU Law 39
VI. Conclusion 43

2. A European Web of Human Rights Regimes: The EU, the ECHR and the National Legal Systems **45**
I. Introduction 45
II. EU Law, the ECHR and the Strasbourg Court 46
III. EU Law, the ECHR and the Luxembourg Court 56
IV. Recent Developments in the Relationship between the Strasbourg and Luxembourg Courts 63
V. EU Law, the ECHR and National Courts 74
VI. Conclusion 87

PART II
CONVERGENCE AND CONFLICTS IN EUROPEAN FUNDAMENTAL RIGHTS STANDARDS

3. Case Study I: The Dublin System ... 91
I. Introduction ... 91
II. Mutual Trust and Recognition in the AFSJ ... 93
III. The Dublin System ... 95
IV. The Evolving Case Law on Dublin Transfers – A Retrospective Outlook ... 98
V. The Systemic Deficiencies Criteria and the Limits to Mutual Trust ... 107
VI. Conclusion ... 110

4. Case Study II: The European Arrest Warrant ... 112
I. Introduction ... 112
II. European Arrest Warrant ... 113
III. Validity Challenge *in Abstracto* ... 117
IV. The Fundamental Rights/Mutual Trust Nexus ... 119
V. The Aftermath of *Aranyosi and Căldăraru* ... 127
VI. The EAW and Independence of the Judiciary ... 130
VII. Execution of the EAW and Compliance with Fundamental Rights – in Search of Guidelines for National Courts ... 135
VIII. Conclusion ... 138

PART III
TOWARDS NORMATIVE CONSISTENCY IN EUROPEAN FUNDAMENTAL RIGHTS LAW

5. Conflict Rules in National, European and International Law ... 143
I. Introduction ... 143
II. Defining Treaty Conflict ... 144
III. National Law and National Constitutions ... 145
IV. Conflict Clauses in the Treaties ... 153
V. Conflict Rules in International Law ... 161
VI. Conclusion ... 172

6. Scenarios from the Member States ... 175
I. Introduction ... 175
II. Conform Interpretation ... 176
III. Giving Priority to the ECHR ... 179
IV. Reframing the Conflict ... 183

V. The Preliminary Reference Procedure 190
VI. National Courts' Approaches to Conflicts between EU and ECHR Law – An Overall Assessment and Conclusions 194

Conclusion 198

Bibliography 204
Index 219

TABLE OF CASES

Court of Justice of the European Union

Case C-1/58 *Friedrich Stork & Cie v High Authority of the European Coal and Steel Community*, ECLI:EU:C:1959:4 18

Joined Cases C-36, 37, 38 and 40/59 *Geitling Ruhrkohlen-Verkaufsgesellschaft and others v ECSC High Authority*, ECLI:EU:C:1960:36 18

Case C-10/61 *Commission v Italy*, ECLI:EU:C:1962:2 154

Case C-6/64 *Costa v ENEL*, ECLI:EU:C:1964:66 84

Case C-40/64 *Marcello Sgarlata and others v Commission*, ECLI:EU:C:1965:36 18

Case C-29/69 *Erich Stauder v City of Ulm – Sozialamt*, ECLI:EU:C:1969:57 19

Case C-11/70 *Internationale Handelsgesellschaft mbH v Einfuhr- und Vorratsstelle für Getreide und Futtermittel*, ECLI:EU:C:1970:114 .... 19, 84

Case C-4/73 *Nold v Commission*, ECLI:EU:C:1975:114 .... 20, 56

Case C-36/75 *Rutili v Ministre de l'intérieur*, ECLI:EU:C:1975:137 20

Case C-106/77 *Amministrazione delle Finanze dello Stato v Simmenthal SpA*, ECLI:EU:C:1978:49 84

Case C-120/78 *Rewe-Zentrale AG v Bundesmonopolverwaltung für Branntwein (Cassis de Dijon)*, ECLI:EU:C:1979:42 93

Case C-812/79 *Attorney-General v Burgoa*, ECLI:EU:C:1980:231 154

Case C-314/85 *Foto-Frost v Hauptzollamt Lübeck-Ost*, ECLI:EU:C:1987:452 190

Case C-286/86 *Ministère public v Gérard Deserbais*, ECLI:EU:C:1988:434 154

Case C-5/88 *Hubert Wachauf v Bundesamt für Ernährung und Forstwirtschaft*, ECLI:EU:C:1989:321 .... 21, 26

Case C-260/89 *Elliniki Radiophonia Tileorassi AE (ERT) v Dimotiki Etairia Pliroforissis and Sotirios Kouvelas*, ECLI:EU:C:1991:254 21

Opinion 1/91 *Draft Agreement relating to the creation of the European Economic Area*, ECLI:EU:C:1991:490 34

Case C-158/91 *Ministère public en Direction du travail et de l'emploi v Jean-Claude Levy*, ECLI:EU:C:1993:332 155

Opinion 2/94 *Accession by the Community to the European Convention for the Protection of Human Rights and Fundamental Freedoms*, ECLI:EU:C:1996:140 .... 22, 35

Case C-84/95 *Bosphorus v Ireland*, ECLI:EU:C:1996:312 48

Case C-84/95 *Bosphorus v Ireland*, ECLI:EU:C:1996:179, Opinion of AG Jacobs 60

Case C-124/95 *The Queen, ex parte Centro-Com Srl v HM Treasury and Bank of England*, ECLI:EU:C:1997:8 ... 154
Case T-163/96 *Connolly v European Commission*, ECLI:EU:T:1999:102 ... 54
Case C-377/98 *Netherlands v EP and Council*, ECLI:EU:C:2001:329, Opinion of AG Jacobs ... 32
Joined Cases C-122/99 and C-125/99 *D and Kingdom of Sweden v Council*, ECLI:EU:C:2001:113, Opinion of AG Mischo ... 32
Case C-270/99 *Z v Parliament*, ECLI:EU:C:2001:180, Opinion of AG Jacobs ... 32
Case C-274/99 P *Connolly v Commission*, ECLI:EU:C:2001:127 ... 54
Joined Cases C-187/01 *Hüseyin Gözütok* and C-385/01 *Klaus Brügge*, ECLI:EU:C:2003:87 ... 94
Case T-315/01 *Kadi v Council and Commission*, ECLI:EU:T:2005:332 ... 162, 164
Case C-540/03 *European Parliament v Council*, ECLI:EU:C:2006:429 ... 32
Case C-144/04 *Mangold v Helm*, ECLI:EU:C:2005:709 ... 38
Case C-467/04 *Gasparini and Others*, ECLI:EU:C:2006:406, Opinion of AG Sharpston ... 94
Case C-303/05 *Advocaten voor de Wereld VZW v Leden van de Ministerraad*, ECLI:EU:C:2007:261 ... 117, 119
Joined Cases C-402/05 P and C-415/05 P, *Kadi and Al Barakaat* ECLI:EU:C:2008:461 ... 163, 165
Case C-465/07 *Meki Elgafaji: Noor Elgafaji v Staatssecretaris van Justitie*, ECLI:EU:C:2009:94 ... 61
Case C-555/07 *Seda Kücükdeveci v Swedex GmbH & Co KG*, ECLI:EU:C:2010:21 ... 32, 38
Opinion 1/09 *Creation of a unified patent litigation system*, ECLI:EU:C:2011:123 ... 34
Joined Cases C-92/09 and C-93/09 *Volker und Markus Schecke GbR and Hartmut Eifert v Land Hessen*, ECLI:EU:C:2010:662 ... 32
Case C-232/09 *Dita Danosa v LKB Līzings SIA*, ECLI:EU:C:2010:674 ... 38
Case C-306/09 *IB v Conseil des ministres*, ECLI:EU:C:2010:404, Opinion of AG Cruz Villalón ... 121
Case C-447/09 *Prigge and Others v Deutsche Lufthansa*, ECLI:EU:C:2011:573 ... 38
Case C-400/10 PPU *McB v LE*, ECLI:EU:C:2010:582 ... 60, 196
Joined Cases C-411/10 *NS v Secretary of State for the Home Department* and C-493/10 *ME: ASM: MT: KP: EH v Refugee Applicationlications Commissioner: Minister for Justice: Equality and Law Reform*, ECLI:EU:C:2011:865 ... 95, 97, 99, 103, 177, 201
Case C-571/10 *Kamberaj*, ECLI:EU:C:2012:233 ... 25, 57–58, 156–57
Case C-617/10 *Åklagaren v Hans Åkerberg Fransson*, ECLI:EU:C:2013:105 ... 26, 57
Case C-648/10 *ASNEF*, ECLI:EU:C:2011:777 ... 38
Case C-4/11 *Puid*, ECLI: EU:C:2013:740 ... 100–01, 179

Case C-283/11 *Sky Österreich*, ECLI:EU:C:2013:28..64
Case C-396/11 *Radu*, ECLI: EU:C:2013:39..113, 116
Case C-396/11 *Radu*, ECLI:EU:C:2012:648, Opinion of AG Sharpston..............121
Case C-399/11 *Stefano Melloni v Ministerio Fiscal*,
ECLI:EU:C:2013:107..34–35, 67, 113, 119, 121–23, 136–37, 157, 186
Case C-131/12 *Google Spain*, ECLI:EU:C:2014:317..4, 64
Joined Cases C-293/12 and 594/12 *Digital Rights Ireland Ltd and Seitlinger and Others*, ECLI:EU:C:2014:238..4, 29–30, 32
Case C-394/12 *Shamso Abdullahi v Bundesasylamt*,
ECLI:EU:C:2013:813..67, 100–01, 105, 179
Opinion 2/13 *Accession of the European Union to the European Convention for the Protection of Human Rights and Fundamental Freedoms*, ECLI:EU:C:2014:48 ....2, 37, 45, 124, 156, 194, 198
Case C-112/13 *A v B and Others*, ECLI:EU:C:2014:2195..86
Case C-168/13 PPU *Jeremy F*, ECLI:EU:C:2013:358..123
Case C-542/13 *M'Bodj*, ECLI:EU:C:2014:2452 66
Case C-562/13 *Abdida*, ECLI:EU:C:2014:2453 66
Case C-105/14 *Ivo Taricco and Others*, ECLI:EU:C:2015:555 189
Case C-129/14 PPU *Zoran Spasic*, ECLI:EU:C:2014:586..64
Case C-72/15 *Rosneft*, ECLI:EU:C:2017:236..72
Case C-157/15 *G4S v Achbita*, ECLI:EU:C:2017:203..200
Case C-188/15 *Bougnaoui*, ECLI:EU:C:2017:204 200
Case C-203/15 *Tele2 Sverige*, ECLI:EU:C:2016:970..201
Joined Cases C-217/15 and C-350/15 *Orsi and Baldetti*,
ECLI:EU:C:2017:264..156
Joined Cases C-404/15 and C-659/15 PPU *Pál Aranyosi and Robert Căldăraru v Generalstaatsanwaltschaft Bremen*,
ECLI:EU:C:2016:198..10, 113, 123, 183, 186, 192, 201
Joined Cases C-404/15 and C-659/15 PPU *Pál Aranyosi and Robert Căldăraru v Generalstaatsanwaltschaft Bremen*,
ECLI:EU:C:2016:140, Opinion of AG Bot..126
Case C-601/15 PPU *JN v Staatssecretaris van Veiligheid en Justitie*,
ECLI:EU:C:2016:84..61, 156, 190
Case C-64/16 *Associação Sindical dos Juízes Portugueses*,
ECLI:EU:C:2018:117..131
Case C-73/16 *Puškár*, ECLI:EU:C:2017:725 195
Case C-73/16 *Puškár*, ECLI:EU:C:2017:253, Opinion of AG Kokott..5
Case C-294/16 PPU *JZ v Prokuratura Rejonowa Łódź – Śródmieście*,
ECLI:EU:C:2016:610..61
Case C-367/16 *Piotrowski*, ECLI:EU:C:2018:27 128
Case C-426/16 *Liga van Moskeeën en Islamitische Organisaties Provincie Antwerpen and Others*, ECLI:EU:C:2018:335..200

Case C-578/16 PPU *CK and others v Republika Slovenija*, ECLI:EU:C:2017:127 .... 103, 105, 110, 201
Case C-578/16 PPU *CK and others v Republika Slovenija* ECLI:EU:C:2017:108, Opinion of AG Tanchev 105
Case C-42/17 *MAS & MB (Taricco II)*, ECLI:EU:C:2017:936 198
C-152/17 *Consorzio Italian Management e Catania Multiservizi*, ECLI:EU:C:2018:264 196
Case C-260/17 *Anodiki Services EPE*, ECLI:EU:C:2018:864 196
Case C-163/17 *Jawo*, ECLI:EU:C:2019:218 .... 107, 110
Joined Cases C-297/17, C-318/17, C-319/17 and C-438/17 *Ibrahim and others*, ECLI:EU:C:2019:219 108
Case C-661/17 *MA and others*, ECLI:EU:C:2019:53 .... 60, 108
Case C-128/18 *Dorobantu*, ECLI:EU:C:2019:857 .... 127, 136, 188
Case C-216/18 PPU *LM*, ECLI:EU:C:2018:586 .... 10, 61, 64, 113, 130, 132, 192
Case C-220/18 PPU *Generalstaatsanwaltschaft*, ECLI:EU:C:2018:589 127
Joined Cases C-585/18, C-624/18 and C-625/18 *AK (Independence of the Disciplinary Chamber of the Supreme Court)*, ECLI:EU:C:2019:982 131
Case C-336/19 *Centraal Israëlitisch Consistorie van België and others*, ECLI:EU:C:2020:1031 200–01
Case C-510/19 *Openbaar Ministerie*, ECLI:EU:C:2020:953 133

European Commission of Human Rights

App no 235/56 *X v Germany* (10 June 1958) 158
App no 342/57 *X v Germany* (4 September 1958) 47
App no 13258/87 *M & Co v Germany* (9 February 1990) 49

European Court of Human Rights

App no 8793/79 *James and Others v UK* (21 February 1986) 77, 78, 89
App no 13258/87 *M & Co v Germany* (9 February 1990) 49
App no 14038/88 *Soering v United Kingdom* (7 July 1989) 68, 92, 116, 133, 158, 178, 180
App no 14234/88 *Open Door Counselling v Ireland* (29 October 1992) 67
App no 20665/92 *Markopoulou v Greece* (6 April 1994) 67
App no 22225/93 *EM v Greece* (1 December 1993) 67
App no 24833/94 *Matthews v United Kingdom* (18 February1999) 47, 48
App no 28524/95 *Peers v Greece* (19 April 2001) 188
App no 45036/98 *Bosphorus Hava Yollari Turizm v Ireland* (30 June 2005) 48–55, 98, 129, 159

App nos 41138/98 and 64320/01 *Moldovan and others v Romania (No 1)* (5 July 2005) ... 181
App nos 41138/98 and 64320/01 *Moldovan and others v Romania (No 2)* (12 July 2005) ... 181
App no 48254/99 *Cobzaru v Romania* (26 July 2007) ... 181
App no 48321/99 *Slivenko and others v Latvia* (9 October 2003) ... 159
App no 67253/01 *Babushkin v Russia* (18 October 2007) ... 188
App nos 71412/01 and 78166/01 *Behrami and Behrami v France and Saramati v France, Germany and Norway* (2 May 2007) ... 164–65
App no 73250/01 *Boivin v 34 Member States of the Council of Europe* (9 September 2008) ... 55
App no 73274/01 *Connolly v 15 Member States of the EU* (9 December 2008) ... 54
App no 76240/01 *Wagner and JMWL v Luxembourg* (28 June 2007) ... 78
App no 37213/02 *Kantyrev v Russia* (21 June 2007) ... 187
App no 35207/03 *Ostrovar v Moldova* (13 September 2005) ... 188
App no 17885/04 *Orchowski v Poland* (22 October 2009) ... 180
App no 36257/04 *Berić and Others v Bosnia and Herzegovina* (16 October 2007) ... 165
App no 13645/05 *PO Kokkelvisserij v The Netherlands* (20 January 2009) ... 50, 51, 54
App no 25664/05 *Lind v Russia* (6 December 2007) ... 187
App no 40382/05 *Rambus Inc v Germany* (16 June 2009) ... 55
App no 36099/06 *Beygo v 46 Member States of the Council of Europe* (16 June 2009) ... 55
App no 37201/06 *Saadi v Italy* (28 February 2008) ... 180
App no 18754/07 *Lopez Cifuentes v Spain* (7 July 2009) ... 55
App no 17502/07 *Avotiņš v Latvia* (23 May 2016) ... 52–54, 73, 128
App no 16574/08 *Fabris v France* (7 February 2013) ... 78
App no 30696/09 *MSS v Belgium and Greece* (21 January 2011) ... 51, 52, 92, 95, 97, 98, 99, 100, 109, 110, 177
App nos 54966/09, 57682/10, 20499/11, 41587/11, 27583/12, 75692/12, 76944/12, 77474/12, 9985/13, 16490/13, 29530/13, 37810/13, 40759/13, 55842/13, 56837/13, 62797/13, 64858/13, 65996/13, 66101/13 and 15822/14 *Oprea and Others v Romania* (18 June 2015) ... 124
App no 8139/09 *Othman (Abu Qatada) v United Kingdom* (17 January 2012) ... 133
App no 41738/10 *Paposhvili v Belgium* (13 December 2016) ... 105
App no 12323/11 *Michaud v France* (6 December 2012) ... 52–53
App no 28761/11 *Al Nashiri v Poland* (24 July 2014) ... 133
App nos 14097/12, 45135/12, 73712/12, 34001/13, 44055/13 and 64586/13 *Varga and Others v Hungary* (10 March 2015) ... 124
App no 29217/12 *Tarakhel v Switzerland* (4 November 2014) ... 68, 102, 177

App no 62116/12 *Nabil and Others v Hungary* (22 September 2015) 191
App no 7334/13 *Muršić v Croatia* (20 October 2016)..128
App nos 40324/16 and 12623/17 *Bivolaru and Moldovan v France* (25 March 2021) 10, 74, 127–30, 160
App no 8351/17 *Romeo Castaño v Belgium* (9 July 2019) 200
App no 4907/18 *Xero Flor w Polsce sp. z o.o. v Poland* (7 May 2021)...................133

International Court of Justice

Ambatielos case (Greece v United Kingdom) [1952] ICJ Rep 28 168
Barcelona Traction, Light and Power Company Ltd (Belgium v Spain) [1970] ICJ Rep 3 171
Case Concerning the Gabčíkovo-Nagymaros Project (Hungary v Slovakia) [1997] ICJ Rep 7 168
Military and Paramilitary Activities in and against Nicaragua (Nicaragua v USA) [1986] ICJ Rep 14 .... 162, 164
Questions of Interpretation & Application of the 1971 Montreal Convention arising from the Aerial Incident at Lockerbie (Libya v UK) and (Libya v USA) [1998] ICJ Rep 115 164

UN Committee on Human Rights

Cox v Canada No 486/1992, UN Doc CCPR/C/45/D/486/1992 158
Kindler v Canada No 470/1991, UN Doc CCPR/C/48/D/470/1991 158
Ng v Canada No 469/1991, UN Doc CCPR/C/49/D/469/1991 158

Domestic Case Law

Austria

Verfassungsgerichtshof, Miltner, VfSlg 11500/1987, Judgment of 14 October 1987..81
Verfassungsgerichtshof, VfSlg U 466/11-18 and U 1836/11-13, Judgment of 14 March 2012..86

Belgium

Cass 16 November 2004 [2005] *Chroniques de Droit Public* 610 81
Cass 9 November 2006 [2005] *Chroniques de Droit Public* 597 81

Czech Republic

Ústavní soud České republiky, Pl ÚS 36/01, published under no 403/2002 Coll. 150

France

Conseil d'État, Ass, 30 October 1998 81
Cour de Cassation, Sarran, Levacher et autres Cass, Ass Plen, 2 June 2000 81
Conseil Constitutionnel, Decision no 2004-505 DC, 19 November 2004 148

Germany

BVerfGE 293, 18 October 1967 149
BverfGE 37, 291, 29 May 1974, *Solange I* 19, 77, 186
BverfGE 73, 339, 22 October 1986, *Solange II* 21, 77, 186
BverfGE 89, 155 of 12 October 1993, *Maastricht* 186
BVerfGE 2 BvL 1/97, *Solange III* (2000) 21, 186
BVerfGE 11, 307 14 October 2004, *Görgülü* 81, 82
BverfGE 123, 267 30 June 2009, *Lisbon* 186
BVerfG, 2 BvR 2735/14, 15 December 2015 184
BVerfG, 2 BvR 424/17, 19 December 2017 187
Verwaltungsgerichtshof, 29 July 2019, ECLI:DE:VGHBW:2019:0729. A4S749.19.00 108

Ireland

Attorney-General v X [1992] 1 IR 1, Supreme Court 85
Minister for Justice and Equality v Artur Celmer (No 5) [2018] IEHC 639, High Court 134, 193
Minister for Justice and Equality v Kelly aka Nolan [2013] IESC 54, Supreme Court 180
Minister for Justice, Equality and Law Reform v Rettinger [2010] IR 783, Supreme Court 180
Minister for Justice and Equality v Rostaş [2014] EHC 391, High Court 180–82
Society for the Protection of Unborn Children (Ireland) Ltd v Grogan [1989] IR 734, Supreme Court 85

Italy

Fragd v Amministrazione delle Finanze dello Stato, Italian Constitutional Court Decision No 232/1989 (1989) 77
Frontini v Ministero delle Finanze, Italian Constitutional Court Decision No 183/73 (1973) 20, 77

SpA Granital v Amministrazione delle Finanze dello Stato, Italian Constitutional Court Decision No 170/84 (1984) 21
Italian Constitutional Court, Decision Nos 348/2007 and 349/2007 (2007) 75, 82
Italian Constitutional Court, Decision No 113/2011 (2011)....150
Italian Constitutional Court, Order No 24/2017 (2017).... 188–89

Spain

Spanish Constitutional Court, STC 91/2000 (30 March 2010)....121

United Kingdom

Chester [2013] UKSC 63....83
EM (Eritrea) v Secretary of State for the Home Department [2012] EWCA Civ 1336 176–77
EM (Eritrea) v Secretary of State for the Home Department [2014] UKSC 12....101, 176–77
Factortame Ltd v Secretary of State for Transport [1991] 1 AC 603 85
F-K v Polish Judicial Authority [2012] UKSC 25 182
Krolik v Regional Court in Czestochova, Poland [2012] EWHC 2357....183
Norris v US (No 2) [2010] UKSC 9 183
R (Ullah) v Special Adjudicator [2004] INLR 381....83
R v Horncastle & others [2009] UKSC 14....83

TABLE OF LEGISLATION

European Union

Council Directive 92/43/EEC of May 1992 on the conservation of natural habitats and of wild fauna and flora, [1992] OJ L206/7........................50
Council Framework Decision 2002/584/JHA of 13 June 2002 on the European arrest warrant and the surrender procedure between Member States, [2002] OJ L190/1 ....34, 112, 114, 180
Council Regulation (EC) No 343/2003 of 18 February 2003 establishing the criteria and mechanisms for determining the Member State responsibility for examining an asylum Applicationlication lodged in one of the Member States by a third-country national, [2003] OJ L50/1 ....51, 126, 177
Directive 2006/24/EC on the retention of data generated or processed in connection with the provision of publicly available electronic communication services or of public communications networks and amending Directive 2002/58/EC (Data Retention Directive), [2006] OJ L105/54 29
Council Decision of 20 March 2007, CS/2007/7404 40
Council Regulation (EC) No 168/2007 establishing a European Union Agency for Fundamental Rights, [2007] OJ L53/1 41
Explanations Relating to the Charter of Fundamental Rights, [2007] OJ C303/20 ....2, 59
Directive 2008/115/EC of the European Parliament and of the Council of 16 December 2008 on common standards and procedures in Member States for returning illegally staying third-country nationals, [2008] OJ L348/98 190
Council Framework Decision 2009/299/JHA of 26 February 2009 amending Framework Decisions 2002/584/JHA, 2005/214/JHA, 2006/783/JHA, 2008/909/JHA and 2008/947/JHA, [2009] OJ L81/24 ....34, 112, 180
Protocol No 30 TEU on the Application of the Charter of Fundamental Rights of the European Union to Poland and to the United Kingdom 38
Directive 2013/33/EU of the European Parliament and of the Council of 26 June 2013 laying down standards for the reception of Applicants for international protection (recast), [2013] OJ L180/96 190

Regulation (EU) No 604/2013 of the European Parliament and of the Council of 26 June 2013 establishing the criteria and mechanisms for determining the Member State responsible for examining an Application for international protection lodged in one of the Member States by a third-country national or a stateless person, [2013] OJ L180/31 96

Council of Europe

Statute of the Council of Europe 1949. 17
European Convention for the Protection of Human Rights and Fundamental Freedoms, 4 November 1950 ....2, 35, 37, 45, 56, 95, 124, 156, 194, 198
Protocol No 14 to the Convention for the Protection of Human Rights and Fundamental Freedoms, amending the control system of the Convention, 13 May 2004 79
Protocol No 16 to the Convention for the Protection of Human Rights and Fundamental Freedoms 3, 66, 69, 78, 79, 194

International Legislation

Geneva Convention Relating to the Status of Refugees of 1951 64

TABLE OF INSTITUTIONAL DOCUMENTS

European Union

The Schuman Declaration, 9 May 1950
Commission of the European Communities, Eighth General Report on the Activities of the European Communities 270 (1974)
Joint Declaration on Fundamental Human Rights [1977] OJ C-103/1
European Council Copenhagen Declaration on Democracy, EC Bull 3-[1978]
Commission Memorandum, Accession of the Communities to the European Convention on Human Rights, Bulletin of the European Communities, Supplement 2/79, COM(1979)
European Council, Presidency Conclusions, Cologne 3–4 June 1999
European Commission, Communication on the Charter of Fundamental Rights of the European Union, COM(2000) 559
European Commission, Decision on the Application of the Charter of Fundamental Rights of the European Union SEC(2001) 380/3
Commission of the European Communities, Written Observations in *Bosphorus Airways v Ireland*, 30 June 2004, JURM (2004) 6026.
European Commission, Communication on Impact Assessment (5 June 2002) COM(2002) 276
Final European Commission Communication, 'Compliance with the Charter of Fundamental Rights in Commission legislative proposals – Methodology for systematic and rigorous monitoring' (27 April 2005) COM(2005) 172
The Hague Programme, Strengthening Freedom, Security, and Justice in the EU [2005] OJ C53/01
European Commission, Report 'On the Practical Operation of the Methodology for a Systematic and Rigorous Monitoring of Compliance with the Charter of Fundamental Rights' (29 April 2009) COM(2009) 205 final
Resolution of the Council of 30 November 2009 on a Roadmap for strengthening procedural rights of suspected or accused persons in criminal proceedings, [2009] OJ C295/01
European Commission Communication, Strategy for the effective implementation of the Charter of Fundamental Rights by the European Union (19 October 2010) COM(2010) 573/4
Council discussion document, 'The Role of the Council in Ensuring the Effective Implementation of the Charter of Fundamental Rights in the Legislative Process', informal meeting of the Justice and Home Affairs Ministers (20–21 January 2011)

Council of the European Union, Guidelines on methodological steps to be taken to check fundamental rights compatibility at the Council's preparatory bodies (18 May 2011) Council Doc No 10140/11
Commission Staff Working Paper, Operational Guidance on taking account of Fundamental Rights in Commission Impact assessments (6 May 2011) SEC(2011) 567 final
Independent External Evaluation of the EU Agency for Fundamental Rights (November 2012)
Fundamental Rights Agency (FRA), 'The EU Charter of Fundamental Rights before national courts and non-judicial human rights bodies', *Annual Report 2013*
European Parliament Resolution of 27 February 2014 with recommendations to the Commission on the review of the European Arrest Warrant (2013/2109(INL))
Council of the European Union, Guidelines on methodological steps to be taken to check fundamental rights compatibility at the Council's preparatory bodies (16 December 2014) Council Doc No 16957/14
European Parliament, Rules of Procedure, 8th parliamentary term (2014–2019)
Outcome of the Council Meeting (23 June 2015) 10228/15
Interinstitutional Agreement between the European Parliament, the Council of the European Union and the European Commission on Better Law-Making, [2016] OJ L123/1
Report on the Application of the EU Charter of Fundamental Rights' (19 May 2016) COM(2016) 265 final
European Parliament, Draft Report on the Annual Report on Human Rights and Democracy in the World 2016 and the European Union's policy on the matter (2017)
Independent External Evaluation of the EU Agency for Fundamental Rights (October 2017)

Council of Europe

Laeken Declaration on the Future of the European Union, 15 December 2001
Interlaken Declaration, adopted by the High Level Conference on the Future of the European Court of Human Rights on 19 February 2010
Brighton Declaration, adopted at the High Level Conference on the Future of the European Court of Human Rights on 19 April 2012
Committee of Ministers, Explanatory Report to Protocol No 16 to the European Convention on Human Rights, CM(2013)31, 2 October 2013
Practical Guide on Admissibility Criteria. Council of Europe/European Court of Human Rights, 2014
ECtHR Annual Report 2014
Protocol No 16 to the European Convention of Human Rights

Introduction

I. Aims and Scope of this Book

The European Union (EU) is often described as a community or union of values.[1] If we agree with this characterisation of the EU (and not everyone would, of course), it is because of the role fundamental or human rights[2] have played in its creation. Indeed, the strength of fundamental rights protection in the EU is vivid, and it derives, to a large extent, from the enforcement of fundamental rights by the European and national courts. However, the environment in which these courts operate is far from simple. So what are the different sources of EU fundamental rights and how do they relate to one another? What exactly is the relationship between EU fundamental rights and the European Convention on Human Rights (ECHR)? Can national courts apply ECHR law in cases that fall within the scope of EU law? If so, should they apply the EU Charter of Fundamental Rights and the ECHR simultaneously? What if the requirements of two European sources clash? This set of questions highlights only some aspects of the highly complex architecture of EU fundamental rights law.

This complexity is caused by the coexistence of at least three legal systems, each with their own bill of fundamental rights and their own enforcement mechanism.[3] First, at the national level, fundamental rights are mainly to be found in constitutions, sometimes complemented by international treaties and sometimes, also, EU law. Second, at the international level, individuals can bring individual complaints before the European Court of Human Rights (ECtHR),[4] alleging violations of their fundamental rights as protected by the ECHR. At the moment, all 27 EU Member States[5] are also Members of the Council of Europe and signatories to the ECHR. Third, fundamental rights are also protected in the context of EU law, where they

[1] See, eg, K Lenaerts 'The Role of the EU Charter in the Member States' in M Bobek and J Adams-Prassl (eds), *The EU Charter of Fundamental Rights in the Member States* (Oxford, Hart Publishing, 2020) 19, 35.

[2] In this book, the terms 'fundamental rights' and 'human rights' are used interchangeably.

[3] There are, of course, more human rights treaties and instruments applicable in Europe and in the EU. The focus in this book is on the interplay between EU fundamental rights, the ECHR and national constitutional rights, because of the special relationship between EU law and the ECHR, as well as the special status they both have in the national legal systems. However, other instruments may be mentioned too, where relevant.

[4] Also 'Strasbourg Court' or simply 'Strasbourg'.

[5] The book has been largely written prior to the exit of the UK from the EU on 31 January 2020 (although EU rules applied until the end of the transition period on 31 December 2020) and the UK as a Member State and the case law of the UK national courts are considered in different chapters.

derive from the Charter, unwritten general principles of EU law and, again, the ECHR. Legal action based on the infringement of EU fundamental rights may thus involve the Court of Justice of the European Union (CJEU),[6] national courts and the ECtHR.

The legal relationships between these component parts of the European human rights architecture and between the actors belonging to each of these systems are contested and still evolving. The most important catalyst for change was the entry into force of the Lisbon Treaty. This Treaty gives the EU a binding Charter of Fundamental Rights and obliges the EU to accede to the ECHR – necessitating a new conception of the relationship between the CJEU and the ECtHR. However, the CJEU rejected the Draft Accession Agreement (DAA) in Opinion 2/13,[7] which seems to foreclose any real possibility for accession in the near future, although the negotiations have recommenced recently.[8] In addition, the text of the Charter introduces an interpretative rule in Article 52(3), which provides that the corresponding Charter and Convention rights shall have the same meaning and scope. The provision is intended to ensure the necessary consistency between the Charter and the ECHR rights without adversely affecting the autonomy of EU law and that of the CJEU.[9]

In the meantime, the CJEU has been increasingly dealing with fundamental rights cases as a consequence of the continued expansion of the scope of EU law and policy in areas that are very important from a human rights perspective, such as asylum and immigration law, criminal law and data protection. The Court has picked up on the increased human rights salience of EU law, positioning itself as a human rights court and placing the Charter at the heart of its human rights adjudication.[10] At the same time, the ECHR system has been struggling with an overburdened Court, whose legitimacy is challenged in several states, as well as with the problems of the non-execution of its judgments.[11] Additionally, political declarations of the Contracting Parties have put a new emphasis on the role of national courts, as well as on a direct relationship between national courts and

[6] Also 'Court of Justice', 'Luxembourg Court' or 'Court'.

[7] Opinion 2/13 *Accession of the European Union to the European Convention for the Protection of Human Rights and Fundamental Freedoms*, ECLI:EU:C:2014:48.

[8] Accession negotiations were meant to recommence in March 2020, but had to be postponed due to the Covid-19 pandemic. An informal virtual meeting was held in June 2020, and negotiations formally continued in Strasbourg from 29 September to 2 October 2020. Both institutions remain committed to EU's accession but there is no indication, at the time of writing, of when a new accession agreement is expected to be reached.

[9] Explanations Relating to the Charter of Fundamental Rights [2007] OJ C303/20.

[10] G de Búrca, 'After the EU Charter of Fundamental Rights: the Court of Justice as a human rights adjudicator?' (2013) 20 *Maastricht Journal of European and Comparative Law* 2, 168.

[11] Criticism has come mainly from 'old' State Parties in relation to the degree of the Court's influence on national law and the Court's legitimacy to exert such influence, as well as to the proliferation of the ECHR rights, which is said to be the result of the Court's dynamic and evolutive approach in their interpretation. For a recent comparative study, see P Popelier, S Lambrecht and K Lemmens (eds), *Criticism of the European Court of Human Rights: Shifting the Convention System: Counter-Dynamics at the National and EU Level* (Antwerp, Intersentia, 2016).

the ECtHR.[12] Following the Brighton Declaration, which called for 'shared responsibility' and 'dialogue' between the courts, the text of Protocol No 16 to the ECHR was drafted, creating a system under which national courts can request advisory opinions from the Strasbourg Court on legal questions relating to the interpretation of the Convention and the protocols thereto, in addition to questions of clarification of the Court's case law.[13] Requests for an advisory opinion can be submitted only by constitutional courts or courts of last instance, but they are optional and the opinions given by the ECtHR are not binding.[14] Protocol No 16 entered into force on 1 August 2018[15] and two advisory opinions have already been issued.[16] However, this new procedure may come at the cost of increased complexity, and it remains to be seen whether it will facilitate or rather further complicate fundamental rights matters in Europe.[17]

The increased focus on fundamental rights in the European legal space poses multiple political and legal challenges for the EU as well as for its Member States. It is particularly problematic for national courts, since they are at the crossroads of three legal systems. As state organs, they ensure compliance of their state with the ECHR. At the same time, they must uphold their national constitution and comply with EU law and EU fundamental rights. Consequently, national courts may be confronted with competing and conflicting obligations for the protection of fundamental rights originating in EU and ECHR law, as well as in national (constitutional) law. After all, the catalogues of rights may not require the same level of protection and are interpreted by different highest courts, while clear rules governing their mutual relationship are lacking. As a result, the multi-level system of protection may have the effect of diminishing legal certainty where legal subjects may be put in an unequal position vis-à-vis others, and where the rights they enjoy may depend on which jurisdiction is compelled to enforce them. This research focuses specifically on divergences between EU and ECHR law and does

[12] Brighton Declaration, adopted at the High Level Conference on the Future of the European Court of Human Rights on 19 April 2012, para 9. See also the Interlaken Declaration, adopted by the High Level Conference on the Future of the European Court of Human Rights on 19 February 2010, para 4.

[13] Committee of Ministers, Explanatory Report to Protocol No 16 to the European Convention on Human Rights, CM(2013)31, 2 October 2013, paras 1 and 9.

[14] ibid paras 1–3. For critical appraisals see J Gerards, 'Advisory Opinions, Preliminary Rulings, and the New Protocol No 16 to the European Convention of Human Rights, a Comparative and Critical Appraisal' (2014) 21 *Maastricht Journal of European and Comparative Law* 4; K Dzehtsiarou and N O'Meara, 'Advisory Jurisdiction of the European Court of Human Rights: A Magic Bullet for Dialogue and Docket-Control?' (2014) 34 *Legal Studies* 3, 444.

[15] The ratification by at least 10 states has been achieved with the French ratification, which is when the protocol entered into force. At the time of writing there are 16 ratifications in total, nine of which are EU states: Estonia, Finland, Lithuania, Slovenia, France, Greece, the Netherlands, Slovakia and Luxembourg.

[16] ECtHR Advisory Opinion on Matters of Surrogacy requested by the French Court of Cassation, 10 April 2019, Request no P16-2018-001; ECtHR Advisory Opinion relating to Article 300.1 of Armenia's Criminal Code requested by the Armenian Constitutional Court, 29 May 2020, Request no P16-2019-001.

[17] K Lemmens, 'Protocol No 16 to the ECHR: Managing Backlog through Complex Judicial Dialogue?' (2019) 15 *European Constitutional Law Review* 691.

not, in principle, consider conflicts between EU and/or ECHR law on the one hand and national (constitutional) law on the other, although mention may also be made of these types of conflicts, where relevant.[18] It is important to note at the outset that divergences (both conceptual and explicit) in the protection of fundamental rights by the CJEU and the ECtHR are not always problematic and will not necessarily result in a conflict; on the contrary, they can be a source of mutual influence, enrichment and cross-fertilisation. However, if the EU standard of fundamental rights protection would fall below the ECHR minimum standard, as interpreted by the case law of the ECtHR, Member States would face conflicting treaty obligations, since they would be required to comply with their EU law obligations and, at the same time, are required to ensure that the ECHR minimum standards, as determined by the ECtHR, are respected.[19] This book thus focuses precisely on divergences between EU and ECHR law where the level of protection provided by the CJEU may be considered to be below the minimum level required by the ECtHR. It does not consider instances in which the CJEU provides higher levels of protection, which would be compatible with the ECHR in light of Article 53 of the Convention.[20] This latter situation would create divergences in the case law in Strasbourg and Luxembourg (and could potentially create issues with national constitutional protection of rights), but not conflicting treaty obligations for the national courts in respect of EU and ECHR law. A good example of the latter situation is the *Menci* case, concerning the application of the *ne bis in idem* principle. In that case, the CJEU departed from the approach of the ECtHR on the application of the said principle, but it did so in such a way as to provide a higher level of protection than that guaranteed by the Convention (yet without mentioning the last sentence of Article 52(3) of the Charter).[21] This, as

[18] It could be said that conflicts are more likely to occur between EU and/or ECHR law and national law than between EU and ECHR law and, as such, they may pose even greater challenges for national courts. However, this is also something that has been dealt with more in the existing literature. See, eg, Popelier, Lambrecht and Lemmens (eds) (n 11); G Martinico and O Pollicino (eds), *The National Judicial Treatment of the ECHR and EU Laws. A Comparative Constitutional Law Perspective* (Groningen, Europa Law Publishing, 2010); A Torres Pérez, *Conflicts of Rights in the European Union – A Theory of Supranational Adjudication* (Oxford, Oxford University Press, 2009).

[19] On the distinction between unproblematic and problematic divergences, see L Besselink, 'The Protection of Fundamental Rights post-Lisbon. The Interaction between the EU Charter of Fundamental Rights, the European Convention on Human Rights (ECHR) and National Constitutions' (2012) 1 *Reports of the FIDE Congress Tallinn* 1, 7.

[20] One example would be digital rights, for which the CJEU has even been criticised for providing too much protection. See Joined Cases C-293/12 and 594/12 *Digital Rights Ireland Ltd and Seitlinger and others*, ECLI:EU:C:2014:238, and Case C-131/12 *Google Spain*, ECLI:EU:C:2014:317. For a discussion, see F Fabbrini, 'The EU Charter of Fundamental Rights and the Rights to Data Privacy: The Court of Justice as a Human Rights Court' in S de Vries, U Bernitz and S Weatherill (eds), *The EU Charter of Fundamental Rights as a Binding Instrument: Five Years Old and Growing* (Oxford, Hart Publishing, 2015) 261. Interestingly, there are also fields in which the ECtHR has been criticised for going too far in the protection provided, although the criticism only came from certain corners. An example would be the protection provided to asylum seekers under Art 3 of the Convention. See, eg, M Bossuyt, 'The European Union Confronted with an Asylum Crisis in the Mediterranean: Reflections on Refugees and Human Rights Issues' (2015) 5 *European Journal of Human Rights* 581.

[21] M Luchtman, 'The ECJ's Recent Case Law on Ne Bis In Idem: Implications for Law Enforcement in a Shared Legal Order' (2018) 55 *CML Rev* 1717.

explained above, is not problematic from the ECHR perspective and does not lead to conflicts between the two. Accordingly, it is also not problematic from the national perspective, because Member State authorities can ensure compliance with both by following the CJEU's higher standards when the matter concerns EU law. What remains crucial, of course, is that the CJEU, when providing more protection in the context of one right when conflict of rights exists, does not cause another fundamental right in the Charter to be accorded protection below the ECHR standards.[22]

The complex architecture of European fundamental rights law is not uncharted territory in academic writing. However, in the debate on the legal issues, the spotlights are usually on the two European courts[23] while the perspective of national courts tends to be overlooked.[24] Nevertheless, as things stand now, national courts are first in line concerning fundamental rights protection, both in the context of the EU, where individuals generally challenge measures adopted by the EU indirectly by questioning their implementation at the domestic level, and in the context of the ECHR, which requires domestic remedies to be exhausted first, with the Strasbourg Court offering only subsidiary protection. This book aims to fill this gap by also considering the national law perspective. Moreover, there is a level of urgency regarding this research: national courts have been struggling with competing and potentially conflicting obligations arising from EU and ECHR law on a more frequent basis in the last few years than in the preceding decades. This is due to several factors, including the already mentioned expansion of EU law and policy into human rights-sensitive areas, such as asylum and criminal law, but also due to the fact that the tools have changed. In the early days, the CJEU had to operate on the basis of general principles and indirectly the ECHR, while the heart of EU fundamental rights law today is the Charter, the EU's own bill of

[22] This will not often be the case for the application of the *ne bis in idem* principle but it is the case for conflicts between rights that are not absolute and have to be balanced. Here the CJEU would have to stick to the balance established in Strasbourg and could provide higher protection of one right only to the extent that it would not go below the minimum level of protection of the other right that is at stake. See in this context the analysis of AG Kokott in Case C-73/16 *Puškár*, ECLI:EU:C:2017:253, paras 118–127.

[23] See, eg, E Ravasi, *Human Rights Protection by the ECtHR and the ECJ* (Leiden, Brill Nijhoff, 2017); S Morano-Foadi and V Vickers (eds), *Fundamental Rights in the EU – A Matter for Two Courts* (Oxford, Hart Publishing, 2015); T Lock, *The European Court of Justice and International Courts* (Oxford, Oxford University Press, 2015); F Korenica, *The EU Accession to the ECHR: Between Luxembourg's Search for Autonomy and Strasbourg's Credibility on Human Rights Protection* (Heidelberg, Springer, 2015); P Gragl, *The Accession of the European Union to the European Convention to Human Rights* (Oxford, Hart Publishing, 2013).

[24] There are a few exceptions. See OM Arnardóttir and A Buyse (eds), *Shifting Centres of Gravity in Human Rights Protection* (London, Routledge, 2016); J Gerards, 'Who decides on fundamental rights issues in Europe? – Toward a mechanism to coordinate the roles of the national courts, the ECJ and the ECtHR' in S Weatherill and S de Vries (eds), *Five Years Legally Binding EU Charter of Fundamental Rights – What is the state of play in the protection of fundamental Rights in the EU?* (Oxford, Hart Publishing, 2015). Note, however, that the former is a compilation of chapters written by experts from different fields and the latter is a book chapter. See also G Martinico, 'Is the European Convention Going to Be "Supreme"? A Comparative-Constitutional Overview of ECHR and EU Law before National Courts' (2012) 23 *The European Journal of International Law* 2, 401.

rights, which is closely tied in with the ECHR and national constitutions. At least symbolically, the Charter consolidates and strengthens the Union's commitment to fundamental rights and the CJEU's mandate with respect to the protection thereof. As a consequence, the judges in Luxembourg are more inclined to invoke human rights arguments in the case law before them; and one could even say that human rights have become part of the daily business of the CJEU, making the coexistence of different sources of law and their interpretations more challenging and the divergences between them more likely. Lastly, and crucially, the EU's accession to the ECHR – a 'landmark in the completion of the system'[25] – no longer seems a viable option. As already stated, the CJEU rejected the DAA in its Opinion 2/13, which has been perceived as a flagrant motion of distrust towards the ECtHR but also the national courts.[26] It is difficult to foresee, keeping in mind the objections in Opinion 2/13, when the recently reinstituted negotiations will deliver desirable results.[27]

When discussing the relationships between the different actors in the European fundamental rights landscape, it is important to note that some authors have conceptualised and discussed them in terms of constitutional pluralism. In essence, constitutional pluralism assumes that the multiple independent claims of constitutional autonomy coexist in a non-hierarchical system of norms.[28] In such a system the focus is on common constitutional space combined with mutual respect for the constituent parts. The European human rights regime should therefore be seen in terms of harmony and convergence and not competition and conflict, which, in turn, should allow for a real dialogue between the courts.[29] This book, by contrast, considers that the relationship between EU law and the ECHR can be

[25] Speech of (former) President of the Spanish Constitutional Court Perez de los Cobos at the 2015 opening of the judicial year at the ECtHR, available at www.echr.coe.int/Documents/Speech_20150130_Perez_Cobos_Orihuel_ENG.pdf (last accessed 15 December 2020). See also M Kuijer, 'The challenging relationship between the European Convention on Human Rights and the EU legal order: consequences of a delayed accession' (2018) 24 *The International Journal of Human Rights* 1; J Polakiewicz, 'EU Law and the ECHR: Will EU Accession to the European Convention on Human Rights Square the Circle?' (2013) 13 *European Human Rights Law Review* 592.

[26] Opinion 2/13 (n 7); ECtHR Annual Report 2014, available at http://echr.coe.int/Documents/Annual_Report_2014_ENG.pdf (last accessed 15 December 2020); D Spielmann, 'Solemn hearing for the opening of the judicial year of the European Court of Human Rights', Strasbourg, 30 January 2015, available at http://echr.coe.int/Documents/Speech_20150130_Solemn_Hearing_2015_ENG.pdf (last accessed 20 December 2020).

[27] For a debate on whether EU's accession is still desirable, see T Lock, 'The Future of EU Human Rights Law: is accession to the ECHR still desirable?' (2020) 7 *Journal of International and Comparative Law* 427; J Callewaert 'Do we still need Article 6(2) TEU? Consideration on the absence of EU accession to the ECHR and its consequences' (2018) 55 *CML Rev* 1685.

[28] N Walker, 'The Idea of Constitutional Pluralism' (2002) 65 *MLR* 317, 337. On constitutional pluralism in the EU, see M Avbelj and J Komarek (eds), *Constitutional Pluralism in the European Union and Beyond* (Oxford, Hart Publishing, 2012).

[29] Notably, albeit with slight variations in the argument, S Besson, 'European Human Rights Pluralism: Notion and Justification' in M Maduro, K Tuori and S Sankari (eds), *Transnational Law: Rethinking European Law and Legal Thinking* (Cambridge, Cambridge University Press, 2014) 170; Torres Pérez (n 18); N Krisch, 'The Open Architecture of European Human Rights Law' (2007) *LSE Working Papers 11/2007*.

seen in hierarchical terms (when it comes to establishing minimum standards), because EU primary law envisages this hierarchy. While judicial dialogue is a valuable and powerful tool that can help reconcile different sources, it does not change the legal hierarchy between them. Moreover, there may simply be instances where an incompatibility cannot be taken away by dialogue and convergence.

In terms of the method, the legal analysis in the book consists primarily of a systematic reading of case law of both European and national courts, recording consistent and inconsistent features, and drawing inferences about their meaning and impact.[30] This approach has allowed a deeper understanding of what courts do, and how and why they do it. The extensive focus on the case law has permitted a greater number of cases to be addressed, which in turn has provided a more accurate account of the different patterns. With regard to the case law analysis of the two European courts, the book offers new insights into the case law in the Area of Freedom, Security and Justice (AFSJ), which has been developing rapidly in the last few years. Of course, the case law in this field has been discussed and criticised extensively already, particularly in the context of the relationship between the principle of mutual trust and fundamental rights.[31] In fact, there is probably no other topic in EU law that has gained as much academic attention in recent years as the principle of mutual trust in the AFSJ.[32] This book builds on these critiques by analysing the case law from the point of view of national courts and focusing on the elements that are relevant for the relationship between EU and ECHR law. Finally, the book incorporates a discussion of the case law of national courts that illustrates the working of EU fundamental rights in practice, something that is often missing in academic literature.

A major overarching goal of this book is to explain the new architecture of EU fundamental rights as it has developed since the entry into force of the Treaty of Lisbon. In that sense, the book also aims to be of use to students and practitioners seeking to gain a deeper understanding of the topic. Nevertheless, given the already existing work examining this subject and its rich content, the scope of the book is limited to examining the relationship between the judicial actors in the system.

[30] This research ended on 31 March 2021 and, accordingly, it does not cover developments after this date. However, there are a few exceptions.

[31] See, eg, E Xanthopoulou, *Fundamental Rights and Mutual Trust in the Area of Freedom, Security and Justice: A Role for Proportionality?* (Oxford, Hart Publishing, 2020); G Anagnostaras, 'The Common European Asylum System: Balancing Mutual Trust Against Fundamental Rights Protection' (2020) 21 *German Law Journal* 1180; M Schwarz, 'Let's talk about trust, baby: Theorizing trust and mutual recognition in the EU's area of freedom, security and justice' (2018) 24 *European Law Journal* 124; A Willems, 'Mutual Trust as a Term of Art in EU Criminal Law: Revealing its Hybrid Character' (2016) 9 *European Journal of Legal Studies* 211.

[32] See the works cited in n 31. See also, with further references, F Maiani and A Miglionico, 'One principle to rule them all? Anatomy of mutual trust in the law of the Area of Freedom, Security and Justice' (2020) 57 *CML Rev* 7; C Ladenburger, 'The Principle of Mutual Trust between Member States in the Area of Freedom, Security and Justice' (2020) 3 *Zeitschrift für Europarechtliche Studien* 373; K Lenaerts, 'La vie après l'avis: Exploring the principle of mutual (yet not blind) trust' (2017) 54 *CML Rev* 805.

II. Structure and Outline of Chapters

The book is structured around three main research questions. First, what are the different component parts of the architecture of EU fundamental rights and how do they relate to one another? Second, what are the main fields in which divergences between EU and ECHR law have materialised, and to what extent are such divergences problematic from the point of view of national courts? Finally, how can and should national courts in the Member States deal with divergences and potential conflicts between EU law and the ECHR and the case law of the Strasbourg and Luxembourg Courts? These questions are addressed, respectively, in the three main parts of the book: 'The New European Fundamental Rights Architecture' (Part I); 'Convergence and Conflicts in European Fundamental Rights Standards' (Part II); and 'Towards Normative Consistency in European Fundamental Rights Law' (Part III).

The first two chapters, which make up Part I of the book, trace the evolution of fundamental rights protection in EU law and analyse the relationships between the EU, the ECHR and national constitutional systems.

Chapter 1 lays down the foundations of the new architecture of fundamental rights protection in EU law and discusses the role and place of fundamental rights in the EU today. The purpose of the chapter is not only to familiarise the reader with the genesis of EU fundamental rights, or remind the reader of it, but also to bring forward one principal observation that deeply underpins the arguments put forward in this book: the EU has become an important player in the field and there is no denying that it is a human rights actor of some sorts.[33] Yet the chapter also shows that the EU is different from other more 'natural' human rights actors in Europe, such as the ECHR and the national constitutional systems. This raises difficult questions as to the interpretation of EU fundamental rights, the already complicated relationship between the EU and the ECHR systems, and, ultimately, the impact on national law and national courts.

Chapter 2 turns more closely to the analysis of the relationship between the EU, the ECHR and national constitutional systems, in order to understand how they relate to each other and how the system works as a whole. Since the relationships are in constant flux and the case law is prone to changes and refinement, a comprehensive analysis was necessary to prepare the ground for what comes in the second and the third parts of the book. Indeed, understanding how the system works as a whole in the post-Lisbon Europe and how exactly the different components relate to one another is imperative for examining and resolving conflicts when these different components clash. The key element in the analysis is that it examines the interactions in a triangular manner, looking at how they are construed from the Strasbourg, Luxembourg and national perspectives. The analysis demonstrates

[33] See further ch 1. See also M Claes, 'Fundamental Rights' in PJ Kuijper et al (eds), *The Law of the European Union* (Alphen a/d Rijn, Wolters Kluwer, 2018) 97.

the various ways in which the systems are intertwined, and explains when and why this can lead to divergences and tensions between the Strasbourg and Luxembourg Courts. At the same time, national courts need a clear understanding of the meaning and scope of the Charter and the Convention rights and, crucially, the relationship between them. While the legal rank of the two supranational sources of fundamental rights may be different in the Member States, most, if not all, EU Member States, and their courts, pay due regard to the case law of both the CJEU and the ECtHR. What is more, in some legal systems national courts are required to apply ECHR law directly, even to the extent that it seems to outweigh the importance of the national constitutional bills of rights.[34] It is therefore incumbent upon the two European Courts to facilitate the central role of national courts in judicial protection of fundamental rights in Europe.[35]

Part II of the book examines divergences in the case law of the Luxembourg and Strasbourg Courts in the AFSJ. This area constitutes one of the most fundamental rights-sensitive areas of EU law and one of the busiest areas of activity for the CJEU, making it particularly suitable for this part of the book.[36] Part II covers two case studies: the so-called Dublin system and the Framework Decision on the European Arrest Warrant (EAW). Special attention is paid to the principles of mutual trust and mutual recognition, as they play a central role in this area and the tensions between Strasbourg and Luxembourg in recent years have been closely linked to it. What is common in these two case studies is that they both concern transfers of individuals from one Member State to another pursuant to EU instruments of cooperation based on the principle of mutual trust. Moreover, they both have been subject to a significant body of case law not only in Luxembourg but also in Strasbourg. The outcome is an in-depth analysis of the relevant case law of the CJEU and the ECtHR, which shows common ground but also points to the divergences between the two, and discusses why and the extent to which they are problematic. It should be emphasised that the purpose of this Part is not to offer a comprehensive and exhaustive account of the numerous cases decided in the AFSJ but, rather, to identify and analyse the most important cases that have caused tensions in the case law of the two European Courts.

Chapter 3 first examines the Dublin system on asylum claims, which is a central piece of the Common European Asylum System. The Dublin system establishes the criteria for determining which EU Member State is responsible for examining an asylum application. The rules aim to ensure quick access to asylum procedure and the examination of an application in substance by a single, clearly determined Member State. This is usually the first country of entry into the EU, which means that asylum seekers who arrive later in another EU country should

[34] The prime example is the Netherlands. See further ch 2.

[35] S O'Leary, 'Courts, charters and conventions: making sense of fundamental rights in the EU' (2016) 56 *Irish Jurist* 4.

[36] The number of cases decided in Luxembourg in the AFSJ has grown rapidly, from 53 in 2015 to 106 in 2019, making it the busiest area of activity for the CJEU in that year. See the statistics available in the CJEU's Annual Report (Judicial Activity) 2019.

in principle be sent back to the country of first entry. The system operates on the basis of mutual trust: the Member States presume that all States treat asylum seekers and examine their claims in accordance with the relevant rules of national, European and international law. The analysis demonstrates that the ECtHR has exerted great influence on the CJEU in this field, leading to the gradual softening of the application of the mutual trust doctrine and greater convergence between the case law of the Luxembourg and Strasbourg Courts. This, in turn, has led the EU legislature to revise the Dublin Regulation, which now includes an exception to mutual trust based on the CJEU's *NS* judgment and an additional interpretative tool in Recital 32, according to which the States are bound by the relevant case law of the Strasbourg Court in the application of the Regulation.

Chapter 4 goes on to consider the relationship between mutual trust and fundamental rights in the context of the Framework Decision on the EAW, the most powerful and frequently used instrument of judicial cooperation in the AFSJ. The EAW facilitates cooperation between EU states in fighting crime by organising swift surrender of crime suspects and convicted criminals between the EU countries. The EAW system operates on the basis of mutual recognition: a warrant issued by one EU Member State's judicial authority is valid across the entire territory of the EU. This chapter engages with the CJEU's case law in this field and demonstrates how the EAW case law developed throughout the years. In the early cases, the CJEU insisted on a strict reading of the EAW, thereby denying the possibility of refusals to surrender on fundamental rights grounds other than those expressly provided by the Framework Decision. In subsequent case law, however, the CJEU recognised that further limitations may be placed on the principles of mutual recognition and mutual trust. Similarly to the Dublin case law, the Court's approach to derogations remains limited to 'exceptional circumstances'. While the influence of the ECtHR in this field is less prominent given that the landmark cases *Aranyosi and Căldăraru* and *LM* make no parallels with the ECHR and the Strasbourg case law on extraditions, there are good reasons to believe that the CJEU was influenced by the ECtHR but also national courts.[37] Nevertheless, the analysis also shows that there are still methodological divergences in the approaches of the two European Courts that could lead to different outcomes and levels of protection.[38] Moreover, unlike the Dublin Regulation, the Framework Decision does not contain a specific and precise instruction to follow the Strasbourg case law. The analysis draws attention to several points of concern that will likely have to be addressed by the CJEU in the coming years. Crucially, it illustrates and reminds that convergence takes place over time, on a voluntary basis, and it always carries risk of new divergences, all the while the number of applications involving EU law and fundamental rights before both European and national courts being on the rise.

[37] Joined Cases C-404/15 and C-659/15 PPU *Aranyosi and Căldăraru*, ECLI:EU:C:2016:198; Case C-216/18 PPU *LM*, ECLI:EU:C:2018:586.

[38] See in particular *Bivolaru and Moldovan v France* App nos 40324/16 and 12623/17 (ECtHR, 25 March 2021).

Part III of this book critically explores different ways for national courts to deal with and overcome what they perceive to be conflicts between EU and ECHR law.

Chapter 5 examines the rules of conflict available to national courts when trying to find a solution for what they perceive as conflicts between EU and ECHR law. It looks at the national constitutions, but also at international law, since both EU treaties and the ECHR are essentially international treaties. It argues that neither national constitutional law nor international law can conclusively determine how conflicts between EU and ECHR law should be resolved. This is due to the special nature and status of both EU law (supranational character) and the ECHR (human rights treaty) in national and international law. The only rules that could be used are those found in the treaties themselves. In this regard, an argument has been made that Article 52(3) of the EU Charter of Fundamental Rights, even though not written as a conflict rule, can be used as such. Article 52(3) of the Charter states that corresponding Charter and ECHR rights shall have the same meaning and scope, while the exact meaning and scope of the Convention rights, pursuant to the explanatory notes on this provision, are determined not only by the wording of the Convention, but also by the case law of the Strasbourg Court. Therefore, as a general rule, when there is a conflict between EU law (which must be interpreted in light of the Charter) and the ECHR, the latter should be followed.[39]

The purpose of Chapter 6, the book's final chapter, is to analyse different ways in which national courts can deal with conflicting 'messages' from Luxembourg and Strasbourg. In so doing, four different scenarios are developed whereby the inspiration is drawn from the actual cases of national courts. It is not the purpose of this chapter to provide a systematic analysis of the case law of national courts in all or selected Member States. Instead, the national decisions are used as illustrations of different ways of approaching the conflicts. The first scenario identified is national courts seeking conform interpretation. Indeed, this is the first thing national courts will try to do. Some national courts will go to great lengths to find the jurisprudence of the Luxembourg and Strasbourg courts consistent and avoid the conflict altogether. However, conform interpretation can also be problematic, because national courts may perceive and/or present the outcome of the case as a conform interpretation, while in fact they give priority to one or to the other. The second scenario refers to situations in which national courts give priority to the ECHR, without sending the question of perceived incompatibility to the CJEU for a preliminary ruling. This carries the risk of failing to comply with the EU law obligations and risking infringement proceedings for breaching EU law. The third scenario features cases in which national courts have decided to reframe the conflict between EU and ECHR law into a conflict between EU law and the national constitution, which is then interpreted in light of the ECHR.

[39] The argument is supported by the preceding analysis of Art 52(3) of the EU Charter of Fundamental Rights in ch 2.

The fourth and last scenario concerns sending the questions of compatibility between EU law and the ECHR to the CJEU for a preliminary ruling in Luxembourg. This has been identified as a preferred scenario, but only when national courts actively engage in a dialogue with the CJEU, questioning the interpretation of EU law, as well as the choices of the CJEU made in that regard where appropriate, and suggesting their own interpretation of the provisions of EU law in light of the Charter (which should then be interpreted in conformity with the ECHR). This should be supported by a reference to Article 52(3) of the Charter, which clearly and convincingly states that corresponding Charter and ECHR rights shall have the same meaning and scope. Even more specifically, it is suggested that Article 52(3) can operate as a rule of conflict: in case of conflicting approaches in the case law of the two European Courts, national courts should give an ECHR conform interpretation of EU law. By emphasising the importance of Article 52(3) of the Charter, the book ultimately contends that there should never be an incompatibility between the two sources if the rights correspond (and they do in the majority of the cases), because complying with the ECHR minimum standards, as interpreted by the ECtHR, would also mean complying with primary law of the EU.

PART I

The New European Fundamental Rights Architecture

1

The Development of EU Fundamental Rights Law

I. Introduction

In the aftermath of the Second World War the European and international institutional system was designed anew. The atrocities committed during the War required action aimed at ensuring that the past could not repeat itself, and as a result, the codification and protection of fundamental rights became a central concern at both international and national level.

At the European level, two main organisations were created for this purpose: the Council of Europe (CoE) and the European Union (EU).[1] At the time of their creation, the CoE and the EU were completely separate systems with different roles and objectives. Today, they both share the same fundamental values – human rights, democracy and the rule of law – but they are still separate entities that perform different yet complementary roles.[2] Nevertheless, the links between the CoE and the EU have been institutionalised progressively, at least to some extent.[3] It is now clear that the EU has an increasingly important role to play in the area of fundamental rights protection, and that the European Convention on Human Rights (ECHR or 'the Convention') has had a tremendous influence on the development of EU fundamental rights law. Even though the two organisations have enriched each other and have worked closely with each other, they have never been able to make themselves permanently complementary. The transition from being completely distinct systems to being partly integrated, partly

[1] On the history of European integration see, inter alia, I Bache, S George and S Bulmer, *Politics in the European Union* (Oxford, Oxford University Press, 2011); D Dinan, *Origins and Evolution of the European Union* (Oxford, Oxford University Press, 2006); D Dinan, *Europe Recast: A History of European Union* (New York, Palgrave Macmillan, 2004); M Stirk, *A History of European Integration since 1914* (London, Pinter, 1996). On the history of the CoE and the ECHR see, eg, B Wassenberg, *History of the Council of Europe* (Strasbourg, Council of Europe Publishing, 2013).

[2] AW Heringa, 'Editorial: Europe's Common Bill of Rights' (1996) 3 *Maastricht Journal of European and Comparative Law* 1.

[3] eg the head of the EU delegation to the CoE participates (without voting rights) in all meetings of the Committee of Ministers. See also the reference in (now) Art 220 of the Treaty on the Functioning of the European Union (TFEU), which has been in the Treaties since the foundation of the EU, as well as the explicit competence for the EU to accede to the ECHR in Art 6(2) of the Treaty on European Union (TEU).

autonomous, complementary and overlapping systems, both charged with protecting fundamental rights, took over 50 years.

The Treaty of Lisbon further extended the scope of the EU action in many areas, including human rights protection, which has led to an increased cooperation between the two European organisations and has even opened the way for the EU's accession to the ECHR. These developments have been characterised as 'fundamentally changing' the architecture of human rights in the EU,[4] taking the protection of human rights 'to a new level',[5] and providing for an 'improved' and 'effective' judicial protection of human rights.[6] Today, more than ever before, the EU portrays itself as an organisation that is committed to human rights protection and that requires respect for those rights, not only by the EU, but also by its Member States and its partners in the international arena. This chapter returns to the EU's origins and explains how the EU evolved from a limited economic Community to a powerful entity in which the protection of fundamental rights has become a central commitment.

The evolution of EU fundamental rights law is divided into three broad periods. The first is the period immediately after the creation of the European Community (now the EU), characterised by the absence of human rights in the EU legal system (section II). The second is the period of the emergence of EU fundamental rights as general principles of EU law, inspired by the common constitutional traditions of the EU Member States and the ECHR, and developed by the Court of Justice of the European Union (CJEU or 'the Court') (section III). The third and final phase is the present-day framework, covering the period after the entry into force of the Treaty of Lisbon in December 2009 (section IV). Section V reflects on the development of EU fundamental rights law and the role and place of fundamental rights in the EU today. Section VI seeks to draw a conclusion about the impact of all of this.

II. The Creation of the European Community and the Silence on Human Rights

'We must re-create the European family in a regional structure called, it may be, the United States of Europe …'[7] In his famous speech in 1946, Winston Churchill

[4] I Pernice, 'The Treaty of Lisbon and Fundamental Rights' in S Griller and J Ziller, *The Lisbon Treaty. EU Constitutionalism without a Constitutional Treaty?* (Heidelberg, Springer, 2008) 235, 252.

[5] K Mathisen, 'The Impact of the Lisbon Treaty, in particular Article 6 TEU, on Member States' obligations with respect to the protection of fundamental rights', *University of Luxembourg, Law Working Paper Series Paper 2010-01*, 4.

[6] D Leczykiewicz, 'Effective Judicial Protection of Human Rights after Lisbon' (2010) 35 *EL Rev* 326, 330.

[7] W Churchill, speech delivered at the University of Zurich, 19 September 1946, available at www.coe.int/t/dgal/dit/ilcd/Archives/selection/Churchill/ZurichSpeech_en.asp (last accessed 16 December 2020).

called on Europe to unite. His words helped generate the first important step in this endeavour taken in May 1948, when a congress, consisting of approximately 800 Ministers, Members of Parliament, trade unionists, artists, journalists, economists and members of the liberal professions, was convened at The Hague to discuss and make proposals for a body to represent democratic Europe. The congress proposed the creation of a European assembly resting on common acceptance and the protection of human rights and democracy, and various other measures for coordinating and harmonising European policies.[8] This programme of unity was undertaken to prevent a return to totalitarian regimes, to defend fundamental rights, peace and democracy, and to encourage economic prosperity and stimulate international cooperation.[9]

After some months of negotiations between the Governments of Belgium, France, Luxembourg, the Netherlands, the United Kingdom, Denmark, Ireland, Italy, Norway and Sweden on the specificities of this new body, the CoE was created. It was an inter-governmental entity comprising 10 Member States (now 47), with the primary mission to promote and protect human rights and fundamental freedoms, the rule of law and democracy.[10] The ECHR – a treaty negotiated under the auspices of the CoE – was the first international human rights treaty with enforcement mechanisms. It came into force on 3 September 1953. Already distinctive at its conception, the ECHR has since evolved into a sophisticated legal system. While creating the CoE was certainly the first milestone on the way to a closer Europe, some states wanted even closer and deeper integration.

It was the French Foreign Minister, Robert Schuman, who took the first step in the process of the foundation of the EU. In his speech, inspired by Jean Monnet, Schuman proposed that France and Germany, and any other European country wishing to join them, pool their coal and steel resources. Schuman argued that '[t]he pooling of coal and steel production should immediately provide for the setting up of common foundations for economic development as a first step in the federation of Europe'.[11] The first agreement created was the Treaty establishing the European Coal and Steel Community (ECSC), signed by Belgium, France, West Germany, Italy, Luxembourg and the Netherlands in 1951. It entered into force on 23 July 1952 and expired on 23 July 2002, exactly 50 years later. Another Treaty that was also created in 1952 was the European Defence Community Treaty (EDC Treaty), initially signed by the six countries but ultimately rejected on a procedural motion by the French National Assembly in 1954. The European

[8] MJ Dedman, *The Origins and Development of the European Union 1945–2008* (Abingdon, Routledge, 2010).

[9] The Preamble to the Statute of the Council of Europe (1949) states 'Reaffirming their devotion to the spiritual and moral values which are the common heritage of their peoples … there is a need of a closer unity between all like-minded countries of Europe'. The Preamble to the EEC Treaty (1957) refers to laying the 'foundation of an even closer union among the peoples of Europe'.

[10] See Preamble to and Art 1 of the Statute of the Council of Europe.

[11] The Schuman Declaration, 9 May 1950.

Political Community Treaty (EPC Treaty), which was never formally signed, was also drafted to accompany the EDC Treaty. Interestingly, however, this EPC Treaty contained provisions that can be found in the EU Treaties today. According to the EPC Treaty, the main objective of the (then) European Community was to contribute towards the protection of human rights and fundamental freedoms in the Member States, and to integrate the ECHR into the system.[12] This is proof that, even at its inception, the EU was a project with goals that went beyond economics, even if the States were not (yet) ready to make such a commitment.[13] The next step was taken in 1957 when the Treaties establishing the European Economic Community (EEC) and the European Atomic Energy Community (EURATOM) were signed in Rome.[14] These Treaties did not contain express human rights clauses, except for a limited number of economic rights, such as freedom from discrimination on the basis of nationality in relation to free movement of workers (Article 7 EEC) and in the workplace (Article 199 EEC).

The silence on human rights was further reflected in Article 2 of the EEC Treaty, which provided that 'the Community shall have as its task … to promote throughout the community a harmonious development of economic activities, a continuous and balanced expansion, an increase in stability, an accelerated raising of the standard of living and closer relations between the states belonging to it'. This is of course very different from Article 2 of the TEU today, which refers to the respect for human dignity, freedom, democracy, equality, the rule of law and respect for human rights, including the rights of persons belonging to minorities, as the EU's founding values.

The early case law of the Court of Justice also reflects the reluctance to engage with human rights. The first time the Court was confronted with claims based on fundamental rights was in the 1959 *Stork* case.[15] The Court refused to annul decisions of the High Authority of the ECSC on the basis of their incompatibility with the rights as protected in the German *Grundgesetz*. In the subsequent *Geitling and Sgarlata* cases,[16] the Court maintained the restrictive approach, limiting itself to matters concerning purely economic integration. Both the lack of a catalogue

[12] See Arts 2 and 3 of the Draft Treaty embodying the Statute of the European Political Community (1952–1953). For a detailed analysis of the draft EPC Treaty, see G de Búrca, 'The Road Not Taken: The EU as Global Human Rights Actor' (2011) 105 *American Journal of International Law* 649.

[13] As Weiler has put it, '[the European project] had a spiritual dimension: Redefining human relations, the very way individuals relate to each other and to their community' in J Weiler, 'On the Values, Virtues (and Vices) of the European Construct: What we can learn from Aristotle, Aquinas and Maimonides', presentation at the Hertie School of Governance (13 March 2012) 2–3.

[14] Weiler commented that '[n]either the Treaty of Paris nor the Treaty of Rome contained any allusion to the protection of fundamental human rights'. See J Weiler, 'Fundamental Rights and Fundamental Boundaries: On the Conflict of Standards and Values in the Protection of Human Rights in the European Legal Space' in J Weiler, *The Constitution of Europe* (Cambridge, Cambridge University Press, 1999) 102, 107.

[15] Case C-1/58 *Friedrich Stork & Cie v High Authority of the European Coal and Steel Community*, ECLI:EU:C:1959:4.

[16] Joined Cases C-36, 37, 38 and 40/59 *Geitling Ruhrkohlen-Verkaufsgesellschaft and Others v ECSC High Authority*, ECLI:EU:C:1960:36; Case C-40/64 *Marcello Sgarlata and others v Commission of the EEC*, ECLI:EU:C:1965:36.

of human rights in Community law and the fact that the Court was not expressly given the power to review Community acts for infringements of human rights, contributed to the Court's early refusal to exercise such a review. This was to change gradually, as we shall see.

III. Fundamental Rights as General Principles of EU Law

Former Advocate General Jacobs wrote some years ago that 'the whole foundations [of the protection of fundamental rights at the EU level] were the work of the Court',[17] and indeed the CJEU has played a central role in developing EU fundamental rights.

A. The New Approach

The new attitude in the case law of the Court of Justice was revealed for the first time in the 1969 *Stauder*[18] judgment, in which the Court implicitly pointed to the fact that fundamental rights were enshrined in the general principles of Community law.[19] The Court based this statement on an assumption of what the intentions of the Treaty drafters had been at the time. In more elaborate wording one year later, the Court confirmed that respect for fundamental rights formed an integral part of the general principles of Community law and that the protection of those rights, whilst inspired by the constitutional traditions common to the Member States, must be ensured within the framework of the structure and objectives of the Community.[20]

The Court's new approach did not end the ongoing debate in Germany concerning the lack of a catalogue of rights in the Community, however. In the decision famously known as *Solange I*,[21] the German *Bundesverfassungsgericht* reserved the right to review the compatibility of Community law with the German Constitution, as long as ('*so lange*') the Community did not have a catalogue of its own, comparable to the catalogue of fundamental rights in the German Basic Law.[22] Another constitutional court that was not convinced was the Italian *Corte*

[17] FG Jacobs, 'Human Rights in the European Union: the Role of the Court of Justice' (2001) 26 *EL Rev* 337. See also A Tizzano, 'The Role of the ECJ in the Protection of Fundamental Rights' in A Arnull, P Eckhout and T Tridimas (eds), *Continuity and Change In EU Law: Essays in Honour of Francis Jacobs* (Oxford, Oxford University Press, 2008) 125.

[18] Case 29/69 *Erich Stauder v City of Ulm – Sozialamt*, ECLI:EU:C:1969:57.

[19] ibid 419.

[20] Case 11/70 *Internationale Handelsgesellschaft mbH v Einfuhr- und Vorratsstelle für Getreide und Futtermittel*, ECLI:EU:C:1970:114, paras 3 and 4.

[21] BVerfGE 37, 271 2 BvL 52/71 *Solange I-Beschluß* (29 May 1974).

[22] The decision was criticised by the Commission (see Commission of the European Communities, *Eighth General Report on the Activities of the European Communities* (1974) 270) as well as by the

Constituzionale. In the *Frontini* decision,[23] the Constitutional Court interpreted Article 11 of the Italian Constitution, which determines conditions under which Italy may transfer part of its sovereignty by means of an international agreement, as requiring that Community competences must not infringe fundamental rights. Notwithstanding the challenges posed by the German and the Italian Constitutional Court, the Luxembourg Court continued developing its own internal control mechanism, reaffirming that human rights and freedoms are general principles of Community law (now Union law), based on the constitutional traditions common to the Member States and pertinent international instruments, in particular the ECHR.

The first reference to international human rights treaties was made in *Nold*,[24] where the Court held that in order to determine the common constitutional standards for the Member States, it would look at the human rights treaties ratified by all states.[25] No specific reference to the ECHR had been made, however, since France had not ratified the Convention at this point. As of 1974, all the Member States had become Contracting Parties to the ECHR,[26] which led the Luxembourg Court to look for inspiration in the ECHR, in addition to common constitutional traditions, in developing its own fundamental rights standards.

The ECHR was referred to for the first time explicitly by the Court in the 1975 *Rutili* judgment,[27] and has since then been referred to numerous more times. In the *Hauer* judgment[28] of 1979, the Court examined the right to property as protected in Article 1 of the First Protocol to the ECHR, as well as specific provisions of the German Basic Law and of the Irish and Italian Constitutions. This is one of the few examples of comparative analysis of constitutional traditions adopted by the Luxembourg Court in the early years. The Court does not often engage in thorough analysis of the constitutional traditions of the Member States and focuses on the ECHR instead.[29] This is not surprising: the ECHR can be seen as a

European Parliament, but also by many commentators. See, eg, W Edeson and F Wooldridge, 'European Community Law and Fundamental Human Rights: Some Recent Decisions of the European Court and National Courts' (1976) 1 *Legal Issues of European Integration* 44.

[23] *Frontini v Ministero delle Finanze*, Corte Constituzionale Case no 183/73 (1973). See also FP Ruggieri Laderchi, 'Report on Italy' in AM Slaughter, AS Sweet and J Weiler (eds), *The European Courts and National Courts* (Oxford, Hart Publishing, 1998).

[24] Case 4/73 *Nold v Commission*, ECLI:EU:C:1975:114.

[25] Even though the applicant specifically referred to the ECHR, the Court of Justice did not make a specific reference to it at this point.

[26] France was the last EC Member State to ratify the ECHR in 1974.

[27] Case 36/75, *Rutili v Ministre de l'intérieur*, ECLI:EU:C:1975:137, para 32.

[28] Case 44/79 *Liselotte Hauer v Land Rheinland-Pfalz*, ECLI:EU:C:1979:290.

[29] C McCrudden, 'Using Comparative Reasoning in Human Rights Adjudication: The Court of Justice of the European Union and the European Court of Human Rights Compared' (2013) 15 *Cambridge Yearbook of European Legal Studies* 383; B De Witte, 'Balancing of Economic Law and Human Rights by the European Court of Justice' in PM Dupuy, F Francioni and EU Petersmann (eds), *Human Rights in International Investment Law and Arbitration* (Oxford, Oxford University Press, 2009).

representative of common standards, to which all Member States are bound. Under its general principles case law, the Court protects and upholds fundamental rights in relation to the actions of the EU institutions, but also against Member States when they act 'within the scope of Community law'.[30] There are two main categories to be distinguished concerning the latter: national measures implementing or applying EU law (*Wachauf* line of cases)[31] and national measures derogating from EU law (*ERT* line of cases).[32]

The political institutions confirmed their commitment to fundamental rights in the Joint Declaration on Human Rights issued in 1977.[33] The European Council endorsed the Joint Declaration the following year, and respect for human rights was said to be one of the 'cherished values' of the Union.[34] The Court of Justice thus succeeded in the endeavour it undertook in the late 1960s, developing fundamental rights case law without the guidance of any express treaty provisions. Both the *Corte Costituzionale* and the *Bundesverfassungsgericht* reconsidered their position after having witnessed the development of the Court's fundamental rights case law, and decided that they would no longer review the compatibility of EU legislation with fundamental rights, as long as the EU, and in particular the Court of Justice, continued to protect fundamental rights adequately.[35] This case law of the Court prompted further steps by other Community institutions and the Member States to underline the Community's political commitment to respect for fundamental rights.

[30] On the notion 'scope of Community law', see J Temple Lang, 'The Sphere in Which Member States are Obliged to Comply with the General Principles of Community Fundamental Rights Principles' (1991) 2 *Legal Issues of European Integration* 23; Jacobs (n 17).

[31] Case 5/88 *Hubert Wachauf v Bundesamt für Ernährung und Forstwirtschaft*, ECLI:EU:C:1989:321. In this line of cases the Court ruled that Member States are bound by Community fundamental rights when they adopt measures to implement regulations or transpose directives, or more generally when they apply national rules whose subject matter is governed by provisions of Community primary and/or secondary legislation.

[32] Case C-260/89 *Elliniki Radiophonia Tileorassi AE (ERT) v Dimotiki Etairia Pliroforissis and Sotirios Kouvelas*, ECLI:EU:C:1991:254. In this line of cases, the Court widened the interpretation of holding that the Member States are also bound by Community fundamental rights when they are trying to justify a national measure that limits any of the Treaty rights, especially free movement rights. For an overview of the *Wachauf/ERT* line of cases, see X Groussot, L Pech and GT Petursson, 'The Reach of EU Fundamental Rights on Member State Action after Lisbon' in S de Vries, U Bernitz and S Weatherill (eds), *The Protection of Fundamental Rights in the EU After Lisbon* (Oxford, Hart Publishing, 2013).

[33] Joint Declaration on Fundamental Human Rights [1977] OJ C-103/1.

[34] European Council Copenhagen Declaration on Democracy, EC Bull 3-1978.

[35] *SpA Granital v Amministrazione delle Finanze dello Stato*, Corte Costituzionale Case no 170/84 (1984) and *Solange II*, BVerfGE 73, 339 2 BvR 197/83 (1986). See also *Solange III*, BVerfGE 2 BvL 1/97 (2000). Yet the concerns of the *Bundesverfassungsgericht* about the lack of robust fundamental rights protections in the EU have not completely disappeared, as demonstrated in the ruling on the Maastricht Treaty in 1993, and more recently in 2009, when it ruled on the Lisbon Treaty (or, more accurately, on the German laws implementing the Lisbon Treaty). For discussion, see M Kumm and VF Comella, 'The Primacy Clause of the Constitutional Treaty and the Future of Constitutional Conflict in the European Union', *Jean Monnet Working Paper 5/04*, available at www.jeanmonnetprogram.org/archive/papers/04/040501-15.pdf (last accessed 16 December 2020).

B. Treaty Amendments – Building in a Human Rights Perspective

The first reference to fundamental rights in the Treaties can be found in the Preamble to the Single European Act (1987), which was the first major treaty reform of the EEC Treaty. The formal reference to fundamental rights was finally inserted in the Maastricht Treaty in Article F(2) of the EU Treaty (now Article 6(2) of the TEU). The provision confirmed the existing case law of the Court, reflecting an increased awareness at the political level of the need for the Union to respect fundamental rights.[36] At the same time, however, it caused confusion, as it was excluded from the jurisdiction of the Court of Justice.[37] In other words, there was no judicial mechanism for enforcing the obligation Article F(2) of the EU Treaty imposed on the Union. Nevertheless, the Court continued to develop its case law, as it did before the Maastricht Treaty: outside of the Treaty framework and on the basis of its general principles.

The Treaty of Amsterdam (1999) deepened the commitment for fundamental rights protection within the Union, inter alia by strengthening the role of the Luxembourg Court in this matter. It corrected the 'mistake' of Maastricht, and formally clarified that the jurisdiction of the Court of Justice applied to Article 6(2) TEU with regard to actions of the EU institutions (Article 46(d) TEU). In addition, the Treaty of Amsterdam introduced a political mechanism for sanctioning Member States guilty of a 'serious and persistent breach' of the principles on which the Union is founded, including respect for fundamental rights. According to Article 7 TEU, as amended by the Treaty of Amsterdam, a 'serious and persistent breach' of fundamental rights may result in the suspension of Member States' rights derived from the Treaty, including voting rights. However, even after Amsterdam, the incorporation of fundamental rights in the Treaty did not go beyond the confirmation of the jurisprudence of the Court of Justice, and thus the codification of rights that already existed.[38]

C. An EU Bill of Rights

The initiative for drafting an EU Bill of Rights dates back to the German presidency of the European Council in the first half of 1999.[39] The EU Charter of Fundamental

[36] A Arnull, 'Opinion 2/94 and Its Implications for the Future Constitution of the Union' in University of Cambridge Centre for European Legal Studies, *The Human Rights Opinion of the ECJ and its Constitutional Implications* (1996) CELS Occasional Paper No 1, available at www.cels.law.cam.ac.uk/publications/occasional%20papers/Paper_1.pdf (last accessed 16 December 2020).

[37] Art L of the TEU excluded Art F(2) from the jurisdiction of the Court of Justice. For a discussion, see G Gaja, 'The protection of Human Rights under the Maastricht Treaty' in D Curtin and T Heukels (eds), *Institutional Dynamics of European Integration* (Dordrecht, Nijhoff Publishers, 1994).

[38] For an overview of the changes brought about by different treaty amendments, see B Moriarty, 'Human Rights in EU Law' in B Moriarty and E Massa, *Human Rights Law* (Oxford, Oxford University Press, 2012) 155.

[39] See European Council, Presidency Conclusions, Cologne, 3–4 June 1999.

Rights, 'solemnly proclaimed' on 7 December 2000, in Nice, was the first formal EU document to combine and declare all fundamental rights and values to which EU citizens are entitled. Its main objective was to 'make more visible and explicit to EU citizens the fundamental rights they already enjoy at European level'.[40] At this initial stage the Charter was a non-binding declaration, however. This confirmed the continuing reluctance of (some of) the Member States[41] to commit themselves to a legally binding catalogue of rights, presumably because they wanted to keep the scope of application of EU law as limited as possible and prevent an unintended extension of the Union's competencies. The lack of binding force did not, of course, mean that the Charter had no legal value. It was referred to in the preambles to texts of secondary legislation and used as a document of reference by the various EU institutions. As such, the Charter had an important role in the construction of a European corpus of human rights law, even when it was not formally binding.[42]

IV. Fundamental Rights Protection in Post-Lisbon Europe

The Treaty of Lisbon came into force on 1 December 2009, marking what EU leaders have described as a 'new era' for the Union.[43] Article 6 TEU sets out three main strands of protection: first, it states that the Union shall respect the Charter of Fundamental Rights, which has the same legal value as the Treaties; second, it makes accession to the ECHR a legal obligation; and, third, it confirms that fundamental rights, as guaranteed by the ECHR and as they result from the common constitutional traditions of the Member States, constitute general principles of EU law. These three strands of protection are examined in turn below. In addition, Article 7 TEU now gives the EU the power to act against a Member State that seriously and persistently violates common values enshrined in Article 2 TEU, thereby entrusting the EU with the protection of the most fundamental values the EU and the Member States have in common, in case national safeguards fail.[44] Thus,

[40] As underlined by the (then) President of the European Commission in 2000, Romano Prodi. As to the doubts whether or not the EU needed the Charter, see J Weiler, 'Editorial: Does the European Union Truly Need a Charter of Rights?' (2000) 6 *European Law Journal* 95.

[41] The firm opposition came from the British Government. The Irish, the Dutch and the Scandinavian Member States also had certain reservations. Belgium, France, Germany and Italy, on the other hand, were strong supporters of giving the Charter a legally binding status.

[42] J Dutheil de la Rochère, 'The EU Charter of Fundamental Rights, Not Binding but Influential: the Example of Good Administration' in A Arnull, P Eeckhout and T Tridimas, *Continuity and Change in EU Law: Essays in Honour of Sir Francis Jacobs* (Oxford, Oxford University Press, 2008).

[43] The Treaty of Lisbon was originally conceived as a 'Constitution for Europe', but its problematic ratification process, meeting popular rejection in France and the Netherlands, resulted in a re-ordering of the first agreed text and partial renegotiations. The majority of innovations proposed in the original Treaty, however, were carried over to the Lisbon Treaty.

[44] On the procedure of Art 7 TEU, see, amongst many, L Besselink, 'The Bite, the Bark and the Howl: Article 7 TEU and the Rule of Law Initiatives' in A Jakab and D Kochenov (eds), *The Enforcement of EU Law and Values* (Oxford, Oxford University Press, 2017); C Closa and D Kochenov (eds), *Reinforcing the Rule of Law Oversight in the European Union* (Cambridge, Cambridge University Press, 2016).

after Lisbon, the EU Treaties not only commit the EU to the values enshrined in Article 2, but they also foresee such a policy in relation to the Member States. Finally, fundamental rights have become part of the entire policy cycle in the EU and are at the centre of the EU's very purpose and identity.[45] All EU institutions, bodies, offices and agencies are under the same duty to respect, observe and promote the Charter when exercising their competences,[46] and thus have a role and a capacity to 'protect' fundamental rights. The obligation to promote and support fundamental rights equally applies in the external relations of the EU, both in trade and investment policies and in the area of Common Foreign and Security Policy (CFSP).[47]

A. EU Charter of Fundamental Rights

i. Legal Status

Article 6(1) TEU states that the EU Charter of Fundamental Rights, proclaimed in 2000, is primary EU law. The text of the Charter itself is not incorporated into the Treaties, but it is accorded the same legal value as the Treaties. In other words, the Charter is primary EU law. The Charter reflects the common values of the peoples of Europe, and is based on the common constitutional traditions of the EU Member States and the international human rights treaties they have concluded in view of safeguarding human rights protection.[48] Its main objective is to make EU fundamental rights more visible and explicit to EU citizens.

ii. Content

The EU Charter of Fundamental Rights comprises 54 articles that fall under seven headings or titles, six of which are devoted to listing specific types of rights, while the last clarifies the scope of application of the Charter and the principles governing its interpretation.

The Charter draws on the ECHR, the European Social Charter and other human rights conventions, as well as the rights and principles resulting from the common constitutional traditions of EU Member States. Furthermore, the Charter contains the rights developed in the case law of the Court of Justice,

[45] M Dawson, *The Governance of EU Fundamental Rights* (Cambridge, Cambridge University Press, 2017).

[46] Regarding the three main institutions, namely, the Commission, the Council and the Parliament, see section IV.A.iv.

[47] Case C-366/10 *Air Transport Association of America and Others*, ECLI:EU:C:2011:864, para 101; and Case C-263/14 *Parliament v Council*, ECLI:EU:C:2016:435, para 47. See also Joint Communication to the European Parliament and the Council: Action Plan on Human Rights and Democracy (2015–2019) 'Keeping human rights at the heart of the EU agenda', 16 final, 28 April 2015.

[48] Preamble to the Charter of Fundamental Rights of the European Union [2000] OJ C364/01.

but it also incorporates some of the 'third generation' rights, such as guarantees on bioethics and transparent administration. These rights do not often appear in national constitutions or in other international conventions ratified by the EU Member States, thus testifying to the Charter's innovative character.[49] Importantly, the Charter makes a distinction between rights and principles. The latter, according to Article 52(5) of the Charter, are to be implemented through additional legislation, and only become justiciable in cases involving the interpretation and legality of such laws. The Charter, however, does not clarify which articles are rights – that are indisputable and can be enforced before courts – and which are principles that need to be implemented through legislative or executive acts before they can give rise to direct claims for positive action. The absence of a clear distinction in the Charter is primarily the result of the reluctance among the drafters to give all rights included in the Charter equal status.[50] The Charter Explanations do not shed much light on this question either, except for giving a few examples of the latter category: Articles 25, 26, 34(1) and 35–38 are identified as principles, and Articles 23, 33 and 34 are said to contain elements of both rights and principles. As becomes clear, most of these provisions are found in Title IV on Solidarity, and concern economic, social and cultural (ESC) rights.

The CJEU's case law in this regard also remains limited. In *Kamberaj*, for example, the Court used the concepts 'right', 'principle' and 'general principle' interchangeably.[51] In *AMS*, a case concerning the right of workers to information and consultation within the undertaking, the Court ruled that for Article 27 of the Charter to be fully effective, it must be given more specific expression in EU or national law, thus suggesting that Article 27 is in fact a 'principle'.[52] In *Glatzel*, a case concerning discrimination on disability grounds, the Court expressly identified Article 26 of the Charter as a 'principle'.[53] However, the Court did not elaborate on the exact consequences of a Charter provision's being identified as a principle. It seemed to adopt a narrow interpretation of Article 52(5), with the focus on measures implementing Article 26, and did not consider the duty incumbent upon the EU and its Member States before the implementation has taken place.[54]

[49] C Ladenburger, FIDE 2012 – Session on 'Protection of Fundamental Rights post-Lisbon – The interaction between the Charter of Fundamental Rights, the European Convention of Human Rights and National Constitutions', Institutional Report, available at www.fide2012.eu/index.php?doc_id=88 (last accessed 16 December 2020).

[50] See, eg, J Krommendijk, 'Principled silence or mere silence on principles? The role of the EU Charter's principles in the case law of the Court of Justice' (2015) 11 *European Constitutional Law Review* 321.

[51] Case C-571/10 *Kamberaj*, ECLI:EU:C:2012:233.

[52] Case C-176/12 *AMS*, ECLI:EU:C:2014:2, para 45.

[53] Case C-356/12 *Wolfgang Glatzel*, ECLI:EU:C:2014:350, para 78.

[54] For discussion of the binding effect of principles, see T Lock, 'Rights and Principles in the EU Charter of Fundamental Rights' (2019) 56 *CML Rev* 1201.

iii. Scope of Application

The scope of application of the Charter is defined in its Article 51(1), which provides that the provisions of the Charter are addressed to the institutions and bodies of the Union with due regard for the principle of subsidiarity, and to the Member States only when they are implementing Union law. The wording of the provision seems to suggest a rather limited scope of application: in order for the Charter to be applicable to actions of the Member States, they must be 'implementing EU law'. This has raised doubts among the legal scholars and practitioners: does the wording of Article 51(1) imply that the scope is more limited than under the pre-Charter case law of the CJEU?[55] Some scholars argued that the Charter should have a more limited scope of application, as intended by the Treaty drafters,[56] while others endorsed a broader interpretation as provided in the Explanations relating to the Charter,[57] contending that the concept of 'implementing EU law' should be seen as equivalent to the case law notion of 'acting within the scope of EU law' for all practical purposes.[58]

The CJEU provided some clarification in the *Åkerberg Fransson* judgment,[59] a case referred by a District Court in Sweden, asking whether the EU principle of *ne bis in idem* prevented a Member State from imposing criminal sanctions for tax evasion where it already had imposed administrative penalties. The Swedish Government, all the intervening Member States,[60] as well as the European Commission argued that the Court had no jurisdiction to answer the questions referred for a preliminary ruling, as the tax penalties and the criminal proceedings in question did not arise from the implementation of EU law. The Court concluded, however, that even though the tax penalties and criminal proceedings did not arise from implementation of EU law, the relevant national law was designed to penalise the infringement of Directive 2006/112 and was therefore intended to implement an obligation of EU law.[61] In other words, the CJEU opted for a broader interpretation of the Charter's scope. In *Iida*, the Court of Justice provided additional guidance for determining the scope of application of the Charter: it held that national courts must determine if the national legislation at stake is intended to

[55] The pre-Charter scope of application of EU fundamental rights appears broader: Member States were bound by EU fundamental rights when they were 'implementing' EU law (*Wachauf*) and when they were acting 'in the scope of [EU] law', also including when they adopted rules on the basis of a derogation conferred by the Treaty freedoms (*ERT*).

[56] eg P Yowell, 'The Justiciability of the Charter of Fundamental Rights in the Domestic Law of Member States' in PM Huber and K Ziegler (eds), *The EU and National Constitutional Law* (Munich, Richard Boorberg Verlag, 2012) 107. For an overview of the drafting history of Art 51(1) of the Charter, see PM Huber, 'The Unitary Effect of the Community's Fundamental Rights: The ERT-Doctrine Needs to be Reviewed' (2008) 14 *European Public Law* 323.

[57] Explanations relating to the Charter of Fundamental Rights, [2007] OJ C303/17.

[58] P Craig, *The Lisbon Treaty: Law, Politics, and Treaty Reform* (Oxford, Oxford University Press, 2010) 210; M Dougan, 'The Treaty of Lisbon 2007: Winning minds, not hearts' (2008) 45 *CML Rev* 663.

[59] Case C-617/10 *Åklagaren v Hans Åkerberg Fransson*, ECLI:EU:C:2013:105.

[60] The Czech Republic, Denmark, Ireland and the Netherlands.

[61] *Åklagaren v Hans Åkerberg Fransson* (n 59) para 28.

implement EU law, what its character is, whether it pursues objectives other than those covered by EU law and whether there are specific EU rules on the matter capable of affecting it.[62] Nevertheless, these criteria are neither cumulative nor exhaustive, and determining the scope of application of the Charter remains tricky for the national bodies and courts.[63] As for the EU institutions, bodies, offices and agencies, the Charter is binding upon them even when they are acting outside the scope of the Treaties.[64]

iv. The Charter and the EU Legislative Process

The EU Charter of Fundamental Rights has had a major impact on the law and policy-making process in the EU, not only in the judicial process but also in the *ex ante* political and legislative processes. This is particularly important because *ex ante* mechanisms seek to protect fundamental rights by preventing violations from occurring, which is different from the *ex post* judicial processes.[65] The EU institutions have all adjusted their procedures in order to ensure that all proposals for EU legislation and policy are in compliance with the newly binding catalogue of human rights. The Commission took the lead and the Council and the Parliament followed suit.

a. The Commission

As early as in 2001, the European Commission committed itself to ensuring the compatibility of all legislative proposals with the Charter.[66] In 2005, the Commission set out its 'methodology for ensuring the Charter is properly implemented in Commission proposals',[67] followed by a report on the operation of the methodology in 2009.[68] The latter report noted the positive developments, but also acknowledged the shortcomings and suggested improvements. As a consequence,

[62] Case C-40/11 *Iida*, ECLI:EU:C:2012:691, para 79.

[63] M Bobek and J Adams-Prassl (eds), *The EU Charter of Fundamental Rights in the Member States* (Oxford, Hart Publishing, 2020). See also annual reports of the Commission and the Fundamental Rights Agency (FRA) on the application of the Charter at national level.

[64] For instance, in the context of the EMS Treaty. See Joined Cases C-8/15 P to C-10/15 P, *Ledra Advertising and Others v European Commission and European Central Bank*, ECLI:EU:C:2016:701, para 67.

[65] M Dawson, 'Fundamental Rights in European Union Policy-making: The Effects and Advantages of Institutional Diversity' (2020) *Human Rights Law Review* 20, 50–73; Dawson (n 45).

[66] European Commission, Decision on the Application of the Charter of Fundamental Rights of the European Union SEC(2001) 380/3.

[67] European Commission Communication, 'Compliance with the Charter of Fundamental Rights in Commission legislative proposals – Methodology for systematic and rigorous monitoring' (27 April 2005) COM(2005) 172.

[68] European Commission Report, 'On the Practical Operation of the Methodology for a Systematic and Rigorous Monitoring of Compliance with the Charter of Fundamental Rights' (29 April 2009) COM(2009) 205 final.

the methodology was reinforced in 2010 with the 'Charter Strategy',[69] the objective of which has been to make the fundamental rights set out in the Charter as effective as possible. The Commission also announced publication of annual reports on the application of the Charter, and several practical measures to start building a 'fundamental rights culture' at all stages of EU legislative procedures.[70]

At the heart of the Charter Strategy is the fundamental rights 'checklist', which has been implemented in the context of impact assessments. It consists of six questions[71] designed to help the drafters identify which fundamental rights could be affected by draft legislation and policies, and to assess the impact on these rights of each envisaged policy option. Legislative proposals are to be accompanied by an explanatory memorandum, which 'must contain a summary explaining how fundamental rights obligations have been met'.[72]

In order to reinforce the Charter Strategy further and make it more effective in practice, the Commission introduced the 'Optional Guidance on Taking Account of Fundamental Rights in Commission Impact Assessments',[73] which complements the Commission's Impact Assessment Guidelines introduced earlier.[74] This was another way of adding a fundamental rights element to the early stages of the EU legislative process. The problem was, however, that the Charter rights have been divided according to the existing economic-social-environmental structure of the impact assessments, without any internal revision. It turned out to be an exercise of fitting fundamental rights into the existing structure, rather than revising the existing structure to accommodate fundamental rights. This kind of integrated approach allows the impact of fundamental rights to be factored into a broader set of considerations, which may have positive effects, but it could also result in some rights being overlooked and/or the consideration of the impact on certain rights being unfocused.

The Commission's strategies and fundamental rights 'checklist' have been criticised in the literature as being inadequate to ensure a systematic fundamental rights assessment of legislation. There are specific arguments to be made in relation to different aspects, but the general criticism concerns the lack of legal expertise on fundamental rights in the Impact Assessment Board and inadequate strategy regarding consultations with the relevant stakeholders, which, taken together, may lead to a 'box-ticking exercise' rather than a systematic, in-depth assessment.[75]

[69] European Commission Communication, Strategy for the effective implementation of the Charter of Fundamental Rights by the European Union (19 October 2010) COM(2010) 573/4.

[70] ibid 2.

[71] ibid 5.

[72] ibid 8.

[73] Commission Staff Working Paper, 'Operational Guidance on Taking Account of Fundamental Rights in Commission Impact Assessments' (6 May 2011) SEC(2011) 567 final.

[74] Communication from the Commission on Impact Assessment (5 June 2002) COM(2002) 276 final.

[75] I de Jesus Butler, 'Ensuring Compliance with the Charter of Fundamental Rights in Legislative Drafting: the practice of the European Commission' (2012) 37 *EL Rev* 4, 397; V Kosta, *Fundamental Rights in EU Internal Market Legislation* (Oxford, Hart Publishing, 2015).

The role of the Charter rights in the Commission's impact assessments has been enhanced gradually. In 2014, following the CJEU's judgment in *Digital Rights Ireland*,[76] in which the Court declared the Data Retention Directive[77] invalid on fundamental rights grounds, the Commission committed itself to revising the Optional Guidance, which was achieved by the Commission's Better Regulation Agenda.[78] The Better Regulation Guidelines and associated 'toolbox' aim to boost transparency and accountability in EU decision making and to improve the quality of laws. One of the key points is the comprehensive involvement of citizens and stakeholders in order to ensure that economic, social and environmental impacts, together with fundamental rights, continue to be considered at all stages of the legislative process. The specific tool 28, entitled 'fundamental rights and human rights', gives an overview of the most salient points to consider when assessing fundamental rights in impact assessments, also including a fundamental rights checklist that is now more elaborate. In addition, in 2015, the Commission trained specific departments to ensure that officials are able to apply a fundamental rights-based approach to policy and law making.[79] More recently, the new Interinstitutional Agreement on Better Law Making[80] now commits all institutions involved in the legislative process to go further, by preparing an impact assessment in certain cases, which would presumably also include considerations related to fundamental rights. While there are still further points of improvement,[81] the Commission's work demonstrates its dedication and willingness to engage further in the discussion, and its search for ways to improve the *ex ante* fundamental rights assessment at all the stages of the legislative process.

b. The Council

The Council of Ministers, unlike the Commission and the Parliament, did not have an established procedure for a fundamental rights assessment when the Charter came into force. In fact, it was only in 2011 that the Council adopted 'Guidelines on methodological steps to be taken to check fundamental rights compatibility at the Council preparatory bodies', framed as 'non-binding advice' intended to help the Council's preparatory bodies to identify and deal with fundamental rights issues arising in connection with the proposals under discussion.[82] The ruling in

[76] Case C-293/12 *Digital Rights Ireland*, ECLI:EU:C:2014:238.

[77] Directive 2006/24/EC on the retention of data generated or processed in connection with the provision of publicly available electronic communication services or of public communications networks and amending Directive 2002/58/EC (Data Retention Directive) [2006] OJ L105/54.

[78] European Commission Communication, 'Better regulation for better results – An EU agenda' (19 May 2015) COM(2015) 215 final.

[79] Report on the Application of the EU Charter of Fundamental Rights' (19 May 2016) COM(2016) 265 final.

[80] Interinstitutional Agreement between the European Parliament, the Council of the European Union and the European Commission on Better Law-Making [2016] OJ L123/1.

[81] See, eg, de Jesus Butler (n 75) 397–418.

[82] Council of the European Union, Guidelines on methodological steps to be taken to check fundamental rights compatibility at the Council's preparatory bodies (18 May 2011) Council Doc No 10140/11.

Digital Rights Ireland was also a red flag for the Council. In December 2014, the Council revised the Guidelines in order to enhance the assessment of the compatibility with fundamental rights.[83] The new Guidelines now include a fundamental rights checklist, which is similar to that of the Commission.[84]

Another point worth noting is that, in the methodologies for assessing the proposal, the revised Guidelines provide expressly for reference to be made to the case law of the European Court of Human Rights (ECtHR), alongside the Charter and the case law of the CJEU, whereas, in the earlier version, the ECHR and the case law of the ECtHR were only listed at the end under 'other sources of interpretation'.[85] This is particularly interesting in the context of the conflicts between EU law and the ECHR, since at least some potential conflicts could be mitigated *ex ante*. Further, the Guidelines recommend involving the FRA in assessing the proposal.[86] In case of doubt, the Guidelines recommend consulting the Council Legal Service, national experts in the Member States, the Working Party on Fundamental Rights, Citizenship and Free Movement of Persons (FREMP Working Party), or any other preparatory body specialising in human rights.[87] It is curious that the Council does not refer to the FRA in the 'in case of doubt' situations, but the real issue seems to be that the opinions on legislative proposals, especially those from the FRA, are not requested very often by the Council or the Commission. The Parliament has been more proactive in engaging the FRA. Finally, the Council also provided training to Council staff in order to make the guidelines more operational, stressing the importance of providing further training in order to raise awareness and enhance the protection of fundamental rights at all levels of the Council's work.[88]

c. The European Parliament

The European Parliament sought to promote fundamental rights much earlier than the Commission.[89] However, its actual role in checking the compatibility of EU legislation with fundamental rights has not been systematic, and the Parliament Legal Service checks compatibility only when the issue has been raised in the committees dealing with the proposal, or when the legislation is being amended.

[83] Council of the European Union, Guidelines on methodological steps to be taken to check fundamental rights compatibility at the Council's preparatory bodies (16 December 2014) Council Doc No 16957/14.
[84] ibid 24 (annex 5).
[85] ibid 8.
[86] ibid 8–9.
[87] ibid 10.
[88] See, eg, Outcome of the Council Meeting (23 June 2015) 10228/15, 17–18.
[89] Already in 1977, the Parliament issued a Declaration on Fundamental Human Rights, which was subsequently adopted by the Commission and the Council on 5 April 1977, [1977] OJ C103/1.

In 2009, the Parliament revised its Rules of Procedure to the Treaty of Lisbon and strengthened the compatibility check with the Charter by adding another procedure: a political group of at least 40 Members can request that a proposal for a legislative act or parts of it is referred to the committee responsible for the interpretation of the Charter, that is the Committee on Civil Liberties, Justice and Home Affairs (LIBE), if they are of the opinion that it does not comply with rights enshrined in the Charter.[90]

In early 2012, the Parliament established the Impact Assessment (IA) unit as a part of the Directorate for Impact Assessment and European Added Value, which deals with various aspects of an *ex ante* or *ex post* evaluation of EU legislation and policies. The IA unit now carries out its own impact assessment, primarily by checking if the Commission complied with the Better Regulation and the Toolbox. Finally, the Parliament may also seek advice from the FRA when in doubt about the compatibility of a proposal or an amendment with fundamental rights. As mentioned before, the Parliament has made use of this more than the Council and the Commission, but the power to request opinions of the FRA is generally under-utilised among the institutions. Overall, it can be concluded that the *ex ante* rights-based review, which is carried out at different phases of EU law-making procedure, is highly relevant in the context of conflicts between EU law and the ECHR, as it can mitigate some of the conflicts and even prevent them. While the relevant EU institutions have taken important steps to ensure that EU legislation is in line with fundamental rights, more efforts can be made in the coming years, such as through the adoption of a more proactive policy by the relevant institutions, as well as the closer involvement of the FRA and other expert agencies in the process.[91]

v. *The Charter and the Case Law of the CJEU*

The EU Charter did not play an important role in the jurisprudence of the Court of Justice in the first years after its proclamation. The Court continued to use general principles of law in fundamental rights cases and remained mostly silent on the Charter, although it was explicitly invited to use it on a number of occasions. There could be several reasons why the Court did not use the Charter in the early years. One reason could be that it simply did not need the Charter in order to rule in the cases before it, or that it was not yet sure how to use it. Another reason could be that the Court may have preferred the flexibility

[90] European Parliament, Rules of Procedure, 8th parliamentary term (2014–2019), rule 38, at www.europarl.europa.eu/sides/getDoc.do?pubRef=-//EP//NONSGML+RULES-EP+20150909+0+DOC+PDF+V0//EN&language=EN (last accessed 16 December 2020).

[91] Such as the European Border and Coast Guard Agency (FRONTEX), the European Institute for Gender Equality (EIGE) and the European Asylum Support Office (EASO). For a thorough assessment, see Dawson (n 45).

of using unwritten general principles, which gave it the possibility to deal with fundamental rights cases while also achieving other objectives along the way, such as advancing European integration. Making the Charter justiciable, either through the Treaties or judicial application, would likely limit, or at least change, the ways in which the Court would develop its fundamental rights jurisprudence.[92] The first (direct) reference to the Charter was made only in 2006.[93] After this judgment, the Court continued to use the concept of general principles of law and, occasionally, specified that these rights are also 'reaffirmed' in the Charter.[94] Interestingly, the Advocates General referred to the Charter more often, but even those references were brief, and sometimes also with an emphasis on the Charter's non-binding character.[95]

After the Treaty of Lisbon entered into force on 1 December 2009, and the Charter became legally binding, the Court started to apply the Charter directly. The first time the Court officially confirmed the new legal status of the Charter was in the *Kücükdeveci* case from 2010.[96] In the same year, the Court struck down secondary EU legislation, in the *Volker and Schecke* judgment,[97] for being incompatible with the Charter. The most prominent example came two years later in the *Digital Rights Ireland Ltd* case,[98] when the Court declared the Data Retention Directive invalid because it did not lay down the precise rules governing the extent of its interference with the fundamental rights enshrined in Article 7 and 8 of the Charter (respect for private and family life and protection of personal data), nor provide sufficient safeguards to ensure the effective protection of the data retained against the risk of abuse or any unlawful access and use of that information.[99] Today, the Charter is the main 'reference point' for the EU political institutions and for the Court when it comes to fundamental rights. The number of decisions in which the CJEU referred to and quoted the Charter increased tremendously in the first years of its binding legal effect, and the trend has continued to this day.

[92] See C Engel, 'The European Charter of Fundamental Rights – A Changed Political Opportunity Structure and its Normative Consequences' (2001) 7 *European Law Journal* 151; J Morijn, 'Judicial Reference to the EU Fundamental Rights Charter: First Experiences and Possible Prospects' Coimbra Human Rights Centre Working Paper (2002).

[93] Case C-540/03 *European Parliament v Council*, ECLI:EU:C:2006:429, para 38.

[94] According to the data provided by Gráinne de Búrca, the Charter was referred to in 59 judgments of the Court over this nine-year period, but many of these references did not entail any serious engagement with Charter provisions. See G de Búrca, 'After the EU Charter of Fundamental Rights: The Court of Justice as a Human Rights Adjudicator?' (2013) 20 *Maastricht Journal of European and Comparative Law* 168.

[95] See, for example, Opinion of AG Jacobs in Case C-270/99 *Z v Parliament*, ECLI:EU:C:2001:180, para 40; Opinion of AG Mischo in Joined Cases C-122/99 and C-125/99 *D and Kingdom of Sweden v Council*, ECLI:EU:C:2001:113, para 97; Opinion of AG Jacobs in Case C-377/98 *Netherlands v EP and Council*, ECLI:EU:C:2001:329, paras 197 and 210.

[96] Case C-555/07 *Kücükdeveci*, ECLI:EU:C:2010:21, para 22.

[97] Joined Cases C-92/09 and C-93/09 *Volker und Schecke*, ECLI:EU:C:2010:662.

[98] Case C-293/12 *Digital Rights Ireland*, ECLI:EU:C:2014:238.

[99] ibid paras 65–71.

vi. The Charter and the ECHR

The relationship between the Charter and the ECHR is mainly regulated in Article 52(3) of the Charter, comprising two complementary rules intended to ensure the consistency between the two documents. According to the first rule, when the Charter rights correspond to the Convention rights, 'the meaning and scope of those rights shall be the same'. This would actually be the case in most disputes, since approximately 90 per cent of the Charter's justiciable rights are borrowed from the Convention or from Strasbourg jurisprudence.[100] According to the Charter Explanations,[101] the meaning and the scope of the guaranteed rights are determined not only by the text of those instruments, but also by the case law of the ECtHR. The Charter's Official Explanations provide more clarification as to the meaning of Article 52(3), and while they are not legally binding, they should nonetheless be given due regard by the EU and Member State courts, in accordance with Article 52(7) of the Charter. The second complementary rule states that EU law is free to provide more extensive protection. In any event, pursuant to the Charter Explanations, the level of protection afforded by the Charter may never be lower than that guaranteed by the ECHR. In other words, Article 52(3) of the Charter operates as a rule of conflict: if there is an incompatibility in the way a specific right is interpreted and applied by the two European courts, EU law should align with ECHR law.[102]

vii. The Charter and National Constitutional Rights

The EU Charter of Fundamental Rights complements national systems of fundamental rights protection but it does not replace them. It comes into play only when Member States are acting within the scope of EU law, as stipulated in Article 51 of the Charter. However, having in mind that the Charter's catalogue of rights is extensive and that, as demonstrated earlier, it may have a wide scope of application in the Member States as a result of its interpretation by the CJEU, interactions between the Charter and national constitutional rights are likely to undergo a significant development in the years to come.

Article 52(4) of the Charter provides that where the Charter recognises fundamental rights 'as they result from the constitutional traditions common to the Member States, those rights shall be interpreted in harmony with those

[100] J Callewaert, 'The European Convention on Human Rights and European Union Law: A Long Way to Harmony' (2009) 6 *European Human Rights Law Review* 768. Note, however, that the wording of the corresponding provisions is not the same because of the Charter drafters' intention to simplify the Convention provisions and make them easier to understand, while sticking to the scope and meaning they have under the Convention.

[101] Explanations relating to the Charter of Fundamental Rights (n 57).

[102] See ch 2, section III.A.ii for further analysis of Art 52(3) of the Charter and the parameters of the relationship between EU law and the ECHR. See also M Claes, 'Fundamental Rights' in PJ Kuijper et al (eds), *The Law of the European Union* (Alphen a/d Rijn, Wolters Kluwer, 2018) 97.

traditions'. By referring to the constitutional traditions common to the Member States, the Charter does not seek to define the lowest common denominator of the Member States' constitutions but rather a higher standard of protection that is adapted to the nature of EU law and is in harmony with the national constitutional traditions.[103]

Furthermore, Article 53 of the Charter provides that nothing within the Charter is to be interpreted as restricting protections already recognised by, inter alia, the ECHR and Member States' constitutions. The text is reminiscent of Article 53 ECHR,[104] but it has been interpreted differently by the CJEU. The CJEU considered that Article 53 fails to address the practical reality of the EU's unique supranational order and the primacy doctrine, which are its essential features,[105] and that, by using the language of minimum and maximum protection, it does not address the potential conflicts between rights when different value systems and institutions are at stake. This issue became obvious in the *Melloni* case,[106] referred by the Spanish *Tribunal constitucional* to the CJEU for a preliminary ruling. The case concerned the issue of divergent levels of protection of fundamental rights at the national and European levels in relation to the execution of the European Arrest Warrant (EAW).

The Spanish *Tribunal constitucional* asked the CJEU whether the EAW Framework Decision[107] must indeed be interpreted in a way that is more restrictive in relation to the defendants' rights than is the case under Spanish law and, if so, whether the relevant provision of the Framework Decision was invalid for a breach of the right to a fair trial contained in the EU Charter of Fundamental Rights. If the answer to the latter question would be negative, the Spanish Constitutional Court asked whether it could apply its own constitutional rights and leave the Framework Decision unapplied, on the basis of Article 53 of the Charter. The Spanish Constitutional Court thus raised one of the most difficult questions for the multilevel system of rights protection in Europe: to what extent does EU law require a lower level of constitutional rights protection?[108] The CJEU essentially ruled that whenever the EU harmonises legislation in a certain

[103] K Lenaerts, 'Exploring the Limits of the EU Charter of Fundamental Rights' (2012) 8 *European Constitutional Law Review* 3.

[104] 'Nothing in this Convention shall be construed as limiting or derogating from any of the human rights and fundamental freedoms which may be ensured under the laws of any High Contracting Party or under any other agreement to which it is a Party.'

[105] See Opinion 1/91 *Draft Agreement relating to the creation of the European Economic Area*, ECLI:EU:C:1991:490, para 21; and Opinion 1/09 *Creation of a unified patent litigation system*, ECLI:EU:C:2011:123, para 65.

[106] Case C-399/11 *Melloni*, ECLI:EU:C:2013:107.

[107] Council Framework Decision 2009/299/JHA of 26 February 2009 amending Framework Decisions 2002/584/JHA, 2005/214/JHA, 2006/783/JHA, 2008/909/JHA and 2008/947/JHA, thereby enhancing the procedural rights of persons and fostering the application of the principle of mutual recognition to decisions rendered in the absence of the person concerned at the trial.

[108] A Torres Pérez, '*Melloni* in Three Acts: From Dialogue to Monologue' (2014) 10 *European Constitutional Law Review* 2.

area in an exhaustive way, the Member States are no longer allowed to require a higher standard of procedural safeguards, not even on the basis of their national constitutions. In those cases, the EU decides on the level of fundamental rights' protection it considers to be adequate, as it strikes a balance between those rights, on the one hand, and the effectiveness of EU law, on the other. According to the Court, national authorities and courts are free to apply higher national standards of protection of fundamental rights, a possibility envisaged by Article 53 of the Charter, 'provided that the level of protection provided for by the Charter, as interpreted by the Court, and the primacy, unity and effectiveness of EU law are not thereby compromised'.[109] *Melloni* can be seen as a step taken by the CJEU towards the centralisation of standards of fundamental rights protection in the EU, at least in areas where Member States' authorities are implementing EU acts.[110]

B. Accession of the EU to the ECHR

The EU's accession to the ECHR is long-awaited. Officially proposed by the European Commission and Parliament in 1979,[111] accession was consistently opposed by a number of Member States for many years, as there was a lack of political will in those countries to submit themselves to supplementary obligations under the ECHR with regard to EU law. Following the CJEU's Opinion 2/94,[112] in which the Court held that EU accession requires a treaty revision, as it would result in a substantial change to its system for the protection of human rights, the idea was put on hold until it re-emerged at the time of the drafting of the Constitutional Treaty. This time around, all Member States expressed political will to achieve accession to the ECHR,[113] and a provision giving the Union the competence to accede was included in the Constitutional Treaty and, later on, in the Treaty of Lisbon. Article 6(2) TEU provides that the Union 'shall accede' to the ECHR.

There are many perceived advantages to the potential of EU accession to the ECHR. First of all, accession would ensure that the actions of the EU institutions, including the decisions of the CJEU, would become subject to an independent external judicial control mechanism. Conversely, accession would enable the EU to participate in the proceedings before the ECtHR and represent itself

[109] *Melloni* (n 106) para 60.

[110] This case is discussed in greater detail in ch 4.

[111] Commission Memorandum, Bulletin of the European Communities: Accession of the Communities to the European Convention on Human Rights, Supplement 2/79, COM (79).

[112] Opinion 2/94 *Accession by the Community to the European Convention for the Protection of Human Rights and Fundamental Freedoms*, ECLI:EU:C:1996:140.

[113] Presumably because the States had accepted the EU's commitment to human rights and then decided to fully realise that commitment both internally (giving the Charter a biding status) and externally (requiring accession to the ECHR).

in cases concerning EU law. This would end the present anomaly whereby all EU Member States are bound by the guarantees and control mechanisms of the ECHR, while the EU institutions are not subject to any kind of external control over human rights compliance. Furthermore, accession would facilitate the harmonious development of European fundamental rights, and would enhance consistency in the case law of the Strasbourg and Luxembourg Courts, as there would be a formal hierarchy between the two systems. Politically, accession would send out important positive signals in several directions. It would be proof of a mature organisation that is willing to submit itself to external review and to close the gap between the focus on human rights in external relations and the alleged lack of a robust system of fundamental rights protection internally.[114] Finally, it could be part of Europe's 'search for a soul' and an expression of the values on which the EU is built.[115]

Accession became crucial as more and more powers were transferred from the Member State level to the EU level in areas that are sensitive in terms of fundamental rights, such as in the Area of Freedom, Security and Justice.[116] After accession, European citizens would be able to bring complaints against the EU and/or its Member States before the ECtHR for alleged violations of the ECHR through acts and omissions in the context of EU law.

Before negotiations could start, some adjustments to the ECHR system were also necessary in order for the EU, which is a non-state entity with a specific and complex legal system, to accede to the Convention (membership was only open to states). Article 59(2), introduced by Protocol 14 to the Convention, now explicitly provides the possibility for the EU to become a contracting party to the ECHR. Although no time limit is set, the European Council envisaged a rapid accession process in the Stockholm Programme.[117] On 26 May 2010, the Committee of Ministers of the CoE gave an ad hoc mandate to its Steering Committee for Human Rights (CDDH) to develop, in cooperation with the European Commission, the necessary legal instruments for the accession.[118] The CDDH entrusted the informal working group CDDH-UE with this task. It was composed of 14 experts

[114] This argument was put forward by *Bundesverfassungsgericht* in several of its judgments relating to European integration. See also, eg, Human Rights Watch World Report 2014, available at www.hrw.org/sites/default/files/wr2014_web_0.pdf (last accessed 16 December).

[115] Laeken Declaration on the Future of the European Union, 15 December 2001. On Europe's values, see A Williams, *EU Human Rights Policies: A Study in Irony* (Oxford, Oxford University Press, 2004); and A Williams, 'Fundamental Rights in the New European Union' in C Barnard (ed), *The Fundamentals of EU Law Revisited: Assessing the Impact of the Constitutional Debate* (Oxford, Oxford University Press, 2007) 71.

[116] For discussion of the problems that accession will create for the implementation of EU legislation adopted within the framework of the former third pillar, see C Costello, 'Courting Access to Asylum in Europe: Recent Supranational Jurisprudence Explored' (2012) 12 *Human Rights Law Review* 287.

[117] The Stockholm Programme – An open and secure Europe serving and protecting the citizens (2 December 2009) 17024/09. The Commission followed suit in the Action Plan Implementing the Stockholm Programme, COM(2010) 171.

[118] CDDH(2010)008 (Strasbourg, 3 June 2010).

from the CoE Member States (seven from EU Member States and seven from non-EU Member States). As for the EU, its Justice Ministers gave the Commission the mandate to conduct the negotiations on their behalf.[119] Official talks on the EU's accession to the ECHR finally started on 7 July 2010. The CJEU also had its role in the negotiations, first as a part of the Council working group in charge of establishing the negotiation mandate and later during the accession negotiations as an observer.[120] On 14 October 2011, the CDDH transmitted a report to the Committee of Ministers on the work done by the CDDH-UE and the draft legal instrument in an appendix.[121] Given the political implications and some of the issues that were raised, on 13 June 2012 the Committee of Ministers instructed the CDDH to pursue negotiations with the EU within the ad hoc group '47+1' and to finalise the legal instrument dealing with the accession modalities. The Draft Accession Agreement (DAA) was finalised in June 2013.[122]

The conditions for the adoption of an accession agreement are set out in Article 218 TEU. It requires unanimity in the Council and the consent of the European Parliament, as well as ratification by all the EU Member States in accordance with their national constitutional requirements. It would, moreover, require the approval of all the 47 signatories to the Convention (Article 50 ECHR). Soon after the DAA was finalised, the CJEU was asked, on the basis of Article 218(11) TFEU, to give its opinion on its compatibility with the EU Treaties. To the surprise (and disappointment) of many, the CJEU held in Opinion 2/13 that the DAA is incompatible with the EU Treaties, because it undermines the specific characteristics and the autonomy of EU law.[123] The expectation of EU accession to the ECHR was set back considerably by this Opinion, although negotiations formally resumed in September 2020. The discussion on accession will be taken up again in the next chapter.

C. General Principles of EU Law

Article 6(3) of the TEU provides that 'fundamental rights, as guaranteed by the ECHR and as they result from the constitutional traditions common to

[119] 10630/1/10 REV 1, press release of the 3018th Council meeting Justice and Home Affairs, Luxembourg, 3–4 June 2010, available at http://europa.eu/rapid/press-release_PRES-10-161_en.htm?locale=en (last accessed 29 January 2015).

[120] See Council Document 17807/09, JAI 948, INST 255 (Brussels, 5 January 2010) and Council Document 13714/10, JAI 747, INST 333 (Brussels, 17 September 2010).

[121] CDDH(2011)009 (14 October 2011).

[122] It consists of a draft agreement on the accession of the EU to the ECHR and a draft explanatory report, a draft declaration by the EU, a draft rule to be added to the Rules of the Committee of Ministers for the supervision of the execution of judgments and of the terms of friendly settlements in cases to which the EU would be a party, and a draft model of a memorandum of understanding; see at www.coe.int/t/dghl/standardsetting/hrpolicy/accession/Meeting_reports/47_1(2013)008rev2_EN.pdf (last accessed 16 December 2020).

[123] Opinion 2/13 *Accession of the European Union to the European Convention for the Protection of Human Rights and Fundamental Freedoms*, ECLI:EU:C:2014:48.

the Member States, shall constitute general principles of the Union's law'. This provision, as well as its earlier versions, reflects the case law of the CJEU in which the Court declared that respect for fundamental rights constitutes an integral part of the general principles of EU law. One may wonder about the purpose of this provision, now that the Charter is legally binding and the EU is required to accede to the ECHR. Perhaps it was simply to show that the Lisbon Treaty does not break from the past, but it is possibly also a way to allow the Court of Justice, if necessary, to integrate new rights into the EU system, rights that are not mentioned in the Charter or the ECHR but which may emerge over time,[124] or, importantly, to protect Charter rights whose impact is limited due to the existence of protocols such as those of the UK and Poland. Lastly, the general principles could also be used to protect rights that already exist but are limited by vertical application.[125]

The situation of rights that already exist but are limited by vertical application is well illustrated in *Kücükdeveci*,[126] decided on 19 January 2010. The case concerned a claim of age discrimination based on German employment law that did not take periods of work served prior to the employee's 25th birthday into account when calculating the notice period prior to dismissal. The German law was incompatible with the requirements of Directive 78/2000, the transposition period for which had passed prior to the applicant's dismissal. However, as the respondent in the case was a private party, the general prohibition on allowing untransposed Directives to be relied upon against a private party would ordinarily have hindered Ms Kücükdeveci's case. Yet the Court held that non-discrimination on grounds of age must be regarded as a general principle of EU law, which was given specific expression in the relevant Directive and, as such, could result in its having horizontal direct effect.[127] The Court also referred to the Charter, which is puzzling. The Charter indeed prohibits any discrimination on the grounds of age, but its scope is limited to EU institutions' and Member States' actions, as discussed earlier, and the reference to the Charter did not seem to help support the horizontal application argument. Similarly, in *Prigge*,[128] the CJEU referred to the Charter only at the advanced stage of analysis, to confirm the prior existence of the corresponding general principle of EU law. There are other examples that could be mentioned in this context,[129] however there does not seem to be a discernible pattern in the CJEU's case law with regard to the use of general principles in its reasoning. Interestingly, Article 6 TEU is silent on the relationship between the

[124] G Arestis, 'Fundamental Rights in the EU: Three years after Lisbon, the Luxembourg Perspective' (2013) *Cooperative Research Paper 02/2013*, College of Europe.

[125] Protocol No 30 TEU on the application of the Charter of Fundamental Rights of the European Union to Poland and to the United Kingdom. See also S Douglas-Scott, 'The European Union and Human Rights after the Treaty of Lisbon' (2011) 11 *Human Rights Law Review* 4, 645.

[126] Case C-555/07 *Kücükdeveci*, ECLI:EU:C:2010:21.

[127] ibid para 50. See also an earlier case concerning non-discrimination on grounds of age, Case C-144/04 *Mangold*, ECLI:EU:C:2005:709.

[128] Case C-447/09 *Prigge*, ECLI:EU:C:2011:573.

[129] See, eg, Case C-232/09 *Danosa*, ECLI:EU:C:2010:674; Case C-648/10 *ASNEF*, ECLI:EU:C:2011:777.

general principles of EU law (and thus indirectly the ECHR and common constitutional traditions) and the Charter, and this silence seems to presume that they will normally coincide or, at least, they will not conflict.[130] It can be concluded that this source will continue to be relevant with respect to the Member States' fundamental rights obligations in parallel with those contained in the Charter and the ECHR, because of the margin the CJEU has in reshaping these principles and their application in contrast to the margin of discretion the CJEU has with regard to written catalogues of rights.[131] Given this state of affairs, one may also wonder whether the system would be any different without the general principles, given the extensive list of rights in the Charter and their broad and comprehensive scope of application.

V. Some Reflections on the Role and Place of Fundamental Rights in EU Law

Weiler and Alston argued in 2000 that the EU should take international leadership in human rights by providing an outstanding example of a comprehensive, coherent and forward-looking human rights policy.[132] The authors stressed the importance of bridging the gap between the EU's voiced commitment to human rights and its actions. In that context, they proposed major organisational and procedural changes, arguing for a move away from negative to positive integration in the field of human rights and the need for a clear commitment to human rights, as well as effective political and organisational structures to give effect to those commitments. This idea was challenged by several authors who were very sceptical about the EU's assuming such a role in the future. One of the key responses came from Armin von Bogdandy.[133] He argued that an EU human rights policy is not desirable, as it would have strong centralising effects and would impact on the existing relationship between the EU and the Member States, overshadowing national constitutions and affecting the independence of the national legal orders. Furthermore, it was doubtful whether the EU (at the time) 'wield[ed] enough political and moral clout' to develop and implement such policies.[134] He also questioned whether a fully-fledged fundamental rights policy would be beneficial to

[130] Claes (n 102).

[131] See, eg, T Tridimas, 'Fundamental Rights, General Principles of EU Law, and the Charter' (2014) 16 *Cambridge Yearbook of European Legal Studies* 361.

[132] P Alston and J Weiler, 'An "Ever Closer Union" in Need of a Human Rights Policy: The European Union and Human Rights' in P Alston (ed), *The EU and Human Rights* (Oxford, Oxford University Press, 1999) 3, also published as 'An Ever Closer Union in Need of a Human Rights Policy' (1988) 9 *European Journal of International Law* 658.

[133] A von Bogdandy, 'The European Union as a Human Rights Organization? Human Rights and the Core of the European Union' (2000) 37 *CML Rev* 1307. See also A Williams, *EU Human Rights Policies: A Study in Irony* (n 115).

[134] von Bogdandy (n 133) 1317.

the EU, the Member States and for fundamental rights themselves. The same query relates to the role of the CJEU, which may not have the necessary legitimacy but also the abilities to assume the role of a human rights court, given its situational logic embedded in the broader EU legal system and the manner in which it functions and communicates.

Fast-forward some 20 years, there is no denying that the EU has become a human rights actor of some sorts.[135] The protection of human rights has climbed high on the EU's agenda and features prominently among the founding values and objectives of the EU: in the Treaties, in the Charter, and increasingly also in the opening recitals of many pieces of secondary legislation and policy documents. The protection of fundamental rights also features prominently and frequently in the case law of the CJEU and the references made by national courts. Increasingly, the EU is expected not only to respect, but also to protect and actively promote human rights. While the EU still lacks a general human rights competence, fundamental rights are at the core of its every action both internally and on the international scene.[136] It has become clear in recent years that the binding force of the Charter and the strengthened mandate of the EU institutions to engage in fundamental rights protection have significantly shaped, and in a way transformed, the EU. One example is the recently proposed ratification of the Istanbul Convention by the Commission, which is a CoE instrument on preventing and combating violence against women and domestic violence.[137] The EU signed the Convention on 13 June 2017 and the Council reiterated its intent to proceed with the ratification in its conclusions on the application of the Charter of Fundamental Rights of the European Union adopted on 13 October 2017. Moreover, the EU is already a party to the UN Convention on the Rights of Persons with Disabilities (UNCRPD)[138] and will accede to the ECHR. These are all signs that the EU is actively pursuing EU fundamental rights policy, notwithstanding the lack of general fundamental rights competence in the Treaties. Further, the EU acquired a more explicit competence to develop policies to protect certain fundamental rights such as data protection, equal treatment, and the rights of migrants and suspected persons in criminal proceedings.[139] At the same time, the EU institutions have called for an

[135] For a similar claim, see Claes (n 102).

[136] 2018 Report on the Application of the EU Charter of Fundamental Rights, available at https://ec.europa.eu/info/aid-development-cooperation-fundamental-rights/your-rights-eu/eu-charter-fundamental-rights/application-charter/annual-reports-application-charter_en (last accessed 18 December 2020).

[137] For more details, see Explanatory Report to the Council of Europe Convention on preventing and combating violence against women and domestic violence, Istanbul, 11 May 2011.

[138] Council Decision of 20 March 2007, CS/2007/7404.

[139] For example, Art 16 TFEU, introduced by the Lisbon Treaty, is the new legal basis for the adoption of comprehensive data protection rules. Another example is European asylum and refugee policy and Art 78 TFEU, which, taken together with Art 18 of the Charter (the right to asylum), is at least partly a human rights policy.

active and consistent pursuit of human rights policies in all areas of EU law.[140] As for its external policies, Article 21 TEU states that

> the Union's action on the international scene shall be guided by the principles which have inspired its own creation, development and enlargement, and which it seeks to advance in the wider world: democracy, the rule of law, the universality and indivisibility of human rights and fundamental freedoms …

This provision calls for a convergence towards a more enhanced fundamental rights protection in all EU external actions, be they trade, investment, development, CSFP or migration. The EU Action Plan on Human Rights and Democracy 2020–2024 additionally reinforces the EU's strong commitment to further advancing universal values for all. Finally, establishing the FRA, which commenced its work on 1 March 2007, was another step in the expansion of an EU policy on fundamental rights. Although the FRA's mandate is relatively limited and arguments have been made for the extension of its powers, its unique contribution to promoting and protecting fundamental rights has been generally considered highly valuable both nationally and at the EU level.[141] Moreover, the FRA (like other EU institutions) has also engaged in mandate stretching and has conducted tasks that are not explicitly mentioned in its founding Regulation.[142] Nevertheless, greater involvement of the FRA in the EU legislative process is needed in order to realise its full potential in EU fundamental rights governance.[143]

It is true that the EU does not have a fully-fledged competence to regulate fundamental rights, and the fields in which it does have such competence are fairly limited. It is also true that the Charter does not explicitly demand an EU human rights policy, while emphasising that it cannot extend the existing competences. Nevertheless, the Charter has become the fundamental rights yardstick for monitoring actions of both the EU and the Member States when implementing EU law in all EU policies. In that sense, it could be argued that the EU has a general obligation to pursue fundamental rights actively and to develop fundamental rights policies when exercising its competences, thus also in the areas where the EU does not have an explicit fundamental rights competence.

The case law of the CJEU also shows the increasingly important role and place of fundamental rights in EU law. The Court has been willing to engage more

[140] eg in various documents issued by the European Parliament. See, eg, European Parliament, Draft Report on the Annual Report on Human Rights and Democracy in the World 2016 and the European Union's policy on the matter (2017/2122) (INI), available at www.europarl.europa.eu/sides/getDoc.do?type=COMPARL&reference=PE-608.041&format=PDF&language=EN&secondRef=01 (last accessed 18 December 2020).

[141] See the First and the Second Independent External Evaluation of the EU Agency for Fundamental Rights (November 2012 and October 2017), available at http://fra.europa.eu/sites/default/files/fra-external_evaluation-final-report.pdf and http://fra.europa.eu/sites/default/files/2nd-fra-external-evaluation-october-2017_en.pdf (last accessed 18 December 2020).

[142] Council Regulation 168/2007/EC establishing a European Union Agency for Fundamental Rights. For discussion, see Dawson (n 45) 126–33.

[143] Dawson (n 45) 126–33.

with fundamental rights arguments, including also arguments against the EU institutions or Member States. It has been tightening its scrutiny of the EU legal acts on the basis of their compliance with fundamental rights and bolstering its fundamental rights jurisprudence, albeit in an inconsistent way. It has done so by focusing on the Charter and making its assessments largely independent from national constitutions and the ECHR. This was also the message conveyed in Opinion 2/13 on the EU's accession to the ECHR – the EU already has a system for human rights protection and a Court that will enforce it. In that sense, the EU sees itself as a human rights organisation, putting fundamental rights at the core of its values and its actions.[144] However, it is not *only* a human rights organisation; it is an international organisation with extensive policies that also (increasingly) include fundamental rights. This means that human rights remain one of the elements of the EU legal order, which have to be balanced with other policies. Moreover, the EU is still learning how to accept and integrate the new reality, and so is its Court. This makes the EU different from other, more 'natural' human rights actors, such as the ECHR and the national constitutional systems, and it illuminates why and how it is different.

The question *should* the EU be a human rights actor is more difficult, and it is not the aim of this chapter to provide a final answer to this more normative part of the question. However, a few comments are in order. The first component of this question and a possible answer concerns negative obligations towards fundamental rights: should the EU comply with fundamental rights in its actions? The answer in this case is obviously affirmative: fundamental rights should guide the exercise of the EU's powers, and there is little discussion in this context. The second component concerns the question whether the EU should also actively pursue human rights policies. As stated earlier, there is no general human rights competence in the Treaties and the EU was not intended to assume this role. In fact, there are some good reasons to be sceptical about the desirability of such a role for the Union, and development in this direction remains contested.[145] However, as argued previously, the EU has already been moving in that direction, and it is already a human rights actor of some sorts. The third component concerns the question whether the EU should actively interfere with EU Member States' human rights issues, first, when they act in the scope of EU law and, second, when the actions are outside of the scope of application of EU law? While the answer to the first part of the question may be more obvious, since Article 51(1) of the EU Charter refers to situations in which the Member States 'are implementing Union law', the second part of the question is an extremely sensitive issue. The more technical answer would be that the EU should not interfere, because this would be outside of the competences

[144] For a critical appraisal, see A Williams, 'Human Rights and the EU' in D Chalmers and A Arnull (eds), *The Oxford Handbook of EU Law* (Oxford, Oxford University Press, 2015) 249; A Rosas, 'Is the EU a Human Rights Organisation?' *Cleer Working Papers 2011/1*. For a broader debate on this and related questions, see the special issue of C Leconte and E Muir, 'Understanding Resistance to EU Fundamental Rights Policy' (2014) 15 *Human Rights Review* 1.

[145] For a discussion on the scepticism of EU human rights, see Dawson (n 45).

that have been transferred to it. However, it is also arguable, particularly in line with the developments as described in this chapter, that the EU should intervene even when the actions of the Member States fall outside of the scope of application of EU law, because the EU constitutes a community of values that Member States should uphold, even when they are acting in an area outside of EU law.

VI. Conclusion

This chapter has sought to explain the origins and historical development of EU fundamental rights law. Indeed, in order to fully appreciate the complexity of the current system of fundamental rights protection in the EU, it is vital to know and understand its genesis.

The EU was originally created as an international organisation with an economic scope of action and, accordingly, the EEC Treaty did not contain – with very few exceptions – provisions concerning protection of fundamental rights. The lack of explicit fundamental rights provisions did not mean, however, the absence of legal protection. As early as 1969, the Court of Justice held that fundamental rights form an integral part of the general principles of law the observance of which the Court ensures. For the next three decades, the Court developed and shaped EU fundamental rights, drawn from the general principles of EU law, which mostly found their basis in the ECHR, and from the common constitutional traditions of the Member States. The absence of a written catalogue of fundamental rights, which would be easily accessible to European citizens, remained an issue of concern, however. Two main proposals were made on repeated occasions with the aim of filling this gap. The first proposal was for the EU to accede to the ECHR, an already existing European instrument aimed at protecting human rights to which, moreover, all Member States are subscribed. The CJEU held that such a fundamental constitutional change in the EU legal system could not be implemented without a Treaty amendment. The second proposal was that the Union should adopt its own Bill of Rights, granting the Court of Justice the power to ensure its correct implementation. After years of vigorous debates, the EU Member States decided to include both in the Treaty of Lisbon: a legally binding Charter of Fundamental Rights and a competence (and legal obligation) for the EU to accede to the ECHR. While the former has been in full operation ever since, accession to the ECHR has been postponed, and it may take a long time before it can be realised.

The purpose of this chapter has been not only to familiarise the reader with, or remind the reader of, the origins of EU fundamental rights law, but also to bring forward one principal observation, which deeply underpins the arguments put forward in this book: the EU has become an important player in the field of fundamental rights protection. Fundamental rights feature prominently among the foundational values of the EU and they guide EU action in all policy fields, both internally and on the international scene. Fundamental rights not only constitute a cornerstone of the Union's constitutional order, they also form a central element of its political culture and impose duties on political actors. While this new reality has been acknowledged at different levels of the EU legal order, the EU is still, at times, hesitant to recognise its new role, and so is its Court.[146] Of course, protection of fundamental rights is not the only mission of the EU, but it is overarching. In the words of the CJEU President Lenaerts:

> In retrospect, the entry into force of the Charter is one of the most important achievements in the history of European integration. It shows that the European integration project is more than its internal market. The EU is, first and foremost, a union of democracies, a union of justice and a union of rights ...'[147]

The result is that now we have two big human rights actors in Europe, the CoE and the EU (to the extent that one considers the EU to be one), which reinforce each other but which also sometimes compete with each other[148] and with the national human rights actors. This results in a multi-layered and multi-sourced architecture of fundamental rights law, which by the very nature of its existence raises difficult questions as to the interpretation of fundamental rights according to the different layers, the already complicated relationship between the EU and the ECHR systems, and, ultimately, the impact on national law and national courts. These are the questions I turn to in the remainder of this book.

[146] For a similar claim see Claes (n 102).

[147] K Lenaerts, 'The Role of the EU Charter in the Member States' in M Bobek and J Adams-Prassl (eds), *The EU Charter of Fundamental Rights in the Member States* (Oxford, Hart Publishing, 2020) 19.

[148] See, for instance, the signs of rivalry between the two European Courts expressed in the interview with David Thór Björgvinsson, a former judge of the ECtHR, in G Butler, 'A Political Decision Disguised as Legal Argument? Opinion 2/13 and European Union Accession to the European Convention on Human Rights' (2015) 31 *Utrecht Journal of International and European Law* 81, 104.

2

A European Web of Human Rights Regimes: The EU, the ECHR and the National Legal Systems

I. Introduction

Former Advocate General Cruz Villalón described the protection of human rights in Europe as 'a crowded house'.[1] Indeed, the European system of fundamental rights protection can be described as an area in which national law, European Union (EU) law and the European Convention on Human Rights (ECHR) coexist, drawing on and incorporating each other, together with other treaties and treaty mechanisms. These national, international and supranational regimes make up the legal and institutional context within which actors belonging to different regimes function. The Lisbon Treaty changed the system and the relationships within it, at least formally. The binding status of the EU Charter and the growing fundamental rights case law, as well as the requirement for the EU to accede to the ECHR, followed by the controversial Opinion 2/13,[2] have all had an impact on the relationships in the web. Nevertheless, these human rights systems continue to overlap, and the number of cases being governed simultaneously by all these norms has been increasing in recent years. This calls for reconsideration of the relationship between the different legal systems and their courts.

As a preliminary point, it is important to remember the fundamental differences between the EU and the ECHR systems and the two European Courts. The European Court of Human Rights (ECtHR) is a specialised court with the sole mission of ensuring compliance with the common minimum standard of human rights protection. States are obliged to execute judgments rendered against them, and they have to give consideration to the general principles that are developed in the case law as a whole (*res interpretata*). Supervision by the Strasbourg Court is subsidiary in character, as reflected inter alia in the principles of exhaustion of domestic remedies and margin of appreciation. The Court of Justice of

[1] P Cruz Villalón, 'Rights in Europe: The Crowded House', *KCL Working Paper in European Law 01/2012*.

[2] Opinion 2/13 *Accession of the European Union to the European Convention for the Protection of Human Rights and Fundamental Freedoms*, ECLI:EU:C:2014:48.

the European Union (CJEU), in contrast, has a broader mission of ensuring that the law is observed in the interpretation and application of the Treaties. Ensuring compliance with EU fundamental rights is thus only part of its mission. In other words, the interpretation and application of EU fundamental rights operates in a different legal environment from that of the ECHR and it has a different scope. Nevertheless, while the CJEU is not a fundamental rights court by origin or experience, its fundamental rights docket continues to grow and expand.[3] This means that the cases before the two European Courts will often involve the same or similar questions.

This chapter explains how these different regimes relate to each other, focusing first on the relationships between the EU and the ECHR systems and the two highest Courts within those systems. This interaction is first construed from the perspective of the ECHR and the Strasbourg Court (section II) and then from the point of view of EU law and the Luxembourg Court (section III). The analysis in these two sections demonstrates that the two European Courts have been engaging in various types of dialogue, most notably by citing each other's case law. The case law of the CJEU provides many examples of the guiding role of the ECHR in EU law, revealing a general tendency, on the part of the CJEU, to avoid conflicts in the form of divergent interpretations and the application of ECHR rights. This interplay is also reflected in the Strasbourg system, where the rulings of the ECtHR show the influence of EU law and the CJEU's case law, as well as the willingness of the Strasbourg Court to go to great lengths to avoid conflicts with EU law. However, the plurality of overlapping human rights sources, in the absence of any formal mechanism regulating them, continues to carry the risk of conflicting perspectives. Section IV goes on to discuss the more recent developments in the relationship between the CJEU and the ECtHR, with a particular focus on Opinion 2/13. Section V examines the status of EU law and the ECHR in the national legal systems, and the role of national courts vis-à-vis the two European Courts. This section paints a broad picture, using selected examples from different Member States in order to illustrate important similarities and differences. Each time, the perspectives shift in order to enable a deeper understanding of the relationships between the different instruments and actors in the web. Section VI brings the different components and perspectives together.

II. EU Law, the ECHR and the Strasbourg Court

At present, the EU is not party to the ECHR and hence not directly bound by it on the international plane. Complaints cannot be brought against the EU acting as a

[3] G de Búrca, 'After the EU Charter of Fundamental Rights: the Court of Justice as a human rights adjudicator?' (2013) 20 *Maastricht Journal of European and Comparative Law* 168; B De Witte, 'The Past and Future Role of the European Court of Justice in the Protection of Human Rights' in P Alston, M Bustelo and J Heenan (eds), *The EU and Human Rights* (Oxford, Oxford University Press, 1999) 859.

defendant in Strasbourg, and the EU itself cannot be held responsible. However, ECHR Contracting Parties can be held responsible for not complying with their ECHR obligations, even if non-compliance would be a result of the states' international obligations.[4] This section explores the responsibility of EU Member States under the ECHR for violation rooted in EU law.

A. Member States' Responsibility under the ECHR for Acts of EU Law

i. Matthews: Responsibility for Primary Law

The case of *Matthews v United Kingdom*[5] was the first in which the ECtHR ruled that an EU Member State was in breach of the Convention for complying with its EU law obligations. Denise Matthews, a British citizen resident in Gibraltar,[6] applied to be registered as a voter in the elections for the European Parliament but was informed that, under the terms of the European Community Act on Direct Elections from 1976, Gibraltar was not included in the franchise for the European Parliament elections. The question before the Strasbourg Court was whether the United Kingdom (UK) was liable for violating Article 3 of Protocol No 1 to the ECHR (the right to free elections), by failing to hold elections for the European Parliament in Gibraltar.

The ECtHR held that the failure to provide for elections did violate Article 3 of Protocol 1, since the very essence of Matthews' right to vote to choose the legislature had been denied. The Court pointed out that Contracting States can transfer their powers to an international organisation, but they remain responsible for ensuring that Convention rights are guaranteed. The Court further stated that the respondent, the UK, could not claim that there was a lack of control over the situation, as it had voluntarily agreed to be bound by the EC Treaty and the 1976 Act on Direct Elections, which had been concluded as a treaty between the Member States of the EU. Importantly, the ECtHR noted that since the 1976 Act is primary EU law, it cannot be challenged before the CJEU.[7] It thus identified a gap in judicial protection in the EU legal system and decided to step in because the applicant would otherwise have been left without a remedy. Ensuring that Convention rights are respected in relation to EU primary law thus lies in the (collective) hands the Member States and the Strasbourg Court.

[4] As held already in 1958 by the now defunct European Commission of Human Rights in *X v Germany* App no 342/57 (EComHR, 4 September 1958).

[5] *Matthews v United Kingdom*, App no 24833/94 (ECtHR, 18 February 1999).

[6] Gibraltar is a Crown Colony of the UK. It is largely self-governing, but it is part of the EU's territory since the UK is responsible for its external relations within the meaning of Art 227(4) of the EC Treaty. Accordingly, EU legislation forms part of the legislation of Gibraltar, thus directly affecting the applicant.

[7] *Matthews v United Kingdom* (n 5) para 33.

ii. Bosphorus: Responsibility for Secondary Law

The *Bosphorus*[8] case reaffirmed the standpoint that the ECtHR adopted in *Matthews*, but with a twist. In this case, the Irish authorities seized an aircraft owned by a Yugoslav airline company but that was leased to Bosphorus, an airline charter company registered in Turkey. Ireland took this action in order to comply with Council Regulation (EEC) 990/93, which had a direct effect in the Irish legal order. The Regulation implemented sanctions by the UN Security Council at the Community level against the former Yugoslavia (Serbia and Montenegro) on the basis of Chapter VII of the Charter of the United Nations. Article 8 of the said Regulation provides:

> All vessels, freight vehicles, rolling stock and aircraft in which a majority or controlling interest is held by a person or undertaking in or operating from the Federal Republic of Yugoslavia (Serbia and Montenegro) shall be impounded by the competent authorities of the Member States.

Bosphorus contested the seizure, arguing that Article 8 of Regulation 990/93 either did not apply in the circumstances, or was contrary to Bosphorus' fundamental right to property. The case thus involved, as in *Matthews*, the question of responsibility of a Member State under the Convention for legal actions induced by the EU. The difference, however, was that *Matthews* concerned EU primary law, while the alleged infringement in *Bosphorus* had its origin in EU secondary law (ie a Regulation). The case was dealt with first in Luxembourg and later on in Strasbourg.

The CJEU ruled that the right to property is not an absolute right and can be restricted if objectively justified. Since the Regulation pursued a general interest of the Union, the interference was not disproportionate and thus the validity of the Regulation under EU law was not affected.[9] Subsequently, the applicant brought the case to the European Commission of Human Rights and the Commission referred it to the ECtHR. It ended up being a long road to Strasbourg, given that the proceedings commenced in the Irish courts in 1993. The ECtHR reaffirmed what was previously stated in *Matthews*, namely, that Contracting Parties are free to transfer sovereign powers to an international organisation and such an organisation cannot be held responsible under the ECHR as long as it is not a party to it. The states that are parties to the ECHR, on the other hand, are responsible to ensure compliance with the Convention at any time, even when they are acting

[8] *Bosphorus v Ireland*, App no 45036/98 (ECtHR, 30 June 2005). For analysis, see C Costello, 'The *Bosphorus* Ruling of the European Court of Human Rights: Fundamental Rights and Blurred Boundaries in Europe' (2006) 6 *Human Rights Law Review* 87. For a more recent discussion including subsequent cases, see C Ryngaert, 'Oscillating between embracing and avoiding Bosphorus: the European Court of Human Rights on Member State responsibility for acts of international organisations and the case of the EU' (2015) 39 *EL Rev* 176.

[9] Case C-84/95 *Bosphorus v Minister for Transport, Energy and Communications and Others*, ECLI:EU:C:1996:312.

under international legal obligations. However, the Court limited such responsibility by introducing the so-called 'presumption of equivalent protection (of fundamental rights)'.[10] It reasoned that as long as an international organisation 'is considered to protect fundamental rights ... in a manner which can be considered at least equivalent to that for which the Convention provides', the Court would presume that a state acted in compliance with the Convention, when it had no discretion in implementing the legal obligations following from its membership of the organisation.[11] The presumption of equivalent protection does not absolve Member States of their responsibility, but rather it acts as a conditional immunity and can thus be rebutted if the protection offered is manifestly deficient.[12] This was contrary to the European Commission's argument (submitted in the written observations) that the 'equivalent protection' doctrine should fully immunise EU acts from Strasbourg scrutiny.[13]

The ECtHR ultimately held that the protection of fundamental rights by EU law in this case was equivalent (defined as 'comparable but not identical' in the judgment) to that of the Convention system, and concluded that the presumption was not rebutted in this case.[14] The *Bosphorus* decision has since been repeatedly confirmed by the Strasbourg Court.

The *Bosphorus* decision received quite some criticism, however.[15] The Strasbourg Court was accused of applying double standards in human rights protection.[16] Indeed, the standard review appears less strict for the EU Member States vis-à-vis non-EU Member States and, conversely, for the EU vis-à-vis other international organisations (as it did not give such leeway to the Contracting States when acting under other international law obligations such as World Trade Organization law). Another criticism relates to the examination of manifest deficiency in the protection, which was dealt with rather superficially. The Court considered the nature of interference, the general interest pursued and the ruling of the CJEU, and concluded, in the two paragraphs it had devoted to the analysis, that it was 'clear that there was no dysfunction of the mechanism of control of the observance of the

[10] It was not an entirely new concept, however. The notion of 'equivalent protection' was first developed by the European Commission of Human Rights in 1990 in *M & Co v Federal Republic of Germany* App no 13258/87 (EComHR, 9 February 1990). The Commission stated that 'equivalent protection' implies that a transfer of powers to an international organisation could exclude a state's responsibility under the Convention with regard to the exercise of the transferred powers, provided that fundamental rights would receive equivalent protection within that organisation.

[11] *Bosphorus v Ireland* (n 8) paras 155 and 156.

[12] Costello (n 8) 87.

[13] Commission of the European Communities: Written Observations in *Bosphorus Airways v Ireland*, 30 June 2004, JURM (2004) 6026, para 19.

[14] *Bosphorus v Ireland* (n 8) para 166.

[15] S Peers, 'Bosphorus. European Court of Human Rights. Limited Responsibility of European Union Member States for Actions within the Scope of Community Law. Judgment of 30 June 2005, *Bosphorus Airways v Ireland*, Application No 45036/98' (2006) 2 *European Constitutional Law Review* 443; Costello (n 8) 87.

[16] K Kuhnert, 'Bosphorus – Double standards in European human rights protection?' (2006) 2 *Utrecht Law Review* 2.

Convention'.[17] Moreover, the criterion for 'manifest deficiency' was left unsettled. It was not clear from the judgment under which conditions a deficiency would be considered to be 'manifest' and – more importantly – why a deficiency should be 'manifest' in order to rebut the presumption. The Concurring Opinion of Judge Ress provides some clarification as to the conditions, namely, that the protection will be considered manifestly deficient when there has been, in procedural terms, no adequate review in the particular case, such as (i) when the CJEU lacks competence; (ii) when the CJEU has been too restrictive in its interpretation of individual access to it; or (iii) where there has been an obvious misinterpretation or misapplication by the CJEU of the guarantees of the Convention right.[18] However, as is reflected in this and other separate concurring judicial opinions, the criterion 'manifestly deficient' appears to establish an particularly high threshold, which is markedly different from the supervision generally carried out by the Strasbourg Court. Nevertheless, the *Bosphorus* doctrine continues to regulate the relationship between the ECHR regime and the EU legal order, when EU secondary law leaves no discretion for the Member States as to its implementation and the subsequent application is at issue.

iii. Kokkelvisserij: Responsibility for Acts of the EU Institutions

The ECtHR extended the *Bosphorus* presumption of equivalent protection to the procedures applied by the EU institutions in the *Kokkelvisserij*[19] case. Kokkelvisserij, an association of individuals and enterprises based in the Netherlands and engaged in mechanical cockle fishing, lodged a complaint before the ECtHR, arguing that the Dutch Council of State had violated the Convention by relying on a preliminary ruling of the CJEU that breached the right to a fair trial, as enshrined in Article 6 ECHR. The Council of State had requested the preliminary ruling from the Court of Justice concerning the interpretation and application of the Netherlands' Nature Conservation Act in the light of EU law and, in particular, Article 6 of the 'Habitats Directive'.[20]

In the case before the CJEU, the applicant association asked the Court to re-open the oral proceedings after hearing the Advocate General's Opinion, but the Court refused the request. The CJEU found that the applicant had failed to submit precise information that made it appear either useful or necessary to re-open the proceedings pursuant to Rule 61 of the Rules of Procedure. In its judgment, however, the Court followed the reasoning of the Opinion of the Advocate General.

Since the case involved purely procedural matters of the CJEU rather than the implementation of EU law, it was not clear whether the *Bosphorus* doctrine would

[17] *Bosphorus* (n 8) para 166.
[18] Concurring Opinion of Judge Ress in *Bosphorus v Ireland* (n 8) para 3.
[19] *PO Kokkelvisserij v The Netherlands*, App no 13645/05 (ECtHR, 20 January 2009).
[20] Council Directive 92/43/EEC of May 1992 on the conservation of natural habitats and of wild fauna and flora.

apply in this case. The ECtHR first established that the violation was imputable to the Netherlands, since the Council of State requested the preliminary ruling and the Netherlands was a party to the proceedings. It held that the *Bosphorus* presumption did apply in this case, given that the obligation to give effect to a preliminary ruling by the CJEU stems from membership in the EU. The Strasbourg Court further considered whether the protection provided in Article 61 of the CJEU's Rules of Procedure was 'manifestly deficient'. The Court ruled that the protection afforded was not 'manifestly deficient' and declared the application manifestly ill-founded and hence inadmissible. *Kokkelvisserij* thus extended the *Bosphorus* presumption of equivalent protection to the procedures applied by EU institutions, *in casu* the CJEU.[21]

iv. Clarifying Bosphorus

The limiting effect was further extended in the *MSS v Belgium*[22] case, which will be discussed in more detail in chapter 3. The case raised the question of compliance of the EU Dublin II Regulation[23] with the Convention rights. The applicant was an Afghan national, who entered the EU through Greece but applied for asylum in Belgium. The Belgian authorities decided to transfer him back to Greece, in accordance with the Dublin rules. The applicant then alleged before the ECtHR that, by sending him to Greece, the Belgian authorities exposed him to a risk of inhuman and degrading treatment, and that he was indeed subjected to such treatment. Even though the act at issue in this case was a Regulation, which, by its nature, is directly applicable in the Member States and does not normally allow discretion to the Member States, the ECtHR still examined whether the Belgian authorities had any discretion when applying the Regulation. Noticing the margin of discretion allowed under Article 3(2) of the Dublin II Regulation,[24] the Strasbourg Court concluded that the presumption of equivalent protection was not applicable to the present case.

The Court used this opportunity to clarify the impact of the presumption of equivalent protection established in *Bosphorus* and the limits of its applicability: State action taken in compliance with its international obligations is justified as long as the relevant organisation is considered to protect fundamental rights in a

[21] C Van de Heyning, 'PO Kokkelvisserij vs The Netherlands, Application no 13645/05, 20 January 2009' (2009) 46 *CML Rev* 2125.

[22] *MSS v Belgium and Greece*, App no 30696/09 (ECtHR, 21 January 2011).

[23] Council Regulation 343/2003 of 18 February 2003 establishing the criteria and mechanisms for determining the Member State responsibility for examining an asylum application lodged in one of the Member States by a third-country national [2003] OJ L50/0001.

[24] 'By way of derogation from paragraph 1, each Member State may examine an application for asylum lodged with it by a third-country national, even if such examination is not its responsibility under the criteria laid down in this Regulation. In such an event, that Member State shall become the Member State responsible within the meaning of this Regulation and shall assume the obligations associated with that responsibility …'

manner that can be considered at least equivalent to that for which the Convention provides. However, a State is fully responsible under the Convention for all acts falling outside its strict international legal obligations, notably where it exercised State discretion.[25]

The ECtHR's decision in *Michaud v France*[26] further clarified the conditions under which the presumption of equivalent protection can be applied. In this case, the applicant claimed that an internal regulation, adopted on the basis of the French Monetary and Financial Code, which was an implementing act of EU Directive 2005/60/CE, was in violation of Articles 6, 7 and 8 ECHR. The main argument of the French Government was that the *Bosphorus* presumption of equivalent protection had to be applied in this case, and thus that the Strasbourg Court should not check the proportionality of the interference. The Court disagreed, however, and explained that there were some crucial differences between the two cases: first, the *Bosphorus* case dealt with an EU Regulation that, by its nature, did not provide discretion for the Member States concerning its application, whereas the present case concerned the implementation of a Directive that, by its nature, did give Member States discretion as to its implementation; and, second, in the *Bosphorus* case the CJEU had already checked whether the Regulation in question was in compliance with the EU fundamental rights standards, while this was not the case in *Michaud* (the *Conseil d'Etat* had dismissed all claims and declared that the internal regulation was in accordance with European human rights standards, without referring the question to the CJEU). Accordingly, the presumption of equivalent protection could not be applied, and the Court tested the proportionality of the interference. The Court concluded that the challenged provisions did not violate the Convention.

v. *Responsibility for Acts of Another Member State – Avotiņš v Latvia*

The more recent case in which the ECtHR discussed the application of the *Bosphorus* presumption was *Avotiņš v Latvia*.[27] It was also the very first case in which the ECtHR was called upon to examine the guarantees of a fair hearing in the context of mutual recognition in EU law.[28]

The case concerned an alleged violation of Article 6 ECHR by the Latvian courts for the recognition and enforcement of a Cypriot judicial decision, which was the result of court proceedings that had allegedly disregarded Avotiņš' defence rights. The ECtHR first examined whether the two conditions for the application of the *Bosphorus* presumption were fulfilled, namely, the absence of a margin of discretion on the part of the domestic authorities and the deployment of the supervisory mechanism provided for in EU law. The Court found that under the

[25] *MSS v Belgium and Greece* (n 22) para 338.
[26] *Michaud v France*, App no 12323/11 (ECtHR, 6 December 2012).
[27] *Avotiņš v Latvia*, App no 17502/07 (ECtHR, 23 May 2016).
[28] ibid para 98.

Brussels I Regulation,[29] the courts of the Member States could not exercise any discretion in ordering the enforcement of a judgment given in another Member State other than the specific grounds provided therein (which did not apply in this case). Accordingly, the Latvian courts were required to order the enforcement of the Cypriot judgment in Latvia. With respect to the second condition, the ECtHR noted that the Latvian Supreme Court did not request a preliminary ruling from the CJEU regarding the interpretation and application of the relevant provisions of the Brussels I Regulation. However, the Court considered that this condition should be applied without 'excessive formalism and taking into account the specific features of the supervisory mechanism in question'.[30] In the Strasbourg Court's view, making the request for a preliminary ruling to the CJEU always and without exception would be disproportionate. The Court added that the applicant did not advance any specific argument concerning the interpretation of the relevant provisions of the Regulation and its compatibility with fundamental rights, such as to warrant a finding that a preliminary ruling should have been requested from the CJEU. Consequently, the Court found the second condition to be fulfilled and the *Bosphorus* presumption to be applicable in this case.[31]

The analysis of the Court concerning the second condition is reminiscent of the *Michaud* case discussed in section II.A.iv, where the Court strongly emphasised the importance of the involvement of the CJEU and the fact that *Conseil d'Etat* had refused to make such a reference. The Strasbourg Court distinguished the two cases, however, by stating that the applicant in the present case did not submit a request for such a preliminary ruling to the Latvian Supreme Court, while Michaud had submitted such a request to the *Conseil d'Etat*.[32]

After having established that the *Bosphorus* presumption was applicable, the Strasbourg Court went on to examine whether the protection afforded by EU law was equivalent to that provided for in the ECHR system. It held that the protection provided for in EU law was not manifestly deficient and, accordingly, there had been no violation of Article 6 of the ECHR by the Latvian courts. It is interesting to note, however, that the application of the presumption in *Avotiņš* appears somewhat stricter than in previous cases, and it could be even said that the ECtHR came very close to rebutting it.[33] This is not surprising given that the case was decided in the aftermath of CJEU Opinion 2/13, when the future of the *Bosphorus* presumption was unsettled.[34] Even though the Court ultimately found the presumption to

[29] Council Regulation (EC) No 44/2001 of 22 December 2000 on jurisdiction and the recognition and enforcement of judgments in civil and commercial matters.

[30] *Avotiņš v Latvia* (n 27) para 109.

[31] ibid paras 111–112.

[32] ibid para 111.

[33] See, eg, P Gragl, 'An Olive Branch from Strasbourg? Interpreting the European Court of Human Rights' Resurrection of *Bosphorus* and Reaction to *Opinion 2/13* in the *Avotiņš* Case' (2017) 13 *European Constitutional Law Review* 551.

[34] The ECtHR President at the time, Dean Spielmann, commented on Opinion 2/13 in unusually strong language, suggesting that the Strasbourg Court might toughen its review of EU law. See the

be applicable and, moreover, found no violation of the Convention, the Court also made critical remarks concerning the principle of mutual trust and recognition, and implicitly suggested reform of the system.[35]

vi. The Protection Gap

The cases just discussed are all examples of the efforts of the Strasbourg Court to balance peaceful coexistence with the Luxembourg Court while retaining the responsibility of the Member States under the ECHR.[36] In doing so, different variations arise, depending on the nature of the EU act. The first step for the Strasbourg Court is to establish that the Member State has acted, and not the EU itself. If the jurisdiction is established, the Court can review the act that is allegedly in violation of the Convention. In that context, the ECtHR will decide whether the *Bosphorus* presumption of equivalent protection is applicable to the case or not. If the presumption is not applicable, the Strasbourg Court will undertake full scrutiny.[37]

Yet cases remain where the jurisdiction of a Member State, and consequently of the ECtHR, cannot be established. An example showing the gap in external protection for individuals is *Connolly*.[38] The case was first dealt with in Luxembourg as it involved a labour dispute between Connolly, an EU employee at the time, and the European Commission. The applicant worked for the Commission in an area related to economic and monetary policy. After having taken leave of absence, Connolly published a book dealing with monetary policy, for which he had not received prior permission.[39] Since this was contrary to the Staff Regulations, Connolly was dismissed. He appealed the decision before the Court of First Instance and subsequently before the CJEU, arguing that Article 17 of the Staff Regulations was unlawful, since it was in breach of the principle of freedom of expression set forth in Article 10 ECHR. Both EU Courts dismissed the appeal.[40] Connolly then brought the case to Strasbourg, arguing, inter alia, that the denial to submit written observations to the Opinion of the Advocate General before the

ECtHR Annual Report for 2014, available at http://echr.coe.int/Documents/Annual_Report_2014_ENG.pdf (last accessed 16 December 2020). See also N Mole, 'Can *Bosphorus* be maintained?' (2015) 16 *ERA Forum* 467; J Polakiewicz, 'Speech: The Future of Fundamental Rights Protection without Accession', 26 June 2006, available at www.coe.int/en/web/dlapil/speeches-of-the-director/-/asset_publisher/ja71RsfCQTP7/content/the-future-of-fundamental-rights-protection-without-accession?inheritRedirect=false (last accessed 16 December 2020); J Morijn, 'After Opinion 2/13: How to Move on in Strasbourg and Brussels?', *EUtopia Law* (5 January 2015), available at https://eutopialaw.com/2015/01/05/after-opinion-213-how-to-move-on-in-strasbourg-and-brussels/ (last accessed 16 December 2020).

[35] This discussion is taken up again in section IV.C.

[36] Van de Heyning (n 21).

[37] See, eg, *Avotiņš v Latvia* (n 27) para 105.

[38] *Connolly v 15 Member States of the European Union*, App no 73274/01 (ECtHR, 9 December 2008).

[39] His book, *The Rotten Heart of Europe*, had criticised the EMU project.

[40] Case T-163/96 *Connolly v European Commission*, ECLI:EU:T:1999:102; Case C-274/99 P *Connolly*, ECLI:EU:C:2001:127.

CJEU constituted a breach of Article 6 of the Convention. Since the EU was (and still is) not a contracting party to the Convention, the indicated respondents were all the (then) EU Member States. The ECtHR held that the respondents did not intervene in the proceedings at any time, which meant that the alleged violation did not occur within their jurisdiction and hence the jurisdiction of the Court. The ECtHR concluded that the complaint was in fact directed against the EU Courts and thus inadmissible *ratione personae*. The same reasoning can be discerned in a number of other labour disputes where the ECtHR consistently held that it had no jurisdiction *ratione personae* to deal with complaints directed against individual decisions given by the competent body of an international organisation.[41]

B. Concluding Remarks

Presently, the EU cannot be held responsible under the ECHR for the acts of its organs, and applications brought against it are incompatible *ratione personae* with the Convention. The EU Member States, however, remain responsible under the ECHR for human rights violations originating in the EU. In that sense, the ECtHR has jurisdiction to review EU law indirectly, as well as a large number of cases decided by the CJEU.

Over the years, the Strasbourg Court has shown that it trusts the level of protection provided for in the EU and enforced by the CJEU. Therefore, in situations in which the Member States do not have any discretion as to how an EU act is applied, the Court will decline full scrutiny and apply the *Bosphorus* presumption of equivalent protection. This is a compromise offered by the Strasbourg Court: it may accept the jurisdiction, but it will not conduct a full review. The Court has struggled along the way in trying to find a balance; sometimes it has been willing to assign responsibility to a Member State, while in other cases it has allowed Member States to escape responsibility. In the efforts to accommodate the autonomy of the EU legal order, the ECtHR has restricted its own competence to review national measures to the detriment of human rights protection.[42] While the future of the *Bosphorus* doctrine after Opinion 2/13 has been debated in the literature[43] and among the Strasbourg judges,[44] it continues to be valid case law in Strasbourg.

[41] *Boivin v 34 Member States of the Council of Europe*, App no 73250/01 (ECtHR, 9 September 2008); *Beygo v 46 Member States of the Council of Europe*, App no 36099/06 (ECtHR, 16 June 2009); *Rambus Inc v Germany*, App no 40382/05 (ECtHR, 16 June 2009); *Lopez Cifuentes v Spain*, App no 18754/07 (ECtHR, 7 July 2009).

[42] Nevertheless, in most cases involving EU law, the ECtHR was able to establish margin of discretion on the part of the national authorities, which means that the *Bosphorus* presumption was not applied often over the years.

[43] Mole (n 34) 467; Polakiewicz (n 34); Morijn (n 34).

[44] G Butler, 'A Political Decision Disguised as Legal Argument? Opinion 2/13 and European Union Accession to the European Convention on Human Rights' (2015) 31 *Utrecht Journal of International and European Law* 81, 104.

III. EU Law, the ECHR and the Luxembourg Court

A. The Status of the ECHR in EU Law

The EU is not a party to the ECHR so, formally speaking, the ECHR is not part of EU law. However, this does not mean that the ECHR is of no avail in EU fundamental rights protection. First, fundamental rights as guaranteed by the ECHR constitute general principles of EU law (Article 6(3) TEU). Second, the EU Charter draws heavily on the ECHR and provides that Charter rights corresponding to rights guaranteed by the ECHR shall have the same meaning and scope as those laid down by the said Convention, while the EU is allowed to offer more extensive protection (Article 52(3) of the Charter). In addition, Article 53 of the Charter clarifies that nothing in the Charter can be interpreted as restricting or adversely affecting human rights and fundamental freedoms as recognised, in their respective fields of application, by the ECHR.

i. Article 6(3) TEU

As early as 1974 the ECHR had become a 'source of inspiration' for the judges in Luxembourg, and later on it had acquired 'special significance' among the legal sources, to be taken into account when identifying the fundamental rights applicable under EU law.[45] This stance was codified for the first time in the Maastricht Treaty in Article F(2) EU, which is now, after some minor modifications, Article 6(3) TEU:

> Fundamental rights, as guaranteed by the European Convention for the Protection of Human Rights and Fundamental Freedoms and as they result from the constitutional traditions common to the Member States, shall constitute general principles of the Union's law.

This provision gives the ECHR a position different from that originally given to it by the Court of Justice, as it provides, rather directly and convincingly, that the ECHR rights *are* the general principles of EU law.[46] This then means that the ECHR is part of EU law after all, as a matter of EU law. However, this interpretation has

[45] The ECHR has been mentioned as a 'source of inspiration' since 1974 (for the very first time in Case 4/73 *Nold v Commission* [1974] ECR 491) and it has been characterised as having 'special significance' since 1989. On the different stages of the role of the ECHR in the case law of the CJEU, see A Rosas, 'The European Union and Fundamental Rights/Human Rights' in C Krause and M Scheinin (eds), *International Protection of Human Rights: A Textbook* (Åbo, Institute for Human Rights, Åbo Academy University, 2009).

[46] On this point, see B De Witte, 'The use of the ECHR and Convention case law by the European Court of Justice', in P Popelier, C Van de Heyning and P Van Nuffel (eds), *Human Rights Protection in the European Legal Order: The interaction between the European and the national courts* (Antwerp, Intersentia, 2011) 22.

been contested in the literature, and the CJEU has given it a different interpretation. Cases in point are *Kamberaj* and *Åkerberg Fransson*.[47]

In *Kamberaj*, the CJEU ruled against the direct application of the ECHR provisions in EU law.[48] The case originated in a reference for a preliminary ruling made by the Italian Court of Bolzano, which had asked, inter alia, whether, in the event of a conflict between the provision of domestic law and the ECHR, the reference to the latter in Article 6 TEU obliged the national court to apply the provisions of the ECHR – in the present case Article 14 ECHR and Article 1 of Protocol 12 – directly, disapplying the incompatible source of domestic law, without first making a reference to the *Corte Costituzionale*.[49] The referring court thus placed the specific issue of the case in the broader context of the European and national fundamental rights architecture, asking how EU law, national constitutional law and the ECHR relate: was the ECHR part of EU law by virtue of Article 6(3) TEU?

It is important to note here that the *Corte Costituzionale* has qualified the ECHR as '*norma interposta*', implying that it ranks between the constitutional and ordinary Italian law, since a conflict between ordinary Italian law and the ECHR can result in an indirect violation of Article 117 of the Constitution. The ECHR rights should thus be observed when applying national law, but national law cannot be disapplied when it is in conflict with the ECHR. Instead, a reference to the *Corte Costituzionale* should be made. This did not prevent Italian judges from sometimes disapplying ordinary legislation for an infringement of the ECHR, and the debate on the status of the ECHR in Italian law is not yet settled.[50]

In response, the CJEU commenced by saying that Article 6 TEU reflected the settled case law of the Court, according to which fundamental rights form an integral part of the general principles of EU law. The Court held, however, that Article 6(3) TEU 'does not govern the relationship between the ECHR and the legal systems of the Member States and nor does it lay down the consequences to be drawn by a national court in case of a conflict between the rights guaranteed by that convention and a provision of national law'.[51] Accordingly, Article 6(3) TEU did not require the national court to apply the ECHR directly and to disapply the provision of national law (which implements EU law) in the case of a conflict with the ECHR.[52]

One can see the importance of the question: holding that the ECHR (and the case law of the ECtHR), as such, is part of EU law, based on the doctrine of incorporation, would imply that the compatibility of national law with the ECHR

[47] Cases C-571/10 *Kamberaj*, ECLI:EU:C:2012:233 and Case C-617/10 *Åkerberg Fransson*, ECLI:EU:C:2013:105.

[48] *Kamberaj* (n 47).

[49] ibid para 59.

[50] G Bianco and G Martinico, 'The Poisoned Chalice: An Italian view on the Kamberaj case', *Working Paper on European Law and Regional Integration no 18* (2013).

[51] *Kamberaj* (n 47) para 62.

[52] ibid para 63.

becomes a question of EU law. The CJEU could then be asked to interpret the ECHR, at least when the case comes within the scope of EU law, and it would be bound by the case law of the Strasbourg Court, not as a matter of international law (this would require accession) but as a matter of EU law. Another consequence could be that some national courts would sidestep the CJEU's interpretative monopoly and would ultimately take *control* over EU law and its relationship with national law, by using the ECHR and the Strasbourg case law instead (when interpreting EU general principles that coincide with the ECHR). Nevertheless, one would expect the Court to take a note of the change in the wording of Article 6(3) TEU and to explain more directly and convincingly how, given this new wording, the ECHR is still merely 'a source of inspiration'. In any case, the reference in *Kamberaj* reflects the struggle of a national judge in determining whether the Charter applies in a particular case, as well as uncertainty regarding the application of general principles of EU law and the role of the ECHR therein.

Many commentators take the same view as the CJEU,[53] considering that the ECHR has not become part of EU law by virtue of Article 6(3) TEU; however, this view has also been contested.[54] This is not surprising, given that the wording of the provision is clear: the ECHR rights 'shall constitute general principles of the Union's law'. What comes to mind immediately is the Court's concern for its own autonomy vis-à-vis the judicial authority of other courts and tribunals, which was often expressed over the years and for which the Court has been heavily criticised. The CJEU reaffirmed its stance again in *Åkerberg Fransson*, ruling that since the ECHR has not been formally incorporated into EU law, the domestic effects of the ECHR and the relationship between the ECHR and national law are not governed by EU law.[55]

ii. Article 52(3) of the Charter

In addition to Article 6 TEU, the interpretative principle in Article 52(3) of the EU Charter of Fundamental Rights further enhances the ECHR's importance and position in EU law:

> In so far as this Charter contains rights which correspond to rights guaranteed by the Convention for the Protection of Human Rights and Fundamental Freedoms, the meaning and scope of those rights shall be the same as those laid down by the said Convention. This provision shall not prevent Union law providing more extensive protection.

This provision formulates a duty to interpret Charter rights corresponding to rights in the ECHR in the same way, and it makes the limitation of those corresponding fundamental rights justifiable only if the limitation would also be permissible

[53] Rosas (n 45) 457–58.
[54] De Witte (n 46) 21–24.
[55] *Åkerberg Fransson* (n 47) para 44.

under the ECHR. In that sense, it is designed to avoid conflicting interpretations of the same fundamental rights guaranteed by the two human rights catalogues. Furthermore, since the ECtHR determines the meaning and scope of the Convention rights (pursuant to Article 32 ECHR), it must be assumed that Article 52(3) of the Charter also intends to make the case law of the ECtHR an integral part of the meaning and scope of those rights, where it functions as a minimum standard. This assumption is not unwarranted in my view; Article 52(3) is only meaningful if it commits the CJEU to take account of the Strasbourg case law.

This argument finds its support in the object and purpose of Article 52(3) as provided in the Explanations relating to the Charter. The Explanations clearly state that the purpose of this provision is to ensure the necessary consistency between the Charter and the ECHR and between the relevant case law of the two European Courts.[56] Importantly, the Explanations specify that the meaning and scope of the ECHR rights are determined by the text of the Convention and by the Strasbourg Court. This is, moreover, backed up by the Preamble to the Charter, which also refers to the Strasbourg case law specifically. Finally, the Explanations make clear that the level of protection afforded by the Charter may never be lower than that guaranteed by the ECHR, but it can of course be higher.

It is nevertheless also important to consider some counterarguments at the outset, particularly relating to the conclusion that the CJEU, when interpreting Charter rights that have a corresponding right in the ECHR, is bound by the interpretations given to the latter by the ECtHR. One is that the text of Article 52(3) is open as to whether there is a duty to follow the case law of the ECtHR, since the provision only mentions the Convention rights and not the Strasbourg case law interpreting it. This is further supported by the evidence of failed instances in the drafting history of the Charter where an attempt was made to include the explicit reference to the ECtHR in the provision.[57] It is thus said that since there is no express reference to the ECtHR's case law in the provision itself, there is little room for arguing that the case law should be considered binding.[58] The idea behind the contention is that while it is true that Explanations relating to Article 52(3) do expressly refer to the Strasbourg case law, Article 52(7) of the Charter only postulates a duty to 'duly regard' these Explanations. Indeed, one can question why the explicit reference to the case law of the ECtHR was not included in the provision itself. However, it would not seem appropriate to claim that it is because the intention of the drafters had been to only include the text of the Convention.

[56] Explanations Relating to the Charter of Fundamental Rights [2007] OJ C303/20.

[57] For further details on the drafting history of the Charter and an argument against the binding nature of ECtHR case law, see S Brittain, 'The Relationship Between the EU Charter of Fundamental Rights and the European Convention on Human Rights: An Originalist Analysis' (2015) 11 *European Constitutional Law Review* 482.

[58] ibid 503. See also T Lock, *The European Court of Justice and International Courts* (Oxford, Oxford University Press, 2015) 181; S Douglas-Scott, 'The Court of Justice of the European Union and the European Court of Human Rights after Lisbon' in S De Vries et al (eds), *The Protection of Fundamental Rights in the EU after Lisbon* (Oxford, Hart Publishing, 2013) 153, 163.

The Convention was drafted in the 1950s, and the meaning and scope of ECHR rights has evolved and developed over the years owing to dynamic and evolutive interpretation by the Strasbourg Court.[59] It would thus be impossible, in practice, to give any meaningful effect to the legal obligation in Article 52(3) without considering Strasbourg case law. It would also be contrary to the primary aim of this provision, which is ensuring the harmonious interpretation of corresponding Charter and ECHR rights, and achieving consistency between Luxembourg and Strasbourg case law. Accordingly, it must be assumed that the case law of the ECtHR forms an integral part of the meaning and scope of ECHR rights, and thus of the meaning and scope of the corresponding Charter rights.

This interpretation is in line with the argument of Advocate General Jacobs in the *Bospohorus* case, when he argued that even though the ECHR may not be formally binding upon the EU, 'for practical purposes the Convention can be regarded as part of Community law and can be invoked as such both in this Court and in national courts where Community law is in issue'.[60] Initially, the CJEU seemed to suggest the same interpretation. In *McB v LE*, the CJEU held that where Charter rights are the same as those in the ECHR, they must be given the same meaning and the same scope, 'as interpreted by the case-law of the European Court of Human Rights'.[61] In *Jaramillo*, the Court went as far as to state that a reference to the case law of the ECtHR 'must be made' when interpreting and applying a Charter right that corresponds to an ECHR right, in accordance with Article 52(3) of the Charter.[62] This judgment seemed to have extended the obligation of following the ECtHR case law to also having to explicitly reference it. In later cases, however, the Court changed its approach. It repeatedly held that whilst Article 52(3) of the Charter requires corresponding rights contained in the Charter and the ECHR to be given the same meaning and scope, the latter 'does not constitute, as long as the European Union has not acceded to it, a legal instrument which has been formally incorporated into European Union law'.[63]

More recently, the Court's practice in this respect has been uneven. There are many examples that follow a reference to Art 52(3) of the Charter and where the CJEU engages extensively with the case law of the ECtHR.[64] At the same time, other judgments contain a brief reference, with an accompanying reminder that

[59] See, eg, E Brems and J Gerards (eds), *Shaping Rights in the ECHR – The Role of the European Court of Human Rights in Determining the Scope of Human Rights* (Cambridge, Cambridge University Press, 2013).

[60] Opinion of AG Jacobs in Case C-84/95 *Bosphorus v Ireland*, ECLI:EU:C:1996:179.

[61] Case C-400/10 PPU *McB* ECLI:EU:C:2010:582, para 53.

[62] Case C-334/12 *Jaramillo and Others* ECLI:EU:C:2013:134, para 43.

[63] See, eg, *Kamberaj* (n 47) para 62; *Åkerberg Fransson* (n 47) para 44. For the academic literature that supports the Court's view, see Lock (n 58) 169; for the opposite view, see W Weiss, 'Human Rights in the EU: Rethinking the Role of the European Convention on Human Rights After Lisbon' (2011) 7 *European Constitutional Law Review* 1, 64 and 71.

[64] This is often the case law in the Area of Freedom, Security and Justice (AFSJ). See, eg, Case C-661/17 *MA*, ECLI:EU:C:2019:53 and Case C-571/17 *Samet Ardic*, ECLI:EU:C:2017:1026.

the ECHR is not part of EU law. In the *N* case, for example, concerning the detention of asylum seekers in the context of their deportation for reasons of public order and safety, the CJEU ruled that it does not consider itself formally bound by the ECHR and the case law of the ECtHR when it interprets EU law. The Court went as far as to state that the validity review of EU secondary law 'must be undertaken solely in the light of the fundamental rights guaranteed by the Charter'.[65] This language in this judgment seems even stronger than usual: a fundamental rights review *must* be undertaken *solely* in the light of the Charter. In that judgment the Court also pointed out that Article 52(3) is intended to ensure the consistency between the rights contained in the Charter and the corresponding rights guaranteed by the ECHR, without thereby adversely affecting the autonomy of EU law and that of the CJEU.[66] The Court indeed uses the autonomy argument in some cases to dismiss national courts' questions regarding the consequences of Article 52(3) of the Charter. However, could it not be said that Article 52(3), by virtue of its wording, necessarily conditions and limits the autonomy of EU law in the field of fundamental rights? Moreover, leaving aside Article 52(3) of the Charter, one might wonder what the benefit would be of autonomously developing EU law in a way that is not compliant with the ECHR minimum standards when the Member States may be answerable for it in Strasbourg?[67] Finally, there are also judgments that are silent on the ECHR and Strasbourg case law, even when it was referenced by the referring court and the Advocate General.[68]

A related problem in the judgments in which the Court of Justice does refer to the ECHR and/or the ECtHR case law is that some decisions contain an extensive analysis of the Strasbourg case law, demonstrating that the two are in conformity, while in other cases the CJEU simply comes to this conclusion without any kind of preceding discussion or analysis (usually doing so at the very end of the reasoning). The fact that the CJEU uses the Charter first and foremost in its analysis is not wrong – the Charter is the EU's catalogue of rights, and it is only logical that the Charter is taken as the main source for identifying and interpreting fundamental rights. It may even be a desirable approach in many cases, since it may afford an opportunity for the CJEU to provide more protection. Having said that, when references are being made to the ECHR, the Court should engage more deeply in explaining how its decision is in conformity with the ECHR and the case law of the ECtHR, rather than simply stating that it is.[69] In this context, Weiler criticised the CJEU's 'notoriously telegraphic style', which is 'not designed to inspire

[65] Case C-601/15 PPU *N*, ECLI:EU:C:2016:84, para 46. This case is discussed in more detail in ch 6.

[66] ibid para 47. For the same expression, see eg Case C-294/16 PPU, *JZ v Prokuratura Rejonowa Łódź – Śródmieście*, ECLI:EU:C:2016:610, para 50.

[67] J Callewaert, 'Do we still need Article 6(2) TEU? Consideration on the absence of EU accession to the ECHR and its consequences' (2018) 55 *CML Rev* 1685, 1706.

[68] The case in point is Case C-216/18 PPU *LM*, ECLI:EU:C:2018:586. See in this context the Opinion of AG Tanchev, which includes over 100 mentions, including an extensive analysis, of the ECHR and ECtHR case law.

[69] See, eg, Case C-465/07 *Meki Elgafaji, Noor Elgafaji v Staatssecretaris van Justitie*, ECLI:EU:C:2009:94, para 44.

confidence'.[70] But Weiler also questioned the appropriateness of references to the ECHR and the case law of the ECtHR more generally, arguing that it is the Strasbourg Court that has the ultimate authority to give a binding interpretation of the provisions of the ECHR and, otherwise, the national (constitutional) courts are better placed than the CJEU to make that judgment.[71] Weiler made a further point questioning the legal duty of national courts in the case of an erroneous interpretation of the Convention by the CJEU, without however providing answers.[72] While these concerns are valid, especially in cases where the CJEU only states that the interpretation of the Charter rights is in conformity with the ECHR and the case law of the ECtHR without any further explanation, in practical terms and from the perspective of the Member States, the references to the ECHR in the CJEU's case law are relevant since they show that the two systems are complementary (rather than in competition) and mutually reinforcing. It is especially important that the national courts see that the approach is the same in Luxembourg and Strasbourg, since they have to ensure that their jurisprudence is in compliance with both. In the event of doubt, national courts can always ask for clarification. In my view, therefore, the references are valuable, but the Court should be more systematic and elaborate in this respect, especially in sensitive cases where it may not be so obvious or clear that its interpretation of the Charter is indeed in conformity with (the ECtHR's interpretation of) the ECHR (and hence that Article 52(3) of the Charter has been upheld).

As a final point and a matter of clarification, it is of course entirely correct to say that the ECHR is not part of EU law since the EU has not acceded to it, and thus has not committed itself to compliance by means of an accession treaty. But the argument is that the EU Member States have decided to adopt this rule unilaterally in Article 52(3) of the Charter, which commits the Union to ensure compliance with the ECHR minimum standards, in accordance with certain rules, regardless of the formal accession.[73] Article 52(3) could thus be seen as imposing an internal obligation to ensure compliance with the ECHR – and, by extension, the case law of the ECtHR – as *a matter of EU law* (and not as a matter of international law, which would indeed require formal accession).[74]

[70] J Weiler, 'Editorial: Human Rights: Member State, EU and ECHR Levels of Protection; PS Catalonia; Why Does it Take So Long for my Article to Be Published?' (2013) 24 *European Journal of International Law* 471, 473.

[71] ibid.

[72] ibid.

[73] President of the CJEU Lenaerts had concluded already in 2001, after the Charter was solemnly proclaimed, that the ECJ 'will be obliged to take over the interpretation given by the ECtHR', at least for ECHR rights corresponding to the rights in the Charter: K Lenaerts and E De Smijter, 'The Charter and the role of the European Courts' (2001) 8 *Maastricht Journal of European and Comparative Law* 90, 99.

[74] De Witte addressed the confusion between the two separate legal questions in his writings: De Witte (n 46).

IV. Recent Developments in the Relationship between the Strasbourg and Luxembourg Courts

The ECHR and the case law of the ECtHR have been instrumental in the development of EU fundamental rights. Over the years, the CJEU showed its commitment to having regard to the Convention and to adhering to Strasbourg's interpretation when applying fundamental rights. It used both the Convention itself and the Strasbourg case law to define and further develop unwritten general principles of EU law and, occasionally, to set the standards of human rights protection in the EU. The Court also demonstrated a willingness to engage with the case law of the Strasbourg Court in order to avoid conflicting judgments. This referencing and mutual accommodation were thus beneficial for avoiding conflicts; however, this practice started to diminish in Luxembourg, in particular since the EU Charter became legally binding, which resulted in the relationship between the two European courts becoming strained and more complicated.

A. Charter Centrism and Limited References to the ECHR

The Court of Justice has played a key role in the post-Lisbon fundamental rights narrative too, developing its own human rights *acquis*. In doing so, the Court has used, almost exclusively, the newly legally binding Charter as the reference text and the starting point for its assessment of fundamental rights. While this development in itself is not problematic (quite the opposite in fact; it would seem beneficial that the EU has its own bill of rights for the sake of both legal certainty and transparency, and it may allow the CJEU to provide more protection)[75] and the ECHR is meant to be subsidiary, several other changes in the Court's case law, coupled with the exclusive focus on the Charter, seem to give cause for concern.

One of those changes is the sharp decline in references to the ECHR and the ECtHR's case law over the past few years. According to Gráinne de Búrca, who conducted a study on the number of references to the Charter of Fundamental Rights by the Court of Justice since it gained binding legal force in December 2009 until the end of 2012, there has been a remarkable lack of referencing on the part of the Court to other relevant sources of human rights law and jurisprudence in that period, notably to the ECHR and the ECtHR case law.[76] She determined that out of 122 cases in which the Charter was mentioned, the CJEU referred to a Convention provision in only 20 cases. Furthermore, the Court referred to the case law of the ECtHR in only 10 out of 27 cases in which the CJEU engaged

[75] Some authors consider Charter centrism problematic for various reasons. See, eg, de Búrca (n 3).
[76] ibid.

substantively with the Charter in that period.[77] Moreover, any references to other international human rights treaties and to the common constitutional traditions of the Member States have been basically absent from the CJEU's case law.[78] Indeed, this trend can be observed in some of the important Grand Chamber judgments from that period, such as *Åkerberg Fransson*,[79] *Sky Österreich*,[80] *Google Spain*[81] and *Zoran Spasic*,[82] none of which explicitly mentions ECHR standards.[83] This is quite remarkable considering that a study of the number of references by the CJEU to the ECHR before the Charter became legally binding (from 1998 to 2005) revealed that the references to the ECHR had been increasing constantly throughout those years, and that the ECHR had in fact become the main rights instrument in the CJEU's jurisprudence.[84]

The decline in references continued in the period after 2012, as noted by some authors. Lambrecht and Rauchegger looked into the references to the case law of the ECtHR in the period between 1 January 2014 and 1 April 2015.[85] In that period, the Court referred to the ECtHR's case law in only 8 of the 43 judgments in which the Charter played a substantive role.

Looking at the more recent cases, the CJEU still refers to the ECHR and the Strasbourg case law occasionally and often in important decisions, but there are also examples where it is obvious that it should refer, especially when national courts refer to it (as well as the Advocates General) but the Court does not mention it.[86] While this sort of number crunching may not tell the full story, it is an important indication that the CJEU is making its human rights jurisprudence more autonomous. This carries the risk of divergent human rights standards in Europe, and potentially conflicting decisions in Strasbourg and Luxembourg.

[77] It should be noted that even though the CJEU did refer to the Charter in all 122 cases, it engaged in a substantive analysis of the Charter rights in 27 cases.

[78] An exception is the Geneva Convention Relating to the Status of Refugees of 1951, which has been cited quite often, and the Convention on the Rights of the Child in cases dealing with expulsion for child sexual offences. See also A Rosas, 'Five Years of Charter Case Law: Some Observations' in S de Vries, U Bernitz and S Weatherill (eds), *The EU Charter of Fundamental Rights as a Binding Instrument: Five Years Old and Growing* (Oxford, Hart Publishing, 2015).

[79] *Åkerberg Fransson* (n 47).

[80] Case C-283/11 *Sky Österreich*, ECLI:EU:C:2013:28.

[81] Case C-131/12 *Google Spain*, ECLI:EU:C:2014:317.

[82] Case C-129/14 PPU *Zoran Spasic*, ECLI:EU:C:2014:586.

[83] Instead, in *Åkerberg Fransson*, for example, the Court held that the ECHR does not constitute, as long as the EU has not acceded to it, a legal instrument that has been formally incorporated into EU law, and consequently EU law does not govern the relations between the ECHR and the legal systems of the Member States, nor does it determine the conclusions to be drawn by a national court in the event of a conflict between the rights guaranteed by the ECHR and a rule of national law.

[84] L Scheeck, 'Competition, Conflict and Cooperation between European Courts and the Diplomacy of Supranational Judicial Networks', *Garnet Working Paper 23/07* (2007).

[85] S Lambrecht and C Rauchegger, 'European Union: The EU's Attitude to the ECHR' in P Popelier, S Lambrecht and K Lemmens (eds), *Criticism of the European Court of Human Rights: Shifting the Convention System: Counter-Dynamics at the National and EU Level* (Antwerp, Intersentia, 2016) 41.

[86] For example, in Case C-216/18 PPU *LM*, ECLI:EU:C:2018:586. For other examples and discussion, see L Glas and J Krommendijk, 'From Opinion 2/13 to Avotiņš: Recent Developments in the Relationship between the Luxembourg and Strasbourg Court' (2017) 17 *Human Rights Law Review* 2.

Moreover, by disregarding other human rights mechanisms, the CJEU is missing the opportunity to develop its expertise in the field of human rights further and to strengthen the legitimacy of its decisions in the eyes of European citizens.[87] Interestingly, in Strasbourg, the number of references to the EU Charter has only increased in the post-Lisbon period.[88] Moreover, in the period after the publication of Opinion 2/13, the relevant figures show that references to the Charter, EU law and the CJEU's case law do not appear to be decreasing in Strasbourg.[89]

While compliance with the ECHR is not measured by the number of references to it, it is important to prevent a sharp decline in references, as noted in the years following the entry into force of the Charter, which would lead to a perception of fragmented and divided fundamental rights protection in Europe. This is exactly what the Lisbon Treaty drafters aimed to prevent by introducing the interpretative principle in Article 52(3) of the Charter, as well as Article 6(2) TEU.[90]

B. Opinion 2/13 on the EU's Accession to the ECHR

The CJEU's Opinion 2/13 is possibly one of the most extreme examples of the Court's 'legal parochialism' in recent years.[91] In the Opinion, the Court (in contrast to all other parties that have submitted observations in the proceedings)[92] ruled that the Draft Accession Agreement (DAA)[93] was incompatible with the autonomy and the specific characteristics of EU law. It firmly rejected the DAA for five main reasons. Some of them are rather technical and other more substantial. The technical objections mainly relate to the arrangements made in the DAA in respect of Article 344 TFEU and arrangements concerning the co-respondent mechanism

[87] de Búrca (n 3).

[88] Gragl (n 33).

[89] Glas and Krommendijk (n 86) 11.

[90] Callewaert (n 67).

[91] Most authors have been very critical of the CJEU's approach in Opinion 2/13. See, amongst many, E Spaventa, 'A Very Fearful Court? The Protection of Fundamental Rights in the European Union after Opinion 2/13' (2015) 22 *Maastricht Journal of European and Comparative Law* 35; S Peers, 'The EU's Accession to the ECHR: The Dream Becomes a Nightmare' (2015) 16 *German Law Journal* 213; B De Witte and Š Imamović, 'Opinion 2/13 on Accession to the ECHR: Defending the EU Legal Order against a Foreign Human Rights Court' (2015) 40 *EL Rev* 683; P Gragl, 'The Reasonableness of Jealousy: Opinion 2/13 and EU Accession to the ECHR' in W Benedek, F Benoit Rohmer W Karl and M Nowak (eds), *European Yearbook on Human Rights* (Vienna, Neuer Wissenschaftlicher Verlag, 2015) 27. For a more nuanced view of the Opinion, see D Halberstam, '"It's the Autonomy, Stupid!" A Modest Defense of Opinion 2/13 on EU Accession to the European Convention on Human Rights' (2015) 16 *German Law Journal* 105; C Krenn, 'Autonomy and Effectiveness as Common Concerns: A Path to ECHR Accession after Opinion 2/13' (2015) 16 *German Law Journal* 147.

[92] This includes the European Commission, the Council of Ministers and the Parliament, as well as 24 EU Member States.

[93] For analysis of the DAA see P Gragl, 'A Giant Leap for European Human Rights? The Final Agreement on the European Union's Accession to the European Convention on Human Rights' (2014) 51 *CML Rev* 13.

and the CJEU's prior involvement. These should not be too difficult to remedy, although it may take time before consensual solutions are worked out between the different actors, even for these more technical objections.

By contrast, the objection relating to the principle of mutual trust and recognition, and the presumption underlying it, is more substantial and more difficult to remedy. The views expressed in the context of the meaning and role of the principle of mutual trust and recognition in EU law affect the core of the Convention system and go to the heart of the very notion of fundamental rights. Other more substantial objections concern the relationship between Article 53 of the Charter and the ECHR, the ECHR Protocol No 16 and, perhaps most controversially, the EU's Common Foreign and Security Policy (CFSP).[94]

Opinion 2/13 is problematic not only for its outcome, but also for its language and underlying tone. In the Opinion, the CJEU depicts the EU legal order as normatively self-sufficient, and does not give any recognition to the ECHR legal system.[95] Article 6(2) TEU, which illustrates the aspirations of the Member States to join the ECHR and, more importantly, make accession to the ECHR a legal obligation, is barely mentioned in the Opinion. Article 52(3) of the Charter – the key provision explaining the relationship between the Charter and the Convention – is not mentioned once.[96] What is even more puzzling in this context is that on the same day as publishing Opinion 2/13, the Court adopted two Grand Chamber judgments in the *M'Bodj* and *Abdida* cases, on the rights of refugees, where it based its reasoning on and made a reference to the Strasbourg case law.[97] In the *Abdida* case, the Court explicitly referred to Article 52(3) of the Charter, stating that '[i]t is the case law of the European Court of Human Rights, which, in accordance with Article 52(3) of the Charter, must be taken into account when interpreting a Charter provision that corresponds to a Convention right'.[98]

This section focuses on the Court's view on the principle of mutual trust, which is explicitly addressed in the first objection and is central in discussion of the divergences in the case law of the CJEU and the ECtHR today. For the sake of completeness and clarity, a brief overview of other objections is also included.

[94] For the sake of clarity, all objections are considered in turn below. For the analysis of the CFSP objection in particular, see G Butler, 'The Ultimate Stumbling Block? The Common Foreign and Security Policy, and Accession of the European Union to the European Convention on Human Rights' (2016) 39 *Dublin University Law Journal* 229.

[95] L Halleskov Storgaard, 'EU Law Autonomy versus European Fundamental Rights Protection – On Opinion 2/13 on EU Accession to the ECHR' (2015) 15 *Human Rights Law Review* 485, 521.

[96] Compare the view of AG Kokott in Opinion 2/13, *Accession of the European Union to the European Convention on Human Rights*, ECLI:EU:C:2014:2475. She concluded, with reference to Art 52(3) of the Charter, that 'the EU is already (that is to say, before its formal accession) applying the standards of fundamental rights protection that flow from the ECHR; therefore, viewed purely in terms of their substance, the restrictions on the exercise of the competences of the EU institutions that may in future result from being a party to the ECHR already apply' (para 42).

[97] Case C-542/13 *M'Bodj*, ECLI:EU:C:2014:2452, paras 39 and 40; and Case C-562/13 *Abdida v Centre public d'action sociale d'Ottignies-Louvain-La-Neuve*, ECLI:EU:C:2014:2453, paras 47 and 52.

[98] *Abdida* (n 97) para 47.

The analysis follows the arguments as presented by the Court of Justice in the Opinion.[99]

i. The Specific Characteristics and the Autonomy of EU Law

The first point the CJEU brought up under this heading was the coordination between Article 53 of the Charter and Article 53 ECHR. Article 53 of the Charter suggests that the protection provided in the Charter shall not restrict or adversely affect the rights contained in the national constitutions, EU law and in the international human rights instruments, including the ECHR. Similarly, Article 53 ECHR states that the Convention rights shall not derogate from or restrict the rights and freedoms stipulated in other human rights instruments. The coordination between the two provisions was considered necessary by the Court in order to secure its own interpretation of Article 53 of the Charter, which, in light of *Melloni*,[100] limits the application of higher national fundamental rights standards if it affects the effectiveness, uniformity and autonomy of EU law. The CJEU considered that somehow Article 53 of the Convention would have an impact on the limits determined in the context of Article 53 of the Charter. However, this argument seems to be flawed, because Article 53 of the Convention is not a conflict rule; it simply states that Contracting States can provide more protection if they wish to do so, but applicants cannot rely on this provision to claim that their rights under national or international law have been violated.[101] Thus, the ECtHR only determines the floor, the minimum level of protection, but not the ceiling. Moreover, the ECtHR has referred to this provision only exceptionally, so it is not clear where the fears of the CJEU are coming from.[102] Nevertheless, this objection, albeit a puzzling one, does not appear as problematic as some other objections discussed further below.

The second point raised by the Court as concerns the principle of mutual trust and recognition is one of the most difficult points – if not the most difficult one – in the Opinion. The Court gives the principle a constitutional ranking and observes that it is of 'fundamental importance' for the EU, as it allows for the creation and the maintenance of an area without internal borders.[103] Drawing on its previous rulings in *NS* and *Abdullahi*, the Court stressed that the principle of mutual trust requires EU Member States to presume that fundamental rights have been observed by other states, save for in 'exceptional circumstances'.[104] In so far

[99] For my analysis of the objections that are not discussed extensively in this book, see De Witte and Imamović (n 91) 683.

[100] Case C-399/11 *Melloni*, ECLI:EU:C:2013:107. For discussion of *Melloni*, see ch 4.

[101] See, eg, *Markopoulou v Greece* App No.20665/92 (ECtHR, 6 April 1994) 4; *EM v Greece* App no 22225/93 (ECtHR, 1 December 1993) 4.

[102] *Open Door Counselling v Ireland* App no 14234/88 (ECtHR, 29 October 1992). See also C Van de Heyning, 'No Place Like Home: Discretionary Space for the Domestic Protection of Fundamental Rights' in Popelier, Van de Heyning and Van Nuffel (eds) (n 46) 73.

[103] Opinion 2/13 (n 2) paras 191–195.

[104] ibid paras 191 and 192.

as the ECHR would, in requiring the EU and the Member States to be considered Contracting Parties not only in their relations with Contracting Parties that are not Member States of the EU but also in their relations with each other, require a Member State to check that another Member State has observed fundamental rights, even though EU law imposes an obligation of mutual trust between those Member States, accession would upset the underlying balance of the EU and undermine the autonomy of EU law.[105] In other words, EU Member States are under a duty either not to perform a fundamental rights scrutiny, or to limit such scrutiny to the most extreme of violations. But how valid is this argument in the context of the ECHR rights, which virtually all European states have in common?[106] Interestingly, the Opinion was released only a few weeks after the ECtHR's *Tarakhel* ruling,[107] in which the Strasbourg Court condemned the automatic application of the Dublin rules. Although the CJEU does not refer to the *Tarakhel* case in Opinion 2/13, some commentators have suggested that it has played a role in the Court's reasoning.[108]

While the Opinion contains several objections to the DAA that will be difficult to overcome, the mutual trust objection is particularly challenging. Imposed mutual trust does not sit well with the ECHR system, which takes the perspective of the individual and requires the ECHR Contracting Parties to ensure that the Convention rights are respected rather than relying on or trusting other states to comply with fundamental rights.[109] One has to wonder if it would even be possible to accommodate the principle of mutual trust and mutual recognition as interpreted and applied by the CJEU within the Strasbourg system, without affecting the core of the Convention system. This mutual trust is also highly problematic from a general human rights perspective, because it has the effect of removing the minimum standard of fundamental rights protection provided for in the ECHR in the fields of EU law that are prone to human rights violations, and in which measures are adopted against the weakest and most marginalised individuals.[110]

Such a one-sided interpretation of the principle by the CJEU is also problematic from the EU law perspective, but not for the reasons indicated by the CJEU. The respect for fundamental rights is a founding principle of the Union and an

[105] ibid para 194.

[106] See also J Callewaert, 'Is EU Accession still a good idea?' in Š Imamović, M Claes and B De Witte (eds), 'The EU Fundamental Rights Landscape After Opinion 2/13' *Maastricht Faculty of Law Working Paper 2016/3*.

[107] *Tarakhel v Switzerland* App no 29217/12 (ECtHR, 4 November 2014). The judgment is discussed in ch 3.

[108] S Peers, 'The EU's Accession to the ECHR: The Dream Becomes a Nightmare' (2015) 16 *German Law Journal* 213; Halleskov Storgaard (n 95).

[109] This is the Soering line of cases. See *Soering v United Kingdom* App no 14038/88 (ECtHR, 7 July 1989). However, the Court has made exceptions too, eg *Povse v Austria* App no 3890/11 (ECtHR, 18 June 2013).

[110] E Spaventa, 'A Very Fearful Court? The Protection of Fundamental Rights in the European Union after Opinion 2/13' (2015) 22 *Maastricht Journal of European and Comparative Law* 35; De Witte and Imamović (n 91) 683.

indispensable prerequisite for its legitimacy.[111] It is also a core principle of the national legal systems. Mutual trust and recognition, on the other hand, are merely principles used to facilitate judicial cooperation among the Member States. This is not to say that fundamental rights are absolute or cannot be balanced, but the way the Court has approached it in Opinion 2/13, and in some of its fundamental rights cases, points to the Court's misunderstanding and misconception of the role and place of fundamental rights in the EU.

The third and final point under this heading concerns Protocol No 16 to the ECHR. The CJEU considered Protocol No 16 problematic because it would allow national supreme courts to engage in a dialogue with the ECtHR, possibly also in relation to EU law matters, and thus circumvent the preliminary reference procedure in EU law. While this may indeed materialise at some point in the future, it is not the responsibility of the ECtHR and is not a consequence of accession. If national supreme courts would indeed decide to refer their questions and concerns to Strasbourg, rather than Luxembourg while there is a legal obligation under EU law to refer questions of EU law to the CJEU, then the problem would lie in the relationship between the CJEU and the domestic courts, and it should not be addressed and remedied in the Accession Agreement. In fact, national supreme courts of the Member States that have ratified Protocol No 16 have been able to engage in a dialogue with Strasbourg concerning the ECHR rights as from 1 August 2018 (which is when the Protocol entered into force), thus having the same effect and consequence even without accession (in the EU states that have ratified it).[112]

ii. Article 344 TFEU

In accordance with Article 344 TFEU, the CJEU has exclusive jurisdiction to decide all disputes between EU Member States and between the EU and the Member State(s) in so far as they concern EU law, thus excluding any other means of dispute settlement in such cases. In this context, the CJEU considered it necessary that a provision be included in the DAA that would exclude the ECtHR's jurisdiction under Article 33 ECHR over disputes between Member States or between Member States and the EU within the scope of EU law as regards the application of the ECHR. Interestingly, Advocate General Kokott, who signalled the same problem, found that there was no need for such an extreme change in the Agreement, as it did not appear to be strictly necessary for the practical effectiveness of Article 344 and it is not common practice in international agreements.[113] Indeed,

[111] As emphasised during the Cologne European Council (3–4 June 1999), Presidency Conclusions, Annex IV.

[112] So far, the ECtHR issued two Advisory Opinions: ECtHR Advisory Opinion on Matters of Surrogacy requested by the French Court of Cassation, 10 April 2019, Request no P16-2018-001; ECtHR Advisory Opinion relating to Article 300.1 of Armenia's Criminal Code requested by the Armenian Constitutional Court, 29 May 2020, Request no P16-2019-001.

[113] View of AG Kokott in Opinion 2/13 (n 96).

it is not common in international treaty law to include a provision in an accession agreement that excludes the jurisdiction of the relevant court in the application of the instrument to which a party is acceding (*in casu* the ECtHR and the ECHR) in disputes involving other Contracting Parties relating to specific content. This seems to be another example of a matter that should be regulated internally.

iii. Co-Respondent Mechanism

One of the key features of the DAA is the co-respondent mechanism. Outlined in Article 3 of the DAA, the co-respondent mechanism was considered necessary to accommodate the specific situation of the EU as a non-state entity with an autonomous legal system that is becoming a party to the Convention alongside its own Member States. The mechanism was thus tabled in order to remedy the scenario where a complaint is brought against a Member State, which could have been avoided only by disregarding an obligation under EU law. Similarly, a complaint may be brought against one of the EU institutions for implementing provisions of the EU Treaties that are in fact agreed upon by the Member States. Therefore, the EU should be able to join as a co-respondent in the proceedings against one or more Member States and, conversely, the EU Member States should be able to become co-respondents to proceedings instituted against the EU.[114]

The DAA refers to two scenarios that trigger the co-respondent mechanism if certain conditions are fulfilled. The first scenario refers to the situation in which an alleged violation of the Convention concerns a provision of EU law that is directly applicable in the national legal order and is directed against one or more EU Member States but not against the EU itself.[115] This would be a situation in which one or more Member States could avoid the alleged violation only by disregarding an obligation under EU law (eg by applying a Regulation that does not leave a margin of discretion as to its implementation). The second scenario concerns the situation in which an alleged violation of the Convention concerns EU primary law and is directed against the EU and not against one or more EU Member States.[116] In both scenarios, the other party would be able to become a co-respondent.

[114] Art 3(6) of the final version of the DAA states 'In proceedings to which the European Union is co-respondent, if the Court of Justice of the European Union has not yet assessed the compatibility with the Convention rights at issue of the provision of European Union law as under paragraph 2 of this Article, then sufficient time shall be afforded for the Court of Justice of the European Union to make such an assessment and thereafter for the parties to make observations to the Court. The European Union shall ensure that such assessment is made quickly so that the proceedings before the Court are not unduly delayed. The provisions of this paragraph shall not affect the powers of the Court.

[115] Art 1(1) DAA indicates that the EU shall accede to the Convention but also to the Protocol to the Convention (commonly referred to as Protocol No 1) and Protocol No 6 to the Convention.

[116] Art 3(3) DAA.

The CJEU essentially has three main problems with the mechanisms developed by the negotiators:

1. The ECtHR's decision on whether a co-respondent can or cannot join the proceedings would involve an assessment of the division of competences under EU law as well as the criteria for the attribution of their acts and omissions, which could encroach upon the autonomy of EU law.
2. The principle of joint responsibility could result in a situation in which a Member State may be held responsible, together with the EU, for the violation of a provision of the ECHR to which that particular Member State has made a reservation under Article 57 ECHR.
3. The ECtHR decision on whether the Member State(s) is (are) responsible solely or jointly with the EU would involve an assessment of the division of competences in the EU, and would consequently impinge on the autonomy of EU law and the CJEU as its final interpreter.

While the second argument is uncalled for, since it presumes that the ECtHR is incapable of accounting for reservations if they are made by the Member States in the ECHR system, the other two seem more legitimate and should be addressed in the new version of the agreement.

iv. Prior-involvement Procedure

Article 3(6) of the DAA introduces another procedural novelty: the possibility of the involvement of the CJEU in proceedings before the ECtHR in cases in which the EU is joined as a co-respondent. The rationale for introducing this possibility for the CJEU is the fact that, in cases where an EU Member State is designated as a respondent and the case concerns an EU act, the situation may be that the EU joins the proceedings as a co-respondent while the condition of the exhaustion of domestic remedies at the EU level has not been fulfilled, that is, if the CJEU has not been involved through the preliminary reference procedure.[117] This would be in situations in which the highest national courts give final decisions concerning (implementing) acts of EU law without making the reference to the CJEU.[118] The Court found this mechanism also to be problematic from the perspective of EU law. First, the CJEU insisted that, under the DAA, the question of whether it had already given a ruling on the same question of law as that at issue in the proceedings in Strasbourg required an interpretation of the case law of the CJEU, which could only be determined 'by the competent EU institution' whose decision should

[117] On the prior-involvement procedure, see R Baratta, 'Accession of the EU to the ECHR: The Rationale for the ECJ's Prior Involvement Mechanism' (2013) 50 *CML Rev* 1305, 1310.

[118] Making the preliminary reference to the CJEU is in principle obligatory for national courts of last instance (under Art 267 TFEU) but it is subject to exceptions, ie if the question raised is irrelevant to the outcome of the case, when the EU law provision has already been interpreted by the CJEU (*acte éclairé*) or when the correct application of EU law is so obvious that it does not leave scope for any reasonable doubt (*acte clair*).

bind the ECtHR.[119] Similarly, Advocate General Kokott argued that it would be incompatible with the autonomy of EU law if the decision regarding the necessity of the prior involvement of the Court of Justice 'were to be left to the ECtHR alone'.[120] Second, the Court found the scope of Article 3(6) DAA, or rather the explanation provided in the explanatory report, too limited, as it provides that the CJEU's prior assessment of the compatibility of EU law with the Convention means ruling on the interpretation of primary EU law and the validity of secondary EU law, and thus omits the 'interpretation' of secondary EU law. As with the co-respondent mechanism, objections relating to the prior-involvement procedure are clearly less problematic to remedy – although they show great distrust towards the competences of the ECtHR – and the Commission has already engaged in finding the appropriate solutions.

v. Common Foreign and Security Policy

In addition to the mutual trust, the objection concerning the CFSP is another highly controversial point in the Opinion, which will be difficult to remedy.[121] The CJEU has limited jurisdiction in this field, and has therefore decided that the ECtHR should not have the jurisdiction if the Court itself does not have it. In other words, if the Member States want to give review powers to the Strasbourg Court, they should first give such competence to the CJEU. This is clearly problematic, because the Member States have made a conscious choice to exclude (for the most part) the jurisdiction of the CJEU in this particular field. Yet the only way to overcome it seems to be to give the jurisdiction also to the CJEU, and in this sense the CJEU has already taken steps in that direction on its own initiative.[122] However, it is not clear how this objection can be fully remedied without a treaty amendment.

C. A Drop in Temperature

Opinion 2/13 evinces distrust towards the ECtHR, so it is not surprising that it was not well received in Strasbourg. The ECtHR President at the time, Dean Spielmann, commented on Opinion 2/13 in unusually strong language, pointing out that

> the principal victims will be those citizens whom this [Opinion 2/13] deprives of the right to have acts of the European Union subjected to the same external scrutiny as

[119] Opinion 2/13 (n 2) para 241.

[120] Opinion 2/13 Opinion of AG Kokott (n 96) para 183.

[121] For a discussion on the CFSP objection, see Butler (n 94). More generally on the CFSP and the CJEU, see C Hillion, 'A Powerless Court? The European Court of Justice and the Common Foreign and Security Policy' in M Cremona and A Thies (eds), *The European Court of Justice and External Relations Law: Constitutional Challenges* (Oxford, Hart Publishing, 2014) 47.

[122] See, eg, Case C-72/15 *Rosneft*, ECLI:EU:C:2017:236. For a discussion and further references, see G Butler, 'The Coming Age of the Court's Jurisdiction in the Common Foreign and Security Policy' (2017) 13 *European Constitutional Law Review* 673.

> regards respect for human rights as that which applies to each Member State. More than ever, therefore, the onus will be on the Strasbourg Court to do what it can in cases before it to protect citizens from the negative effects of this situation.[123]

An important question in the relationship between EU law and the ECHR viewed from the Strasbourg perspective was the future of the *Bosphorus* presumption after Opinion 2/13.[124] In *Avotiņš v Latvia*,[125] discussed earlier in the chapter, the ECtHR applied the presumption for the first time after Opinion 2/13. Although the decision may seem EU- and CJEU-friendly at first sight, given that the Court found the *Bosphorus* presumption to be applicable and found no manifest deficiency in the protection provided, a careful reading reveals hidden messages and a somewhat stricter application of the presumption. In particular, the ECtHR's assessment of the principle of mutual trust and recognition is worth noting.

The Strasbourg Court commenced by stating that it is mindful of the importance of the mutual recognition mechanism for the construction of the AFSJ and of the mutual trust it requires. The Court thus considers, *in principle*, the means necessary for the creation of the AFSJ to be legitimate.[126] It is apparent to the Court, however, that effectiveness pursued by some of those means results in a 'tightly regulated or even limited' review of the observance of fundamental rights.[127] Here the Court referred to paragraph 192 of Opinion 2/13, where the CJEU suggested that accession to the ECHR would undermine mutual trust among Member States because they would be required to check whether other States observe human rights, and noted that such an interpretation of mutual trust could, in practice,

> run counter to the requirement posed by the Convention according to which the court in the State addressed must at least be empowered to conduct a review commensurate with the gravity of any serious allegation of a violation of fundamental rights in the State of origin, in order to ensure that the protection of those rights is not manifestly deficient.[128]

The ECtHR warned that the application of the *Bosphorus* presumption in the case of *Avotiņš*, and in similar cases, leads to a paradoxical situation in which national courts are precluded from a fundamental rights review due to the principle of mutual trust (as interpreted by the CJEU in Opinion 2/13) and the ECtHR is

[123] ECtHR Annual Report 2014, available at http://echr.coe.int/Documents/Annual_Report_2014_ENG.pdf (last accessed 16 December 2020).

[124] Mole, 'Can *Bosphorus* be maintained?' (n 34); L Glas and J Krommendijk, 'From Opinion 2/13 to Avotiņš: Recent Developments in the Relationship between the Luxembourg and Strasbourg Court' (2017) 17 *Human Rights Law Review* 2; X Groussot et al, 'The Paradox of Human Rights Protection in Europe: Two Courts, One Goal?' in OM Arnardóttir and A Buyse (eds), *Shifting Centres of Gravity in Human Rights Protection* (London, Routledge 2016).

[125] *Avotiņš v Latvia* (n 27).

[126] ibid para 113.

[127] ibid para 114.

[128] ibid.

precluded from conducting a thorough assessment due to the applicability of the (self-imposed) presumption of equivalent protection.[129]

The Court ended its appraisal by referring to national courts and their duty under the Convention. It developed a test to be applied in the context of the mutual recognition instruments: if a serious and substantiated complaint is raised before national courts to the effect that the protection of a Convention right has been manifestly deficient, and this situation cannot be remedied by EU law, national courts cannot refrain from examining that complaint on the sole ground that they are applying EU law, and hence cannot rely on the *Bosphorus* presumption in those cases.[130] This position was reaffirmed most recently in *Bivolaru and Moldovan v France*, which is also the first case in which the Strasbourg Court rebutted the presumption finding a violation of Article 3 ECHR.[131]

V. EU Law, the ECHR and National Courts

After having discussed the status of EU law in ECHR law, the status of the ECHR in EU law, and the relationship between the Strasbourg and Luxembourg Courts, this section examines (separately) the status of EU and ECHR law in national law and the national courts' case law. The examination will address selected constitutional experiences. The analysis does not examine the question of how national courts view the relationship between EU and ECHR law. This latter question is considered in Part III of the book.

A. General Considerations

The two traditional theoretical approaches to the relationship between national and international law are monism and dualism. In countries that are monist, international treaties are automatically integrated into the national legal order. In dualist systems, national and international norms are separate, each regulating their own sphere of competence, and international norms become part of national law through a separate transposition act. Only after this incorporation can the provisions of international law be relied upon in the national courts. In the EU, for instance, Ireland, Germany, Italy, Sweden, Denmark and (formerly) the UK can be considered dualist states. However, many national constitutions contain both monist and dualist elements,[132] and this classification does not always correspond

[129] ibid para 115.
[130] ibid para 116.
[131] *Bivolaru and Moldovan v France* App nos 40324/16 and 12623/17 (ECtHR, 25 March 2021). For a further analysis of this case see ch 4.
[132] A Aust, *Modern Treaty Law and Practice* (Cambridge, Cambridge University Press, 2007).

to the way international law is given effect in practice, especially with regard to EU and ECHR law.[133] France, for example, is a monist country, and pursuant to Article 55 of the French Constitution, ratified treaties have priority over domestic legislation, but because of the prohibition of the judicial review of statutes that already existed, Article 55 was not applied. On the other hand, the UK and Ireland are dualist countries, but the courts often use and refer to both the national implementing legislation and the ECHR itself in their fundamental rights decisions. Nevertheless, the discussion below will continue to refer to the distinction between monist and dualist systems when explaining the relationships from the national perspective, using a few examples from each group, since the monist and dualist nature of the legal system still largely determines the way in which international treaties are applied domestically.

There are important differences between the Member States as to the status of EU and ECHR law in the national legal order. Some countries reserve a special status for EU law and other countries do so for international human rights treaties, distinguishing them from other international law. Italy, for example, provides for the special status of EU law in Article 117 of the Constitution, which states that '[l]egislative power belongs to the state and the regions in accordance with the constitution and within the limits set by European Union law and international obligations', thus making a distinction between EU law and other international law. There is no similar provision for the ECHR in the Italian Constitution, but the *Corte Costituzionale* has ruled that the ECHR is situated somewhere between ordinary laws and the Constitution.[134] Spain (Article 10), Portugal (Article 16) and Romania (Article 20) are among the countries that give constitutional status to human rights treaties in their national legal order. Spain does not have a similar provision for EU law; in fact, the Spanish Constitution contains only a generic transfer of powers clause in Article 93, but the Portuguese and Romanian Constitutions do contain provisions devoted to EU law (Articles 8 and 148 respectively), thus also giving it a special status.

The Netherlands is special in this respect, because both EU law and the ECHR have a special status and primacy over national law, including over national constitutional law. Article 94 of the Dutch Constitution provides that statutory regulations – including Acts of Parliament – shall not be applicable if such application is in conflict with provisions of treaties that are binding on all persons. The ECHR and all the ratified Protocols are considered by the courts to be 'binding on all persons' within the meaning of Article 94 of the Constitution. The same applies to EU law, although the Dutch courts have developed a doctrine according to which EU law is said to have primacy because the EU Treaties require it and not by

[133] H Keller and A Stone Sweet (eds), *A Europe of Rights: The Impact of the ECHR on National Legal Systems* (Oxford, Oxford University Press, 2009). More recently, see, Popelier, Lambrecht and Lemmens (eds) (n 85).

[134] Italian Constitutional Court, Decisions nos 348/2007 and 349/2007.

virtue of the constitutions of the Member States.[135] This is contested by those who argue that, logically, EU law has primacy in the domestic legal order because the Dutch courts recognise such primacy based on the Dutch Constitution and not (only) because the CJEU requires it based on the Treaties.[136] Be that as it may, the Dutch courts are required to interpret and apply national law in light of the international legal obligations, and they use different techniques to avoid conflicts; when avoiding conflict is not possible, Dutch courts may disapply and declare non-binding the provision of national law in order to ensure that supremacy is given to the rule of international law. This practice, however, only applies in cases of conflicts with international law, since Article 120 of the *Grondwet* stipulates, somewhat paradoxically, that the constitutionality of Acts of Parliament shall not be reviewed by the courts. Accordingly, Acts of Parliament cannot be reviewed in light of the rights contained in the Constitution, but they can be reviewed in light of the rights found in international treaties. Belgium is similar in the sense that both EU and ECHR law have a super-legislative rank, but the underlying structure is different.[137]

Dualist countries, such as the UK and Ireland, have a completely different approach to international law. In the UK, international law and treaties have no immediate application domestically, even though they are binding upon the state itself in international law. This is due to its dualist nature and the doctrine of parliamentary sovereignty, according to which a valid Act of Parliament cannot in principle be questioned by the courts. Both EU law and the ECHR have been given effect in national law by an Act of Parliament, the 1972 European Communities Act and the 1998 Human Rights Acts, respectively. Even though they do not operate in the same way, both EU and ECHR law have had an extensive influence on the UK's unwritten constitution, and have somewhat diluted the traditional dualist orthodoxy and the parliamentary sovereignty doctrine.[138] In Ireland, the ECHR was incorporated into national law through the Irish ECHR Act only in 2003, given the fact that Ireland has its own Bill of Rights and strong judicial review of legislation, and therefore the incorporation of the ECHR was not considered urgent. Thus, in both the UK and Ireland, the ECHR has been incorporated through an Act of Parliament and thus applies only indirectly. Nevertheless, as will be demonstrated in chapter 6, the ECHR is also sometimes directly applied in both the UK and Ireland.

[135] J Fleuren, 'The Application of Public International Law by Dutch Courts' (2010) 57 *Netherlands International Law Review* 245; LFM Besselink, 'The Proliferation of Constitutional Law and Constitutional Adjudication, or How American Judicial Review Came to Europe After All' (2013) 9 *Utrecht Law Review* 2, 19.

[136] Besselink (n 135) 19.

[137] See, eg, P Popelier, 'Report on Belgium' in G Martinico and O Pollicino (eds), *The National Judicial Treatment of the ECHR and EU Laws. A Comparative Constitutional Law Perspective* (Groningen, Europa Law Publishers, 2010) 81. For a more recent report in relation to the ECHR specifically, see P Popelier, 'Belgium: Faithful, Obedient, and Just a Little Irritated' in Popelier, Lambrecht and Lemmens (eds) (n 85) 103.

[138] K Ziegler, E Wicks and L Hodson (eds), *The UK and European Human Rights: A Strained Relationship?* (Oxford, Hart Publishing, 2015); R Masterman, 'The United Kingdom' in J Gerards and J Fleuren (eds), *Implementation of the European Convention on Human Rights and the Judgments of the ECtHR in National Case-Law* (Antwerp, Intersentia, 2014).

Germany and Italy could be said to belong to the same group as the UK and Ireland with regard to the formal status of the ECHR in the domestic legal order, but the Constitutional Courts in those countries have accorded it a special place in the hierarchy of domestic legal sources in comparison to other international law.[139] Concerning EU law, both Italy and (especially) Germany have set express limits to EU integration, and their Constitutional Courts do not accept the unconditional primacy of EU law.[140]

In spite of all the differences outlined above, the national courts[141] in most Member States give a special status to ECHR law either because it is prescribed in the constitution, or because of its nature and the way it is embedded in the national legal systems. As for EU law, national courts generally accept the primacy and direct effect of EU law and apply EU law uniformly in all jurisdictions, even though the acceptance of primacy is not unconditional in most states.

B. The Status of the ECHR in National Law

i. *The ECHR Perspective*

The ECHR does not require any specific mode of incorporation of the Convention into the national legal systems, and some states even refused incorporation of the Convention in the early years of its ratification.[142] Unlike the EU, the ECtHR does not have a doctrine of primacy and direct effect, and it has never directly imposed the application of ECHR law on the national courts. Even though Article 13 ECHR provides that 'everyone whose rights and freedoms as set forth in this Convention are violated shall have an effective remedy before a national authority notwithstanding that the violation has been committed by persons acting in an official capacity', the Strasbourg Court initially refused to interpret this provision as mandating the direct enforceability of the ECHR or judicial remedies. In the case of *James and Others v United Kingdom*, the Court held:

> The Convention is not part of the domestic law of the United Kingdom, nor does there exist any constitutional procedure permitting the validity of laws to be challenged for non-observance of fundamental rights. There thus was, and could be, no domestic remedy in respect of the applicants' complaint that the [contested] legislation itself

[139] See Order 2 BvR no 1481/04 and *Corte Costituzionale*, judgments nos 348 and 349/2007.

[140] See the *Solange* line of cases of the German Constitutional Court and the *controlimiti* doctrine in the case law of the Italian Constitutional Court. See eg BverfGE 37, 291, 29 May 1974 *Solange I*; BverfGE 73, 339, 22 October 1986 *Solange II*; *Corte Costituzionale* judgment of 18 December 1973, No 183/1973, *Frontini*; *Corte Costituzionale* judgment of 5 June 1984, No 170/1984, *Granital*; *Corte Costituzionale* judgment of 13 April 1989, No 232/1989, *Fragd*. For discussion see, eg, A von Bogdandy and S Schill, 'Overcorning Absolute Primacy: Respect for National Identity under the Lisbon Treaty' (2011) 48 *CML Rev* 1417.

[141] By national courts, I primarily refer to ordinary national courts, as they are responsible for the day-to-day application of EU law, but a reference may also be made, where relevant, to national constitutional courts.

[142] Until the 1980s, the French authorities denied the ECHR any legal status domestically.

> does not measure up to the standards of the Convention and its Protocols. The Court, however, concurs with the Commission that Article 13 does not go so far as to guarantee a remedy allowing a Contracting State's laws as such to be challenged before a national authority on the ground of being contrary to the Convention or to equivalent domestic legal norms.[143]

The Strasbourg system does not provide a clear mandate for the national courts as to their duties under the ECHR: there is no direct effect or primacy doctrine in ECHR law.[144] Nevertheless, the obligation for applicants to exhaust domestic remedies under Article 35(1) ECHR presumes that national courts at all levels are structurally involved in the process. This further follows from Article 53 of the Convention, as well from a number of principles and rules of interpretation developed by the ECtHR – in particular the principle of subsidiarity and the margin of appreciation – which reaffirm the key role of the national courts in interpreting and giving effect to the rights guaranteed in the Convention.

However, over the past decade, more emphasis has been placed on the application of the ECHR by domestic authorities and on making Convention rights effective domestically. In the case of *Wagner and JMWL v Luxembourg*, the ECtHR imposed a general obligation on national courts to examine alleged violations of Convention rights with 'particular rigour and care', and to ensure their full effect in the domestic legal order.[145] These changes of tone in the Strasbourg case law have implied a shift from an exclusively subsidiary role as 'secondary guarantor of human rights' in individual cases to a more central and crucial position as a constitutional adjudicator.[146] Therefore, even though the ECHR system does not have a doctrine of direct effect and of primacy, in may have similar effects in practice.[147]

Concerning compliance with the Strasbourg Court's judgment, the Contracting States only have an *obligation de résultat*.[148] For example, a state that has infringed Convention rights can either change the legislation causing the breach, or it can simply change the interpretation of the relevant legislation. States are also not required to re-open the proceedings domestically to revise the domestic judgment that was challenged in Strasbourg; a revision is recommended but it is not mandated under the Convention system. In that sense, the Member States have much more leeway as to how they comply with their ECHR obligations in comparison to the EU legal system. Furthermore, there is no preliminary reference procedure as yet in the ECHR system, but Protocol No 16 to the ECHR does offer a

[143] *James and Others v UK* App no 8793/79 (ECtHR, 21 February 1986) para 85.

[144] This is not to say that ECHR law cannot have direct effect and primacy in the domestic legal orders of the Contracting States.

[145] See, eg, *Wagner and JMWL v Luxembourg* App no 76240/01 (ECtHR 28 June 2007) para 96; and *Fabris v France* App no 16574/08 (ECtHR, 7 February 2013) para 72.

[146] G Martinico and O Pollicino, *The Interaction between Europe's Legal Systems Judicial Dialogue and the Creation of Supranational Laws* (Cheltenham, Edward Elgar Publishing, 2012) 240.

[147] This claim is supported in a number of recent comparative studies. See Martinico and Pollicino (eds) (n 136); H Keller and A Stone Sweet (eds), *A Europe of Rights. The Impact of the ECHR on National Legal Systems* (Oxford, Oxford University Press, 2012).

[148] *Swedish Engine Drivers v Sweden* App no 5614/72 (ECtHR, 6 February 1976).

similar mechanism.[149] Nevertheless, there are some important differences between the two mechanisms: the advisory opinion under Protocol No 16 is available only to the highest courts and tribunals of a Contracting Party; the decision to refer questions to the ECtHR is entirely voluntary and at the discretion of the national court; and the advisory opinion issued in Strasbourg is not formally binding on the national authorities.[150] The envisaged procedure thus has a legal structure different from the preliminary reference procedure in EU law and, importantly, it is for the national authorities to decide on how to implement opinions issued in Strasbourg. Finally, it is available only in those Contracting Parties that have ratified it.

At the same time, however, there are also notable gradual changes in the ECtHR's jurisprudence that have resulted in the impact of its judgments in the domestic legal orders becoming more direct. Several factors of change can be identified.[151] First of all, more recent judgments of the Strasbourg Court leave the states with fewer options to remedy the violations other than amending or annulling the legislation. Furthermore, certain countries have introduced a new procedure before domestic courts that allows the re-opening of the case and a revision of the judgment deemed contrary to the Convention by the Strasbourg Court. This, again, may have an invalidating effect in practice. Second, the mechanisms available for the enforcement of the ECtHR's judgments have changed. Generally, the Committee of Ministers[152] is in charge of monitoring the execution of the Court's judgments, and it can use different political means to pressure states in the case of non-compliance. Since the entry into force of Protocol No 14, however, it can also start an infringement procedure against a state for failing to fulfil its obligations under Article 1 ECHR.[153] The Strasbourg Court has also adopted measures to enhance the enforcement of its decisions, on the recommendation of the Committee of Ministers, such as introducing the so-called 'pilot judgments'. Adopted to combat repetitive claims from a number of Contracting Parties that face structural difficulties in complying with the ECHR, pilot judgments contain specific instructions for the states as to the way in which the violations can be remedied. The change in approach is also evident outside of the pilot judgments: the Court has become more specific in its decisions, going beyond the usual declaratory judgments, indicating specific individual and general measures, thereby limiting the choice of means that states usually have to

[149] The EU member states that have ratified the Protocol at the time of the writing are Estonia, Finland, France, Greece, Lithuania, Luxembourg, Netherlands, Slovak Republic, and Slovenia.

[150] For a critical assessment of the mechanism see J Gerards, 'Advisory Opinions, Preliminary Rulings, and the New Protocol No. 16 to the European Convention of Human Rights, a Comparative and Critical Appraisal' (2014) 21 *Maastricht Journal of European and Comparative Law* 4.

[151] S Besson, 'European Human Rights, Supranational Judicial Review and Democracy. Thinking outside the judicial box' in Popelier, Van de Heyning and Van Nuffel (eds) (n 46) 97.

[152] The executive organ of the CoE.

[153] Protocol No14 to the Convention for the Protection of Human Rights and Fundamental Freedoms, amending the control system of the Convention, 13 May 2004.

remedy the infringement.[154] The judgments are thus written in a way that implies an *erga omnes* effect, rather than being binding only on the state against which the judgment has been rendered. Indeed, one of the objectives stated in the Action Plan adopted during the Interlaken Conference on the Reform of the Court was to generalise the *erga omnes* effect of all judgments of the Court in all Contracting States.[155]

ii. The National Perspective

The ECHR system is subsidiary to the domestic systems and becomes operational only when all domestic remedies have been exhausted.[156] In this respect, therefore, it differs greatly from the EU legal system. Nevertheless, the ECHR is deeply rooted in the legal orders of the EU Member States and important areas of national law have changed as a result of it. This is due to the specificities of the ECHR system, in particular the individual complaint mechanism, which allows individuals to bring a complaint against their own state.[157] The status of the ECHR varies between the Contracting Parties, but the countries can roughly be put into three groups: (i) countries that accord the ECHR constitutional and even supra-constitutional status; (ii) countries in which the ECHR has a quasi-constitutional rank (superior to domestic legislation but below the Constitution); and (iii) countries that give the ECHR at least the status of ordinary legislation.

The first group refers mainly to monist countries, such as Belgium, France and the Netherlands, in which the ECHR is superior to national law and national courts are competent to give direct effect to the ECHR provisions.[158] The Netherlands and Belgium give priority to the ECHR even above the Constitution, when necessary to avoid violations of the Convention rights.[159] The Netherlands is probably the most extreme example: the ECHR is a substitute for constitutional review of primary legislation, which is explicitly forbidden in the Constitution, and the ECHR outranks national law, including the national Constitution. It is therefore not surprising that Dutch judges seem to be more familiar with ECHR rights than the rights contained in the Dutch Constitution.[160] In Belgium, both the *Hof van*

[154] H Keller and C Marti, 'Reconceptualizing Implementation: The Judicialization of the Execution of the European Court of Human Rights' Judgments (2015) 26 *European Journal of International Law* 829.

[155] Interlaken Conference on the Reform of the European Court of Human Rights, 19 February 2010.

[156] Art 35 ECHR.

[157] On the national level, similar mechanisms exist in Germany (the *Verfassungsbeschwerde*) and Spain (the *recurso de amparo*).

[158] This may, however, affect the balance and create competition between ordinary courts and the Constitutional Court. The constitutional legislature in France and Belgium has sought to (re-)establish the superiority of the Constitutional Court in those countries, by introducing a system of obligatory preliminary reference to the Constitutional Court where an alleged breach of fundamental rights concerns at the same time overlapping human rights bills, the ECHR and the national Constitution.

[159] J Gerards and J Fleuren (eds), *Implementation of the ECHR and the case law of the European Court of Human Rights in National Case Law. A Comparative Analysis* (Antwerp, Intersentia, 2014).

[160] J Gerards, 'The Netherlands: Political Dynamics, Institutional Robustness' in Popelier, Lambrecht and Lemmens (eds) (n 85) 327.

Cassatie (the highest court in civil and criminal matters) and *Raad van State* (the highest court in administrative cases) accept the primacy of EU and ECHR law.[161] The Belgian Constitutional Court takes a more balanced view, considering international treaties as being inferior in rank to the Constitution, since under Article 167 of the Constitution they require legislative approval, which is then subject to constitutional review. Notwithstanding this attitude, the ECHR takes a prominent place in the case law of the Belgian Constitutional Court, even more so than in the case law of *Hof van Cassatie*, for example, and the Constitutional Court devotedly and consistently takes the ECtHR's case law into account. Interestingly, the Belgian Constitutional Court often refers to multiple judgments of the ECtHR in its decisions, at times quoting more than 15 Strasbourg judgments in one single decision.[162] In France, the Council of State ruled that 'the superiority conferred upon international agreements by Article 55 of the French Constitution does not, in the internal legal order, apply to provisions of a constitutional nature'.[163] The position of the French Court of Cassation is the same.[164] Uniquely, in Austria (which is a dualist country), the ECHR (as well as most of its Protocols) was incorporated into the Federal Constitutional Law already in 1964 through a federal constitutional amendment, which means that it enjoys constitutional status.[165] The Austrian Constitutional Court has stressed, however, that the case law of the ECtHR could be disregarded if it would be in violation of the Constitution.[166]

Other dualist systems have incorporated the ECHR through either a statute, or a decision of a supreme or constitutional court. These are mainly countries that belong to the second group referred to above, such as Germany and Italy. In Germany, a federal law adopted by the German Parliament on 7 August 1952 introduced the ECHR into the domestic legal order.[167] This means that the ECHR has the rank of an ordinary federal law[168] and, as such, has priority over ordinary statute law but not over constitutional law. Over time, however, the ECHR has acquired a quasi-constitutional rank through the case law of the *Bundesverfassungsgericht*. In the *Görgülü* case, the *Bundesverfassungsgericht* held:

> The guarantees of the Convention influence the interpretation of the fundamental rights and constitutional principles of the Basic Law. The text of the Convention and the case-law of the European Court of Human Rights serve, on the level of constitutional law, as guides to interpretation in determining the content and scope of fundamental

[161] Cass 16 November 2004 [2005] *Chroniques de Droit Public* 610; Cass 9 November 2006 [2005] *Chroniques de Droit Public* 597.

[162] P Popelier, 'Belgium: Faithful, Obedient, and Just a Little Irritated' in Popelier, Lambrecht and Lemmens (eds) (n 85) 103.

[163] CE, ass, 30 October 1998.

[164] *Sarran, Levacher et autres* Cass, Ass Plen, 2 June 2000.

[165] BVG BGBl Nr 59/1964. For further details see A Gamper, 'Austria: Endorsing the Convention System, Endorsing the Constitution' in Popelier, Lambrecht and Lemmens (eds) (n 85) 75.

[166] Austrian Constitutional Court, *Miltner*, VfSlg 11500/1987.

[167] Act of the Convention for the Protection of Human Rights and Fundamental Freedoms (*Gesetz über die Konvention zum Schutze der Menschenrechte und Grundfreiheiten*) BGBl 1952 Teil II S 685.

[168] Art 59(2) of the German Constitution.

> rights and constitutional principles of the Basic Law, provided that this does not lead to a restriction or reduction of protection of the individual's fundamental rights under the Basic Law.[169]

The German Constitutional Court thus ruled that national courts are required to interpret national constitutional rights in conformity with the ECHR and the relevant case law of the ECtHR.[170] At the same time, it also clarified that a Convention right cannot be applied to a case if the application would result in limiting or derogating from the level of protection provided under the Basic Law (and other human rights instruments).[171] Similarly, in Italy the ECHR was considered statutory legislation for a long time, albeit with some exceptions, until the Italian *Corte Costituzionale* decided to revisit its position. In its 2007 landmark decisions,[172] the Italian Constitutional Court held that the ECHR has supra-legislative status (*norma interposta*): it has a privileged position in comparison to ordinary law, but it still must abide by all constitutional norms.

The third group of countries refers to those states that have given the ECHR at least the status of ordinary law. This is true for the UK and Ireland, and for the Scandinavian countries. In the UK, the Human Rights Act (HRA) 1998 provides that primary and subordinate legislation must be read and given effect in a way that is compatible with the Convention rights, and attention has to be given to the case law of the Strasbourg Court.[173] In the pre-incorporation period (1973–2000), the UK's membership of the EU played a role in the reception of the Convention in the UK.[174] If an ECHR right was recognised (by the CJEU) as being part of EU law, it had to be enforced in the UK courts in relation to EU matters. In this way, Convention rights became part of UK law even before the HRA 1998 'through the back door'.[175] In Ireland, Convention rights function as a supplement to its strong constitutional rights tradition and the highly effective domestic system of human rights protection.

National courts in some Member States already see themselves as 'ECHR courts' and have jurisdiction under national law to review the compatibility of national law with the ECHR, and they can set it aside in the event of incompatibility (eg the Netherlands, Belgium, France). In Germany, as explained above, national courts are required to interpret national constitutional rights in conformity with the ECHR, but ECHR rights cannot be applied to a case if the application would result in limiting or derogating from the level of protection provided under the Basic Law and other international human rights instruments. In the UK, the situation

[169] BVerfGE 11, 307 *Görgülü*.

[170] BVerfGE 111, 307 (317, 324).

[171] BVerfGE 111, 307 (317); 128, 326 (371); 131, 268 (295). This is also reflected in Art 53 ECHR.

[172] Italian Constitutional Court, Decisions nos 348/2007 and 349/2007.

[173] The HRA 1998, s 2 provides that '[a] court or tribunal determining a question which has arisen in connection with a Convention right must take into account any – (a) judgment, decision, declaration or advisory opinion of the European Court of Human Rights'.

[174] S Besson, 'The Reception Process in Ireland and the United Kingdom' in Keller and Stone-Sweet (eds) (n 145) 31.

[175] In the words of Lord Slynn, a former UK judge at the CJEU. See *Hansard* HL Deb 26 November 1992, vol 540, col 1095.

is more complex. National courts are competent to apply provisions of the ECHR and are under a statutory obligation to seek a treaty-consistent interpretation,[176] but they are not permitted to resolve conflicts between primary legislation and the ECHR. In such cases, they may issue a 'declaration of incompatibility' or signal to Parliament that it should consider amending the legislation. Lord Bingham stated in *Ullah* that '[t]he duty of national courts is to keep pace with the Strasbourg jurisprudence as it evolves over time: no more, but certainly no less'.[177] However, the duty of national courts in the context of the ECHR has also been expressed in different terms by Lord Phillips:

> The requirement to 'take into account' the Strasbourg jurisprudence will normally result in [the Supreme Court's] applying principles that are clearly established by the Strasbourg Court. There will however be rare occasions where [the Supreme Court] has concerns as to whether a decision of the Strasbourg Court sufficiently appreciates or accommodates particular aspects of our domestic process. In those circumstances it is open to [the Supreme Court] to decline to follow the Strasbourg decision, giving reasons for adopting this course. This is likely to give the Strasbourg Court the opportunity to reconsider the particular aspect of the decision that is in issue, so that there takes place what may prove to be a valuable dialogue between this court [the Supreme Court] and the Strasbourg Court.[178]

More recently, however, Lord Mance stated:

> It would have then to involve some truly fundamental principle of our law or some most egregious oversight or misunderstanding before it could be appropriate for this Court to contemplate an outright refusal to follow Strasbourg authority at the Grand Chamber level.[179]

Generally, the attitude in the UK seems to be that national courts try to ensure consistency with international law, and the HRA 1998 is no exception to this. They also tend to accept the authority of the Strasbourg Court in interpreting the Convention in the majority of the cases.

In conclusion, it could be said that the ECHR has become the law of the land in almost all Contracting Parties, and the level of 'embeddedness'[180] in domestic legal systems is, by and large, especially in the EU Member States, very high, regardless of the system's being predominantly monist or dualist – and notwithstanding the fact that the Convention operates, unlike EU law, in the absence of the doctrines

[176] Pursuant to HRA 1998, s 2(1), courts and tribunals are required to take into account the jurisprudence of the ECtHR when deciding cases that relate to the rights under the ECHR. Section 3(1) requires primary and subordinate legislation to be interpreted in a way that is compatible with Convention rights, 'as far as possible'.

[177] *R (Ullah) v Special Adjudicator* [2004] INLR 381.

[178] *R v Horncastle & Others* [2009] UKSC 14 [11]. For scholarly literature on this point, see eg E Bjorge, 'National supreme courts and the development of ECHR rights' (2001) 9 *International Journal of Constitutional Law* 5; B Hale, 'Argentoratum Locutum: Is Strasbourg or the Supreme Court Supreme?' (2012) 12 *Human Rights Law Review* 65.

[179] *Chester* [2013] UKSC 63 [27].

[180] LR Helfer, 'Redesigning the European Court of Human Rights: Embeddedness as a Deep Structural Principle of the European Human Rights Regime' (2008) 19 *The European Journal of International Law* 1, 125.

of primacy and direct effect. According to Gerards and Fleuren, it is incorrect to think that monist states, such as the Netherlands, France or Belgium, are more compliant with the ECHR than dualist states such as the UK; the Convention and the judgments of the Strasbourg Court can have equal importance for national fundamental rights in dualist states.[181]

C. The Status of EU Law in National Law

The status of EU law in national law has been discussed extensively in the literature.[182] The discussion that follows is therefore brief and concerns only the most important points.

i. The EU Law Perspective

In contrast to the ECHR system and the approach of the ECtHR, the Court of Justice developed the doctrine of primacy and direct effect almost from the beginning.[183] Formulated in *Costa v ENEL*,[184] the principle of primacy means that EU law 'cannot be overridden by domestic legal provisions, however framed'. The Court clarified in *Internationale Handelsgesellschaft* that EU law takes precedence over all forms of national law, including national constitutional law.[185] The principle was further elaborated in the *Simmenthal* case,[186] in which the Court concluded that EU law would also take precedence over national legislation that was adopted after the passage of the relevant EU norms. It held that 'every national court must, in a case within its jurisdiction, apply Community law in its entirety and protect rights which the latter confers on individuals and must accordingly set aside any provision of national law which may conflict with it, whether prior or subsequent to the Community rule'.[187] Naturally, the same principles apply to EU fundamental rights law.

Using the doctrines of direct effect and primacy, the Court of Justice formulated an EU mandate for national judges.[188] As a part of this mandate, national judges are under an obligation to apply EU law and, after the Treaty of Lisbon, to do so

[181] Gerards and Fleuren (eds) (n 159).

[182] See, amongst many, M Claes, 'The Validity and Primacy of EU Law and the "Cooperative Relationship" between National Constitutional Courts and the Court of Justice of the European Union' (2016) 23 *Maastricht Journal of European and Comparative Law* 1; M Claes, 'The Primacy of EU Law in European and National Law' in D Chalmers and A Arnull (eds), *The Oxford Handbook of European Union Law* (Oxford, Oxford University Press, 2015) 178.

[183] For a general introduction to the principles of direct effect and primacy, see eg A Rosas and L Armati, *EU Constitutional Law: An Introduction* (Oxford, Hart Publishing, 2018).

[184] Case 6/64, *Costa v ENEL*, ECLI:EU:C:1964:66.

[185] Case 11/70 *Internationale Handelsgesellschaft*, ECLI:EU:C:1970:114.

[186] Case 106/77 *Simmenthal*, ECLI:EU:C:1978:49.

[187] ibid para 21.

[188] M Claes, *The National Courts' Mandate in the European Constitution* (Oxford, Hart Publishing, 2006).

in light of the EU Charter of Fundamental Rights. Sometimes they are required to request a preliminary ruling from the CJEU in accordance with Article 267 TFEU, which 'highlights the role of the national judge as the EU judge'.[189] They are also required to enforce CJEU decisions. In that sense, as indicated earlier, the relationship between national courts and Luxembourg is very different from the relationship between national courts and Strasbourg.

ii. The National Perspective

The primacy and direct effect of EU law has in principle been accepted by the national authorities and courts, but there is still resistance in some countries, especially in the field of EU fundamental rights, which is why it is interesting to consider this question. Some states provide for the unconditional acceptance of EU law in their constitutions (eg the Netherlands and Belgium), while other states set explicit limits on its acceptance in cases when certain core elements of the national constitution are at stake (eg Italy, Germany and Ireland).[190] Nevertheless, these limits are reserved for exceptional cases of manifest infringements of fundamental rights or other elements of constitutional identity. Some Member States have adapted their constitutions prior to accession in order to remove any constitutional limits to integration, such as in Ireland.[191] In the UK, the major problem was the perceived irreconcilability of its traditional doctrine of parliamentary sovereignty and the primacy of EU law. Over time, however, the doctrines of the supremacy and direct effect of EU law were gradually recognised as having been incorporated into the UK national law through the European Communities Act 1972.[192]

All national courts are thus EU courts: they are 'the common courts of EU law', and as such are part of the EU judicial system. Article 19 TEU, as amended by the Treaty of Lisbon, reminds us of the role of national courts by instructing the Member States to 'provide remedies sufficient to ensure effective legal protection in the fields covered by Union law'. This obligation follows from EU law, but also from the case law of the CJEU. In order to become EU courts, national judges have employed a variety of techniques to accommodate the primacy and direct effect of EU law, and thus also of the Charter.[193]

[189] A Rosas, 'When is the EU Charter of Fundamental Rights Applicable at National Level?' (2012) 19 *Jurisprudence* 1269, 1274.

[190] For Italy and Germany see the decisions cited in n 140. For Ireland, see *Society for the Protection of Unborn Children (Ireland) Ltd v Grogan* [1989] IR 734; and *Attorney-General v X* [1992] 1 IR 1.

[191] The Third Amendment of the Constitution Act, 1972. According to Art 29(4), 'no provision of this Constitution invalidates laws enacted, acts done or measures adopted by the State necessitated by the obligations of membership of the European Communities or prevents laws enacted, acts done or measures adopted by the European Union or by the Communities, or institutions thereof, or by bodies competent under the Treaties establishing the Communities, from having the force of law in the State'.

[192] *Factortame Ltd v Secretary of State for Transport* [1991] 1 AC 603, 658.

[193] Only some Member States accept absolute primacy. In most Member States, constitutional and other highest courts do not fully accept the primacy of EU law and insist on placing the fundamental structures and values of national constitutional orders beyond the reach of European integration. For discussion, see A Von Bogdandy and S Schill, 'Overcoming Absolute Primacy: Respect for National Identity under the Lisbon Treaty' (2011) 48 *CML Rev* 1417, 1435–36.

While national courts generally do act as EU courts, they also sometimes struggle with the application of EU law, including the Charter. This is particularly true for Austria, for example, where ordinary courts do not normally deal with fundamental rights questions. If they doubt the compatibility of national law with constitutional rights or the ECHR, ordinary courts have to refer the matter to the Constitutional Court. Now, with the application of the Charter, ordinary courts in Austria have suddenly become human rights courts too, without having had this competence previously, which has led to competition between ordinary courts and the Constitutional Court. The Constitutional Court initially adopted the same approach with regard to incompatibility between national legislation and the EU Charter.[194] But the Charter is also EU law, which means that ordinary courts are also required to apply the Charter. It is not surprising that the CJEU did not accept the distinction made by the Austrian Constitutional Court between EU law and the Charter, and in the rather unusual case of *A v B and Others*[195] – which dealt, inter alia, with the role (and duty) of the national court when faced with national legislation that seemed incompatible with EU law – it ruled that Article 267 TFEU precludes national law under which ordinary courts, if they consider a national statute to be contrary to the Charter, would not be able to refrain from applying that statute and would have to apply to the Constitutional Court for that statute to be struck down. In other words, an obligation to first make a reference to the Constitutional Court violates EU law, since national courts must remain free to disapply a national provision they consider to be contrary to EU law and to make a reference to the CJEU in that regard. This has, of course, significantly impacted the way in which the Austrian legal system has always functioned and has caused issues to arise between ordinary courts and the Constitutional Court. It is not entirely clear whether the approach has fully changed in the practice of Austrian courts following the judgment of the CJEU, but it illustrates the struggle with the application of EU law and – perhaps especially – the Charter. The latter is true for several other Member States, such as Ireland, Spain and Portugal, which tend to focus on national constitutional rights and/or the ECHR presumably because they are more familiar with those sources.[196] Nevertheless,

[194] *Verfassungsgerichtshof* Judgment U 466/11 of 14 March 2012. The Austrian Constitutional Court went as far as to say that in situations in which a right guaranteed by the Austrian Constitution has the same scope as a right guaranteed by the Charter, it is not necessary to make a request for a preliminary ruling under Art 267 TFEU, because the interpretation of the Charter would not be relevant for the purposes of ruling on an application for a statute to be struck down, that being a decision that may be given on the basis of rights guaranteed by the Austrian Constitution.

[195] Case C-112/13 *A v B and Others*, ECLI:EU:C:2014:2195. The referring court – *Oberlandesgericht Wien* (Higher Regional Court, Vienna) – asked whether EU law, and in particular Art 267 TFEU, precludes rules of national law, such as those at issue in the main proceedings, under which ordinary courts hearing an appeal or adjudicating at final instance are under a duty, if they find that a national statute is contrary to Art 47 of the Charter, to apply, in the course of the proceedings, to the Constitutional Court for that statute to be generally struck down and may not simply refrain from applying that statute in the case before them.

[196] See national reports and comparative analyses in M Bobek and J Adams-Prassl (eds), *The EU Charter of Fundamental Rights in the Member States* (Oxford, Hart Publishing, 2020). With respect to Ireland in the early years of the Charter's binding force, see G de Búrca, 'The Domestic Impact of the EU Charter of Fundamental Rights' (2013) 49 *Irish Jurist* 49.

in most countries, the Charter is viewed as part of EU law and there are no particular issues in that respect.

VI. Conclusion

The relationship between EU and ECHR law and the two European Courts is much more closely knit than the relationship between other sources of international law or international courts.[197] The first part of the analysis has shown that the ECtHR already has jurisdiction to review EU law and the cases decided by the CJEU. The only cases that are not admissible in Strasbourg are those involving direct actions by the EU institutions, as seen in *Connolly*. The Strasbourg Court has, however, limited its own competence to review EU law by introducing the *Bosphorus* presumption of equivalent protection. It has done so in cases that involve directly applicable acts of EU law that leave no discretion for the Member States and where the enforcement mechanism through the CJEU can be employed, thus trusting EU fundamental rights standards and the CJEU as their guarantor. In cases in which the Member States have a margin of manoeuvre, the Strasbourg Court exercises full scrutiny.

The ECHR has always played an important role in EU law and the CJEU's case law, first in determining the general principles of EU law and later on in drafting the Charter. This is reflected in Article 6 TEU and in provisions of the Charter itself. The key provision in this respect is Article 52(3) of the Charter, which provides that the meaning and scope of Charter rights that have a corresponding right in the ECHR shall be the same as those laid down in the said Convention, but the EU may offer higher protection. Accordingly, an argument has been made that since the ECHR is interpreted by the ECtHR in its case law, the CJEU should follow the latter when determining the meaning and scope of the corresponding Charter rights. The CJEU's practice in this respect has not been consistent, however. In the early post-Charter cases, the Court seemed to have indicated that the case law of the ECtHR must be followed and even explicitly referenced. In some more recent judgments, the Court held that Strasbourg case law must be taken into account, but the need to ensure consistency between the Charter and the Convention must not adversely affect the autonomy of EU law and that of the CJEU. Regrettably, Opinion 2/13 on the EU's accession to the ECHR does not clarify this point further as it does not contain a single reference to Article 52(3) of the Charter. The reality today is that the Luxembourg Court often refers to the ECHR in its jurisprudence, but the references are neither systematic nor coherent. Sometimes they entail extensive analysis of the Strasbourg case law and at other times they are very brief and made in passing. Even though the absence of the references in some cases does not necessarily mean that the CJEU detracts from that case law, there is a danger that it could be the way the national courts perceive

[197] For the comparison of the relationship between the CJEU and ECtHR and that between the CJEU and other international courts, see Lock (n 58).

it in certain cases – a point to which I will return in Part III of the book. At the same time, both EU fundamental rights law and the ECHR, as well as the case law of the two European Courts, play an important role in the national legal systems and protection of fundamental rights domestically. The legal ranking of the two supranational sources of fundamental rights is not the same in all the Member States, but most, if not all, EU States and their courts pay due regard to the case law of the CJEU and ECtHR, and interpret domestic fundamental rights in light of it in order to guarantee respect for their supranational obligations and avoid conflicts.

Nevertheless, the relationship between national courts and the CJEU, on the one hand, and national courts and the ECtHR, on the other, has been very different. The former relationship is characterised by obligations imposed on the national courts as to their duties in the context of EU law. The CJEU developed an EU mandate for national courts based on the doctrines of direct effect and primacy, which directly involves them in the application and enforcement of EU law. The national courts engage in direct dialogue with the CJEU, given that there is a specific procedure for this, although this is not the case for all courts in all Member States and for courts at all levels. Some courts are more willing to engage and refer questions for a preliminary ruling, while other national courts are more hesitant, or even make a conscious decision not to refer. By contrast, the relationship between national courts and the ECtHR is characterised by the subsidiary nature of the system. The ECHR does not impose obligations directly on national courts but rather on the Contracting States. Fairly recently, however, the Strasbourg Court started to intervene more in domestic systems, gradually developing what could be called an ECHR mandate for national courts. But it has also made efforts to build the relationship with domestic courts indirectly.[198] Notwithstanding the obvious differences in the relationships, the national courts have become involved with both EU and ECHR law and apply them regularly, even routinely. At the same time, they may find themselves caught between conflicting obligations when there is a discrepancy between EU law as interpreted by the CJEU, on the one hand, and the ECHR as interpreted by the ECtHR, on the other. In the absence of formal institutionalised relationship between the two systems and with no clear guidance from the CJEU, the question of divergences and how national courts should deal with them remains open. Part II of this book goes on to consider the divergences between the case law of the two European Courts in the AFSJ.

[198] This is, for example, exemplified in yearly judicial seminars. The focus of the seminar in 2012 was on the greater involvement of national courts in the Convention system, and in 2014 it was on shared judicial responsibility. The mission is very much focusing on the involvement of national courts.

PART II

Convergence and Conflicts in European Fundamental Rights Standards

3

Case Study I: The Dublin System

I. Introduction

Part I of the book analysed the new architecture of European fundamental rights law. It sought to illustrate that European Union (EU) fundamental rights often overlap with national constitutional rights and rights deriving from international human rights treaties, most conspicuously the European Convention on Human Rights (ECHR), which, in turn, is deeply rooted in domestic legal systems and in the EU fundamental rights themselves. In many situations, therefore, a case can be governed simultaneously by several norms, ultimately interpreted by a different court, without clear rules regarding their coexistence. This, in turn, may lead to divergences and tensions both between the two European Courts and between each of them and national (constitutional) courts. After all, these courts may have different roles in their legal systems, they may apply different methodologies, and they may simply have different normative preferences. This part of the book looks more closely into the interactions and divergences between the Luxembourg and Strasbourg Courts in the Area of Freedom Security and Justice (AFSJ), which is one of the most fundamental rights-sensitive areas of EU law and the busiest area of activity for the Court of Justice of the European Union (CJEU).[1] It analyses two prominent legal instruments of the AFSJ: the Dublin Regulation, which is a central piece of the Common European Asylum System (CEAS), and the Framework Decision on the European Arrest Warrant (EAW), which is the first EU instrument of mutual recognition in criminal matters. While only the latter is an instrument of mutual recognition, both the Dublin system and the EAW operate on the basis of mutual trust between the Member States. As already discussed in chapter 2, the principles of mutual trust and recognition have gained constitutional importance in EU law in recent years, particularly in the AFSJ. In essence, the principle of mutual recognition, which presupposes mutual trust, requires Member States to trust, inter alia, one another's fundamental rights protection in both substantive and enforcement terms. However, the reality is that some

[1] The number of cases decided in Luxembourg in the AFSJ has grown rapidly, from 53 in 2015 to 106 in 2019, making it the busiest area of activity for the CJEU in that year. See the statistics available in the CJEU's Annual Report (Judicial Activity) 2019.

Member States have questionable human rights track records, as witnessed, inter alia, in the judgments of the European Court of Human Rights (ECtHR), and unconditional mutual trust is simply untenable.[2] Indeed, the CJEU President Lenaerts and other commentators have been emphasising in recent years that mutual trust is not blind trust, but setting its exact limits has proved to be a challenging task. Moreover, the idea of mutual trust does not sit well with the ECHR system, since the ECHR Contracting Parties are required to ensure that Convention rights are respected, rather than relying on or trusting other states to comply with the ECHR standards.[3]

This chapter examines the gradual introduction of fundamental rights consideration in EU asylum law through the case law of the CJEU, as well as the revisions of the Dublin Regulation by the EU legislature. At the heart of the discussion is the relationship between the principle of mutual trust and recognition and the protection of fundamental rights.

The chapter first traces the origins of the principle of mutual trust and recognition in EU law and discusses its legal effects (section II). It then briefly outlines the main features of the Dublin system, which operates on the basis of mutual trust (section III). It shows that the main goal of the system has been to assign the responsibility for processing an individual asylum application to a single Member State, which has resulted in asylum seekers' being sent back to countries with questionable human rights track records. Section IV explores the gradual introduction of fundamental rights consideration in EU asylum law in the case law of the CJEU, as well as the changes introduced by the EU legislature in the Dublin III Regulation. The analysis of the cases focuses specifically on the aspects that have caused tension in the case law of the Strasbourg and Luxembourg Courts and omits detailed discussion of other aspects that have already been addressed extensively in the academic literature.[4] The case law analysis reveals incompatibilities between the way in which the Dublin Regulation has been applied in the early years and the requirements of the ECHR. This has led the CJEU to change its approach in interpreting the Dublin Regulation, and the EU legislature to revise it. As this chapter highlights, the CJEU appears to have acted under pressure from the ECtHR, which had set high standards of protection of fundamental rights of asylum seekers in the *MSS* and *Tarakhel* judgments.

[2] It is often forgotten that of the top 10 violators of the ECHR in the period 1959–2020, seven countries are EU Member States (Italy, Romania, Poland, France, Greece, Bulgaria and Hungary). For further details, see Overview of the ECHR statistics 1959 to 2020, available at www.echr.coe.int/Documents/Overview_19592020_ENG.pdf (last accessed 16 December 2020).

[3] This is the *Soering* line of cases. See *Soering v United Kingdom* App no 14038/88 (ECtHR, 7 July 1989).

[4] For a useful account of the case law, see, with further references, E Xanthopoulou, 'Case Study II: Dublin Transfers' in E Xanthopoulou, *Fundamental Rights and Mutual Trust in the Area of Freedom, Security and Justice: A Role for Proportionality?* (Oxford, Hart Publishing, 2020) 164.

II. Mutual Trust and Recognition in the AFSJ

The origins of the principle of mutual recognition in the EU can be found in the internal market context. It emerged in the Court of Justice 1979 *Cassis de Dijon* judgment,[5] as a solution to the obstacles to the free movement of goods. The Court held 'there is … no valid reason why, provided that they have been lawfully produced and marketed in one of the Member States, alcoholic beverages should not be introduced into any other Member State' and that

> [o]bstacles to movement within the Community resulting from disparities between the national laws relating to the marketing of the products in question must be accepted in so far as those provisions may be recognized as being necessary in order to satisfy mandatory requirements relating in particular to the effectiveness of fiscal supervision, the protection of public health, the fairness of commercial transactions and the defence of the consumer.[6]

Since the mutual recognition argument was not put forward by the parties to this case, and it was not included in the Treaties at the time, it could be said that it was truly an invention of the Court of Justice.

While the Court first introduced the principle of mutual trust in the context of the internal market, it has gained major importance more recently in the AFSJ.[7] Shortly after the Treaty of Amsterdam entered into force, formulating the ambitious aim of transforming the Union into an AFSJ, the European Council recognised the need to enhance the ability of national legal systems to work closely together, and asked the Council to determine the scope for greater mutual recognition of judicial decisions. As part of the Vienna Action Plan of the Commission and the Council on this topic, the European Council was asked to initiate a process that would facilitate the mutual recognition of decisions and the enforcement of judgments in both civil and criminal matters within the Union.[8] Subsequently, at a meeting in Tampere on 15–16 October 1999, the European Council endorsed the principle of mutual recognition and declared that it should become 'the cornerstone of

[5] Case C-120/78 *Rewe-Zentrale AG v Bundesmonopolverwaltung für Branntwein* (*Cassis de Dijon*), ECLI:EU:C:1979:42. See also White Paper from the Commission to the European Council, Completing the Internal Market, COM(1985) 310, 17.

[6] *Cassis de Dijon* (n 5) para 14.

[7] See, eg, Xanthopoulou, *Fundamental Rights and Mutual Trust* (n 4); C Ladenburger, 'The Principle of Mutual Trust between Member States in the Area of Freedom, Security and Justice' (2020) 3 *Zeitschrift für Europarechtliche Studien* 373; F Maiani and S Migliorini, 'One Principle to Rule Them All? Anatomy of Mutual Trust in The Law of the Area of Freedom, Security and Justice' (2020) 57 *CMLRev* 7; M Schwarz, 'Let's talk about trust, baby: Theorizing trust and mutual recognition in the EU's area of freedom, security and justice' (2018) 24 *European Law Journal* 124; K Lenaerts, 'La vie après l'avis: Exploring the principle of mutual (yet not blind) trust' (2017) 54 *CML Rev* 805.

[8] Action Plan of the Council and the Commission on how best to implement the provisions of the Treaty of Amsterdam on an area of freedom, security and justice, text adopted by the JHA Council of 3 December 1998, [1999] OJ C19/01.

judicial cooperation within the Union'.[9] At this point mutual recognition was not explicitly linked to a requirement of mutual trust, and the latter was in fact not even mentioned in the Tampere Conclusions. Many policy documents followed in which the principle of mutual recognition maintained the central position.

Today, the principle of mutual recognition is explicitly recognised in the Treaties, as reformed by the Treaty of Lisbon;[10] however, the Treaties do not mention mutual trust. Nevertheless, the European Council noted already in the Hague Programme in 2005 that, in order for the principle of mutual recognition to become effective, mutual trust must first be strengthened 'by progressively developing a European judicial culture based on the diversity of legal systems and unity through European law'.[11]

It was not long before mutual trust came into the picture, as a prerequisite for a successful application of the principle of mutual recognition. The European Commission provided a definition in its Communication of 26 July 2000:

> MR [mutual recognition] is a principle that is widely understood as being based on the thought that while another state may not deal with a certain matter in the same or even a similar way as one's own state, the results will be such that they are accepted as equivalent to decisions by one's own state. Mutual trust is an important element, not only trust in the adequacy of one's partners [*sic*] rules, but also trust that these rules are correctly applied. Based on this idea of equivalence and the trust it is based on, the results the other state has reached are allowed to take effect in one's own sphere of legal influence. On this basis, a decision taken by an authority in one state could be accepted as such in another state, even though a comparable authority may not even exist in that state, or could not take such decisions, or would have taken an entirely different decision in a comparable case.[12]

In essence, mutual trust could be described as the reciprocal trust between the Member States in the legality and quality of each other's legal systems, while mutual recognition refers to the products of these systems.[13] The two concepts have been used interchangeably,[14] but the former is mostly seen as a precondition (for the effective operation) of the latter.[15]

The CJEU, for its part, introduced the duty of the mutual recognition of judicial decisions in the AFSJ in the *Gözütok* and *Brügge* cases.[16] The formulation

[9] Tampere European Council Presidency Conclusions, 15 and 16 October 1999, para 33.

[10] It is expressly mentioned in Arts 67, 70, 81 and 82 TFEU.

[11] The Hague Programme: Strengthening Freedom, Security, and Justice in the EU [2005] OJ C53/01, 3.2.

[12] COM(2000) 495, 26 July 2000.

[13] E Brouwer, 'Mutual Trust and the Dublin Regulation: Protection of Fundamental Rights in the EU and the Burden of Proof' (2013) 9 *Utrecht Law Review* 1.

[14] Opinion of AG Sharpston in Case C-467/04 *Gasparini and Others* [2006] ECR I-9199, fn 87.

[15] K Lenaerts, 'The Principle of Mutual Recognition in the Area of Freedom, Security and Justice', The Fourth Annual Sir Jeremy Lever Lecture, All Souls College, University of Oxford, 30 January 2015, available at www.law.ox.ac.uk/sites/files/oxlaw/the_principle_of_mutual_recognition_in_the_area_of_freedom_judge_lenaerts.pdf (last accessed 16 December 2020).

[16] Joined Cases C-187/01 *Hüseyin Gözütok* and C-385/01 *Klaus Brügge*, ECLI:EU:C:2003:87. In these landmark cases, the Court ruled that the *ne bis in idem* principle precludes criminal proceedings in a

of the duty of mutual recognition indicates a broad scope of application: competent authorities are required to recognise not only decisions of courts from other Member States, but also their (substantive and procedural) criminal law provisions and policy.[17] The lack of reference to the principle of mutual trust in the Treaties has left considerable room for the CJEU to determine its meaning and scope of application. In order to give it a status of a constitutional principle, the CJEU has used unusually strong language: the principle of mutual trust is a 'founding' principle of EU law, alongside the principles of autonomy and primacy.[18] In a nutshell, the principle of mutual trust 'requires each [Member] State, save in exceptional circumstances, to consider all the other Member States to be complying with EU law and in particular with the fundamental rights recognised by EU law'.[19] The words 'to be complying with EU law' have a broad meaning: mutual trust encompasses the idea that acts of other EU Member States are accepted because they reflect the same principles and values, as provided in Article 2 of the Treaty on European Union (TEU), even though these states may not deal with a certain matter in the same or even a similar way as one's own state. The premise that those values are recognised and respected implies – and justifies – mutual trust between the states. However, as is well known by now, the automatic application of the principle of mutual trust and recognition has proved untenable due to the lack of, or at least insufficient, mutual trust between Member States. Nonetheless, the principle became strongly embedded in EU law, and it continues to play a crucial role in the functioning of the AFSJ.[20] The CEAS constitutes one of the principal areas in which the fundamental rights of individuals are placed in competition with the core principle of mutual trust and the need to preserve the effectiveness of EU law.

III. The Dublin System

The issue of responsibility for asylum applications was initially regulated by the Dublin Convention drawn up in 1990, which was replaced in 2003 by the Dublin II Regulation. The Dublin II Regulation, which was subject of controversy[21] and of a number of important judgments of both the ECtHR and the CJEU,[22] was then

Member State where prosecution is sought on the same facts that had been discontinued in another Member State.

[17] C Janssens, *The Principle of Mutual Recognition in EU Law* (Oxford, Oxford University Press, 2013).

[18] Opinion 2/13, EU:C:2014:2454, paras 157 et seq.

[19] ibid para 191.

[20] See, eg, F Maiani and S Migliorini, 'One Principle to Rule Them All? Anatomy of Mutual Trust in The Law of the Area of Freedom, Security and Justice' (2020) 57 *CML Rev* 7; Xanthopoulou, *Fundamental Rights and Mutual Trust* (n 4).

[21] J Lenart, '"Fortress Europe": Compliance of the Dublin II Regulation with the European Convention for the Protection of Human Rights and Fundamental Freedoms' (2012) 28 *Utrecht Journal of International and European Law* 4.

[22] *MSS v Belgium and Greece* App no 30696/09 (ECtHR, 21 January 2011); Joined Cases C-411/10 and C-493/10 *NS and others*, ECLI:EU:C:2011:865.

replaced by the Dublin III Regulation,[23] adopted in summer 2013 and applicable from 1 January 2014. These rules apply to all Member States and four associated non-EU countries (Norway, Iceland, Switzerland and Liechtenstein) bound by the Regulation's provisions on the basis of bilateral agreements.[24] The European Commission proposed a new Dublin IV Regulation in 2016 but it was never adopted.[25]

The Dublin III Regulation lays down the criteria and mechanisms for determining which Member State is responsible for examining an asylum application, with the aim of having every asylum claim in the Union processed by a single Member State. The implementation of the Regulation is facilitated by EURODAC,[26] an EU asylum fingerprint database, and together these two instruments make up the EU machinery for the distribution of asylum-processing responsibility, which is commonly referred to as the 'Dublin system'. As from the Dublin III Regulation, this rule applies to all applications for international protection, not only asylum as set out in the UN Refugee Convention.

The main aim of the Dublin system was to coordinate applications for international protection and to accelerate their processing in the interests of both applicants and participating states. The goal was thus to create a mechanism that quickly assigns the responsibility for processing an individual asylum application to a single Member State, in order to ensure quick access for those in need, but also to avoid abuses of the system where individuals would submit asylum applications in several countries. The criterion used by states is the 'first point of entry' – the Member State responsible for examining an individual's asylum application is the one he or she first entered.[27]

While the Dublin system is not a system of mutual recognition, it does operate on the principle of mutual trust, that is, on the presumption that all states respect the rights of asylum seekers in accordance with European and international law.[28] This presumption relates in particular to the examination of the request for asylum by the responsible Member State and the treatment of the asylum seeker during this examination. The Dublin system is underpinned by the idea of equivalence of Member States' asylum systems, thus presuming that asylum seekers would not

[23] Regulation (EU) No 604/2013 of the European Parliament and of the Council of 26 June 2013 establishing the criteria and mechanisms for determining the Member State responsible for examining an application for international protection lodged in one of the Member States by a third-country national or a stateless person (recast).

[24] The association agreements extended the Schengen *acquis* and the Dublin and EURODAC Regulations (see n 23 and n 26 respectively) to these four states.

[25] European Commission Proposal for a Dublin IV Regulation COM(2016) 270.

[26] EURODAC Regulation (EU) 603/2013 of 26 June 2013.

[27] On the intricacies of the Dublin system, see S Fratzke, *Not Adding Up: The Fading Promise of Europe's Dublin System*, EU Asylum: Towards 2020 Project (Migration Policy Institute Europe, 2015).

[28] Mutual trust is mentioned in Recital 22 of the Dublin III Regulation.

benefit from having their application examined in a specific country. In reality, it is a system designed to avoid forum shopping by asylum seekers. Mutual trust between the states is additionally based on the presumption that all Member States respect the principle of *non-refoulement* and can thus be considered safe countries for third-country nationals.[29]

This presumption does not explicitly feature in the Regulation, except for a brief mention in Recital 22,[30] but the CJEU has consistently held that it must be assumed that all participating states observe and comply with fundamental rights, including the rights contained in the EU Charter of Fundamental Rights, the Geneva Convention and the ECHR.[31] The competitive relationship between mutual trust and fundamental rights becomes particularly evident when applicants for international protection rely on alleged violations of their fundamental rights in order to contest their transfer to the Member State that is responsible for examining their asylum request, and for quite some time the EU Member States have been invoking the principle of mutual trust as a justification for the Dublin transfers of asylum seekers to EU States with questionable records of human rights compliance.[32] This presumption of fundamental rights compliance has come under strain however, initially from the Strasbourg Court and later on from the national courts too.

[29] Dublin II Regulation, Preamble, Recital 2; Dublin III Regulation, Preamble, Recital 3.

[30] Dublin III Regulation, Recital 22: 'A process for early warning, preparedness and management of asylum crises, serving to prevent a deterioration in, or the collapse of, asylum systems, with EASO [European Asylum Support Office] playing a key role, using its powers under Regulation (EU) No 439/2010, should be established in order to ensure robust cooperation within the framework of this Regulation and to develop mutual trust among Member States with respect to asylum policy. Such a process should ensure that the Union is alerted as soon as possible when there is a concern that the smooth functioning of the system set up by this Regulation is being jeopardised as a result of particular pressure on, and/or deficiencies in, the asylum systems of one or more Member States. Such a process would allow the Union to promote preventive measures at an early stage and pay the appropriate political attention to such situations. Solidarity, which is a pivotal element in the CEAS, goes hand in hand with mutual trust. By enhancing such trust, the process for early warning, preparedness and management of asylum crises could improve the steering of concrete measures of genuine and practical solidarity towards Member States, in order to assist the affected Member States in general and the applicants in particular. In accordance with Article 80 TFEU, Union acts should, whenever necessary, contain appropriate measures to give effect to the principle of solidarity, and the process should be accompanied by such measures. The conclusions on a Common Framework for genuine and practical solidarity towards Member States facing particular pressures on their asylum systems, including through mixed migration flows, adopted by the Council on 8 March 2012, provide for a "tool box" of existing and potential new measures, which should be taken into account in the context of a mechanism for early warning, preparedness and crisis management.'

[31] *NS and others* (n 22) para 80.

[32] In the Netherlands, for example, the authorities have relied strongly on the presumption of fundamental rights compliance by other EU Member States in the context of the Dublin transfers. They had decided to suspend returns to Greece only pending the outcome in the *MSS* case. See conclusions of the Workshop on Migration and Human Rights in Europe at www.icj.org/wp-content/uploads/2012/06/Non-refoulement-Europe-summary-of-the-workshop-event-2011-.pdf (last accessed 16 December 2020).

IV. The Evolving Case Law on Dublin Transfers – A Retrospective Outlook

A. The Impetus from Strasbourg – *MSS v Belgium and Greece*

One of the first cases in which the ECtHR ruled on the matter of transferring asylum seekers in the context of the Dublin system was *MSS v Belgium and Greece*,[33] a decision delivered by the Grand Chamber in January 2011. The case concerned the expulsion of an Afghan asylum seeker to Greece by Belgium in the application of the Dublin II Regulation.

The ECtHR held that Dublin transfers were subject to review by the Strasbourg Court and that the *Bosphorus* presumption[34] was not applicable in this case, since those transfers were never mandated and domestic authorities enjoyed a margin of discretion under the 'sovereignty clause' or 'discretionary clause' contained in Article 3(2) of the Dublin II Regulation.[35] The ECtHR acknowledged, in principle, the relevance of the principle of mutual trust in the context of the Dublin Regulation, but it determined that its application was not unconditional. The presumption of compliance with fundamental rights could be rebutted if there were substantial grounds for believing that a person whose return was being ordered would face a real risk of treatment contrary to the Convention in the receiving country.[36]

The ECtHR held that Greece violated Article 3 ECHR (absolute prohibition of torture and inhuman and degrading treatment) in terms both of the risk of return to Afghanistan and the poor detention and living conditions. The evidence of these violations was found in well-documented and easily verifiable reports by non-governmental organisations and international bodies, all of which had given similar accounts on the deplorable situation in Greece at the time. In addition, the Court also found a violation of Article 13 ECHR (the right to effective remedy) taken together with Article 3 ECHR, because the Greek authorities had not examined the applicant's asylum request, nor had they taken any steps to communicate with him or any decision about him. In respect of Belgium, the Strasbourg Court held that it had violated the *non-refoulement* principle in Article 3 ECHR

[33] *MSS v Belgium and Greece* (n 22). For an earlier case see, eg, *KRS v United Kingdom* App no 32733/08 (ECtHR, 2 December 2008).

[34] *Bosphorus v Ireland* App no 45036/98 (ECtHR, 30 June 2005). For discussion of the presumption see ch 2.

[35] The 'sovereignty clause' in Art 3(2) of Dublin II Regulation means that, by way of derogation from the general rule, each Member State may examine an application for asylum lodged with it by a third-country national, even if such examination is not its responsibility under the criteria laid down in the Dublin Regulation. In such cases, the State concerned becomes the Member State responsible and assumes the obligations associated with that responsibility. The clause is now included in Art 17(1) of Dublin III Regulation.

[36] *MSS v Belgium and Greece* (n 22) paras 345 et seq.

because of the poor living conditions in Greece. In the Court's view, the Belgian authorities at the time of the transfer 'knew or ought to have known' the deficiencies of the asylum procedure in Greece.[37] The Court clarified that the applicant should not have been expected to bear the entire burden of proof as regards the risks he faced by being returned to Greece. The Belgian authorities should not have simply assumed that the applicant would be treated in conformity with the Convention standards; they should have verified how the Greek authorities applied their asylum legislation in practice.[38] Finally, the Court found a violation of Article 13 taken together with Article 3 ECHR, because Belgium failed to closely and rigorously scrutinise the substance of the complaint of the applicant and afford proper redress. Accordingly, the assumption that Member States' asylum systems could be considered equivalent and that automatic transfer of asylum seekers absolved a sending state of responsibility for the procedure applied and the living conditions in the receiving state turned out to be misconceived. The judgment interrupted the system of transfers under the Dublin II Regulation, calling into question mutual trust in EU law.[39] With this judgment, it became clear that automatic application of the principle of mutual trust is incompatible with the ECHR, in any case when the absolute prohibition of inhuman and degrading treatment is at stake.

B. The *NS* Judgment

Not long after the judgment in *MSS*, the CJEU was faced with a comparable scenario in the *NS* case.[40] The case involved returns of asylum seekers from Greece to the UK based on the Dublin II Regulation. The applicants claimed that they risked being subjected to inhuman and degrading treatment in Greece, within the meaning of Article 4 of the EU Charter of Fundamental Rights.

The CJEU seemingly followed suit. It commenced by stating that the CEAS is based on mutual confidence and a presumption of compliance with fundamental rights, but that such a presumption is not absolute:

> [It] is not … inconceivable that that system may, in practice, experience major operational problems in a given Member State, meaning that there is a substantial risk that asylum seekers may, when transferred to that Member State, be treated in a manner incompatible with their fundamental rights.[41]

The Court of Justice held that, pursuant to Article 4 of the Charter, the Member States, including the national courts, may not transfer an asylum seeker to the

[37] ibid para 358.
[38] ibid para 352.
[39] P Gragl 'The Shortcomings of Dublin II: Strasbourg's M.S.S. Judgment and Its Implications for the European Union's Legal Order' in W Benedek et al (eds), *European Yearbook on Human Rights* (Vienna, Neuer Wissenschaftlicher Verlag, 2012) 123.
[40] *NS and others* (n 22).
[41] ibid para 81.

Member State responsible within the meaning of the Dublin II Regulation where they

> cannot be unaware that systemic deficiencies in the asylum procedure and in the reception conditions of asylum seekers in that Member State amount to substantial grounds for believing that the asylum seeker would face a real risk of being subjected to inhuman or degrading treatment, within the meaning of that provision.[42]

However, the Court explained that this does not mean that *any* infringement of a fundamental right by the Member State responsible will affect the obligations of the other Member States to comply with the provisions of the Dublin II. In other words, Member States may be required under EU law to presume compliance with fundamental rights in certain cases, even though there may be signs of infringement, and carry on with the transfer.[43]

The CJEU was thus careful not to condemn the Dublin system as a whole. It allowed for an exception, but only in cases of systemic deficiencies and only in relation to Article 4 of the Charter. It made clear that departure from the rules in the Dublin Regulation is and should remain an exceptional case – making the threshold of incompatibility with fundamental rights very high. This is arguably a narrower approach to the exceptions when compared to the *MSS* judgment, because the ECtHR did not make the refusal of the transfer conditional upon the presence of systemic deficiencies in the receiving state. In fact, the Strasbourg Court never used the term 'systemic deficiencies' in its *MSS* ruling, and it clearly distanced itself from it in the *Tarakhel* judgment, discussed in section IV.D.

C. *Puid* and *Abdullahi*

The CJEU confirmed and further clarified its position in the *Puid* and *Abdullahi* judgments,[44] both delivered late in 2013. In *Puid*, the CJEU simply restated its findings from the *NS* judgment and concluded that it was for the referring court to examine whether systemic deficiencies existed on the date on which the decision to transfer Mr Puid to Greece was enforced, which provided substantial grounds for believing that the applicant for asylum would face a real risk of being subjected to inhuman or degrading treatment within the meaning of Article 4 of the Charter. In *Abdullahi*, however, the Court held that

> the *only* way in which the applicant for asylum can call into question the choice of that criterion is by pleading systemic deficiencies in the asylum procedure and in the conditions for the reception of applicants for asylum in that Member State, which provide

[42] ibid para 106.

[43] See, eg, JP Gauci, M Giuffré and E Tsourdi (eds), *Exploring the Boundaries of Refugee Law: Current Protection Challenges* (Leiden, Brill Nijhoff, 2015).

[44] Case C-4/11 *Puid*, ECLI:EU:C:2013:740; and Case C-394/12 *Abdullahi*, ECLI:EU:C:2013:813.

> substantial grounds for believing that the applicant for asylum would face a real risk of being subjected to inhuman or degrading treatment within the meaning of Article 4 of the Charter.[45]

The finding that systemic deficiencies in the responsible Member State represented the only situation where an applicant could challenge a transfer is highly problematic, not least because of the classic conception of individual rights that exists under both EU and ECHR law. While clarifying that this would be the only way to challenge the transfer, the Court left the interpretation of the term 'systemic deficiencies' open. It remained unclear at the time if it was a synonym for the 'Greek' systemic deficiencies, or if other (less grave) deficiencies in asylum systems of the Member States could be considered 'systemic'. What seemed clear, though, was that the exceptions were allowed only when systemic deficiencies in a State could be identified.[46]

Interestingly, the UK Supreme Court interpreted the *NS* judgment differently. In a case decided in early 2014, the Supreme Court concluded that proving 'systemic deficiencies' is only one route to establishing a real risk of ill-treatment, rather than 'a hurdle to be surmounted'.[47] The Supreme Court considered that the CJEU could not have intended to make 'systemic deficiencies' a necessary condition to stop a Dublin return, and ruled that asylum seekers who appealed against their removal to another Member State under the Dublin II Regulation were not required to prove 'systemic deficiencies' in the asylum system of the destination state in order to prevent removal successfully. What is remarkable here is that the Supreme Court based its decision entirely on the *NS* judgment, seeking to determine the intended meaning of some aspects of that judgment, without taking into account or even mentioning the *Abdullahi* judgment, even though it had been rendered two months earlier. While the CJEU refrained from stating that only risks stemming from systemic deficiencies could preclude a transfer in the *NS* judgment, it clearly stated this in the *Abdullahi* decision.[48] It remains unclear whether the Supreme Court was unaware of the latter judgment. The Court's 'systemic deficiencies' test was consolidated in the second and third subparagraphs of Article 3(2) of the Dublin III Regulation, which is applicable as from January 2014.[49]

[45] *Abdullahi* (n 44) para 62 (emphasis added).

[46] Admittedly, the CJEU was not compelled to clarify this point since all the cases (ie *NS*, *Puid* and *Abdullahi*) related to a Dublin transfer of asylum seekers to Greece.

[47] *EM (Eritrea) v Secretary of State for the Home Department* [2014] EWCA Civ 1336 [63]. For detailed analysis of this case, see ch 6.

[48] *Abdullahi* (n 44) para 60.

[49] Art 3(2), second and third subparas of the Dublin III Regulation now provide:

> Where it is impossible to transfer an applicant to the Member State primarily designated as responsible because there are substantial grounds for believing that there are systemic flaws in the asylum procedure and in the reception conditions for applicants in that Member State, resulting in a risk of inhuman and degrading treatment within the meaning of Article 4 of the Charter of Fundamental Rights of the European Union, the determining Member State shall continue to

D. Increasing the Standard of Protection in Strasbourg? The *Tarakhel* Case

In November 2014, the ECtHR arguably increased the standard of protection under the ECHR in the *Tarakhel* judgment, requiring Contracting Parties to undertake a thorough and individualised examination of the situation of the person concerned in the context of a Dublin transfer, if there is evidence indicating violations of the ECHR in the receiving country.[50] The case concerned an Afghan couple with six children, the youngest being born in 2012, after the family had arrived in Switzerland. They had entered the Dublin system at the Italian border in July 2011, where they were registered and placed in a reception facility. Due to poor living conditions in particular, they left the centre, travelling first to Austria and subsequently to Switzerland. The Swiss authorities rejected their application and ordered their return to Italy.

Even though the applicants invoked both Article 3 and Article 8 ECHR, the Strasbourg Court decided to assess the case solely under Article 3, which protects individuals from inhuman and degrading treatment. The principal issue in the case at hand was to ascertain whether the circumstances of the case met the minimum threshold of severity required under the ECHR. In this regard, the Court recalled that a child's vulnerability is a decisive factor in such an assessment, even if the children are accompanied by their parents.[51] Further, examining the applicants' particular situation, the Court emphasised that asylum seekers are part of a 'particularly underprivileged and vulnerable' population group, as such needing special protection under Article 3. This led the Court to accept that the applicants' fears of poor living conditions, especially concerns about being placed in facilities incompatible with their children's needs and the risk of being separated, were not unfounded. The Court held that the circumstances of the case required the Swiss authorities to obtain specific assurances from their Italian counterparts that, on arrival, the family would not be separated and would be received in facilities adapted to the children's ages. Their removal in the absence of such assurances would be contrary to Article 3 ECHR.

In other words, the real risk of ill-treatment in the receiving state precludes the removal of the individual, irrespective of whether the source of risk is systemic or individualised. Thus, and contrary to the CJEU, the ECtHR finds that there is no additional requirement of 'systemic deficiencies'.[52] Hence, following the *Tarakhel*

examine the criteria set out in Chapter III in order to establish whether another Member State can be designated as responsible.

Where the transfer cannot be made pursuant to this paragraph to any Member State designated on the basis of the criteria set out in Chapter III or to the first Member State with which the application was lodged, the determining Member State shall become the Member State responsible.

[50] *Tarakhel v Switzerland* App no 29217/12 (ECtHR, 4 November 2014) para 104.

[51] ibid para 99.

[52] See also C Costello and M Mouzourakis, 'Reflections on Reading Tarakhel: Is "How Bad Is Bad Enough" Good Enough?' (2014) 10 *Asiel en Migrantenrecht* 404.

judgment, national authorities are required under the ECHR to examine all the facts of the case carefully, including any individual characteristics that might make an asylum seeker more vulnerable and warrant a decision not to transfer.

E. Systemic Deficiencies v Individualised Approach in EU Law: The Case of *CK and Others*

In *CK and others*,[53] decided in 2017, the CJEU further qualified its approach concerning the systemic deficiencies requirement. The reference was made in the proceedings between CK, HF and their child AS and the Republic of Slovenia, represented by its Ministry of the Interior, concerning their transfer to Croatia, the Member State responsible for examining their application for international protection in accordance with the provisions of the Dublin III Regulation. This is the first case in which the Court was given the opportunity to comment on the relationship between the new versions of Article 3(2) and Article 17(1) of the Dublin III Regulation. Article 3(2) now enshrines a derogation from the duty to transfer asylum seekers among Member States where 'there are substantial grounds for believing that there are systemic flaws in the asylum procedure and in the reception conditions for applicants in [the Member State primarily designated], resulting in a risk of inhuman or degrading treatment within the meaning of Article 4 of the Charter of Fundamental Rights'. As previously mentioned, this derogation is inspired by the ruling of the CJEU in the *NS and others*,[54] according to which the Member States could use the discretion provided for by the former so-called 'sovereignty clause' – which has now become a distinct provision and appears in Article 17(1) of the Dublin III Regulation – in the event of such systemic flaws.

The facts of the case are as follows. Ms CK, a Syrian national who was six months pregnant, and her husband, Mr HF, an Egyptian national, entered the territory of the Member States via Croatia on 16 August 2015. They were in possession of tourist visas issued by Croatia. The following day, Ms CK and Mr HF entered Slovenia with false Greek identity papers and lodged an application for international protection. Following the application, the Slovenian authorities submitted a request to Croatia, the Member State responsible pursuant to the Dublin III Regulation, to take over the responsibility for examining the applications. In the meantime, Ms CK gave birth to a son, AS, and lodged an application for international protection on his behalf. In January 2016, the Slovenian authorities received the medical records of the applicants, which described Ms CK's high-risk pregnancy and her difficulties following childbirth, providing that she and her new-born son should remain at the reception centre in Slovenia because they were in need of care. Further psychiatric assessments indicated that Ms CK had suffered

[53] Case C-578/16 *CK and others*, ECLI:EU:C:2017:127.
[54] *NS and others* (n 22).

from depression and periodic suicidal tendencies, attributable to the uncertainty surrounding her status. Due to the critical circumstances in the case, the Slovenian authorities sought assurances from their Croatian counterparts concerning the appropriate reception conditions for the applicants, and the Croatian authorities confirmed that the applicants would be provided with accommodation, appropriate care and the necessary medical treatment. As a result, the Slovenian authorities requested the transfer of the applicants to Croatia.

In a judgment of 1 June 2016, the Administrative Court in Slovenia annulled the transfer decision and suspended its enforcement, pending the adoption of a final decision in the administrative proceedings. Subsequently, the Supreme Court set aside the judgment of the Administrative Court, holding that the second subparagraph of Article 3(2) of the Dublin III Regulation was not applicable, since the existence of systemic flaws in the asylum procedure and reception conditions in Croatia had not been established. On the contrary, a report by the United Nations High Commissioner for Refugees (UNHCR) made it clear that the situation in Croatia was good, the access to care was guaranteed and emergency situations were provided for. This was especially true for the Kutina Centre in Croatia, which was intended for vulnerable groups of asylum seekers and to which the applicants would be transferred.

After the decision of the Supreme Court, the last step for the appellants was a constitutional complaint before the Constitutional Court in Slovenia. On 28 September 2016, the Constitutional Court set aside the Supreme Court's judgment and referred the case back to that court. While the Constitutional Court agreed that the second subparagraph of Article 3(2) of the Dublin III Regulation was not applicable, since there were no systemic flaws in the asylum procedure and in the reception conditions in Croatia that might result in a risk of inhuman or degrading treatment within the meaning of Article 4 of the Charter, it considered that that the applicants could not be transferred to Croatia before the Slovenian authorities had examined all the relevant circumstances, including the personal situation and state of health of the applicants. In the Constitutional Court's view, the transfer itself could be injurious to the state of health of Ms CK and her son, and this was something the Slovenian authorities needed to examine before executing the transfer. In construing this argument, the Constitutional Court referred to Recital 32 of the Dublin III Regulation, which provides that Member States are bound by their obligations under the relevant case law of the Strasbourg Court, pointing out that the criterion for an examination under the latter is wider than that of 'systemic flaws' provided in Article 3(2) of the Dublin III Regulation. Interestingly, the Constitutional Court did not make reference to the EU Charter of Fundamental Rights.

Following the judgment of the Constitutional Court, the Supreme Court decided to stay the proceedings and refer four questions to the Court of Justice in Luxembourg. The main question was whether Article 4 of the Charter must be interpreted as meaning that, in circumstances in which the transfer of an asylum seeker with a particularly serious mental or physical illness would result in a real and proven risk of a significant and permanent deterioration in the state of health of the person concerned, that transfer would constitute inhuman and degrading treatment within the meaning of that Article. If the answer to the latter question would be affirmative, the referring court also asked whether it would be required to apply the 'discretionary clause' (Article 17(1) of Dublin III) and examine the asylum application itself.

In his Opinion, Advocate General Tanchev concluded that only systemic flaws in the responsible state could require the prevention of a Dublin transfer.[55] The Advocate General based his reasoning on the *NS* and *Abdullahi* judgments of the CJEU, as well as on the importance of the principle of mutual trust between Member States and the need to ensure the effectiveness of the CEAS. As for the ECHR standards, Advocate General Tanchev acknowledged that his position did not meet the ECHR standards[56] but insisted that the CJEU was not required to follow the approach taken by the ECtHR, as 'it would … be wrong to regard the case-law of the European Court of Human Rights as a source of interpretation with full validity in connection with the application of the Charter'.[57] The CJEU, by contrast, based its reasoning on the duty of the Member States to comply with the case law of the ECtHR, as provided in Recital 32 of the Dublin III Regulation. Curiously, though, the judgment does not contain a reference to *Tarakhel v Switzerland*, but the CJEU did refer to the ECtHR's decision in *Paposhvili v Belgium*,[58] which is based on *Tarakhel*.

The Luxembourg Court ruled that the transfer of the asylum seeker should be suspended if the particular medical condition of the applicant was so serious as to provide 'substantial grounds for believing' that the transfer would result in 'a real risk of inhuman or degrading treatment, within the meaning of Article 4 of the Charter'.[59] National courts should determine if this was indeed the case and, if so, suspend the transfer until the health of the applicant permitted it.[60]

In this case, there was no evidence that there were substantial grounds for believing that there were systemic flaws in the asylum procedure and the conditions for the reception of asylum seekers in Croatia; on the contrary, it was clear from the assurances obtained that the appellants in the proceedings would receive accommodation, the necessary medical treatment and appropriate care.[61] Nevertheless, the Court emphasised that it could not be ruled out that the *transfer itself*, irrespective of the reception conditions in Croatia, might result in a real

[55] Opinion of AG Tanchev in Case C-578/16 PPU *CK and others*, ECLI:EU:C:2017:108.

[56] ibid para 47. AG Tanchev pointed out that the Court Justice requires 'systemic' flaws in the Member State responsible in order to prohibit the transfer of an applicant to that Member State; the ECtHR merely requires existence of flaws that affect the applicant's individual situation.

[57] ibid para 53.

[58] *Paposhvili v Belgium* App no 41738/10 (ECtHR, 13 December 2016).

[59] *CK and others* (n 53) para 90.

[60] ibid.

[61] ibid para 71. This was also acknowledged in the decisions of both the Supreme Court and the Constitutional Court.

risk of inhuman and degrading treatment for the person concerned due to her particularly serious state of health.[62] Accordingly, the Slovenian authorities were under an obligation to assess the risk of such consequences before deciding on the transfer.[63]

The CJEU argued that this change in the case law, whereby it now allows for a derogation from the duty to transfer, in addition to that found in Article 3(2) on 'systemic flaws', stemmed from the increased standard of fundamental rights protection in the Dublin III Regulation in comparison to Dublin II.[64] As for the Member States' responsibility under the discretionary clause contained in Article 17(1) of the Dublin III Regulation, the Court held that the Member State in question had the possibility to examine the asylum application itself if the state of health of the asylum seeker was not expected to improve. The Court emphasised, however, that this provision did not oblige a Member State to examine any application lodged with it, even when read in the light of Article 4 of the Charter.[65]

This ruling seems like an ECHR-friendly development, and in many ways it is. It shows the CJEU's readiness to compromise and bring its case law into line with the Strasbourg standards. However, the judgment also leaves room for questions, since it concerns a very exceptional situation of an asylum seeker whose state of health is particularly serious. It also concerns the question whether the transfer itself would result in a treatment contrary to Article 4 of the Charter and not reception conditions in the receiving state.[66] In other words, the judgment does not seem to call into question the 'systemic deficiencies' test or the application of the principle of mutual trust. This is apparent in the wording of the Court throughout the judgment, where the Court emphasised the exceptional nature of the situation, the seriousness of the state of health of the applicants and – most importantly – the fact that the derogation applied when the *transfer itself* could lead to inhuman and degrading treatment within the meaning of Article 4 of the Charter. Thus, it remained unclear at that time whether the same exception would apply if it were not the actual transfer that could lead to inhuman and degrading treatment but rather the asylum procedure and reception conditions in the Member State responsible, where no systemic flaws had been established in those respects.[67] Indeed, only this latter finding would ensure compliance with the ECHR standards post-*Tarakhel*.

[62] ibid paras 65–66 and 73.

[63] ibid para 75.

[64] ibid paras 62–63 and 94.

[65] ibid para 88.

[66] ibid para 74. On this points see also Š Imamović and E Muir, 'The Dublin III System: More Derogations to the Duty to Transfer Individual Asylum Seekers?' (2017) 2 *European Papers* 719.

[67] The Court made this distinction too in para 94 of the judgment, stating that the outcome in this case differed from the outcome in *Abduallahi*, since the latter judgment involved a national who had not claimed that his transfer would, in itself, be contrary to Art 4 of the Charter.

V. The Systemic Deficiencies Criteria and the Limits to Mutual Trust

More recent case law in the context of Dublin transfers in Luxembourg provides more clarity with regard to the responsibilities of the Member States under Article 4 of the Charter. In *Jawo*,[68] a case concerning transfer of an asylum seeker from Germany to Italy, the referring court considered, inter alia, that the examination of whether there are systemic flaws, within the meaning of the second subparagraph of Article 3(2) of the Dublin III Regulation, cannot be confined to the asylum procedure and the reception conditions during that procedure, but must also include the situation thereafter. The case arose amidst the discussion of the inadequate system of social assistance in Italy, where asylum seekers are allegedly left in misery by the Italian state after having been granted asylum. The referring court thus considered that the granting of optimal reception conditions during the asylum procedure would be insufficient if, having been granted international protection, the person concerned were subsequently to be threatened with living conditions contrary to Article 4 of the Charter. According to the national court, the obligation to carry out such an overall examination of the applicant's situation before the transfer is the necessary reverse side of the Dublin system, which denies those seeking protection a free choice of country of refuge, and in any event, it is an obligation that stems from Article 3 ECHR.[69]

The CJEU held that it follows from the general and absolute nature of the prohibition laid down in Article 4 of the Charter that the transfer of an applicant to that Member State is ruled out in any situation in which there are substantial grounds for believing that the applicant runs such a risk during his transfer or thereafter, even though the second subparagraph of Article 3(2) of the Dublin III Regulation envisages only the *NS* type of situation, namely, that in which the real risk of inhuman or degrading treatment stems from systemic flaws in the asylum procedure and the reception conditions in the Member State designated as responsible for examining the application. It is immaterial, according to the Court, whether it is the moment of the transfer, the time during the asylum procedure or following it that the person concerned would be exposed to a substantial risk of suffering inhuman or degrading treatment.[70] In that regard, the Court of Justice found that national courts are obliged to carry out an assessment of evidence provided by the person concerned, and to determine, on the basis of information that is objective, reliable, specific and properly updated, and having regard to the standard of protection of fundamental rights guaranteed by EU law, whether there are deficiencies, which, importantly, may be systemic or generalised, or which may affect certain groups of

[68] Case C-163/17 *Jawo*, ECLI:EU:C:2019:218.
[69] ibid para 45.
[70] ibid para 88.

people. Finally, the CJEU established the criteria to guide the assessment carried out by the national courts in determining whether the flaws in the asylum system of a Member State are capable of leading to a real risk of inhuman or degrading treatment. The Court held that the flaws must attain a particularly high level of severity, which is attained when

> the indifference of the authorities of a Member State would result in the person wholly dependent on State support finding himself … in a situation of extreme material poverty that does not allow him to meet his most basic needs, such as, inter alia, food, personal hygiene and a place to live, and that undermines his physical or mental health or puts him in a state of degradation incompatible with human dignity …[71]

If this high threshold of 'extreme material poverty' is reached, the applicant must not be transferred because of the real risk of inhuman or degrading treatment.

The Court provided a lengthy illustration of all the circumstances that would *not* be sufficient to block a transfer. It underlined, for example, that 'a high degree of insecurity or a significant degradation of the living conditions of the person concerned' would not suffice.[72] More specifically, the Court explained that the circumstances such as those mentioned by the referring court, namely the absence of integration programmes, less favourable social protection and lack of family support structure, would not attain the level of severity required to reach the threshold. The message that the CJEU conveyed to the national courts is that the exceptions should still be construed narrowly. It is thus not surprising that the referring court ultimately ruled that Jawo could be transferred to Italy.[73]

On the same day, the CJEU restated its findings in the Joined Cases *Ibrahim and others*.[74] The cases concerned the interpretation of the EU Directive on common procedures for granting and withdrawing international protection,[75] and the Court of Justice was asked to consider, inter alia, the question of expected living conditions in the responsible Member State. The CJEU reiterated that an asylum seeker may be transferred to the Member State that is responsible for processing the application or that has previously granted the applicant subsidiary protection, unless the expected living conditions in that Member State would expose him or her to a situation of extreme material poverty, contrary to the prohibition of inhuman or degrading treatment. Here, again, the Court pointed out that inadequacies in the social system of the Member State concerned do not warrant the conclusion that there is a risk of such treatment. Finally, in *MA*,[76] concerning

[71] ibid para 92.
[72] ibid para 93.
[73] Verwaltungsgerichtshof Baden-Württemberg, Judgment of 29 July 2019, ECLI:DE:VGHBW:2019:0729.A4S749.19.00.
[74] Joined Cases C-297/17, C-318/17, C-319/17 and C-438/17 *Ibrahim and others*, ECLI:EU:C:2019:219, paras 81–101.
[75] Directive 2013/32/EU of the European Parliament and of the Council of 26 June 2013 on common procedures for granting and withdrawing international protection.
[76] Case C-661/17 *MA and others*, ECLI:EU:C:2019:53.

a transfer of the applicants from Ireland to the UK, the CJEU explicitly held that fundamental rights in the framework of Dublin transfers are protected not only by Article 3(2) concerning systemic flaws, but also by the Member States' obligations under Article 4 of the Charter, as well as Article 3 ECHR and the relevant case law of the ECtHR.[77] Accordingly, what we see is a high degree of convergence in the case law of the Luxembourg and Strasbourg Courts in the area of asylum law. Indeed, the Court of Justice consistently follows the Strasbourg jurisprudence, adjusting its case law and pushing the limits of mutual trust in order to make it ECHR compliant.[78] It has also referred to the ECtHR judgments extensively, making an effort to show that that the two are in agreement.

Nevertheless, it is not entirely certain that the CJEU's vision of derogations to mutual trust as being possible only in exceptional cases – an argumentative stance the Court of Justice continues to uphold – is in fact in conformity with the ECtHR's approach. The question is thus whether limiting the power of national courts to check compliance with fundamental rights in other Member State to 'exceptional cases' corresponds to what is expected from national courts on the basis of the ECHR. This is particularly so because the Strasbourg Court does not use that terminology even though the States do use it in their submissions,[79] so it remains unclear whether the two approaches are in complete harmony.

Additionally, the manner in which the case law developed warrants a number of comments and reservations. First, it is arguable that the CJEU changed its approach in response to the warning signals from Strasbourg. Indeed, it could be that the CJEU was concerned about the possibility that its decisions would be reviewed by the ECtHR in the context of a Dublin transfer case and the ECtHR would find a violation. After all, the Court of Justice was aware of the fact that the presumption of equivalent protection would not be applicable, and the position of the ECtHR in respect of the Dublin transfers was already clear.[80] It would seem problematic, however, to consider that ensuring minimum standards of fundamental rights protection at the EU level required warning signs from Strasbourg. In fact, one would expect fundamental rights to be protected more robustly and extensively by the EU, going beyond the ECHR minimum standards where possible and appropriate.[81] The second and related point is that the CJEU's more forceful change in approach coincides with the amendments made by the EU legislature in the

[77] ibid para 84.

[78] On this point see V Pergantis, 'The "Sovereignty Clause" of the Dublin Regulations in the Case-Law of the ECtHR and the CJEU: The Mirage of a Jurisprudential Convergence?' in GC Bruno, FM Palombino and A Di Stefano (eds), *Migration Issues before International Courts and Tribunals* (Rome, CNR Edizioni, 2019); C Ladenburger, 'The Principle of Mutual Trust between Member States in the Area of Freedom, Security and Justice' (2020) 3 *Zeitschrift für Europarechtliche Studien* 373, 390.

[79] See, eg, *MSS v Belgium and Greece* (n 22) paras 326 and 331.

[80] T Lock, 'The future of EU human rights: Is accession to the ECHR still desirable?' (2020) 7 *Journal of International and Comparative Law* 2.

[81] M Claes, 'Fundamental Rights' in PJ Kuijper et al (eds), *The Law of the European Union* (Alphen a/d Rijn, Wolters Kluwer, 2018) 97.

Dublin III Regulation. The latter now includes, inter alia, Recital 32, which states that the Member States are bound by the case law of the ECtHR in the application of the Regulation. This is further evidenced by the Court's references to the recital in both *CK and others* and *Jawo*, as well as a more general statement that the change in its approach is a consequence of the more explicit and expanded fundamental rights safeguards included in the Dublin III Regulation.[82] It could thus be that the efforts made by the CJEU are a result of the changes in the Dublin III Regulation and not because of a more general obligation to ensure consistency between EU and ECHR law. This, in turn, shows, how important the role of the EU legislature can be when there is divergence between EU and ECHR law.

VI. Conclusion

The chapter has sought to illustrate how the case law of the Strasbourg Court has influenced a gradual softening of the application of the principle of mutual trust in EU law in the area of asylum law. Indeed, the *MSS* judgment called into question the underlying idea that Member States can and should trust each other's compliance with fundamental rights. The ECtHR ruled that transferring States should not just presume that other Member States comply with their international obligations. When an issue arises under Article 3 ECHR, they are obliged to apply the 'sovereignty clause'. The CJEU followed suit in its *NS* judgment, but restricted the rebuttal of the presumption of fundamental rights compliance to cases of systemic deficiencies. When the ECtHR in *Tarakhel v Switzerland* held that the States are obliged to conduct an individual assessment of the risk even there are no systemic deficiencies in the receiving country, the CJEU re-aligned its case law again. It did so in steps: first, in *CK and others* it ruled that the national authorities have a duty to ensure that the transfer of the person concerned would not result in treatment incompatible with Article 4 of the Charter, even when there were no systemic deficiencies in the receiving country. In *Jawo*, the Luxembourg Court clarified that the duty to check applies to any situation in which there are substantial grounds for believing that the applicant runs such a risk of being exposed to treatment contrary to Article 4 of the Charter, during his transfer or *thereafter*, even though the second subparagraph of Article 3(2) of the Dublin III Regulation envisages only the *NS* type of situation, namely, that in which the real risk of inhuman or degrading treatment stems from systemic flaws in the asylum procedure and the reception conditions in the Member State designated as responsible for examining the application. What we thus see in the case law today is a high degree of convergence in the approaches of the Luxembourg and Strasbourg Courts.

While these landmark decisions represent a welcome development in the European fundamental rights architecture, an argument has been made that

[82] See, eg, *CK and others* (n 53) paras 62 and 94.

the CJEU was acting under pressure from the ECtHR. It is indeed likely that the CJEU was trying to avoid the consequence of having its decisions challenged in Strasbourg and, ultimately, risk the ECtHR's finding a violation of the Convention. It would seem problematic, however, to consider that ensuring minimum standards of fundamental rights protection at the EU level required warning signals from Strasbourg. Moreover, the Dublin III Regulation also includes Recital 32, according to which Member States are bound by the relevant Strasbourg case law in the application of the Regulation. This interpretative tool has played an important role in the CJEU's reasoning in the more recent cases, as demonstrated previously. In other words, it is likely that the CJEU changed its approach in part also because of the existence of Recital 32, and not because of a more general obligation to ensure consistency between EU and ECHR law, which, as argued in chapter 2, already exists on the basis of Article 52(3) of the Charter. This, in turn, would mean that although there is a high degree of convergence in the case law of the two European Courts in the context of the Dublin Regulation this may not be the case for other EU legal instruments, in the AFSJ or outside of it.

Another point worth mentioning, by way of a conclusion, relates to the critical aspect of time that is needed to achieve convergence. While it is true that the jurisprudential dialogue between the two European Courts has been particularly valuable in this field, not least for national courts, there is no guarantee that new divergences will not develop. Moreover, while the process of convergence between the case law of the CJEU and the ECtHR is ongoing, national courts are asked to decide cases before them. Nevertheless, the requirement to ensure compliance with the case law of the ECtHR is now explicitly stated in the Dublin III Regulation, which, if maintained and followed, will allow continued convergence between EU and ECHR law in this area of EU law. It is to be hoped, from a general human rights perspective, that the CJEU will be ready to go beyond the ECHR minimum standards when deciding cases in the area that covers among the most disadvantaged and vulnerable individuals and groups.[83]

[83] On the concept of vulnerability and how it relates to the need for extensive safeguards in the asylum process under EU law, see the Report of European Council on Refugees and Exiles, *The Concept of Vulnerability in European Asylum Procedures* (2017), available at https://reliefweb.int/report/world/concept-vulnerability-european-asylum-procedures (accessed 16 December 2020).

4

Case Study II: The European Arrest Warrant

I. Introduction

Over the last two decades, the European Union (EU) has progressively developed a European area of criminal justice. The first EU instrument of mutual recognition in criminal matters was the Framework Decision on the European Arrest Warrant (EAW), adopted following the terrorist attacks in the United States on 11 September 2001.[1] Today, the EAW is the EU's most powerful and frequently used mechanism of judicial cooperation. It is based on the idea that all the countries involved respect fundamental rights guaranteed by the EU and that the requested persons can be extradited safely. Generally, the courts of the Member States have accepted this premise and have been willing to place high levels of confidence in each other's criminal justice systems.[2] However, it was also clear from the outset that the fundamental rights records of the Member States vary considerably. As a result, the relationship between the effectiveness of this instrument and the protection of fundamental rights has also been fiercely debated over the years.

The Framework Decision on the EAW contains an exhaustive list of grounds that can justify non-execution of a warrant. Other grounds – such as degrading prison conditions or controversial judicial reforms – are in principle not permissible. At the same time, the Framework Decision also contains a general clause in Article 1(3), according to which it is not to have the effect of modifying the obligation to respect fundamental rights as enshrined in Articles 2 and 6 of the Treaty on European Union (TEU), and the Court of Justice of the European Union (CJEU, 'the Court' or 'the Court of Justice') has recognised that additional limitations may be placed on the principles of mutual recognition and mutual trust but only 'in exceptional circumstances'. The EAW Framework Decision is thus a particularly interesting instrument for this case study, since national courts may

[1] Council Framework Decision 2002/584/JHA of 13 June 2002 on the European arrest warrant and the surrender procedure between Member States, [2002] OJ L190/0001. It has been in use since 1 January 2004.

[2] See, eg, P Albers et al, 'Towards a Common Evaluation Framework to Assess Mutual Trust in the Field of EU Judicial Cooperation in Criminal Matters' (March 2013) available at www.government.nl/documents/reports/2013/09/27/final-report-towards-a-common-evaluation-framework-to-assess-mutual-trust-in-the-field-of-eu-judicial-cooperation-in-criminal-m (last accessed 16 December 2020).

face directly conflicting obligations in the application of the Decision because ensuring the protection of fundamental rights may mean a failure to execute an EU law obligation.

This chapter analyses the Court's reasoning in cases concerning execution of arrest warrants where there is a risk of human rights violations in the issuing state. It starts with the early case law, in which the Court of Justice insisted on a strict reading of the EAW, seemingly denying the possibility of refusals to surrender that are not expressly provided for by the Framework Decision itself. It then analyses the more recent leading cases, such as *Aranyosi* and *LM*,[3] where the Court was given an opportunity to reassess the balance between the principle of mutual trust and the need to protect fundamental rights. As with chapter 3, the analysis of the case law focuses on aspects that have caused tensions between the case law of the two European Courts (Luxembourg and Strasbourg) and omits a detailed discussion of other aspects, which have already been addressed extensively in scholarly literature.[4]

The chapter thus seeks to identify whether the Court of Justice was successful in drawing a 'new balance' between mutual trust and fundamental rights in the more recent case law, and whether the latter is in conformity with the law under the European Convention on Human Rights (ECHR). As will be shown, the CJEU conceded that there can be exceptions to mutual trust based on human rights grounds, even where these are not expressly stipulated in legislation, but it maintains its view that derogations should be exceptional. For that purpose, the CJEU established a 'two-step test', which national executing authorities must perform before refusing to execute an EAW. In the meantime, the European Court of Human Rights (ECtHR) has also had the opportunity to rule in a number of cases concerning mutual recognition instruments including cases concerning execution of an EAW. The case law analysis demonstrates that the approach of the ECtHR in this regard is methodologically different and it is arguable that the differences in the approaches of the two European Courts can lead to different outcomes and levels of protection in Luxembourg and Strasbourg.

II. European Arrest Warrant

An arrest warrant is a judicial decision issued by a Member State with a view to the arrest and surrender of a requested person by another Member State, for the

[3] Joined Cases C-404/15 and C-659/15 PPU *Aranyosi and Căldăraru*, ECLI:EU:C:2016:198; Case C-216/18 PPU *LM*, ECLI:EU:C:2018:586.

[4] For recent, more thorough account of the case law, see E Xanthopoulou, *Fundamental Rights and Mutual Trust in the Area of Freedom, Security and Justice: A Role for Proportionality?* (Oxford, Hart Publishing, 2020), in particular ch 6. See also A Tinsley, 'The Reference in Case C-396/11 Radu: When does the Protection of Fundamental Rights Require Non-execution of a European Arrest Warrant?' (2012) 2 *European Criminal Law Review* 3; A Torres Pérez, '*Melloni* in Three Acts: From Dialogue to Monologue' (2014) 10 *European Constitutional Law Review* 308; G Anagnostaras, 'Mutual Confidence is not Blind Trust! Fundamental Rights protection and the execution of the European

purposes of conducting a criminal prosecution or executing a custodial sentence or detention order.[5] A warrant may be issued when the person whose return is sought is accused of an offence for which the law establishes a maximum period of the penalty of at least one year in prison or when the person has already been sentenced to a prison term of at least four months.[6] The EAW is described as 'the first and most symbolic measure applying the principle of mutual recognition',[7] which implies that Member State courts will abstain from second-guessing decisions issued by judicial authorities of other Member States and execute the warrants.

Generally, the EAW Framework Decision has been considered to be a successful mutual recognition instrument in the area of judicial cooperation in criminal matters, with significant advantages compared to the traditional extradition system.[8] However, in spite of its initial success, it quickly became controversial from a human rights perspective. There are several reasons for the controversy. Initially, the Framework Decision was criticised because of its partial abolition of the double criminality requirement with respect to 32 crimes.[9] In international extradition law, double criminality requires that the acts for which an extradition is requested constitute a criminal offence in the criminal laws of both the issuing and the executing states. However, the double criminality requirement, as curtailed under the new EAW regime, removes the possibility of examining double criminality for the 32 enumerated offences.[10] More recently, further problems have arisen in relation to the adequate protection of the fundamental rights of individuals who are subject to a warrant, in particular the right to

Arrest Warrant: *Aranyosi and Căldăraru*' (2016) 53 *CML Rev* 165; S Gáspár-Szilágyi, 'Joined Cases Aranyosi and Căldăraru: Converging Human Rights Standards, Mutual Trust and a New Ground for Postponing a European Arrest Warrant' (2016) 24 *European Journal of Crime, Criminal Law and Criminal Justice* 197; P Gragl, 'An Olive Branch from Strasbourg? Interpreting the European Court of Human Rights' Resurrection of *Bosphorus* and Reaction to *Opinion 2/13* in the *Avotiņš* Case' (2017) 13 *European Constitutional Law Review* 551.

[5] As provided in Art 1(1) of the Framework Decision on the EAW (n 1).

[6] Art 2(1) of the Framework Decision on the EAW (n 1).

[7] COM(2006) 8 final 24 January, 2006.

[8] Most notably, the EAW system is faster and more efficient. See reports by the Commission and the Council concerning the implementation of the EAW: COM(2005) 63 and SEC(2005) 267, dated 23 February 2005; COM(2007) 407 and SEC(2007) 979, dated 11 July 2007; COM(2011) 175 final and SEC(2011) 430 final, dated 11 April 2011; Council, Final report on the fourth round of mutual evaluations, Doc No 8302/4/09, 28 May 2009. These reports are primarily based on their analysis of national laws giving effect to the EAW Framework Decision and the response to questionnaires addressed to the Member States.

[9] In the EAW, the verification of double criminality is abolished for a list of 32 offences punishable by a prison sentence of a maximum of three years. This was problematic in some Member States, because not all Member States construe the list in the same way. For example, Belgium excluded acts of abortion and euthanasia from the offence of 'murder or grievous bodily harm' in the list of offences, while there are circumstances in which such acts may be unlawful, which raises difficult fundamental rights questions.

[10] Examples are participation in a criminal organisation, terrorism, trafficking in human beings, sexual exploitation of children and child pornography, corruption and fraud. For the full list see Art 2(2) of the Framework Decision on the EAW (n 1).

a fair trial, the right to liberty, and the prohibition of inhuman and degrading treatment, as well as the national courts' possibility – or rather lack thereof – to decide not to execute a warrant in cases where there is a risk that the requested person's human rights may be violated in the issuing state.[11] Pursuant to the Framework Decision, the refusal is only permissible in the circumstances provided for in Articles 3 and 4, under which courts of the executing Member State must (Article 3)[12] or may (Article 4)[13] refuse the warrant's execution. The Court has held that the list of grounds provided in Articles 3 and 4 is exhaustive, since a refusal

[11] M Fichera, *The Implementation of the European Arrest Warrant in the European Union: law, policy and practice* (Antwerp, Intersentia, 2011).

[12] Art 3 provides:

Grounds for mandatory non-execution of the European arrest warrant

The judicial authority of the Member State of execution (hereinafter 'executing judicial authority') shall refuse to execute the European arrest warrant in the following cases:

1. if the offence on which the arrest warrant is based is covered by amnesty in the executing Member State, where that State had jurisdiction to prosecute the offence under its own criminal law;
2. if the executing judicial authority is informed that the requested person has been finally judged by a Member State in respect of the same acts provided that, where there has been sentence, the sentence has been served or is currently being served or may no longer be executed under the law of the sentencing Member State;
3. if the person who is the subject of the European arrest warrant may not, owing to his age, be held criminally responsible for the acts on which the arrest warrant is based under the law of the executing State.

[13] Art 4 provides:

Grounds for optional non-execution of the European arrest warrant

The executing judicial authority may refuse to execute the European arrest warrant:

1. if, in one of the cases referred to in Article 2(4), the act on which the European arrest warrant is based does not constitute an offence under the law of the executing Member State; however, in relation to taxes or duties, customs and exchange, execution of the European arrest warrant shall not be refused on the ground that the law of the executing Member State does not impose the same kind of tax or duty or does not contain the same type of rules as regards taxes, duties and customs and exchange regulations as the law of the issuing Member State;
2. where the person who is the subject of the European arrest warrant is being prosecuted in the executing Member State for the same act as that on which the European arrest warrant is based;
3. where the judicial authorities of the executing Member State have decided either not to prosecute for the offence on which the European arrest warrant is based or to halt proceedings, or where a final judgment has been passed upon the requested person in a Member State, in respect of the same acts, which prevents further proceedings;
4. where the criminal prosecution or punishment of the requested person is statute-barred according to the law of the executing Member State and the acts fall within the jurisdiction of that Member State under its own criminal law;
5. if the executing judicial authority is informed that the requested person has been finally judged by a third State in respect of the same acts provided that, where there has been sentence, the sentence has been served or is currently being served or may no longer be executed under the law of the sentencing country;
6. if the European arrest warrant has been issued for the purposes of execution of a custodial sentence or detention order, where the requested person is staying in, or is a national or a resident of the executing Member State and that State undertakes to execute the sentence or detention order in accordance with its domestic law;

on grounds other than those explicitly stated would undermine the effectiveness of the Framework Decision and the principle of mutual trust and recognition.[14] Article 1(2) of the Framework Decision indeed reaffirms that Member States are expected to execute any EAW on the basis of the principle of mutual recognition and in accordance with the provisions of the Framework Decision. At the same time, however, the obligation to ensure respect for fundamental rights could not be ignored. According to Article 1(3) of the Framework Decision, it 'shall not have the effect of modifying the obligation to respect fundamental rights and fundamental legal principles as enshrined in Article 6 of the Treaty on European Union'. This implies that the Decision should be implemented while taking into consideration the overall framework in which EU law functions, including its human rights protection. Additionally, Recital 13 of the EAW Framework Decision sets out guarantees against the surrender of an individual 'to a State where there is a serious risk that he or she would be subjected to the death penalty, torture or other inhuman or degrading treatment or punishment'. Accordingly, a more general argument can be made that Article 1(3) of the Framework Decision, in conjunction with Article 6 TEU, may in itself be interpreted as providing sufficient grounds to refuse execution of an EAW in case the latter would result in human rights violations. Many states have indeed introduced an explicit ground for refusal based on fundamental rights claims, albeit with different formulations and thresholds. In Belgium, for example, national law requires 'serious grounds to believe' that the execution of an EAW would infringe fundamental rights.[15] The extradition law in the Netherlands stipulates that the execution of a warrant can be refused where there is a 'substantiated reason to believe' that its execution would lead to a 'flagrant' breach of human rights.[16] The Dutch legislature actually took over the wording of the ECtHR in extradition cases,[17] while also making a reference to the ECHR. The Irish and the British implementing laws simply state that the execution of an EAW could be refused if it would result in a violation of the Convention rights.[18] In Germany, national law generally provides that the requests for surrender shall not be granted if compliance would violate the principles in Article 6 of the TEU.[19] When addressing the constitutional challenges at the national level, the courts usually confined their analyses and decisions to the acts implementing the Framework Decision

7. where the European arrest warrant relates to offences which:
   (a) are regarded by the law of the executing Member State as having been committed in whole or in part in the territory of the executing Member State or in a place treated as such; or
   (b) have been committed outside the territory of the issuing Member State and the law of the executing Member State does not allow prosecution for the same offences when committed outside its territory.

[14] Case C-396/11 *Radu*, ECLI:EU:C:2013:39, para 36.
[15] Art 4(5) of the *Wet betreffende het Europees aanhoudingsbevel* of 19 December 2003.
[16] Art 11 of the *Overleveringswet* of 29 April 2004.
[17] *Soering v United Kingdom* App no 14038/88 (ECtHR, 7 July 1989) para 113.
[18] European Arrest Warrant Act 2003 (Ireland), s 37(1); Extradition Act 2003 (UK), s 21(1).
[19] Act on International Cooperation in Criminal Matters of 23 December 1982, s 73.

rather than the Decision itself, despite the fact that the Framework Decision and the underlying principle of mutual trust and recognition had been challenged.

The fundamental rights concerns resulting from the EAW were thus identified quite early in the Member States, having also led to a number of constitutional challenges in several countries,[20] and discussion in academia;[21] however, they were broadly overlooked in the EU legislative process and by the EU institutions.[22] Nevertheless, the institutions have also voiced their concern more recently regarding the erosion of fundamental rights as a consequence of judicial cooperation based on mutual recognition, and have recommended several changes. In 2009, the Council of the EU adopted a Resolution on a Roadmap for strengthening procedural rights of suspected or accused persons in criminal proceedings.[23] The aim of the Roadmap was to strengthen the rights by employing a 'step-by-step' approach. The starting point was to adopt five measures on basic procedural rights, and the Commission was invited to propose EU legislation to this end. In this context, a number of Directives have been adopted to strengthen different aspects of the rights of suspects or accused persons in criminal proceedings.[24]

III. Validity Challenge *in Abstracto*

Soon after the EAW Framework Decision was adopted (pre-Charter period), the Belgian *Arbitragehof* (Arbitration Court, later renamed 'Constitutional Court') made a reference to the CJEU in the proceedings between Advocaten voor de Wereld, a non-profit association of legal practitioners, and the Council of Ministers.[25] Advocaten voor de Wereld challenged the validity of the legislation implementing the EAW, alleging a violation of several provisions of the Belgian Constitution, as well as Articles 5, 6 and 7 ECHR, and seeking an annulment. The first question concerned the correct legal basis and the second one addressed a number of specific fundamental rights implications of the principle of

[20] In 2005 the EAW was challenged in Poland, Germany, Cyprus and Greece, culminating in the Belgian case *Advocaten voor de Wereld* in 2007, which is discussed further in section III. For an overview and analysis, see E Guild (ed), *Constitutional Challenges to the European Arrest Warrant* (Nijmegen, Wolf Legal Publishers 2006); J Komárek, 'European constitutionalism and the European arrest warrant: In search of the limits of contrapunctual principles' (2007) 44 *CML Rev* 9.

[21] See various chapters in Guild (ed) (n 20).

[22] A Albi, 'The European Arrest Warrant, constitutional rights and the changing legal thinking. Values once recognised lost in transition to the EU level?' in M Fletcher, E Herlin-Karnell and C Matera (eds), *The European Union as an Area of Freedom, Security and Justice* (London, Routledge, 2016).

[23] Resolution of the Council of 30 November 2009 on a Roadmap for strengthening procedural rights of suspected or accused persons in criminal proceedings [2009] OJ C295/01).

[24] See, for instance, Directive 2010/64/EU on the right to interpretation and translation in criminal proceedings, 20 October 2010; Directive 2012/13/EU on the right to information in criminal proceedings, 22 May 2012; Directive 2013/48 on the right of access to a lawyer in criminal proceedings, 22 October 2013.

[25] Case C- 303/05 *Advocaten voor de Wereld*, ECLI:EU:C:2007:261.

mutual recognition. Ten Member States were involved in the case, indicating the importance of the issues.

With respect to the first claim, that the subject matter of the EAW ought to have been regulated by means of a convention and not a framework decision, as the latter may be adopted only for the purpose of the approximation of the laws and regulations of the Member States pursuant to Article 34(2)(b) of the EU Treaty, the Court of Justice ruled that it is within the discretion of the Council to choose the legal instrument it deems appropriate, as long as the conditions governing the adoption of such a measure are satisfied. The conditions in this case were fulfilled, according to the Court, since implementing the principle of mutual recognition of arrest warrants requires the approximation of the laws and regulations of the Member States, in particular the rules relating to the conditions, procedures and effects of surrender.[26]

The second question concerned the fundamental rights implications of the partial renunciation of the double criminality requirement in Article 2(2) of the Framework Decision, which contains a list of 32 offences, if those offences are punishable in the issuing Member State by a custodial sentence or a detention order for a maximum period of at least three years. Traditionally, double criminality requires that the acts for which an extradition is requested constitute a criminal offence in the criminal laws of both the issuing and the executing states. Article 2(2), however, removes the possibility of examining double criminality for those 32 non-defined categories of offences. Advocaten voor de Wereld challenged this provision, arguing that it breaches Article 6(2) of the EU Treaty and, more specifically, the principle of legality in criminal proceedings guaranteed by that provision and the principle of equality and non-discrimination. The CJEU ruled that the principle of legality was not infringed, as the challenged provision does not seek to harmonise the criminal offences in question. Instead, the definitions of the offences and penalties continue to be matters determined by the law of the issuing Member State and, as such, it is the responsibility of that state to ensure compliance with the principle of legality.[27] The Court also rejected the claim concerning the infringement of the principles of equality and non-discrimination. It found that the distinction between the 32 categories and the other offences is objectively justified, because the listed offences are serious enough, in terms of adversely affecting public order and public safety, to justify dispensing with the verification of double criminality. Based on this assessment, the Court ruled that there are no grounds capable of affecting the validity of the EAW Framework Decision.

While the first part of the judgment concerning the procedural matter of the correct legal basis is more elaborate and contains an extensive analysis of the relevant provisions of the Treaty, the second part, which deals with the more critical

[26] ibid para 29.
[27] ibid paras 52–53.

question of fundamental rights objections and mutual trust, is rather limited. The Court did not engage properly with the arguments of the plaintiff, and it provided weak arguments in order to resolve – or, in fact, avoid – some difficult human rights issues.[28] The Belgian Constitutional Court has also been criticised in the context of this decision for providing very little or no guidance to the CJEU regarding the interpretation of the fundamental rights implicated in the case.[29] If national courts truly are EU courts as well, they should – especially supreme or constitutional courts – get more involved in explaining their views as regards the interpretation of EU law.

IV. The Fundamental Rights/Mutual Trust Nexus

In the years following the *Advocaten voor de Wereld* case, which was an abstract review of the Framework Decision, concrete cases of alleged fundamental rights violations in the context of the EAW had emerged in the Member States and subsequently in Luxembourg. This section examines cases in which the infringement of fundamental rights either occurred in the process prior to the issue of the EAW, or when it might occur after the warrant had been executed. Determining the relevance of a past or future breach of fundamental rights perpetrated by the authorities of the issuing Member State can be very difficult in practice and problematic from an EU law perspective.

The *Radu*, *Melloni* and *Aranyosi and Căldăraru* cases invited the CJEU to take a stance on, inter alia, the tension between the effectiveness of the EAW mechanism and respect for fundamental rights. All three instances dealt in essence with the same question: can the executing judicial authority refuse to execute an EAW if the execution would lead to infringements of the requested person's fundamental rights? However, *Radu* and *Melloni* concerned a challenge to the EAW based on an alleged breach of the right to a fair trial; *Aranyosi and Căldăraru* concerned the absolute prohibition of inhuman and degrading treatment. Additionally, *Melloni* is different from the other two cases because it also addresses the issue of the conflicting levels of human rights' protection. The Court's approach differs in all cases.

[28] F Geyer, 'European arrest warrant: Court of Justice of the European Communities: judgment of 3rd May 2007, case C-303/05, *Advocaten voor de Wereld VZW v Leden van de Ministerraad*' (2008) 4 *European Constitutional Law Review* 149. For further criticism of the Court's approach, see D Sarmiento, 'European Union: the European arrest warrant and the quest for constitutional coherence' (2008) 6 *International Journal of Constitutional Law* 171; A Albi, 'From the banana saga to a sugar saga and beyond: could the post-communist Constitutional Courts teach the EU a lesson in the rule of law?' (2010) 47 *CML Rev* 791.

[29] E Cloots, 'Germs of Pluralist Judicial Adjudication: Advocaten voor de Wereld and Other References from the Belgian Constitutional Court' (2010) 47 *CML Rev* 645, 652.

A. *Radu*

In *Radu*,[30] the CJEU was asked, inter alia, to clarify whether the executing judicial authority can refuse to execute the EAW if the execution would lead to infringements of the requested person's fundamental rights, as protected in the Charter of Fundamental Rights and in the ECHR. The question was raised in proceedings brought by Radu, a Romanian national, before a Romanian court against a German EAW seeking his surrender on charges of aggravated burglary. The defendant claimed that the Romanian court should refuse to execute the warrant, since the issuing state had breached his right to a fair trial. Despite the Romanian court's long list of questions in the request for a preliminary ruling, the CJEU's response was rather short and thinly reasoned. The CJEU's Grand Chamber reformulated the questions posed by the Romanian court and limited its decision to answering whether issuing an EAW obliges Member State authorities to give the suspect the opportunity to be heard. The response did not amount to much more than a clear 'no'. It was held that such an obligation 'would inevitably lead to the failure of the very system of surrender provided for by Framework Decision 2002/584 and, consequently, prevent the achievement of the area of freedom, security and justice' and that 'the European legislature has ensured that the right to be heard will be observed in the executing Member State in such a way as not to compromise the effectiveness of the European arrest warrant system'.[31] Accordingly, the executing judicial authorities cannot refuse to execute an EAW on the ground that the requested person was not heard in the issuing Member State before that arrest warrant was issued. The Court, however, failed to clarify, as a matter of principle, whether a court executing an EAW must do so having regard to the person's Charter and ECHR rights – which surely would have been helpful – and whether it may consider matters in the issuing state, past or future, when deciding whether those rights are respected. What it seems to suggest is that regard must be had to the system as a whole and, essentially, that it would be sufficient if rights are protected by one state. The Court also failed to address the general tension between the principle of mutual trust and fundamental rights.[32] Once again, the Court placed great emphasis on the efficiency of the EAW but did not consider Article 1(3) of the Framework Decision, which specifically provides that it is not to have the effect of modifying the obligation to respect fundamental rights.[33]

Contrary to the Court, Advocate General Sharpston had argued that, although silent on the point, the Framework Decision must be interpreted as subject to

[30] *Radu* (n14).

[31] ibid para 41.

[32] On the general tension between fundamental rights and the EAW (or more broadly the mutual trust principle), see Meijers Committee, *The Principle of Mutual Trust in European Asylum, Immigration and Criminal Law: Reconciling Trust and Fundamental Rights* (2011).

[33] 'This Framework Decision shall not have the effect of modifying the obligation to respect fundamental rights and fundamental legal principles as enshrined in Article 6 of the Treaty on European Union.'

the provisions of both the ECHR and the EU Charter as a *matter of EU law*, and thus that under primary EU law a Member State executing an EAW can refuse the request for surrender where it is shown that the human rights of the person whose surrender is requested have been infringed, or will be infringed, as part of or following the surrender process.[34] The key difference in the reasoning lies in the reference to and interpretation of Article 1(3) of the Framework Decision as well as Recitals 10, 12, 13, and 14, which the Advocate General carried out extensively, concluding that 'to interpret Article 1(3) otherwise would risk its having no meaning – otherwise, possibly, than as an elegant platitude'.[35] Moreover, she referred to Advocate General Cruz Villalón's Opinion in *IB*,[36] where he concluded that although mutual recognition is an instrument for strengthening the Area of Freedom Security and Justice (AFSJ), the protection of fundamental rights and freedoms is a necessary precondition that gives legitimacy to the very existence and development of this area.[37]

B. *Melloni*

Mr Melloni was arrested and charged with bankruptcy fraud in 1996 in Italy but, having made bail, he fled to Spain. In 2003, the Italian court handed down an *in absentia* ruling, sentencing Mr Melloni to 10 years' imprisonment for bankruptcy fraud. Subsequently, the Italian authorities issued an EAW for his surrender. After the Spanish police arrested him, the competent court (*Audiencia Nacional*) ordered his surrender to the Italian authorities. However, the defendant filed a constitutional complaint before the Spanish *Tribunal constitucional* (Constitutional Court), claiming that his right to a fair trial had been violated. Mr Melloni argued that the absolute requirements deriving from the right to a fair trial, stated in Article 24(2) of the Spanish Constitution, had been indirectly violated, since Italian procedural law made it impossible for him to appeal against sentences imposed *in absentia*. Additionally, such a violation disregarded the very essence of a fair trial and undermined human dignity by allowing surrender to countries that allowed convictions made *in absentia* without the possibility to appeal. Finally, the defendant argued that the EAW should only be executed if the Italian authorities could guarantee the possibility of appealing against the judgment. Confronted with these facts, the Spanish Constitutional Court was aware that, if it were to uphold its well-established case law on the right to a fair trial regarding persons convicted *in absentia*,[38] it would be in conflict with Article 4a(1) of the Framework Decision as amended in 2009, so it decided to send the request for a preliminary ruling.

[34] Opinion of AG Sharpston in Case C-396/11 *Radu*, ECLI:EU:C:2012:648.
[35] ibid para 70.
[36] Opinion of AG Cruz Villalón in Case C-306/09 *IB*, ECLI:EU:C:2010:404.
[37] Opinion of AG Sharpston in *Radu* (n 34) para 71.
[38] See, eg, Spanish Constitutional Court, STC 91/2000 (30 March 2010).

In its first ever request for preliminary ruling to the CJEU, the Spanish *Tribunal constitucional* asked whether the revised EAW Framework Decision precluded Member States from making the execution of an EAW conditional upon the conviction in question being open to review, in order to guarantee the rights of defence of the person requested under the warrant and, if so, whether such a prohibition was compatible with the right to an effective judicial remedy and to a fair trial (Article 47 of the Charter) and the rights of defence (Article 48(2) of the Charter). The third question, which drew most attention, concerned the interpretation of Article 53 of the Charter and the case of 'a higher national level of protection'.

With respect to the first question, the Court maintained the same reasoning as in the *Radu* decision, which was rendered only a few weeks earlier. Once again, the Court regarded the grounds for a refusal to execute an EAW listed in the Framework Decision to be exhaustive. With respect to the second question – whether the Framework Decision was compatible with the Charter – the Court held that the right of an accused to be present at his or her trial was not absolute and that he or she might waive that right of his or her own free will, either expressly or tacitly, provided that the waiver was established in an unequivocal manner, was attended by minimum safeguards commensurate to its importance and did not run counter to any important public interest. In particular, a violation of the right to a fair trial had not been established, even where the accused did not appear in person, if he or she was informed of the date and place of the trial or was defended by a legal counsellor to whom he or she had given a mandate to do so. At the end of the analysis the Court added that 'this interpretation of Articles 47 and 48(2) of the Charter is in keeping with the scope that has been recognised for the rights guaranteed by Article 6(1) and (3) of the ECHR by the case-law of the European Court of Human Rights'.[39] The statement that the interpretation of the Charter is consistent with Article 6 ECHR and the case law of the ECtHR is rather blunt and contains no further explanation. While it is to be commended that the CJEU aims to ensure consistency with the ECHR when interpreting the Charter rights, the way in which it does so in some cases is inadequate. The Court only mentions it at the end of the analysis, in order to support a conclusion already arrived at independently. There is no assessment of the Strasbourg case law that would substantiate this claim, which in turn may create a perception that there are in fact inconsistencies and which, in any case, precludes constructive dialogue.[40] This is in stark contrast to the Opinion of Advocate General Bot, who made an extensive analysis of the Strasbourg case

[39] Case C-399/11 *Melloni*, ECLI:EU:C:2013:107, para 50.

[40] On inconsistencies in the case law of the two European Courts and the position of national courts, see M Claes and Š Imamović, 'National Courts in the New European Fundamental Rights Architecture' in V Kosta, N Skoutaris and V Tzevelekos (eds), *The EU Accession to the ECHR* (Oxford, Hart Publishing, 2013); M Claes and Š Imamović 'Caught in the middle or leading the way? National courts in the new European fundamental rights landscape' (2013) 4 *European Journal of Human Rights* 627.

law and ultimately concluded that the interpretation of the relevant Charter provisions is consistent with the ECHR and the ECtHR case law.[41]

In its third point of examination, concerning Article 53 of the Charter, the Court emphasised that a Member State cannot make use of Article 53 to refuse the surrender of a person for the reason that the standard of protection of the right to a fair trial in its national constitution is higher than the one established in the national legislation of the issuing Member State. According to the Court, the possibility of invoking Article 53 in order to refuse the execution of an EAW would undermine 'the principle of primacy of EU law' and 'the principles of mutual trust and recognition' guaranteed by the uniform level of fundamental rights protection defined in the Framework Decision.[42] The Court thus rejected the view that Article 53 can be read as a general authorisation to apply the higher national constitutional standard of protection and that rules of national law, even of a constitutional order, must not undermine the primacy and effectiveness of EU law on the territory of that state. While this approach is perfectly in line with EU law and the CJEU's traditional approach to the construction of the EU legal order, in practical terms and from a national law perspective, *Melloni* is very problematic, as it results in two different levels of protection in the Member States depending on whether EU law applies or not. This again puts national courts in a rather difficult position, as they may be required to lower the level of constitutional protection they would otherwise be able to provide, and thus jeopardise the uniform application of the Constitution domestically.[43] If the CJEU expects national courts to accept this, it needs to build its authority further. This authority cannot only be formal; it requires substantive reasoning and a reasoned discussion. It is regrettable, with regard to the position of the Spanish Constitutional Court, that the CJEU did not show awareness of the problem with which the referring court found itself confronted.

The Spanish Constitutional Court did not accept the absolute constitutional primacy of EU law, but it managed to avoid a conflict with the CJEU by lowering its autonomous fundamental rights standard – to the detriment of human rights.[44]

C. A 'New Balance' between Mutual Trust and Fundamental Rights – Joined Cases of *Aranyosi and Căldăraru*

The joined cases of *Aranyosi* and *Căldăraru*[45] provided a new possibility for the Court of Justice to develop its position on the limits to mutual trust and the

[41] Opinion of Advocate General Bot in Case C-399/11 *Melloni* EU:C:2013:107, paras 74–84.

[42] *Melloni* (n 39), paras 58 and 63.

[43] Admittedly, application of Art 53 of the Charter does not always result in the lowering of constitutional standards. For instance, in Case C-168/13 PPU *Jeremy F*, ECLI:EU:C:2013:358, a higher level of constitutional protection was accommodated since there was a margin of discretion for the Member States and, importantly, providing the higher level of protection did not undermine the effectiveness of the Framework Decision on the EAW.

[44] L Besselink, 'The parameters of constitutional conflict after Melloni' (2014) 39 *EL Rev* 531.

[45] *Aranyosi and Căldăraru* (n 3).

relationship between the EAW mechanism and fundamental rights. Mr Aranyosi, a Hungarian national accused of committing burglary, was arrested in Germany on an EAW issued by Hungary. Mr Aranyosi resisted the surrender, referring to reports from the Committee on the Prevention of Torture and the case law from the ECtHR, which documented massive over-crowding in Hungarian prisons to an extent that could be considered a violation of Article 3 ECHR (which corresponds to Article 4 of the EU Charter of Fundamental Rights).

Mr Căldăraru was arrested in Germany on a Romanian EAW, after he was convicted *in absentia* to eight months in prison by a court in Romania for driving without a driver's licence. The defendant resisted the surrender, arguing that he would be subjected to inhuman and degrading treatment due to the awful detention conditions in the Romanian prisons. He too relied on the case law of the Strasbourg Court in order to support his claim. Indeed, the ECtHR found that both Romania and Hungary had infringed Convention rights due to the poor detention conditions.[46] Since Căldăraru was detained in Germany from the moment of his arrest, his case was dealt with under the urgent preliminary ruling procedure provided for in the Court's Rules of Procedure. Nevertheless, the Court decided to join the two cases, as they concerned essentially the same issue and were submitted by the same *Hanseatisches Oberlandesgericht* in Bremen, Germany.

The key issue for the CJEU was thus to determine and clarify whether the responsible executing authority can refuse the execution of an EAW on the ground that Article 4 of the Charter may be violated and, if so, under which conditions. In its judgment from 5 April 2016, the CJEU started off in a similar fashion, as in the cases discussed earlier, stating that the EAW system is based on the principle of mutual recognition, which itself is founded on the mutual trust between the Member States that their national legal systems are capable of providing equivalent and effective protection of the fundamental rights recognised at the EU level, and particularly in the Charter. Further, with reference to Opinion 2/13,[47] the Court stated that both the principle of mutual trust between the Member States and the principle of mutual recognition are of fundamental importance in EU law, given that they allow an area without internal borders to be created and maintained. More specifically, the principle of mutual trust requires each of those States, save in exceptional circumstances, to consider all the other Member States to be complying with EU law, and particularly with the fundamental rights recognised by EU law.[48] The Court then, rather unexpectedly, continued its assessment by referring to Recital 10 and Article 1(3) of the Framework Decision, which provide, respectively,

[46] *Varga and Others v Hungary* App nos 14097/12, 45135/12, 73712/12, 34001/13, 44055/13 and 64586/13 (ECtHR, 10 March 2015); *Oprea and Others v Romania* App nos 54966/09, 57682/10, 20499/11, 41587/11, 27583/12, 75692/12, 76944/12, 77474/12, 9985/13, 16490/13, 29530/13, 37810/13, 40759/13, 55842/13, 56837/13, 62797/13, 64858/13, 65996/13, 66101/13 and 15822/14 (ECtHR, 18 June 2015).

[47] Opinion 2/13 *Accession of the European Union to the European Convention for the Protection of Human Rights and Fundamental Freedoms*, ECLI:EU:C:2014:48.

[48] ibid paras 77–78.

that the implementation of the mechanism of the EAW, as such, may be suspended in the event of a serious and persistent breach of the principles referred to in Article 2 TEU and that the Framework Decision is not to have the effect of modifying the obligation to respect fundamental rights.[49] Furthermore, the Court focused specifically on Article 4 of the Charter, stating that when the authority responsible for the execution of a warrant has in its possession evidence of a real risk of inhuman or degrading treatment of persons detained in the Member State where the warrant was issued, it must assess that risk before deciding on the surrender of the individual concerned. In essence, the Court established a two-step procedure for the national courts, as executing judicial authorities, to follow before declining to execute an EAW. First, the authority must make a finding of general or systemic deficiencies in the protection provided in the issuing state and, second, it must conduct further assessment, specific and precise, of whether there are substantial grounds to believe that the individual concerned will be exposed to inhuman and degrading treatment. The first procedural step requires 'objective, reliable, specific and properly updated' information and evidence.[50] If the judicial authority considers that there is a real risk of inhuman or degrading treatment at the systemic or general level, it moves to the second step which is the individual test. In line with the requirements of the second step, the authority responsible for the execution of the warrant must ask the issuing authority to provide, as a matter of urgency, all the necessary information concerning the conditions of detention, which the issuing judicial authority is obliged to provide. If, in light of the information provided or any other information available to it, the authority in the executing state finds that there is, for the individual who is the subject of the warrant, a real risk of inhuman or degrading treatment, the execution of the warrant must be deferred until additional information is obtained on the basis of which that risk can be discounted. If the existence of that risk cannot be discounted within a reasonable period of time, that authority must decide whether the surrender procedure should be brought to an end.[51]

The CJEU did not follow the Opinion of Advocate General Bot, who concluded that EU law, and in particular the Framework Decision on the EAW, provided no basis for Germany to refuse to execute the arrest warrants. Instead, the Advocate General assigned the responsibility for ensuring that human rights were sufficiently protected to the Hungarian and Romanian authorities – they should be the ones to consider whether or not an EAW should be issued in the first place. In cases in which the warrants had already been issued, the issuing countries (ie Hungary and Romania), and not the executing state, should then undertake all the necessary measures to guarantee the protection of fundamental rights in the individual case. It can be said that the Advocate General's assessment of the case is not surprising, as it is more in line with the Court's earlier case law.

[49] ibid paras 81–84.
[50] ibid paras 91–94.
[51] ibid paras 95–104.

Advocate General Bot raised one interesting point worth noting. It concerns the comparability of the EAW Framework Decision with the Dublin Regulation,[52] and the extent to which the *NS* rationale could be extended to the EAW cases. The comparison relates to the fact that, in Dublin cases, the Court held that the Member States, including the national courts, may not transfer an asylum seeker to the 'Member State responsible' within the meaning of Regulation No 343/2003 where they are aware, from the instruments available to them, that systemic deficiencies in the asylum procedure and in the reception conditions of asylum seekers in that Member State are likely to expose the asylum seeker to inhuman or degrading treatment within the meaning of Article 4 of the Charter. The Advocate General argued that despite the resemblance between the cases, the principle established in the *NS* case is not applicable by analogy to the interpretation of the provisions of the Framework Decision on the EAW, as there are important determining differences between the two instruments. After pointing out some of the obvious differences,[53] the Advocate General explained that the transposition of the principle established in the *NS* case to EAW cases would lead to a situation in which the executing judicial authorities could no longer surrender the requested person for the purposes of prosecution, but they would also not have, as a general rule, jurisdiction to prosecute that person in place of the issuing State. Consequently, there would be a clear and obvious risk in such cases that the offence would remain unpunished and that the offender would reoffend, thus infringing the rights and freedoms of the other citizens of the Union.[54] The CJEU, on the other hand, did not comment on the parallel between the Dublin cases and the EAW. Moreover, while the Advocate General extensively discussed the relevant case law of the ECtHR on extradition of persons, the Court's judgment contained no such analysis or reference to that case law. Evidently, though, the Court was aware of it.

One additional and important difference between the two instruments that was not explicitly mentioned by the Advocate General concerns the discretion that is left to the States in the application of the two instruments. In the Dublin transfer cases, Member States have the discretion to decide whether or not they will transfer the asylum seeker to the responsible Member State; while in the context of the EAW, the surrender is compulsory unless one of the exceptions based on the CJEU's case law would apply. This is an important point from the perspective of the ECHR, where the Strasbourg Court continues to apply the presumption of equivalent protection in cases where Member States do not have discretion. In other words, the ECtHR is more likely to apply the presumption of equivalent protection when the execution of an EAW is challenged, as opposed to a case where the alleged violation concerns a Dublin transfer. Notwithstanding the arguments proposed by the Advocate General and the fact that Member State authorities

[52] For the discussion of the Dublin Regulation and the referenced case law see ch 3.

[53] Opinion of AG Bot in Cases C-404/15 and C-659/15 PPU *Aranyosi and Căldăraru*, ECLI:EU:C:2016:140, paras 45–53.

[54] ibid paras 54–60.

may be exempted from responsibility in Strasbourg in the application of the EAW, national courts should not dispose of the obligation to comply with fundamental rights.[55] If it applies to the Dublin Regulation, it must also apply in the context of the EAW Framework Decision and other instruments of EU law. After all, the presumption of fundamental rights compliance between the EU Member States that exists in ECHR law is not absolute and can be rebutted.[56]

V. The Aftermath of *Aranyosi and Căldăraru*

There are many questions and implications arising from the decision of the Court in *Aranyosi and Căldăraru*. In *ML*,[57] the referring court raised questions relating to the extent of the assessment that is required to rule out the existence of a real risk of inhuman and degrading treatment. The case concerned the legality of the surrender from the point of view of detention conditions in Hungarian prisons. The CJEU held that the executing judicial authority cannot rule out the existence of a real risk merely because of the existence of a (new) legal remedy permitting the person to challenge the conditions of his or her detention. However, the existence of such a remedy may be taken into account when deciding on the surrender of the person concerned. Furthermore, the Court specified that the executing judicial authority is required to assess only the conditions of detention in the prisons in which, according to the information available to it, it is likely that that person will be detained, including on a temporary or transitional basis. To that end, the executing judicial authority must assess solely the actual and precise conditions of detention of the person concerned that are relevant for determining whether that person will be exposed to a real risk of inhuman or degrading treatment within the meaning of Article 4 of the Charter. Finally, regarding the assurances provided by authorities of the issuing Member State other than the judicial authority, that the individual concerned will not be subject to inhuman or degrading treatment, the CJEU found that the executing judicial authority may take that information into account.

In *Dorobantu*,[58] the CJEU Grand Chamber clarified further the conditions under which the surrender of a person sought by an EAW can be refused because standards of detention in the issuing State could be regarded contrary to Article 4 of the Charter of Fundamental Rights. It ruled that executing judicial authorities must take account of all the relevant physical aspects of the conditions of

[55] A Torres Pérez, 'A predicament for domestic courts: caught between the European Arrest Warrant and fundamental rights' in B De Witte et al (eds), *National Court and EU Law: New Issues, Theories and Methods* (Cheltenham, Edward Elgar, 2016) 191, 210.

[56] This is indeed what happened in the recent case concerning EAW *Bivolaru and Moldovan v France* App nos 40324/16 and 12623/17 (ECtHR, 25 March 2021) where the presumption was rebutted for the first time since it was introduced in the case law in 2005.

[57] Case C-220/18 PPU *Generalstaatsanwaltschaft*, ECLI:EU:C:2018:589.

[58] Case C-128/18 *Dorobantu*, ECLI:EU:C:2019:857.

detention in the prison in which the person concerned will be detained, such as the personal space available to each detainee, sanitary conditions and the extent of the detainee's freedom of movement within the prison, and that such an assessment is not limited to the review of obvious inadequacies. For the purposes of that assessment, the executing judicial authority must request from the issuing judicial authority the information that it deems necessary and must rely, in principle, on the assurances given by the issuing judicial authority, in the absence of any specific indications that the conditions of detention infringe Article 4 of the Charter of Fundamental Rights. In particular, with regard to the personal space of each detainee and how to calculate it, the Court of Justice held that the executing judicial authorities must take account of the minimum requirements set by the ECtHR when interpreting Article 3 ECHR. The CJEU specified that it must (at least) be possible for the detainee to move around normally within the cell. It also specifically referred to the Strasbourg case law in which the ECtHR indicated that 'a strong presumption of a violation of Article 3 of the ECHR arises when the personal space available to a detainee is below $3m^2$ in multi-occupancy accommodation'.[59] At the same time, however, there are still judgments in which the CJEU adopts a restrictive approach to derogations from the application of mutual trust and recognition. In *Piotrowski*,[60] for example, the referring court inquired about the scope of the examination as to the ground for refusal in Article 3(3) of the EAW Framework Decision under Article 24(2) of the Charter concerning minors. The CJEU held that the executing judicial authority must only verify whether the individual concerned has reached the minimum age required to be regarded as criminally responsible in the executing State for the acts on which the warrant is based, and cannot consider whether additional conditions relating to an assessment of the circumstances of the minor in the case, to which the prosecution and conviction are specifically subject under the law of that Member State, have been met. The CJEU pointed out that the observance of fundamental rights and the rights of children falls primarily within the responsibility of the issuing Member State, which must be presumed to be complying with EU law in line with the principle of mutual recognition and mutual trust between the Member States.[61]

The ECtHR, on the other hand, requires an assessment of individual circumstances in the context of all mutual recognition instruments every time national courts are presented with a serious and substantiated complaint that there is a manifest deficiency in the protection of a right guaranteed by the Convention, which cannot be waived on the sole ground that they are applying EU law. This requirement was set out in *Avotiņš*[62] and confirmed most recently in *Bivolaru and*

[59] *Muršić v Croatia* App no 7334/13 (ECtHR, 20 October 2016) para 76.
[60] Case C-367/16 *Piotrowski*, ECLI:EU:C:2018:27.
[61] ibid paras 49–50.
[62] *Avotiņš v Latvia* App no 17502/07 (ECtHR, 23 May 2016) para 116. The Court held that if a serious and substantiated complaint is raised before national courts to the effect that the protection of a Convention right has been manifestly deficient, and this situation cannot be remedied by EU law, national courts cannot refrain from examining that complaint on the sole ground that they are applying

Moldovan v France.[63] The latter case, which concerned surrender of the applicants from France to Romania in the application of the EAW, is highly interesting for at least two reasons. First, it is the very first case in which the ECtHR had rebutted the presumption of equivalent protection since it was introduced in the case law in 2005.[64] The Court found a violation of Article 3 ECHR in respect of one of the applicants (Mr Moldovan) on the ground that the French courts had transferred the applicant notwithstanding the fact that there had been sufficient factual basis to establish a real risk that the applicant would be exposed to inhuman and degrading treatment as a result of detention conditions in the Gherla prison in Romania, and hence to refuse execution of the EAW in question. In other words, the French courts had failed correctly to assess the individual risk incurred by Mr Moldovan.[65] This finding of the Strasbourg Court is remarkable in terms of architecture of fundamental rights in Europe as it shows that the ECtHR is effectively checking whether national courts are applying EU law correctly and, by extension, what the correct application of EU law would be.[66] It is all the more remarkable because of a possible alternative scenario: the ECtHR could have ruled that that the presumption does not apply because the national judge failed to correctly apply EU law and assessed the case under the standards generally applied in Strasbourg. It would have still found a violation of Article 3 ECHR, but it would not have gone as far as to rebut the presumption and find a flagrant breach of the Convention in the application of EU law. While this approach in Strasbourg could be perceived as problematic from the perspective of EU law, it can also be seen as a positive development as it puts an additional check on whether national courts apply EU law correctly and in line with the ECHR. It is a check that does not exist in EU law.

Secondly, the Strasbourg Court noted that there is convergence between its own case law and the case law of the CJEU as regards the assessment of the individual risks of ill-treatment to which persons can be exposed as a consequence of the execution of an EAW.[67] While the ECtHR focused on the convergence with regard to the individual assessment what was left on the table, and what is problematic from the perspective of national courts, is the difference concerning the first step: while the CJEU insists on the first step to be performed, whereby executing authority is required to establish systemic or generalised deficiencies in the issuing State before moving to the individual assessment, the ECtHR focuses solely

EU law, and hence cannot rely on the Bosphorus presumption in those cases. See also J Callewaert, 'Do we still need Article 6(2) TEU? Consideration on the absence of EU accession to the ECHR and its consequences' (2018) 55 *CML Rev* 1685.

[63] *Bivolaru and Moldovan v France* (n 56) para 100.

[64] *Bosphorus v Ireland*, App no 45036/98 (ECtHR, 30 June 2005).

[65] ibid paras 121–126. Interestingly, in the case of the other applicant, Mr Bivolaru, the ECtHR found the presumption not to be applicable and it concluded that there was no violation of the ECHR because in his case EU law was correctly applied.

[66] This is exactly one of the reasons why the CJEU rejected the accession agreement in Opinion 2/13. For analysis see ch 2, section IV.B.

[67] *Bivolaru and Moldovan v France* (n 56) para 114.

on the individual risk incurred by the person. In other words, national judges are required under ECHR law to assess cases in which applicants allege individual risk, even if there is no systemic deficiency in the relevant state; under EU law, they should not engage with such allegations because of mutual trust.[68] These are arguably two very different messages to national courts in terms of their obligations under EU and ECHR law, which could ultimately generate different outcomes and levels of protection. In a hypothetical scenario, where a case originates from a country where there are no systemic or generalised deficiencies but where the individual circumstances provide a sufficient basis to conclude that there is a real risk of human rights violations, the result would be that an extradition cannot be postponed or refused on the basis of the CJEU's test (because the first condition is not fulfilled), while it must be refused on the basis of ECHR law (if the second condition – which is also the only condition from the perspective of the ECHR – is indeed fulfilled). In fact, these would be situations in which national courts would possibly not even reach the individual assessment stage because systemic deficiency could not be established. This, in turn, could lead to different levels of protection under EU and ECHR law and possibly also to conflicting treaty obligations for the national courts. Admittedly, the chances of such a scenario arising are quite limited, given the fact that the two stages of the procedure will often coincide, since proving individual risk will likely also involve showing some general or systemic issues (as was the case for Mr Moldovan), but they cannot be excluded. It is to be hoped that as the case law develops on these aspects the CJEU will draw parallel with Dublin case law on Article 3 ECHR/Article 4 of the Charter and allow for derogations from mutual trust on fundamental rights grounds also in cases where no systemic deficiencies can be established.

VI. The EAW and Independence of the Judiciary

The case law analysis so far has mainly focused on the prohibition of torture and inhuman and degrading treatment, as protected in Article 4 of the Charter and Article 3 ECHR. In *LM*,[69] the CJEU was faced with a different legal challenge: the consequences of restrictions imposed upon judicial independence in one Member State for other Member States of the Union. The case concerned an arrest warrant issued by the Polish authorities concerning surrender of a Polish national residing in Ireland. The High Court in Dublin decided to seek guidance from the CJEU about the course of action that would be needed in light of the reasoned proposal

[68] There are very few comments published on the judgment at the time of writing. See eg J Callewaert, 'Manifest deficiency in the execution of a European arrest warrant – judgment of the European Court of Human Rights in the case *Bivolaru and Moldovan v. France*', available at https://johan-callewaert.eu/manifest-deficiency-in-the-execution-of-a-european-arrest-warrant-judgment-of-the-european-court-of-human-rights-in-the-case-of-bivolaru-and-moldovan-v-france/ (last accessed 31 May 2021).

[69] *LM* (n 3).

of the European Commission issued in 2017 pursuant to Article 7(1) TEU, in which it had found that there was a clear risk of a serious breach by Poland of the rule of law principle.[70]

The central issue was thus whether LM, a suspected drug trafficker, should be surrendered from Ireland to Poland when the executing judicial authority had serious doubts as to whether the suspect would receive a fair trial in the issuing State, due to the lack of independence of the judiciary resulting from the legislative changes to the Polish judicial system that challenge the system as a whole.[71] In that respect the Irish court inquired whether and to what extent the joined cases of *Aranyosi and Căldăraru*, which carved out exceptions for surrender on fundamental rights grounds, could be followed in the context of a possible violation of the right to a fair trial. Specifically, the Irish judge asked if following the first step of *Aranyosi* would be sufficient in this case, given the evidence that the conditions in the issuing Member State were incompatible with the fundamental right to a fair trial. If the answer to that question was in the negative, the judge wondered whether it was mandatory, in the context of the second step, to revert to the issuing judicial authority for any further necessary information, and what kind of guarantees would be required to enable the executing authority to discount the existence of the risk to an unfair trial.

There are different ways in which the CJEU could have responded.[72] First, it could have refrained from assessing the impact of the restrictions of judicial independence on the EAW mechanism, following Poland's argument that the issue was hypothetical and that in any event only the European Council was empowered to do so, on the basis of Article 7 TEU. Second, it could have ruled that the first step of *Aranyosi* test would indeed suffice in this case and that cooperation with a Member State that breaches the obligation to ensure the independence of its courts should be suspended altogether. While the former is rather unlikely, the latter scenario seems plausible, given the fact that effective judicial protection before an independent and impartial court is a core element of the rule of law and an obligation stemming from EU law, as held in a number of seminal cases on judicial independence in Poland.[73] At the same time, however, taking this road

[70] COM(2017) 0835, 20 December 2017. It should be noted that the wider topic of the rule of law crisis in the EU is outside of the scope of this book. The discussion in this section is limited to the aspects of the CJEU's *LM* judgment that relate to its compatibility with the ECHR and the perspective of national courts in that regard. For discussion on the rule of law in the EU more broadly see, among many, C Closa and D Kochenov (eds), *Reinforcing Rule of Law Oversight in the European Union* (Cambridge, Cambridge University Press, 2016).

[71] See eg European Commission for Democracy through Law (Venice Commission), Opinion on the amendments to the Act of 25 June 2015 on the Constitutional Tribunal of Poland, CDL-AD(2016)001, 11 March 2016.

[72] See also A Frąckowiak-Adamska, 'Mutual trust and independence of the judiciary after the CJEU judgment in LM – new era or business as usual?' EU Law Analysis 15 August 2018, available at http://eulawanalysis.blogspot.com/2018/08/mutual-trust-and-independence-of.html (last accessed 16 December 2020).

[73] Joined Cases C-585/18, C-624/18 and C-625/18 *AK (Independence of the Disciplinary Chamber of the Supreme Court)*, ECLI:EU:C:2019:982; Case C-64/16 *Associação Sindical dos Juízes Portugueses*, ECLI:EU:C:2018:117.

would have meant that the EAW was de facto suspended in relation to Poland, and it would have resulted in an immense risk of impunity for Polish offenders in the EU. The third option for the CJEU was to find a middle way: allowing an exception to mutual trust under certain specific conditions. This could have been done following *Aranyosi* approach, or by developing a different approach tailored to this specific situation.

The Luxembourg Court went with the third option, giving way to an exception to the mutual trust also in the context of the right to a fair trial. In doing so, the Court followed the two-pronged approach developed in *Aranyosi* in the context of Article 4 of the Charter. It ruled that a risk of a breach of the right to a fair trial as laid down in Article 47 of the Charter in the issuing Member State could indeed warrant the non-execution of an EAW, because the requirement of judicial independence forms part of the essence of the fundamental right to a fair trial, a right that is of cardinal importance in upholding EU values as recognised in Article 2 TEU.[74] However, the Court did not accept that the systemic deficiencies in Poland potentially affecting the independence of judiciary would suffice as a ground for not executing an EAW. Instead, the national court still has to determine, specifically and precisely, whether, having regard to the personal situation of the person concerned, as well as to the nature of the offence and the factual context, and in light of the information provided by the issuing Member State, there are substantial grounds for believing that the individual concerned will run the risk of a breach of the right to a fair trial if he or she is surrendered to that State. In other words, the executing authority must strictly follow the two stages of the test and establish both systemic deficiencies and individual risk. The Irish judge applied the two stages of the test and eventually decided to execute the warrant and surrender LM to Poland.

The position of the Court seems reasonable. Nevertheless, the practical hurdles imposed on both appellants in proving such violations and executing judicial authority accepting them in individual cases are problematic. First of all, it is much more difficult to perform the second step of *Aranyosi* in this context.[75] Indeed, the national courts are required to have regard to the personal situation of the individual concerned, the nature of the offence for which he or she is prosecuted and/or convicted, and the factual context in which the EAW was issued. They are thus asked to assess complex legal matters outside their own jurisdiction and in collaboration with the authorities whose independence may be questioned.[76] It is strange, to say the least, that national courts have to make enquiries of the courts in the issuing

[74] *LM*, (n 3) para 48.

[75] P Bárd and W van Ballegooij, 'The effect of CJEU case law concerning the rule of law and mutual trust on national systems' in V Mitsilegas, A di Martino and L Mancano (eds), *The Court of Justice and European Criminal Law: Leading Cases in a Contextual Analysis* (Oxford, Hart Publishing, 2019).

[76] Some commentators have argued that the individual test is not an adequate tool to ensure respect for the rule of law and that the Court should have fully suspended cooperation with Poland. See, eg, A Frąckowiak-Adamska, 'Drawing Red Lines with No (Significant) Bites: Why an Individual Test is Not Appropriate in the *LM* Case' in A von Bogdandy et al (eds), *Defending Checks and Balances in EU Member States: Taking Stock of Europe's Actions* (Berlin, Springer, 2021).

state regarding, essentially, their impartiality and independence in an individual case.[77] Nevertheless, the Luxembourg Court has since maintained the position that limitations to mutual trust may be possible but must be construed strictly, and that national courts are required to perform both stages of the procedure.[78]

The Strasbourg Court has not yet taken a position on whether the two-step procedure conforms to the requirements of Article 6 ECHR, and it remains to be seen whether the approaches of the two European Courts are compatible in this respect. One might immediately think of the landmark case of *Ástráðsson* on judicial independence,[79] where the Grand Chamber unanimously found a violation of Article 6(1) of the Convention on account of grave breaches in the appointment of a judge to the Icelandic Court of Appeal. The case concerned an allegation made by the appellant that the new Icelandic Court of Appeal, which had upheld his conviction for road traffic offences, was not 'a tribunal established by law' due to irregularities in the appointment of one of the judges who heard his case. Perhaps even more importantly, one could consider in this context the Chamber ruling in *Xero Flor w Polsce sp. z o.o. v Poland*, where it was held that the Polish Constitutional Court was not 'a tribunal established by law'.[80] However, as pointed out by ECtHR President Spano, writing extra-judicially, the factual context in these cases is different from the one that arises in the application of the EAW.[81] Indeed, EAW cases resemble more the *Soering* type of cases which are concerned with extraterritoriality. It is therefore more likely that the ECtHR would examine such a case in the extraterritorial EAW context, and hence apply the 'flagrant denial of justice' test. This test was first developed in *Soering v the United Kingdom*[82] and has been confirmed subsequently in several extradition cases decided in Strasbourg.[83] The term 'flagrant denial of justice' has been described as applying to a trial that is manifestly contrary to the principles embodied in Article 6 of the Convention. It allows a state to refuse extradition only *exceptionally*, when the individual concerned would face a violation of a right to a fair trial that amounts to 'a nullification or destruction of the very essence of that right'.[84]

[77] T Konstadinides, 'Judicial independence and the Rule of Law in the context of non-execution of a European Arrest Warrant: *LM*' (2019) 56 *CML Rev* 743.

[78] In Case C-510/19 *Openbaar Ministerie*, ECLI:EU:C:2020:953, the referring court explicitly asked if it is indeed necessary to also follow the second step in situations in which it is well documented that there are general and systemic deficiencies in the protection of fundamental rights in an EU Member State. The CJEU maintained its position and answered in the affirmative.

[79] *Guðmundur Andri Ástráðsson v Iceland* App no 26374/18 (ECtHR, 1 December 2020).

[80] *Xero Flor w Polsce sp. z o.o. v Poland* App no 4907/18 (ECtHR, 7 May 2021).

[81] R Spano, 'The rule of law as the lodestar of the European Convention on Human Rights: The Strasbourg Court and the independence of the judiciary' (2021) *European Law Journal* 1.

[82] The Court held that 'an issue might exceptionally be raised under Article 6 [of the ECHR] by an extradition decision in circumstances where the fugitive has suffered or risks suffering a flagrant denial of a fair trial': *Soering v United Kingdom* (n 17) para 113.

[83] See, eg, *Al Nashiri v Poland* App no 28761/11 (ECtHR, 24 July 2014); *Othman (Abu Qatada) v the United Kingdom* App no 8139/09 (ECtHR, 17 January 2012); *Pirozzi v Belgium* App no 21055/11 (ECtHR, 17 April 2018).

[84] *Al Nashiri v Poland* (n 84) para 563; *Othman (Abu Qatada) v the United Kingdom* (n 84) para 260.

Now, are the two tests, the CJEU's two-step test and the ECtHR's flagrant denial of justice test, the same or, at least, do they lead to the same result? Justice Donnelly in the *LM* case suggested indeed that the concepts of 'breach of the essence of the right', used by the CJEU, and that of 'flagrant denial of justice', elaborated by the ECtHR, are to be understood as 'one and the same'.[85] Advocate General Tanchev appears to have suggested the same in his Opinion.[86] It does indeed seem that the individual assessment part of the CJEU's two-stage examination corresponds to the ECtHR's 'flagrant denial of justice' test, because the latter also allows the obligation to transfer to be affected only in exceptional circumstances when the essence of the right is affected. However, it cannot be said with certainty that the thresholds are the same. This is due to the fact that the *LM* judgment does not make a reference to the flagrant denial of justice test and to the relevant case law of the ECtHR (other than when summarising the argument put forward by the referring court and the applicant). In chapter 2, I have criticised the fact that the CJEU does not refer to the ECHR and the relevant Strasbourg case law when needed or expected, for example in order to fully answer the national court's question.[87] This is precisely one of those cases where one would expect the Court of Justice to address the relationship with the Strasbourg case law, not least because Justice Donnelly explicitly referred to it in one of her questions. Moreover, one would hope, keeping in mind Article 52(3) of the Charter, that the threshold for finding a violation would be lower in EU law compared to the very stringent test in ECHR law. This is something Advocate General Sharpston had suggested already in *Radu*.[88] She found the flagrant denial of justice test to be 'unduly stringent' and suggested an alternative.[89]

On the other hand, similarly to the extradition case law in the context of Article 3 ECHR, the issue remains with respect to the first step of the test because existence of systemic or general deficiencies does not appear to be a pre-condition (ie the necessary first step) to finding that there is a breach in Strasbourg.[90] This approach reflects well the overall functioning of the Convention system: the Strasbourg Court approaches a case in the context of an individual application under Article 34 of the Convention, thus focusing directly on the particular circumstances of the individual concerned. It thus seems that the approach of the two European Courts diverges on this methodological aspect, not only in the context of Article 3 but also Article 6 of the Convention.

I do not see issues arising in the context of the individual test in relation to Article 6 because the Strasbourg Court applies a very high threshold in finding a violation, which indeed has happened only in a handful of very exceptional

[85] Irish High Court, *Minister for Justice and Equality v Artur Celmer (No 5)* [2018] IEHC 639, para 24.
[86] Opinion of AG Tanchev in Case C-216/18 PPU *LM* ECLI:EU:C:2018:517, paras 78–85.
[87] See ch 2, section IV.A.
[88] Opinion of AG Sharpston in *Radu* (n 34).
[89] ibid paras 83 and 97.
[90] See, eg, the ECtHR's assessment in *Pirozzi v Belgium* (n 83) paras 57–72.

circumstances.[91] It seems difficult to imagine how the threshold could be even higher.[92] Accordingly, if the CJEU were to diverge from the flagrant denial of justice test, it would likely be to lower the threshold in finding a breach of a right to a fair trial and hence offer a higher level of protection, which, as argued before, would not cause a conflict with the ECHR. The problem could arise, however, in the context of the first stage of the procedure, which, for the CJEU, is a necessary prerequisite for applying the individual test. As already suggested in the context of the previous discussion of Article 3 ECHR, the fact that the CJEU requires it could lead to a lowering of the protection because the burden of proof on the applicant is higher: for the CJEU, the applicant must provide evidence that there are systemic or generalised deficiencies as well as how he will be affected individually; for the ECtHR, only the individual circumstances are relevant. Conversely, the possibility for a national court to refuse a warrant because there are serious fundamental rights concerns in an individual case may be more limited when the two-step test is applied, because national courts must first determine the existence of systematic or generalised deficiencies based on objective and reliable evidence before moving on the individual assessment. It appears thus that the national judges are being asked to act differently: under EU law they are required to first check for systemic deficiency, which can then trigger individual assessment, and under the ECHR they are required to check whenever there are substantial reasons for believing that the person concerned will be exposed to human rights violations regardless of systemic deficiency. These are ultimately two different messages for the national courts concerning the approach they are supposed to take in EAW cases. The exact effects and consequences of these methodological differences in the approaches of the two European Courts, especially for the national courts, are in a need of urgent clarification.

VII. Execution of the EAW and Compliance with Fundamental Rights – in Search of Guidelines for National Courts

Finding a balance between mutual trust and fundamental rights in the context of the EAW appears an even more challenging task when compared to the asylum law cases, because fundamental rights concerns are now coupled with the rule of law concerns, as well as with limited discretion afforded to the Member States in the application of the Framework Decision. The dilemma for national judges, but

[91] AG Tanchev notes that there have been only four occasions on which an extradition or expulsion was found to be in breach of Art 6 ECHR. Three of these concerned suspected terrorists detained at Guantanamo Bay and one concerned the admission of evidence obtained by torture. See Opinion of AG Tanchev in *LM* (n 86) paras 83–85.

[92] Opinion of AG Sharpston in *Radu* (n 34) para 78.

also for prosecutors and defence attorneys working in EU cross-border criminal cases, is very real: how to comply with instruments of EU criminal law when the underlying principles of cooperation – mutual recognition and mutual trust – are no longer justified because other States are failing to protect fundamental rights and uphold the rule of law.

In the early EAW case law such as *Radu* and *Melloni*, the CJEU insisted on a strict reading of the EAW Framework Decision, denying the possibility of refusals to surrender on the grounds that were not expressly provided by the Decision itself. Even if one were to agree with the final outcome in these cases, the way in which the Court reached its conclusions is problematic.[93] The Court did not engage sufficiently with the (legitimate) fundamental rights concerns of the national courts, and the quest for the effectiveness and primacy of EU law is overwhelmingly present in the early cases. Nevertheless, a number of national courts expressed concern for the fundamental rights of the suspected or convicted persons and refused surrenders on this ground, as exemplified by the decision of the German Constitutional Court issued just a few months before the CJEU's judgment in *Aranyosi* and *Căldăraru*.[94]

The joined cases of *Aranyosi* and *Căldăraru* gave the Court of Justice a new occasion on which to examine the balance between the principle of mutual trust and the need to protect fundamental rights. This judgment, and the subsequent clarifications and affirmations in the *ML* and *Dorobantu* decisions, have made it clear that executing judicial authorities must seek objective and up-to-date information about prison conditions in EAW cases, when an issue about the compliance of those conditions with fundamental rights arises. For that purpose, the Court established the two-step procedure that must be followed when assessing whether the requested person would be exposed to inhuman or degrading treatment in the issuing Member State. Nevertheless, the Court had initially limited this type of situation to 'exceptional cases' relating to the absolute prohibition of inhuman and degrading treatment. The *LM* case was an opportunity for the Court to decide whether the same exception would apply when a potential breach of the right to a fair trial was at stake. The Court held that the exception would apply, and it strictly followed the two-pronged approach it had developed in *Aranyosi* and *Căldăraru*.

The landmark decisions in *Aranyosi* and *Căldăraru* and *LM* are welcome developments in the Court's fundamental rights case law.[95] From the perspective of

[93] For a general discussion of the legitimacy of the CJEU's decisions, see M Adams et al (eds), *Judging Europe's Judges: The Legitimacy of the Case Law of the European Court of Justice* (Oxford, Hart Publishing, 2013).

[94] It is unclear whether this decision of the German Federal Constitutional Court influenced the CJEU to change its approach in *Aranyosi*, as there is no reference to it in the judgment, but it may well be that it has played a role in the reasoning and deliberations in the CJEU.

[95] See, for instance, the blog post of Fair Trials International (FTI), which has been very active in advocating fundamental rights protection in this field, at www.fairtrials.org/tag/pre-trial-detention-2/ (last accessed 16 December 2020); or S Peers, 'Human Rights and the European Arrest Warrant: Has the ECJ turned from poacher to gamekeeper?', EU Law Analysis 12 November 2016 available at http://eulawanalysis.blogspot.nl/2016/11/human-rights-and-european-arrest.html (last accessed 16 December 2020).

national courts, the judgments are long overdue indications of how they should proceed when faced with evidence that the person being subject to an arrest warrant may be exposed to human rights violations. However, the procedure that they have to follow is far from simple, and there are a number of other open questions concerning the application of the two-step test.

First of all, as a preliminary comment, the Court has been very slow in dealing with the matter. It is remarkable that the Court that identifies itself as a constitutional court of the EU[96] was slower to react than the EU legislature, national courts and national legislatures, who all introduced exceptions to mutual recognition much earlier. For example, the European Commission recognised early on that while the EAW is a very useful tool for Member States in the fight against crime, there is certainly room for improvement in the transposition and application of the Framework Decision, particularly regarding the protection of fundamental rights, which must remain central to the operation of the system.[97] The European Parliament, for its part, recommended a fundamental rights-based refusal ground to be applied to Union mutual recognition instruments when there are substantial grounds to believe that the execution of a measure under those instruments would be incompatible with the executing Member State's obligations under Article 6 TEU and the Charter.[98]

Second, it is unclear if the Court overruled its previous case law. *Aranyosi* is inherently different from the previous cases, as it deals with a separate and specific human rights issue relating to the absolute prohibition of inhuman and degrading treatment. The *LM* judgment, on the other hand, deals with a right to a fair trial, which is the same right as the one invoked in *Radu* and *Melloni*. But similarly to *Aranyosi*, the *LM* case concerns a separate and specific issue regarding the independence of the judiciary in the context of the ongoing rule of law crisis in Poland. The Court has stressed the importance of the independence of the judiciary, which forms part of the essence of the right to a fair trial, and has linked it to the values in Article 2 TEU. It could thus be that the CJEU would adopt a more restrictive approach in a different factual context or when a different right is at stake, and cases like *Piotrowski* point in that direction.

Third, it is not clear if the approach of the CJEU is fully in conformity with the ECHR. As discussed earlier, the CJEU requires national authorities to perform a two-step test examining systemic and general deficiencies in the issuing State as well as individual circumstances, while the ECtHR only requires the latter examination. The key question is whether this *methodological* difference can lead to

[96] See, for example, Report of the Court of Justice on certain aspects on the application of the Treaty on European Union (Luxembourg, 5 May 1995). See also B Vesterdorf, 'A Constitutional Court for the EU?' (2006) 4 *International Journal of Constitutional Law* 607.

[97] See, eg, COM(2011) 175 final and SEC(2011) 430 final, 11 April 2011.

[98] See European Parliament Resolution of 27 February 2014 with recommendations to the Commission on the review of the European Arrest Warrant (2013/2109(INL)) and Annex to the Resolution.

divergent levels of protection. An argument has been made in this chapter that it *could*, since the CJEU requires national courts to conduct an additional step that, if not satisfied, precludes refusal to execute an EAW, which might be required under the ECHR. Since EAW cases are on the rise at both the national and the European level, there is a pressing need for the CJEU to clarify the extent to which its case law corresponds to that of the Strasburg Court.

VIII. Conclusion

This chapter has shown that the CJEU has long relied on the principle of mutual trust to uphold the effectiveness of judicial cooperation in the EU. In the early cases, the Court found the grounds for refusing to execute an arrest warrant listed in the Framework Decision to be exhaustive. With time, and as the challenges to the Framework Decision became more problematic, the Court adopted a more nuanced approach and introduced the two-step procedure, which must be followed when there are reasons to believe that executing an EAW may lead to human rights violations. Both *Aranyosi* and *LM* seek to reconcile the need to protect fundamental rights and uphold the principle of mutual trust. In both judgments, the CJEU underlined the duty of national courts to first establish systematic or generalised deficiencies in the protection provided in the (issuing) State and then scrutinise the individual circumstances of the case in order to decide whether a substantiated risk of violation of fundamental rights exists. As a result, national courts have to follow two procedural steps and make an assessment of fundamental rights standards in other Member States. The extent to which they are actually able to do so depends on the specific circumstances of the case, the ability of the applicant to present clear and coherent evidence concerning human rights violations, as well as the willingness of the issuing authority to provide clear and convincing evidence that fundamental rights will be respected. While the change in the approach of the CJEU is a welcome development, the starting point remains the application of the principle of mutual trust between the Member States, which the Court had declared to be a constitutional principle of the EU legal order. Derogations are to be strictly construed and are possible only in exceptional circumstances.

The ECtHR, for its part, has held that the presumption of equivalent protection is in principle applicable in the context of the EAW system, because the discretionary power of the judicial authority of the executing State has to be exercised within the framework strictly defined by the case law of the CJEU. This means that the Strasbourg Court will only check if the protection of Convention rights has been manifestly deficient. When it comes to the methodology used to assess whether the protection offered is manifestly deficient, the ECtHR only requires the individual test to be conducted. This implies that establishing a systemic or generalised deficiency is not necessary from the Strasbourg perspective. The crux of the matter is whether this difference in methodology of the two European Courts can lead to different levels of protection, whereby the EU level would fall below the ECHR minimum standards.

This chapter has put forward an argument that the different methodology could lead to different outcomes and levels of protection in Strasbourg and Luxembourg. In the hypothetical scenario described above, arrests warrants issued in States where no systemic or generalised deficiencies can be established would in principle have to be executed without or notwithstanding the individual assessment. The national court may not even reach the stage of individual assessment because of the absence of systemic deficiency in a country. This would be in accordance with the CJEU's two-step procedure and the idea that Member States should trust each other and that derogations are possible only in exceptional cases. However, the outcome in the same hypothetical could be different in Strasbourg, because the ECtHR only requires that the national authorities conduct an individual assessment. In practical terms, this could mean that following the different approaches leads to opposing outcomes, to execute or refuse execution of a warrant. It remains to be seen whether this scenario will actually materialise and how the CJEU (and the ECtHR) will address it in the future case law.

My overall aim in Part II has been to illustrate that convergence and harmony in the case law of the two European Courts is achieved over time and with great effort on the part of all the actors involved in the process. In the meantime, however, the national courts are in the eye of the storm, since the problem lies not only in the end result, where it may seem that the CJEU has complied with the ECHR or that the ECtHR has decided to be lenient and accommodating towards the EU legal system, but also in the approach and in the messages they send to national courts in the process. Moreover, convergence in European fundamental rights standards cannot be guaranteed if there are no shared rules about the way in which the systems relate to one another and how conflicts and divergences between them should be resolved. It is that aspect Part III goes on to consider.

PART III

Towards Normative Consistency in European Fundamental Rights Law

5

Conflict Rules in National, European and International Law

I. Introduction

Part II of the book sought to illustrate how and when the divergences between European Union (EU) law and the European Convention on Human Rights (ECHR) are problematic from the perspective of national courts. It outlined instances in which the Court of Justice of the European Union (CJEU) and the European Court of Human Rights (ECtHR) have adopted different approaches in interpreting and balancing fundamental rights, particularly in the context of the Member States' mutual trust and recognition obligations under EU law, which has led to diverging and sometimes also conflicting decisions. The purpose of this final part of the book is to explore the different ways in which national courts can deal with conflicting messages coming from Luxembourg and Strasbourg.

This chapter examines the conflict rules found in the different applicable sources of law that national courts may use to deal with what they may perceive to be conflicts between EU law and the ECHR. Given that the objective is to consider different conflict rules from the point of view of national courts, the analysis begins with the status of EU law and the ECHR in national law, usually found in national constitutions. The investigation covers selected constitutional experiences, which are put into different categories. Furthermore, the chapter also considers the rules of conflict in international law, which is something often overlooked in the literature. Yet both the EU and the ECHR are conceived as international treaties, and a national judge could view conflicts between EU and ECHR law as conflicts between two international treaties, in which case the rules of conflict in international law may become relevant. In that context, conflict clauses in the treaties themselves are examined, as well as general rules of international law, in particular the 1969 Vienna Convention on the Law of Treaties (VCLT or 'Vienna Convention').

The fundamental assumption on which this chapter is based is that both the EU and the ECHR are international organisations founded on and governed by international treaties, which exist alongside other international treaties and rules of customary international law.[1] At the same time, however, both the ECHR and the EU Treaties may be considered *special* treaties in both national and international law – the ECHR because it is a human rights treaty, which gives it a special status compared to other treaties, and the EU Treaties because of the autonomy and supranational character of EU law. The aim of this chapter is to explore these assumptions further, and to determine whether and to what extent national and international (treaty) law is helpful when it comes to resolving conflicts between EU and ECHR law.

The chapter proceeds in the following way. Section II provides a definition of a treaty conflict, making a distinction between conflicts in the narrow and broad senses. Section III starts with the rules of conflicts in national law and national constitutions, since this is the first source that national courts will consider when confronted with a conflict between EU and ECHR law. Section IV examines the question of conflicts between EU and ECHR law from the perspective of EU law and from the perspective of ECHR law. Section V looks into the rules of conflict resolution in international law, more specifically the VCLT, and customary international law, in order to determine whether they are helpful in resolving conflicts between EU and ECHR law. The analysis mainly focuses on Article 30 VCLT, which provides the 'tool-box' for dealing with treaty conflicts. Finally, section VI reflects on the usefulness of the different rules for resolving conflicts between EU and ECHR law.

II. Defining Treaty Conflict

A treaty conflict in the strict sense can be defined as a conflict between provisions of different treaties that cannot be resolved using interpretative techniques such as 'conform interpretation' or 'balancing'.[2] A conflict in the strict sense occurs when a party to two treaties finds itself in a situation in which it cannot simultaneously comply with obligations under both, because treaty A prescribes what treaty B prohibits.[3] This is the situation of direct incompatibility: an obligation may be fulfilled only by thereby failing to fulfil another obligation. However, treaty

[1] On the general responsibility of international organisations, see eg ICJ, Interpretation of the Agreement of 25 March 1951 between the WHO and Egypt, Advisory Opinion (1980) para 37. See further J Klabbers, 'Contending approaches to international organizations: Between functionalism and constitutionalism' in J Klabbers and A Wallendahl (eds), *Research Handbook on the Law of International Organizations* (Cheltenham, Edward Elgar, 2011).

[2] 'Balancing' or 'proportionality balancing', with its origins in Germany, has become a dominant technique of rights adjudication. See, eg, A Stone Sweet and J Mathews, 'Proportionality Balancing and Global Constitutionalism', *47 Faculty Scholarship Series Paper 1296* (2008), available at http://digitalcommons.law.yale.edu/cgi/viewcontent.cgi?article=2296&context=fss_papers (last accessed 16 December 2020).

[3] This definition was first formulated by Wilfred Jenks. See W Jenks, 'The Conflict of Law-making Treaties' (1953) 30 *British Yearbook of International Law* 401, 426.

conflicts can be conceived of more broadly too, including situations in which compliance with one norm *may* result in a breach of the other and where obligations and performance under one treaty frustrate the purpose of another treaty, without there being any strict incompatibility between their provisions.[4] I have referred to those broader conflicts as divergences or inconsistencies.

The VCLT itself does not contain a definition of treaty conflict, and most international treaties are silent on the matter. Most treaties are also hardly ever equipped with solutions in terms of coordination mechanisms or conflict resolution provisions. This is even more the case when the conflicting interpretation concerns normative preferences, since these are never explicitly addressed in the treaties themselves. It will usually be that the judge who is confronted with the conflict will have to figure out how to deal with it.

Limiting the definition to a narrow description seems too restrictive, however, particularly in the context of human rights treaties,[5] where their application will more often involve inconsistencies and divergences rather than directly conflicting obligations. Therefore, the analysis in this chapter will use the broader definition of a treaty conflict, thus also including inconsistencies and divergences in Strasbourg and Luxembourg, which may not necessarily result in directly conflicting obligations but which may be perceived as such by the national courts, or where compliance with one obligation considerably limits or frustrates the purpose of the other. While it may be possible, theoretically, to comply with both treaty obligations ultimately, in cases of broader conflicts the situation is more complex in practice. Time is an important factor too, because it may take a while before it becomes clear whether the two obligations are truly conflicting but the national courts are required to deal with it in the meantime. Moreover, both narrow and broad conflicts remain problematic from the perspective of coherence and legal certainty and have the negative effect of weakening international law as a whole.[6]

III. National Law and National Constitutions

The first place a national judge will look for an answer when confronted with conflicting treaty obligations in most countries is the national constitution. What does the national constitution say about the status of international treaties in the domestic legal order, and in particular of EU Treaties and the ECHR, and (how) can those rules be interpreted as giving priority to one over the other?

[4] H Kelsen, *General Theory of Norms* (Oxford, Oxford University Press, 1991) 123; J Pauwelyn, *Conflict of Norms in Public International Law: How WTO Law Relates to Other Rules of International Law* (Cambridge, Cambridge University Press, 2003) 164–200.

[5] Kelsen (n 4); Pauwelyn (n 4). Furthermore, for the argument that the narrow definition is inadequate, see E Vranes, 'The Definition of "Norm Conflict" in International Law and Legal Theory' (2006) 17 *European Journal of International Law* 395.

[6] R Wolfrum and N Matz, *Conflicts in International Environmental Law* (Berlin/London, Springer, 2003) 6.

There are two preliminary points to be made here. The first one concerns the domestic effect of international (treaty) law in the national legal system, and the traditional description of the relationship between states and international law in terms of monism and dualism. In monist countries, international treaties are incorporated directly into the domestic legal orders. In dualist countries, on the other hand, international treaties have to be transposed into the domestic legal order. This means that an incompatibility between EU law and the ECHR in those countries would in principle be seen as an incompatibility between EU law and an act of national law, incorporating the ECHR into the national legal system. However, as will be shown in this and the next chapter, even in dualist countries the Convention is often used and applied directly by the national courts, presumably due to its special character as a human rights treaty and also because of the authoritative role played by the Strasbourg case law. This means that the traditional way in which the effect of international treaties is examined, namely through the monist or dualist approach, may no longer be as relevant when it comes to the ECHR. The second point relates to the fact that national courts in some countries may consider EU law to be different from other international law and give it a different (higher) status in the domestic legal order in comparison to all other sources of international law. The consequence would then be that the EU Treaties and EU law would have priority over other international treaties in the national legal order. The same may be applicable in relation to the ECHR for states that grant special status to international human rights treaties in their constitutions, requiring an interpretation of all applicable law in conformity with those treaties. These preliminary points are developed further in this section.

A. The Special Status of EU Law in Domestic Legal Orders

Article 1 of the Treaty of Lisbon provides:

> By this Treaty, the High Contracting Parties establish among themselves a European Union … on which the Member States confer competences to attain objectives they have in common.

By using the language of international law, it thus confirms the EU's international character. Even though there have been several proposals over the years to modify the existing treaty architecture, none of these attempts resulted in a clear and explicit change in the nature of the EU and EU law.[7] The legal regime of the amendments, including its latest Treaty of Lisbon, is still set out in Articles 39, 40 and 41 of the Vienna Convention, which govern amendments to and modifications of international treaties. In fact, the Treaty of Lisbon abandoned the idea of changing the nature of the EU in the Treaties, which arguably had been attempted in the

[7] B De Witte, 'The European Union as an International Legal Experiment' in G de Búrca and J Weiler (eds), *The Worlds of European Constitutionalism* (Cambridge, Cambridge University Press, 2012) 19.

preceding Constitutional Treaty, which, according to its title, aimed to 'establish a Constitution for Europe'.[8] As is well known, the Constitutional Treaty, or the 'EU Constitution' as it was often referred to, never entered into force after being rejected by the French and Dutch electorates. As for any future amendments to the EU Treaties, Article 48 of the Treaty on European Union (TEU) provides that any amendment to the Treaties 'shall enter into force after being ratified by all the Member States in accordance with their respective constitutional requirements', again using the traditional language of the law of international treaties, referring to 'treaties' and 'ratification'.[9] The EU legal system and everything built on it is thus not self-sustaining; it is reliant on the Treaties and owes its validity to them. The Treaties, in turn, owe their validity to international law.

Ultimately, therefore, the EU Member States are the main actors that establish the EU Treaties, bound only by their national constitutional rules and the rules of international treaty law. The EU (or previously the EC) was and still is a voluntary association of states in which many decisions are taken as a result of negotiations among the leaders of the states. The Member States remain in a privileged position within the EU, because they can change the general institutional framework of the Union through treaty amendment, which still requires unanimous consent from all the Member States, and they can even decide to withdraw from it, as we have witnessed with the recent exit of the UK.[10] Moreover, the EU Member States have referred to the EU as an international organisation or as a regional economic integration organisation (REIO) in many of the multilateral treaties and conventions to which the EU is a Contracting Party.[11]

The qualification of the EU as an international organisation and EU law as international law is not only part of state practice in the international arena, it is also preserved internally, in the constitutional laws of the Member States. Indeed, the national constitutions in some countries contain a generic transfer of powers

[8] ibid.

[9] It should be noted, however, that the amendment rules under EU law are actually more rigid than those of general international law, since Art 48 TEU provides less flexibility than Art 39 VCLT. In the latter provision, the Contracting Parties are free to arrange the manner of later amendments, or to change the procedure formulated in the preceding treaty. In contrast, the EU Treaties contain the mandatory treaty revision procedure in Art 48, which the Member States must follow. See also 1976 *Defrenne* case [ECLI:EU:C:1976:56], where the Court of Justice confirmed this duty of the Member States.

[10] On the withdrawal agreement and its various effects and consequences, see eg L Van Middelaar, 'Brexit as the European Union's "Machiavellian moment"' (2018) 55 *CML Rev* 3; RA Wessel, 'Consequences of Brexit for international agreements concluded by the EU and its Member States' (2018) 55 *CML Rev* 101; F Fabbrini (ed), *The Law and Politics of Brexit* (Oxford, Oxford University Press, 2017); M Gordon, 'The UK's Sovereignty Situation: Brexit, Bewilderment and Beyond' (2016) 27 *King's Law Journal* 333.

[11] There are several examples of such references in multilateral treaties. See, eg, the UN Framework Convention on Climate Change (1992), Art 20, or the Convention on International Trade in Endangered Species of Wild Fauna and Flora (2015), Art XXI. For discussion of this particular aspect, see E Paasivirta and PJ Kuiper, 'Does One Size Fit All? The European Community and the Responsibility of International Organizations' (2005) 26 *Netherlands Yearbook of International Law* 169.

provision without a specific reference to the EU.[12] An example is Spain, as already discussed in chapter 2, but also, for instance, the Czech Republic, Poland and the Netherlands. Other countries, however, specifically single out a provision on the transfer of powers to the EU, which arguably shows that the EU is viewed differently from other international treaties. Some examples include Germany, Croatia, Finland and Denmark.[13]

It is not surprising that the national courts do not often make specific statements about the nature of the EU and EU law. One of the few examples is the French *Conseil constitutionnel*, which has stated, albeit in a somewhat controversial way, that EU law is distinct from international law.[14] It first stated that 'the provisions of the "Treaty establishing a Constitution for Europe" … show that said instrument retains the nature of an international treaty entered into by the States'.[15] But it then continued, 'pursuant to Article 88-1 of the Constitution … the drafters of this provision thus formally acknowledged the existence of a Community legal order integrated into the domestic legal order and distinct from the international legal order'.[16] It is therefore not entirely clear what the position of the *Conseil connstitutionnel* is, but it seems that even though the Constitutional Treaty, as was the case (but the same argument could be made for the Lisbon Treaty), retained the nature of an international treaty, it has become distinctive from the French perspective due to the special reference to the EU in Article 88(1) of the French Constitution. This may be different in other states that do not have such a reference in their constitutions.

Another attempt to define the nature of EU law was made by the German *Bundesverfassungsgericht*. Already in 1967, the German Constitutional Court described the (then) Community legal order as follows:

> The Community is not a state and not even a federal state. Rather it is a Community of a special nature in the process of an ever closer integration, in intergovernmental institution within the meaning of article 24/1 of the Basic law, to which the Federal Republic of Germany, in common with other Member States has transferred certain sovereign rights. A new public authority has thereby been created, which is autonomous and independent vis-à-vis the public authorities of each Member State. Consequently its acts do not require approval/ratification by the Member States, nor can they be annulled by those States. The EEC Treaty to a certain extent constitutes the Constitution of the Community, … it forms its own legal order which is part of neither public international law nor the national law of the Member States. Community law and municipal law of

[12] For an overview of 'transfer of power' clauses in (then) 28 Member States, see L Besselink, M Claes, Š Imamović and JH Reestman, *National Constitutional Avenues for Further EU Integration*, Report for the European Parliament's Committees on Legal Affairs and on Constitutional Affairs No PE 493.046, Brussels: European Union (2014).

[13] For further discussion of this aspect, see ch 2.

[14] *Conseil Constitutionnel*, Decision no 2004-505 DC of 19 November 2004, *The Treaty establishing a Constitution for Europe*.

[15] ibid para 9.

[16] ibid para 11.

> Member States are two internal legal orders which are distinct and different from each other ...[17]

While the French and German highest courts may have followed the CJEU's view considering the EU to be a 'new legal order', it does not seem enough to conclude that the EU would take a position of priority over the ECHR in the French and German domestic legal orders. Moreover, most national courts try to avoid making a pronouncement on this particular question, especially in fundamental rights cases.

B. The Special Status of ECHR Law in Domestic Legal Orders

While the label 'supranational' used to be reserved in Europe for the EU and its Court, it has become more common in recent years also to characterise the ECtHR as a supranational jurisdiction, and the national courts as 'ECHR courts'.[18] Indeed, the ECtHR has been referred to as 'the Constitutional Court for Europe',[19] and national courts frequently refer to its case law and adapt national law so as to comply with the requirements imposed by the Convention as interpreted by the ECtHR. Martinico suggested, after having conducted a detailed analysis of national case law, that there is a partial convergence in the way EU Member States apply EU and the ECHR's norms.[20] In practical terms, thus, ECHR law is a vital component of the daily work of national courts in most EU states. Moreover, the fact that states adopt a monist or dualist approach to international treaties does not appear as relevant when it comes to the ECHR, since national courts in traditionally dualist states, such as Germany or Italy, have been directly applying the ECHR and Strasbourg case law in their decisions.[21]

In some states, human rights treaties, as a category of international treaties, have a special status. In such cases, national constitutions distinguish between human rights treaties and other treaties, giving the former a special overriding status, either in the provisions of the constitution or in the case law of (constitutional) courts. For instance, Article 20(2) of the Romanian Constitution states that 'where any inconsistencies exist between the covenants and treaties on the fundamental human rights Romania is a party to, and the national laws, the international

[17] Order of 18 October, 1967, 22 BVerfGE 293, para 19.

[18] For the argument on ongoing convergence in the application of EU and ECHR law domestically, see G Martinico and O Pollicino (eds), *The Interaction between Europe's Legal Systems. Judicial dialogue and the creation of supranational laws* (Cheltenham, Edward Elgar Publishing, 2012).

[19] S Greer, *The European Convention on Human Rights* (Cambridge: Cambridge University Press, 2006) 173.

[20] G Martinico, 'Is the European Convention Going to Be "Supreme"? A Comparative-Constitutional Overview of ECHR and EU Law before National Courts' (2012) 23 *European Journal of International Law* 401.

[21] H Keller and A Stone Sweet (eds), *A Europe of Rights. The Impact of the ECHR on National Legal Systems* (Oxford, Oxford University Press, 2008) 686.

regulations shall take precedence, unless the Constitution or national laws comprise more favourable provisions'. In the Czech Republic, international human rights treaties had a special position in comparison to other treaties until 2001, as they were the only treaties that were directly incorporated and were, moreover, granted constitutional status. In 2001, the incorporation provision was extended to all ratified and promulgated international treaties. As this could have impacted the already attained constitutional status of the incorporated human rights treaties, the Constitutional Court of the Czech Republic declared in 2002 that human rights treaties ratified prior to the constitutional amendment would not be affected by the change in the regulation.[22] Another example is the Constitution of Slovakia, which refers to human rights treaties in a separate paragraph, stipulating, somewhat vaguely, that

> international treaties on human rights and fundamental freedoms and international treaties for whose exercise a law is not necessary, and international treaties which directly confer rights or impose duties on natural persons or legal persons and which were ratified and promulgated in the way laid down by a law shall have precedence over [national] laws.[23]

Other countries that give a special status to international human rights treaties are Spain and Portugal, which provide interpretative support for constitutional human rights provisions. Section 10(2) of the Spanish Constitution provides that '[p]rovisions relating to the fundamental rights and liberties recognized by the Constitution shall be construed in conformity with the Universal Declaration of Human Rights and international treaties and agreements thereon ratified by Spain'. Similarly, Article 16 of the Portuguese Constitution states that the fundamental rights enshrined in the Constitution shall not exclude rights set out in applicable international laws. In Italy, the Constitutional Court interpreted Article 117(1) of the Italian Constitution, which mandates the country's exercise of powers to be within the limits set by the international obligations, as meaning that international human rights treaties, and in particular the ECHR, are 'intermediary norms' (*norme interposte*), positioned somewhere between constitutional and ordinary norms.[24]

Constitutions in other states contain more general provisions giving priority to international treaties over national law, but without a distinction between human

[22] Czech Constitutional Court, Pl ÚS 36/01, published under no 403/2002 Coll.

[23] Art 7(5) of the Constitution of Slovakia.

[24] Criminal Proceedings against Paolo Dorigo, Constitutional review no 113/2011; ILDC 1732 (IT 2011). Mr Dorigo had been the victim of a violation of Art 6 ECHR, as found by the European Commission of Human Rights. He had asked the *Corte di Appello* of Bologna to review his (final) conviction in accordance with the international decision. The Appellate Court decided to raise a constitutionality claim before the Constitutional Court with regard to Art 630 of the Italian Code of Criminal Procedure. The Constitutional Court agreed with the reasoning of the *Corte di Appello*, according to which the provision at issue violates the international obligations undertaken by Italy to which Art 117(1) of the Constitution makes reference. Accordingly, the Court declared the partial unconstitutionality of Art 630 of the Italian Code of Criminal Procedure.

rights and other treaties. The Constitution of Bulgaria, for example, stipulates that ratified and promulgated international treaties shall have primacy over any conflicting provision of the domestic legislation.[25] A similar primacy clause can be found in Poland (Article 91), Croatia (Article 141) and Greece (Article 28). In Germany, primacy is only given to international customary law. Article 25 of the German Basic Law states that the general rules of international law 'shall be an integral part of federal law' and 'shall take precedence over the laws and directly create rights and duties for the inhabitants of the federal territory'. However, the case law of the ECtHR is a consistent source of interpretation in the judgments of the German *Bundesverfassungsgericht*, including – and perhaps especially – in decisions concerning EU law.[26]

The Netherlands is another legal system that gives priority to international treaties in the domestic legal order without making a distinction between different types of international treaties. The example of the Netherlands is different, however, because Articles 93 and 94 of the Constitution have been interpreted as also applying to national constitutional law. In other words, international treaty law (hence both EU and ECHR law) has direct effect and primacy over national law, including over the national Constitution. The general practice of Dutch courts, including that of the *Hoge Raad*, is that they consider themselves bound by the ECHR, as interpreted by the ECtHR, and by EU law, as interpreted by the CJEU. Curiously, in the case of the latter, the Dutch courts take the position that there is primacy of EU law because it is required by the EU's special autonomous nature as proclaimed by the CJEU.[27] While this is controversial – since one would assume that primacy of EU law can be or is accepted because the national constitution permits it – the effect remains the same.[28] Nevertheless, even if it were EU law that was in conflict with a human rights treaty, such as the ECHR, priority would be given to the latter.[29]

Finally, there are also national legal systems that do not contain written rules in their constitutions with respect to the legal status of international treaties, such as in Austria and Belgium. Article 9 of the Austrian Constitution states very generally that recognised rules of international law are valid parts of federal law (first paragraph) and that specific sovereign rights can be transferred to intergovernmental institutions and their organs by means of a treaty, which then has to be ratified in accordance with Article 50 of the Constitution (second paragraph). Similarly,

[25] Art 5(4) of the Constitution of Bulgaria.

[26] See, eg, BVerfG, Order of the First Senate of 6 November 2019 – 1 BvR 276/17; BVerfG, Orders of the Second Chamber of 30 October 2019 – 2 BvR 828/19 – and 22 November 2019 – 2 BvR 517/19.

[27] J Fleuren, 'The Application of Public International Law by Dutch Courts' (2010) 57 *Netherlands International Law Review* 245.

[28] See in this context L Besselink, 'The Proliferation of Constitutional Law and Constitutional Adjudication, or How American Judicial Review Came to Europe After All' (2013) 9 *Utrecht Law Review* 2, 19.

[29] L Besselink, 'Constitutional Adjudication in the Era of Globalization: The Netherlands in the Comparative Perspective' (2012) 18 *European Public Law* 231.

Article 34 of the Belgian Constitution provides that '[t]he exercising of specific powers can be assigned by a treaty or by a law to institutions of public international law'. In such situations, the case law of national (constitutional) courts is particularly relevant in determining the status of treaties in national law. In Austria, the ECHR is in fact given constitutional status through a federal constitutional amendment.[30]

There is thus a great variety with regard to the status of human rights treaties in the national legal orders: some states give priority to such treaties, and others do not make a distinction between human rights treaties and other treaties. Notwithstanding the differences, and as already discussed in chapter 2, the ECHR has become deeply embedded in the domestic legal orders of the EU Member States, shaping fundamental rights domestically either directly or through the interpretation of the national constitutional bill of rights.[31] Its special character, in comparison to other international treaties, is represented in different ways, but the authorities in most Convention states consider themselves bound by the ECHR and the ECtHR case law, and they adapt national law so as to comply with it. A recent comparative study, which covered 18 EU Member States, concluded, inter alia, that the ECHR and the Strasbourg case law feature more prominently in the case law of national courts in comparison to the EU Charter of Fundamental Rights, even in cases falling within the scope of EU law.[32] There could be many different reasons for this, and such a discussion would go beyond the scope of this book, but it does not take away from the overall conclusion that the Convention system appears to have acquired a special status in the legal systems of most (EU) Contracting Parties, not only in the countries in which national constitutions give it such a status but also in other Convention states in which the national judicial authorities have accepted it, even without its being an official requirement in the national constitution.

National constitutions and/or the case law of the national constitutional courts have made both EU and ECHR law special in the domestic legal orders, despite the fact that both are, strictly speaking, based on international treaties and are

[30] BVG BGBl Nr 59/1964. For further details, see A Gamper, 'Austria: Endorsing the Convention System, Endorsing the Constitution', in P Popelier, S Lambrecht and K Lemmens (eds), *Criticism of the European Court of Human Rights: Shifting the Convention System: Counter-Dynamics at the National and EU Level* (Antwerp, Intersentia, 2016) 75.

[31] See also LR Helfer, 'Redesigning the European Court of Human Rights: Embeddedness as a Deep Structural Principle of the European Human Rights Regime' (2008) 19 *European Journal of International Law* 125. See also H Keller and A Stone Sweet (eds), *A Europe of Rights. The Impact of the ECHR on National Legal Systems* (Oxford, Oxford University Press, 2008); G Martinico and O Pollicino (eds), *The National Judicial Treatment of the ECHR and EU Laws. A Comparative Constitutional Perspective* (Groningen, European Law Publishing, 2010); P Popelier, C Van de Heyning and P van Nuffel (eds), *Human Rights Protection in the European Legal Order: The interaction between the European and the national courts* (Antwerp, Intersentia, 2011); J Gerards and J Fleuren (eds), *Implementation of the European Convention on Human Rights and of the judgments of the ECtHR in national case law. A comparative analysis* (Antwerp, Intersentia, 2014).

[32] M Bobek and J Adams-Prassl (eds), *The EU Charter of Fundamental Rights in the Member States* (Oxford, Hart Publishing, 2020).

thus international law. At the same time, the national constitutions lack clear rules in the case of a conflict between the two, and national constitutional courts have avoided addressing this matter. Therefore, the next logical step is to look beyond the domestic legal orders, at the Treaties themselves and general international law.

IV. Conflict Clauses in the Treaties

If a national constitution does not offer a solution to a conflict between executing an obligation under EU law and ensuring compliance with the ECHR, national courts may turn to rules of conflict existing in the treaties themselves. Indeed, the VCLT refers to the so-called 'conflict clauses' that can be included in treaties and can act as conflict rules between different treaties.[33] These clauses may be of a more general nature, or they can be designed to cover specific treaties, thus giving priority to the treaty in question or to another treaty in the event of a conflict. This section discusses the conflict clauses contained in the EU Treaties and in the ECHR.

A. Conflict Clauses in the EU Treaties

The primary law of the EU contains several rules that may be applicable in the event of a conflict between the EU Treaties and other international treaties and laws. First of all, the EU Treaties recognise the right of the Member States to conclude new or to continue to adhere to existing international agreements: Article 34(2) TEU refers to the Member States' participation in international organisations; and Articles 165(3), 166(3), 167(3), and 168(3) of the Treaty on the Functioning of the European Union (TFEU) provide that the EU and the Member States shall foster cooperation with third countries and international organisations in certain fields.

These agreements are generally perceived as acts pertaining to national law, however, as in the event of a conflict with EU law, the latter will prevail, as would be the case with any other act of national law.[34] But there is an exception to this general rule: by virtue of Article 351 TFEU, a Member State may be able to invoke an international agreement concluded by it before it became an EU Member State in order to derogate from the EU law obligation. Article 351 TFEU reads in full:

> The rights and obligations arising from agreements concluded before 1 January 1958 or, for acceding states, before the date of their accession, between one or more Member States on the one hand, and one or more third countries on the other, shall not be affected by the provisions of the Treaties.

[33] In particular Art 30 of the VCLT.

[34] A Rosas, 'The Status in EU Law of International Agreements Concluded by EU Member States' (2011) 34 *Fordham International Law Journal* 1304.

> To the extent that such agreements are not compatible with the Treaties, the Member State or states concerned shall take all appropriate steps to eliminate the incompatibilities established. Member States shall, where necessary, assist each other to this end and shall, where appropriate, adopt a common attitude.
>
> In applying the agreements referred to in the first paragraph, Member States shall take into account the fact that the advantages accorded under the Treaties by each Member State form an integral part of the establishment of the Union and are thereby inseparably linked with the creation of common institutions, the conferring of powers upon them and the granting of the same advantages by all the other Member States.

Article 351 TFEU thus refers to agreements concluded between one or more Member States, on the one hand, and one or more third countries, on the other, where conflicts are resolved in favour of obligations that pre-date EU membership. This would also be in accordance with the international law maxim *pacta sunt servanda*. Since the ECHR is the older Treaty, one might argue that, in the event of a conflict between Member States' obligations under the ECHR and those under EU law, the former would prevail.[35] This logic was used by Italy in the first case to invoke Article 351 TFEU (then Article 307 TEC) in relation to its rights and obligations under the General Agreement on Tariffs and Trade (GATT), which seemingly clashed with EU law obligations.[36] However, the third paragraph of Article 351 TFEU also imposes an obligation to interpret, as far as possible, the agreements concluded with third countries in conformity with the EU law obligations of the Member State concerned. Unsurprisingly perhaps, the Court of Justice focused on that third paragraph in its analysis and ruled, following the Opinion of Advocate General Lagrange and the Commission's argumentation, that what is now Article 351 TFEU only protected the rights of third countries under the earlier agreement; the Member States themselves should refrain from exercising those rights to the extent necessary for the performance of their obligations under the (then) EEC Treaty.[37] This stance has been upheld in the subsequent case law with some minor variations.[38] Accordingly, Article 351 TFEU has not been interpreted as a conflict rule – it seems to be about balancing EU law with the international commitments of the Member States, rather than a rule giving priority to the latter.[39]

But what about human rights treaties? Human rights treaties are not about the reciprocal relationships between states, so the reasoning above would not

[35] The exception would be in France, because France joined the EEC before it ratified the ECHR in 1974. See also T Lock, *The European Court of Justice and International Courts* (Oxford, Oxford University Press, 2015) 188.

[36] Case 10/61 *Commission v Italy*, ECLI:EU:C:1962:2.

[37] ibid 10.

[38] See, inter alia, Case 812/79 *Attorney-General v Burgoa*, ECLI:EU:C:1980:231, para 8; Case 286/86 *Ministère public v Gérard Deserbais*, ECLI:EU:C:1988:434, para 17; Case C-124/95 *The Queen, ex parte Centro-Com Srl v HM Treasury and Bank of England*, ECLI:EU:C:1997:8, para 56.

[39] J Klabbers, *Treaty Conflict and the European Union* (Cambridge, Cambridge University Press, 2009) 118; P Koutrakos, *EU International Relations Law* (Oxford, Hart Publishing, 2006) 304.

directly apply. The case law of the Luxembourg Court does not address this matter, except in one case in which the Court accepted a treaty obligation arising from an earlier (individual rights) treaty as a justification for non-compliance with EU law on the basis of what is now Article 351 TFEU. The case in point is *Levy*.[40] Prior to joining what was then the EEC, France had concluded an International Labour Organization (ILO) agreement that required the prohibition of night work for women. In order to comply with it, France had passed legislation prohibiting women from working at night. Subsequently, the EEC adopted a directive on the equality of men and women in employment,[41] which gave women the same rights as men with regard to night work. There was thus a conflict between the French legislation implementing the ILO agreement and the Directive. The Court of Justice ruled that the Directive would not take effect in France to the extent that it would prevent France from complying with the obligations that were incumbent on it under an earlier agreement, in accordance with what is now Article 351 TFEU. The Court made clear, however, that this would be accepted only if the other agreement was concluded with non-member countries. The Court also explained that equal treatment of men and women constitutes a fundamental right recognised by the Community legal order but that its implementation had been gradual, requiring the Council to take action by means of directives, which allow, temporarily, certain derogations from the principle of equal treatment. Even with these reservations in mind the case is important, because it shows that the Court has accepted the principle of earlier treaties having priority over later treaties under certain conditions as safeguarded by the first paragraph of Article 351 TFEU. Thus, an argument could be made that the ECHR obligations should prevail over EU law obligations in the event of a conflict in all EU states that ratified the ECHR before joining the EU. After all, Article 351 TFEU is a clear conflict of law provision, and one that has never been removed from the Treaties. However, the argument is also problematic. First, the rule would not be applicable in all states. France, for example, only ratified the ECHR in 1974, which means that the French authorities could not use Article 351 to argue that the Convention has priority over EU law. Second, and more importantly, the rule contains a very formalistic time criterion that gives precedence to an earlier treaty, while the ECHR, as well as most other treaties, are living instruments that change over time. It would be very odd, therefore, if the question of priority were to depend on what was agreed almost 70 years ago.

Furthermore, and as already asserted, primary EU law also contains specific provisions with respect to the ECHR. The ECHR is deeply embedded in EU law, and in particular in EU human rights law, and the EU Charter (which is part of primary EU law since the entry into force of the Treaty of Lisbon) makes several

[40] Case C-158/91 *Ministère public en Direction du travail et de l'emploi v Jean-Claude Levy*, ECLI:EU:C:1993:332.

[41] Directive 76/207/EEC of 9 February 1976 on the implementation of the principle of equal treatment for men and women as regards access to employment, vocational training and promotion, and working conditions.

references to the ECHR as a source of both inspiration and reference. The most important provision in this context is Article 52(3) of the Charter, which provides that the Charter rights that correspond to the Convention rights should have the same meaning and scope. Article 52(3) is thus a conflict avoidance rule: conflicts between EU and ECHR law should not arise. If, however, conflicts were to arise, this provision could act as a conflict rule. National courts could use Article 52(3) to argue that if there is a conflict between EU law and the ECHR, the provision of EU law is invalid because it violates the Charter, which should be interpreted in accordance with the ECHR.[42]

As demonstrated in chapter 2, the CJEU has not accepted Article 52(3) of the Charter as a conflict rule, and its case law in this regard has been inconsistent.[43] The Court ruled that the ECHR 'does not constitute, as long as the European Union has not acceded to it, a legal instrument which has been formally incorporated into European Union law',[44] and in some judgments, the Court even held that national courts must check the compliance of EU law (which most often will be implementing legislation) with fundamental rights solely on the basis of the Charter.[45] The Court has also ruled that Article 52(3) of the Charter does not require national courts to apply the provision of the ECHR directly in the event of a conflict with national law implementing EU law.[46] At the same time, there are many examples of cases where the Court of Justice has paid due regard to the ECtHR's case law. This leads to uncertainties at the national level, which is probably why national courts keep coming back to Luxembourg with questions regarding the application of this provision. The way in which Article 52(3) of the Charter is interpreted is not at issue if there are no divergences between the case law of the two European Courts, but if there is a discrepancy, the national courts could use this provision as a conflict rule. They could argue that this Treaty provision governs the relationship between the Charter and the Convention and dictates that EU law should provide at least the same level of protection as the ECHR when Charter and Convention rights correspond. Otherwise, national courts risk being in breach of EU law, because EU law itself requires a conform interpretation. Of course, Article 52(3) only refers to the Convention and does not mention the case law of the Strasbourg Court, but the text of the Convention is meaningless without the case law, hence its interpretation must also include the case law of the ECtHR.[47]

It should be remembered, however, that even if Article 52(3) were to be accepted as a conflict rule by the national courts and ultimately even the CJEU, it

[42] This argument is developed further in the next chapter.

[43] This is particularly true if read alongside Opinion 2/13 on the accession of the EU to the ECHR (Opinion 2/13 *Accession of the European Union to the European Convention for the Protection of Human Rights and Fundamental Freedoms*, ECLI:EU:C:2014:48). The subsequent case law has been less clear as to the exact meaning of Art 52(3) and the role it plays in the CJEU's case law.

[44] See, eg, Case C-617/10 *Åkerberg Fransson*, ECLI:EU:C:2013:280, para 44; Case C-217/15 *Orsi*, ECLI:EU:C:2017:264, para 15.

[45] Case C-601/15 PPU *JN*, ECLI:EU:C:2016:84, para 45.

[46] Case C-571/10 *Kamberaj*, ECLI:EU:C:2012:233, paras 62–63.

[47] For an extensive analysis of Art 52(3) of the Charter, see ch 2.

would still not cover all possible conflicts between EU law and the ECHR, since it only covers rights that correspond to each other. The Explanations relating to the Charter provide a list of the Charter and Convention rights that correspond to each other, leaving a gap, albeit small, containing rights that are not covered by this provision. This is where a different provision comes to mind that could help remedy this gap, namely, Article 6(3) TEU. This provision states rather straightforwardly and convincingly that fundamental rights, as guaranteed by the ECHR, 'shall constitute general principles of the Union's law'.[48] An argument could thus be made that all ECHR rights are general principles of EU law, and hence that there should never be a conflict between EU law and the (whole) ECHR, thus also covering Convention rights that do not correspond to the Charter rights.[49] This argument is harder to make, however, since the CJEU has consistently rejected this interpretation of Article 6(3), which had been suggested by some national courts.[50] Thus, if the national courts were to use this provision to give priority to the ECHR and the Strasbourg Court, they would openly disregard the judgments of the CJEU. By contrast, the jurisprudence on Article 52(3) is inconsistent, so it cannot be concluded that applying it in a manner that ensures compliance with the ECHR, as interpreted by the ECtHR, would be contrary to EU law.

Finally, Article 53 of the Charter stipulates that the Charter cannot restrict the level of protection offered by the Convention, nor the rights protected by Union law, international law and in the Member States' constitutions. This means that the level of protection provided in the Charter should correspond to that of the ECHR, EU law, international law and the national constitutions, unless the level of protection offered by the Charter is higher. However, this provision was also interpreted differently by the CJEU in its *Melloni* judgment and in Opinion 2/13, discussed earlier in this book,[51] and Article 52(3) of the Charter remains *lex specialis* when it comes to the relationship between the Charter (and EU law interpreted in light of it) and the Convention.

The last point concerns a completely different approach to dealing with conflicts between EU and ECHR law, namely, through the intervention of the EU legislature, which could amend the conflicting legislation and, in this way, try to resolve the problem of incompatibility with the ECHR. One could say that since the Treaties presume that EU law complies with the ECHR, and otherwise it imposes an obligation to ensure that compliance with Article 51 of the Charter, this could be another way of 'managing' the conflicts available in EU law. Indeed, as

[48] For discussion of this particular point, see ch 2, section III.A.i.

[49] As Bruno De Witte concluded, 'There is therefore no doubt, in my view, that Article 6(3) TEU gives formal binding status to the entire content of the ECHR within the EU legal order, and it is quite curious that the Court of Justice and most legal literature have failed to draw that conclusion.' See B De Witte 'The Use of the ECHR and Convention Case Law by the European Court of Justice' in P Popelier, C Van de Heyning and P van Nuffel (eds), *Human Rights Protection in the European Legal Order: The interaction between the European and the national courts* (Antwerp, Intersentia, 2011) 22.

[50] See, eg, the phrasing of the preliminary references in *Kamberaj* (n 46).

[51] Case C-399/11 *Melloni*, ECLI:EU:C:2013:107; Opinion 2/13 (n 43). See further ch 4, section IV.B and ch 2, section IV.B respectively.

demonstrated in chapter 3, it seems to have worked in the context of the Dublin III Regulation in terms of achieving alignment between the case law of the CJEU and the ECtHR, even though it still remains to be seen how the Regulation will be interpreted and applied by the CJEU in new cases.

B. Conflict Clauses in the ECHR

The ECHR does not contain conflict rules in its text, except for Article 53, which is intended to maintain the (minimum) level of protection afforded under the Convention. Generally speaking, the ECHR Contracting Parties are required to ensure compliance with the minimum standards of the ECHR at all times. As far back as 1958, the European Commission of Human Rights ruled that 'if a State contracts treaty obligations and subsequently concludes another international agreement which disables it from performing its obligations under the first treaty, it will be answerable for any resulting breach of its obligations under the earlier treaty'.[52]

In 1989, in its famous *Soering*[53] decision, the ECtHR addressed the issue of treaty conflicts and ruled that the extradition of a criminal suspect from the UK to the US was contrary to the UK's obligations under the Convention, even when required under the bilateral extradition treaty concluded between the two countries. This judgment changed the traditional understanding of the state's capacity to extradite and its responsibilities in that respect, with significant effects beyond the ECHR itself. The case concerned a German national, Jens Soering, who was accused in the US on two counts of capital murder, which he and his girlfriend had allegedly committed. They fled to the UK, where they were subsequently arrested. The US requested their extradition under the terms of the existing extradition treaty between the UK and the US.

The Strasbourg Court unanimously upheld the previous case law of the defunct European Commission on Human Rights, by which extradition of an individual to a state where he would be likely to be subjected to torture or inhuman or degrading treatment engaged the responsibility of the requested state under Article 3 of the Convention. Stressing the absolute nature of Article 3 and the need to interpret the ECHR in a way that rendered its safeguards practical and effective, the ECtHR ruled that the loss of control after extradition did not absolve the state from responsibility for the foreseeable consequences of extradition suffered outside its jurisdiction.[54]

[52] *X v Germany* App no 235/56 (ECommHR, 10 June 1958).

[53] *Soering v United Kingdom* App no 14038/88 (ECtHR, 7 July 1989).

[54] The general applicability of international guarantees has been acknowledged by the UN Committee on Human Rights in several landmark cases, which explicitly refer to the *Soering* decision and the principles contained therein. See, eg, *Kindler v Canada* No 470/1991, UN Doc CCPR/C/48/D/470/1991; *Ng v Canada* No 469/1991, UN Doc CCPR/C/49/D/469/1991; *Cox v Canada* No 486/1992, UN Doc CCPR/C/45/D/486/1992.

The ECtHR did not accept the argument advanced by the UK that it was bound by the extradition treaty concluded with the US. However, the Strasbourg Court did not explicitly consider the question of the priority of the treaty obligations or how to balance them. Instead, it proceeded to examine whether there was a violation of the ECHR, which in effect resulted in giving primacy to the ECHR over the extradition treaty. The ECtHR did emphasise the particular importance of the right at issue in this case, but it did not clarify whether only certain rights qualified as potential obstacles to extradition (ie absolute rights), or if there was a need to balance the state's interest in criminal law enforcement and the respect for individual rights in the extradition process in every case.

In *Slivenko and others v Latvia*,[55] the ECtHR's Grand Chamber maintained its approach even in the context of a qualified right. The case concerned the expulsion of a family of a former Soviet (later Russian) military officer following the withdrawal of Soviet troops from Latvia, as required by the treaty of April 1994 on the withdrawal of Russian troops. The applicants argued that their removal constituted an interference with respect for their private life and home. The ECtHR ruled that by expelling the Slivenko family from the country, Latvia had disproportionately interfered in their private life and their right to a home, and in so doing had violated Article 8 ECHR. The Strasbourg Court concluded that a prior bilateral treaty between Latvia and Russia could not be invoked to limit the application of the ECHR. It stated:

> In any event, the Court reiterates that the treaty cannot serve as a valid basis for depriving the Court of its power to review whether there was an interference with the applicants' rights and freedoms under the Convention, and, if so, whether such interference was justified (see the admissibility decision in the present application, § 62, ECHR 2002-II).[56]

Moreover, in the Strasbourg Court's opinion, the same principles must apply with regard to any provision of international treaties a Contracting State has concluded prior to the ratification of the Convention and which might result in an inconsistency with some of its provisions.

The incompatibility between EU law and the ECHR was considered by the Strasbourg Court in the *Bosphorus* decision.[57] In this case, the Irish authorities impounded an aircraft used by JAT, an undertaking established in the Federal Republic of Yugoslavia (FRY), on the basis of EC Regulation 990/93 (implementing the UN Security Council (UNSC) Resolution that had introduced sanctions again the FRY). Even though the incompatibility had its origin in a UNSC Resolution, the ECtHR focused solely on the incompatibility between the ECHR and EU law (implementing the UNSC Resolution). The ECtHR reiterated that a Contracting Party is responsible under Article 1 ECHR for all acts and omissions

[55] *Slivenko and others v Latvia*, App no 48321/99 (ECtHR, 9 October 2003).
[56] ibid para 120.
[57] *Bosphorus v Ireland* App no 45036/98 (ECtHR, 30 June 2005).

of its organs, regardless of whether the act or omission in question is a consequence of domestic law or the necessity to comply with international obligations. In the Strasbourg Court's view, Article 1 does not exclude any part of the Contracting Party's jurisdiction from scrutiny under the ECHR.[58] However, it also held that it presumes that the 'the protection of fundamental rights by Community law [is] … "equivalent" … to that of the Convention system'. The presumption is only applicable if the Member States have no discretion, in which case the Strasbourg Court will presume that they are in compliance and will check only if there are signs of manifest deficiency. If the Member States have any discretion as to how they implement and apply EU law, they are fully responsible under the ECHR and the presumption of equivalent protection does not apply.[59]

Thus, if Ireland in this case had had discretion as to whether to impound the aircraft or not, the applicant's claim would have been assessed like any other claim in Strasbourg. The presumption of equivalent protection was also not rebutted in this case. If, however, the ECtHR were to find that the presumption had been rebutted and rule in favour of the applicant, the defendant (Ireland) would be faced with an unresolvable conflict between the ECHR and EU law, requiring Ireland to apply the Regulation. This means that, in the case of a conflict between EU and ECHR law, the ECtHR will first determine if the state had discretion when acting and then, on that basis, will decide whether it will exercise a full test of compatibility between EU law and the Convention or limit itself to assessing whether there is a manifest deficiency in the protection provided. If the ECtHR determines that there has been a violation of the Convention that cannot be justified, the Contracting State is required to put an end to that violation, regardless of the fact that the violation originates in EU law.

The *Bosphorus* doctrine could thus be viewed as a kind of conflict rule as well. The national court could potentially use it to argue that, in a case where the conditions are fulfilled – the state had no discretion as to how EU law is applied domestically and the CJEU had ruled on the matter, concluding that EU fundamental rights had not been breached – EU law should prevail over the Convention, because the Strasbourg Court presumes that the protection provided is equivalent and will only check if there is manifest deficiency in the protection. If the national court establishes that there is no manifest deficiency, it could give priority to EU law. Caution is advised, however, since the *Bosphorus* doctrine is a vague rule – to the extent that it can be considered a conflict rule – and the presumption of equivalent protection is always rebuttable. In *Bivolaru and Moldovan v France*, decided in March 2021, the Strasbourg Court rebutted the presumption for the first time, finding that the protection of fundamental rights in respect of the latter applicant had been manifestly deficient.[60]

[58] ibid para 153.
[59] For a more detailed discussion of *Bosphorus* and other cases in which the *Bosphorus* presumption has been applied, see ch 2.
[60] *Bivolaru and Moldovan v France* App nos 40324/16 and 12623/17 (ECtHR, 25 March 2021).

V. Conflict Rules in International Law

Having examined the question of conflicts between EU and ECHR law from a purely national perspective, looking at national constitutions and the relevant case law of the national courts, as well as from the EU and the ECHR perspective, this subsection explores the international law perspective. Treaty conflicts have been at the centre of the scholarly debate for many years,[61] because of the growing number of international treaties as well the fact that the existing conflict rules provided in treaty law – part of which reflects customary international law – are often considered inadequate to resolve conflicts between (multilateral) international treaties. The most important source is the VCLT.

A. The Vienna Convention on the Law of Treaties

The Vienna Convention, completed in 1969 and in force since 1980, is the 'treaty on treaties'. It determines general rules governing the operation of treaties, but it is also a means of avoiding or resolving potential conflicts between treaties. Most of its rules have been recognised as customary international law by the International Court of Justice (ICJ) and other international courts and tribunals.

In general, international law has a strong presumption against treaty conflicts, and conflict avoidance is often used as an interpretation technique to avoid conflicts altogether.[62] If, however, it is not possible to avoid a conflict, it is necessary to resolve it, which requires concrete rules. The main rules concerning treaty conflicts in the VCLT can be found in its Article 30, entitled 'Application of Successive Treaties Relating to the Same Subject-Matter'. In addition to Article 30, the VCLT contains other important rules, such as Articles 53 and 64 concerning *jus cogens* norms (also referred to in Article 30); Article 41, which deals with the so-called *inter se* agreements; and Article 59 regarding the termination or suspension of a treaty implied by the conclusion of a later treaty. The following discussion focuses on *jus cogens* norms and Article 30 VCLT, since other provisions do not seem to be applicable to conflicts between EU and ECHR law.

i. Jus Cogens

If a norm can be identified as *jus cogens*, it invalidates any other conflicting treaty provision. *Jus cogens* or peremptory norms are defined in Article 53 VCLT:

> A treaty is void if, at the time of its conclusion, it conflicts with a peremptory norm of general international law. For the purposes of the present Convention, a peremptory

[61] See, amongst many, Pauwelyn (n 4); Wolfrum and Matz (n 6); SA Sadat-Akhavi, *Methods of Resolving Conflicts between Treaties* (Leiden, Brill, 2003); JB Mus, *Verdragsconflicten voor de Nederlandse rechter* (Zwolle, WEJ Tjeenk Willink, 1996).

[62] On the so-called presumption against conflicts in international law, see Pauwelyn (n 4) 240–44; J Finke, 'Regime-collisions: Tensions between treaties (and how to solve them)' in CJ Tams et al (eds), *Research Handbook on the Law of Treaties* (Cheltenham, Edward Elgar Publishing, 2014) 421.

> norm of general international law is a norm accepted and recognized by the international community of States as a whole as a norm from which no derogation is permitted and which can be modified only by a subsequent norm of general international law having the same character.

Article 63 VCLT adds that if a new peremptory norm were to emerge, any existing conflicting treaty would become void.[63] The ICJ recognised the rules of *jus cogens* as part of international law in the *Nicaragua Case*.[64] These norms can develop from treaty law, international customary law and general principles of law, but the notion still remains underdeveloped, and there is much uncertainty and dispute about how *jus cogens* norms acquire such status.[65]

The *jus cogens* rule is not a classical conflict rule, as it does not give priority to one norm over another but invalidates the other norm. Nevertheless, it can be used as such if it is possible to identify a certain norm as being an internationally recognised *jus cogens* norm. Thus, if the ECHR (or part of it), being a human rights treaty, can be considered to embody *jus cogens* norms, it could be argued that EU law that is in breach of one or more Convention rights is null and void.[66] It would be difficult, however, to find support for this position in international law, since identifications of *jus cogens* norms are limited and invalidations of other norms on that basis hardly ever occur in practice.[67] The few examples of rights that are generally recognised as being *jus cogens* are the prohibition of genocide and the prohibition of torture.[68]

The European Court of First Instance (CFI) considered *jus cogens* rules in the *Kadi* case.[69] Mr Kadi, a Saudi resident, and the Al Barakaat International Foundation, established in Sweden – both listed in the annex to EU Regulation 881/2002 as suspected of supporting terrorism – brought actions for annulment before the CFI,[70] claiming that the Council was not competent to adopt the

[63] O Dörr and K Schmalenbach (eds), *Vienna Convention on the Law of Treaties: a commentary* (Heidelberg, Springer, 2012).

[64] *Military and Paramilitary Activities in and against Nicaragua (Nicaragua v USA)* [1986] ICJ Rep 14.

[65] U Linderfalk, 'The Effect of Jus Cogens Norms: Whoever Opened Pandora's Box, Did You Ever Think About the Consequences?' (2007) 18 *European Journal of International Law* 853; D Shelton, 'Normative Hierarchy in International Law' (2006) 100 *American Journal of International Law* 291, 304.

[66] A Bianchi, 'Human Rights and the Magic of Jus Cogens' (2008) 19 *The European Journal of International Law* 491.

[67] M Milanović, 'Norm Conflict in International Law: Whither Human Rights?' (2009) 20 *Duke Journal of International and Comparative Law* 69; Bianchi (n 66).

[68] For a more inclusive list, see Venice Commission Report, *Are There Differentiations Among Human Rights? Jus Cogens, Core Human Rights, Obligations Erga Omnes and Non-Derogability*, CDL-UD(2005)020rep-e. On the prohibition of torture specifically, see E De Wet, 'The Prohibition of Torture as an International Norm of Jus Cogens and Its Implications for National and Customary Law' (2004) 15 *European Journal of International Law* 97. On the prohibition of genocide as *jus cogens*, see J Wouters and S Verhoeven, 'The Prohibition of Genocide as a Norm of Ius Cogens and Its Implications for the Enforcement of the Law of Genocide' (2005) 5 *International Criminal Law Review* 401.

[69] Case T-315/01 *Kadi* v *Council and Commission*, ECLI:EU:T:2005:332.

[70] Note that the CFI was renamed the 'General Court' after the entry into force of the Lisbon Treaty on 1 December 2009.

above-mentioned Regulation and that the Regulation violated their fundamental rights, in particular the right to property and the rights of defence. The Regulation imposed sanctions on the applicants, in particular freezing their financial assets.[71] The applicants argued that they had never been involved in terrorism or supported it in any way. In response, the EU Council and the Commission contended that the EU, as well as its Member States, was bound by international law and was thus obliged to give effect to the mandatory measures of the UNSC. To question the lawfulness of those measures by means of judicial review 'would cause serious disruption to the international relations of the Community'.[72]

The CFI dismissed these actions and ruled that the EU Member States were indeed required to comply with UNSC resolutions, in accordance with customary international law and Article 103 of the UN Charter. Furthermore, the Court held that UNSC resolutions have primacy over EU law, as well as over any other obligations of domestic or international law, including those under the ECHR. The CFI considered that the only way EU courts might review the legality of the Regulation at issue would be in the light of higher norms of public international law, that is *jus cogens*, from which even the UN bodies cannot derogate. It found that these higher rules – to the extent that the right to property and defence rights can be considered as part of *jus cogens* – were not infringed in this case.[73]

On appeal to the Court of Justice, the Court reversed the judgment of the CFI, annulling the relevant implementing measures and declaring that they had violated fundamental rights protected by the EU legal order.[74] The Court concluded that the CFI erred in law by holding that the EU judiciary was only competent to review the legality of the Regulation at issue with regard to *jus cogens*. In other words, the Court of Justice held that the EU legal order is autonomous in relation to the rest of international law.

ii. Article 30 VCLT

Article 30 VCLT reads as follows:

1. Subject to Article 103 of the Charter of the United Nations, the rights and obligations of States and international organizations parties to successive treaties

[71] The EU Regulation was implementing a number of UNSC resolutions concerning the suppression of international terrorism and adopted under Chapter VII of the UN Charter. These include SC Res 1267, 15 October 1999, S/RES/1267 (1999); SC Res 1333, 19 December 2000, S/RES/1333 (2000); and SC Res.1390 of 28 January 2002, S/RES/1390 (2002).

[72] *Kadi* (n 69) para 162.

[73] The CFI's assessment of the content of *jus cogens* was criticised by several commentators. See, with further references, P Eeckhout, 'Community Terrorism Listing, Fundamental Rights, and UN Security Council Resolutions: In Search of the Right Fit' (2007) 3 *European Constitutional Law Review* 183.

[74] Joined Cases C-402/05 P and C-415/05 P, *Kadi and Al Barakaat* [2008] ECLI:EU:C:2008:461. The judgment has been met with mixed criticism; see, eg, J Weiler 'Editorial' (2009) 19 *European Journal of International Law* 895; K Ziegler, 'Strengthening the Rule of Law, but Fragmenting International Law: The Kadi Decision of the ECJ from the Perspective of Human Rights' (2009) 9 *Human Rights Law Review* 288; G Harpaz, 'Judicial Review by the European Court of Justice of UN "Smart Sanctions"

relating to the same subject-matter shall be determined in accordance with the following paragraphs.

2. When a treaty specifies that it is subject to, or that it is not to be considered as incompatible with, an earlier or later treaty, the provisions of that other treaty prevail.
3. When all the parties to the earlier treaty are parties also to the later treaty but the earlier treaty is not terminated or suspended in operation under article 59, the earlier treaty applies only to the extent that its provisions are compatible with those of the later treaty.
4. When the parties to the later treaty do not include all the parties to the earlier one:
   (a) as between 2 parties each of which is a party to both treaties, the same rule applies as in paragraph 3;
   (b) as between a party to both treaties and a party to only one of the treaties, the treaty to which both States are parties governs their mutual rights and obligations.
5. Paragraph 4 is without prejudice to article 41, or to any question of the termination or suspension of the operation of a treaty under article 60 or to any question of responsibility which may arise for a State or for an international organization from the conclusion or application of a treaty the provisions of which are incompatible with its obligations towards another State under another treaty.

The principle *lex superior derogat legi inferiori*, contained in Article 30(1) VCLT, refers to situations in which one law is subordinate to another law. This rule is well established in many domestic law hierarchies and has been traditionally applied to resolving conflicts within a single legal system, where rules exist in the form of hierarchy. In federal systems, for example, federal law takes precedence over state law,[75] and in unitary and devolved systems primary legislation is higher in rank than secondary legislation. Similarly, there are norms in international law that are considered to rank higher than all other norms. Article 30(1) VCLT explicitly refers to Article 103 of the UN Charter as *lex superior*. Article 103 gives the UN Charter supremacy, providing:

> In the event of a conflict between the obligations of the Members of the United Nations under the present Charter and their obligations under any other international agreement, their obligations under the present Charter shall prevail.[76]

Against Terror in the Kadi Dispute' (2009) 14 *European Foreign Affairs Review* 65; G de Búrca, 'The European Court of Justice and the International Legal Order After *Kadi*' (2010) 51 *Harvard International Law Journal* 1; G de Búrca, 'The ECJ and the International Legal Order: A Re-evaluation' in de Búrca and Weiler (eds) (n 7) 105.

[75] See, inter alia, Art 32 of the German Constitution.

[76] The legitimacy of the rule in Art 103 of the UN Charter stems from the fact that it is widely accepted by the UN Member States, international courts and tribunals, as well as by other international treaties and organisations, including the VCLT. For the confirmation of its supremacy over other international agreements in the case law of international courts, see *Questions of Interpretation & Application of the 1971 Montreal Convention arising from the Aerial Incident at Lockerbie (Libya v UK) and (Libya v USA)* [1998] ICJ Rep 115, paras 39–41; *Military and Paramilitary Activities in and against Nicaragua (Nicaragua v United States of America)* [1985] ICJ Rep 14, para 107; *Kadi* (n 69) paras 183–204; Case T-306/01 *Yusuf Al Barakaat v Council*, ECLI:EU:T:2005:331, paras 233–254; *Behrami and Behrami v*

As a result, the obligations of the UN members under the UN Charter take precedence over their obligations under any other international agreement.[77] This effect of Article 103 has been challenged before, however, in the context of its relationship with international customary law, with *jus cogens* and human rights norms, as well as in the context of agreements made between UN and non-UN members.[78]

Article 30(2) VCLT refers to the specific conflict clauses that may be included in the treaties themselves. As already explained, such clauses regulate the relationship between the provisions of the treaty that is being drafted and other treaties, in order to resolve or prevent conflicts between provisions stemming from different legal instruments.[79] Conflict clauses can be categorised in three ways: they may provide expressly for the derogation from earlier treaties; they may give priority to the treaty over later treaties; and they may provide that the later treaty is compatible with an earlier treaty. Conflict clauses may be limited to certain specific treaties or apply to all treaties. The International Law Commission (ILC) Fragmentation Study stated that '[a]lthough such [conflict resolution] clauses are undoubtedly useful, there is a limit to what they can achieve', and that 'sometimes conflict clauses may themselves conflict or cancel each other out'.[80] While it may indeed be difficult to implement them in practice, since it is generally hard to predict the impact other (new) treaties may have on the existing obligations and, moreover, such rules are open to interpretation, specific conflict resolution clauses may also prove to be a useful tool in resolving conflicts. This will of course depend on the treaty itself and how the conflict clause has been formulated. When the wording of such a provision gives rise to difficulties and controversy concerning its interpretation, a conflict clause may indeed fail to achieve its aim.

The *lex posterior derogat legi priori* principle, as articulated in Article 30(3) and (4)(a) VCLT, regulates conflicts between treaties concluded between the same parties, where the relationship between those treaties is not regulated in one of them. The principle translated literarily means 'later law overrides earlier law'. The

France, Saramati v France, Germany and Norway App nos 71412/01 and 78166/01 (ECtHR, Decision on Admissibility of 2 May 2007) para 61, respectively at para 141; *Berić and Others v Bosnia and Herzegovina* App no 36257/04 (ECtHR, Decision on Admissibility of 16 October 2007) para 29. It is of course interesting in this context to mention the decision of the Court of Justice in *Kadi*, where the Court disregarded the relevance of Art 103 – without even referring to it – by ruling that the EU is exempted from complying with the UN sanctions adopted under Chapter VII of the UN Charter if they are in conflict with 'higher' EU law. See *Kadi and Al Barakaat* (n 74).

[77] J Vidmar, 'Norm Conflicts and Hierarchy in International Law: Towards a Vertical International Legal System?' in E de Wet and J Vidmar (eds), *Hierarchy in International Law: The Place of Human Rights* (Oxford, Oxford University Press, 2012) 13, 18.

[78] See the discussion, with further references, in V Jeutner, *Irresolvable Norm Conflicts in International Law* (Oxford, Oxford University Press, 2017) 49–50.

[79] International Law Commission (ILC), 'Draft Articles on the Law of Treaties with Commentaries' (1996) 2 *Yearbook of International Law Commission* 187, Art 26(2).

[80] International Law Commission (ILC), *Report of the International Law Commission on the Fragmentation of International Law: Difficulties arising from the diversification and expansion of International Law* (13 April 2006) A/CN.4/L.663/Rev.1 (ILC Fragmentation Study) paras 269–270.

legal consequence is thus that the rule in the older treaty is not applied but its validity is not affected. There are, however, two requirements that need to be fulfilled: first, the parties to the earlier and later treaty must be the same; and, second, the conclusion of the later treaty must not imply the termination or suspension of the earlier one in accordance with Article 59 VCLT. The main justification for giving the later treaty priority is that it is the most recent, and presumably most accurate, reflection of the will of the relevant actors. Determining which treaty is earlier or later should be done on the basis of the date of adoption of the treaty rather than the entry into force. Even though the rights and obligations stemming from the treaty become effective only when the treaty enters into force, it was considered necessary to go back to the moment of adoption in order to understand the priorities at the time fully.[81]

iii. Application of Article 30 VCLT

Article 30 VCLT contains conflict rules that should be applied to treaty conflicts, but it also restricts that same application. What becomes immediately obvious is that the normative framework of Article 30 only applies in certain defined instances. Its title suggests a limited scope of application: it applies only when the treaties are successive and when they relate to the same subject matter. The latter limits the scope of the very notion of treaty conflict, since the most serious conflicts tend to be between provisions from different fields covering – strictly speaking – different subject matters (eg trade versus environment, investment versus labour, or extradition versus human rights). It could be argued, however, that even though the provisions may originate in treaties that cover different subject matters, the boundaries between them are (often) blurred: a treaty on trade may contain human rights and environmental provisions, for example, although in principle they all cover different subject matters. Moreover, there is no pre-determined classification scheme of different subjects that could be used to determine which subject matter is covered in which treaty.[82] This strict interpretation of the wording of Article 30 VCLT is therefore often considered inadequate, and an argument has been made for its broader interpretation and application.[83] Indeed, the conflict rules provided in Article 30 are restrictive if interpreted narrowly; and even when they are interpreted and applied more broadly, they appear not to be very useful with regard to resolving difficult conflicts between EU and ECHR law.

[81] O Corten and P Klein, *The Vienna Convention on the Law of Treaties: A Commentary* (Oxford, Oxford University Press, 2011).

[82] International Law Commission, Report of the Study Group of the International Law Commission finalised by M Koskenniemi, *Fragmentation of International Law: Difficulties Arising from the Diversification and Expansion of International Law* (13 April 2006) UN Doc A/CN.4/L.682.

[83] B Conforti, *Consistency among Treaty Obligations* (Oxford, Oxford University Press, 2011); C Borgen, 'Resolving Treaty Conflicts' (2005) 37 *George Washington International Law Review* 573, 578. See also ILC, *Fragmentation of International Law: Difficulties Arising from the Diversification and Expansion of International Law* (n 81).

The *lex superior* rule refers to norms recognised to rank higher than any other norms of international law. These include Article 103 of the UN Charter and the *jus cogens* norms, which were discussed in section IV.C.ii. Article 103 of the UN Charter only comes into play when there is a conflict between states' obligations under EU and/or ECHR law and the UN Charter, giving priority to the latter. This rule is therefore not relevant in the context of conflicts between EU and ECHR law.

Lex posterior is another conflict rule contained in Article 30 VCLT that does not seem to be helpful in the context of conflicts between EU and ECHR law. While the application of *lex posterior* to bilateral treaties is rather straightforward, this is not the case with regard to multilateral treaties that are 'living instruments',[84] continuously evolving through judicial and non-judicial interpretation and application. The rationale behind the *lex posterior* principle is that the later treaty will reflect the intention of the parties more accurately. This, again, is applicable to bilateral treaties and, more generally, to treaties that deal with the same subject matter, but it is difficult to apply it to conflicts between multilateral treaties. Indeed, it would not make much sense to say, for instance, that the EU Treaty should have priority because it was adopted later than the ECHR, or vice versa. In fact, Pauwelyn has argued that Article 30 VCLT would generally not apply to multilateral treaties of a 'living' or 'continuing' nature, as it presupposes that the treaties are fixed in and do not evolve through time.[85] Moreover, Article 30(4) VCLT includes an exception to the *lex posterior* rule, allowing for parallel application, even if parties to the earlier and later treaties are not the same. In such cases, the *lex posterior* rule applies only to the countries that are Contracting Parties to both treaties, and thus it covers only a limited set of cases.

Since the rules contained in Article 30 of the Vienna Treaty offer little guidance concerning conflicts between EU and ECHR law, it is be important to check whether guidance can be sought elsewhere: in the treaties themselves, for example. In that context, Article 52(3) of the EU Charter is relevant, as it is a specifically designed conflict rule in primary EU law that requires consistency between the corresponding rights in the Charter and in the Convention. It is arguable that an international judge, in an assessment of conflicts between EU and ECHR law and the application of the VCLT, would simply make reference to this provision giving priority to the ECHR.

iv. Lex Specialis

The maxim *lex specialis derogat legi generali*, even though it is not specifically mentioned in the VCLT, is generally accepted as a principle of public international law.[86] It entails the rule that, whenever two or more norms deal with the

[84] See eg G Letsas, 'The ECHR as a living instrument: its meaning and legitimacy' in A Føllesdal, B Peters and G Ulfstein, *Constituting Europe* (Cambridge, Cambridge University Press, 2013).

[85] Pauwelyn (n 4) 378.

[86] S Borelli, 'The (Mis)-Use of General Principles of Law: Lex Specialis and the Relationship between International Human Rights Law and the Laws of Armed Conflict' in L Pineschi (ed), *General*

same subject matter, precedence should be given to the norm that is more specific over the more general norm. It is recognised and applied by the international courts and tribunals, in particular with regard to conflicts between treaties on the same subject matter or those being part of the same regime.[87] Similar to the rules in Article 30 VCLT, the rationale behind *lex specialis* is the fact that a more specific rule would be a more accurate expression of state consent. In practical terms, however, *lex specialis* is mainly used as a conflict avoidance rule rather than conflict resolution rule.[88]

Lex specialis as a rule of conflict resolution is also problematic. The most contentious point is how to determine which measure is more specific, especially in cases of the so-called genuine or true conflicts, where one treaty prescribes and the other one prohibits certain behaviour. In such cases, it is difficult to determine which norm is *lex generalis* and which is *lex specialis*. Consequently, this conflict resolution rule also only addresses a limited set of cases and cannot be taken as a generally applicable rule. In addition, as with previous conflict rules, there are not many examples in international practice where *lex specialis* has been used as a rule of conflict resolution, which may also imply that it is not widely applicable or indeed useful in different types of treaty conflicts.[89]

The notion of *lex specialis* does not appear to be helpful in the conflicts between the ECHR and EU law, since such conflicts mainly concern obligations arising from the ECHR (a human rights treaty) and the application and implementation of EU secondary law (obligations arising under the EU Treaties), whereas a *lex specialis* rule, as defined above, is more suitable for treaties on the same subject matter or treaties that are part of the same regime.[90] It could possibly apply in cases of conflicts between the ECHR and the EU Charter of Fundamental Rights, but conflicts that are considered in this research are mainly between the ECHR and EU secondary law (interpreted in the light of the Charter). Moreover, *lex specialis* seems to be a rule of conflict avoidance rather than conflict resolution – it can tell us which treaty to choose if both are saying the same thing, one being more specific or recent than the other, but if the two norms require conflicting actions it

Principles of Law: The Role of the Judiciary (Cham, Springer, 2015) 265. For an argument that it is factually incorrect to say that *lex specialis* enjoys general acceptance as a principle of international law or that it is entrenched in long-standing custom, see M Milanović, 'The Lost Origins of Lex Specialis: Rethinking the Relationship between Human Rights and International Humanitarian Law' in JD Ohlin, *Theoretical Boundaries of Armed Conflict and Human Rights* (Cambridge, Cambridge University Press, 2016) 78.

[87] The ECtHR, for instance, has considered Art 6 ECHR, providing the right to a fair trial, *lex specialis* in relation to Art 13, providing for the right to an effective remedy – see *Yankov v Bulgaria* App no 39084/97 (ECtHR, 11 December 2003) para 150. See also *Case Concerning the Gabčíkovo-Nagymaros Project (Hungary v Slovakia)* [1997] ICJ Rep 7, para 132; *Ambatielos case (Greece v United Kingdom)* [1952] ICJ Rep 28, para 44.

[88] For the two different understandings of *lex specialis* (as a conflict avoidance and a conflict resolution rule), see ILC, *Fragmentation of International Law: Difficulties Arising from the Diversification and Expansion of International Law* (n 81), paras 56–57 and 88. See also Pauwelyn (n 4) 396.

[89] Milanović (n 67).

[90] Finke (n 62).

may be difficult to determine which one is more specific and on that basis resolve the conflict.

v. *Lex Specialis* and Self-contained Regimes

The notion of *lex specialis* can also be conceptualised in a different way. In addition to its application to specific treaty provisions, it could also apply to the whole treaty regime, which is self-contained and thus *lex specialis*. Such regimes contain sets of rules that form a separate system in international law containing its own rules on substance, interpretation and enforcement. The EU has been considered a self-contained regime,[91] but this idea has also been contested.[92] If EU law could be considered *lex specialis* then it would have priority over other international treaties (which cannot be identified as *lex specialis*). The question arises, is EU law *lex specialis*?

Looking at the EU and EU law from a general international law perspective, we see an association of sovereign states that cooperate very intensely and that have decided to limit their sovereignty for that purpose. This is not problematic from an international law perspective, since the rules of international law, and more specifically international treaty law, are flexible and allow for such a high level of integration. The VCLT does not contain any rules or limitations in this regard, other than that the states are not permitted to make treaties that would be in conflict with *jus cogens*, which is not applicable in this case.[93] The VCLT in fact accepts distinct legal orders pursuant to Article 5, which states that the VCLT applies to any treaty without prejudice to any relevant rules of the organisation. International treaty law thus gives a lot of freedom to the states to decide on the different aspects concerning the international organisation they are creating, including the domestic enforcement of international obligations. In that sense, there is no obvious reason why the special characteristics of EU law, such as the principle of primacy and direct effect, would not be compatible with international treaty law or would imply that EU law should be treated differently in international law. Limitations of national sovereignty for the sake of a high level of integration in international organisations only accounts for the further development of international law and does not in itself give a higher hierarchical status to such treaties.[94] If it were to do so, it would mean that any group of states could create a highly integrated international organisation with unique characteristics and claim hierarchical superiority in international law. Moreover, the idea of self-contained

[91] J Weiler, 'The Transformation of Europe' (1990-1991) 100 *Yale Law Journal* 2403, 2422.

[92] B Simma and D Pulkowski, 'Of Planets and the Universe: Self-Contained Regimes in International Law' (2006) 17 *European Journal of International Law* 483, 519.

[93] Art 53 VCLT.

[94] De Witte (n 7); B De Witte, 'Rules of Change in International Law: How Special is the European Community?' (1994) 25 *Netherlands Yearbook of International Law* 299.

regimes, as such, is disputed and several other regimes are considered to be self-contained, such as international human rights law, international trade law and so on.[95] This is thus not something that can be considered to be an established rule in international law.

Human rights treaties could also be considered *lex specialis* because of their special nature. The argument that human rights treaties are special and therefore hierarchically superior to other treaties in international law has been evolving over the years in both doctrine and court practice, and many debates have arisen about how the law of treaties applies to human rights agreements and how it may accommodate their special characteristics.[96] The doctrinal premise used in this argument is that there is an ongoing process of constitutionalisation in international law,[97] and that the international legal order is moving towards a vertical legal system with human rights at its apex.[98] The question is whether this is indeed the case.

The underlying reason most international treaties are concluded is for the establishment of reciprocal obligations between states for a specific purpose. While this is also true for human rights treaties, they are also different in a number of ways: they are not based on reciprocity; they operate between states and individuals rather than just states, creating obligations for the states towards individuals; and the compliance of states' obligations with human rights treaties is sometimes monitored by the institutions and procedures employed to ensure their enforcement. The Human Rights Committee described human rights treaties as treaties providing 'the endowment of individuals with rights' rather than 'a web of inter-state exchanges of mutual obligations'.[99] In some cases, those rights are directly effective at the national level, but they can also be vindicated at the international level through a complaint procedure before international courts (this is the case under the ECHR machinery). This means that human rights treaties are not static elements of international law, as many other international treaties are, but comprise universal norms driven by the common concerns of the international society. This has been confirmed in the human rights treaties themselves and is mirrored in the ethical and legal foundations of those treaties, including references to human dignity, equality, fairness and justice for all without distinction. In that sense, human rights treaties create obligations towards the international community as a whole, and thus generally have an *erga omnes* character.

[95] J Klabbers, A Peters and G Ulfstein, *The Constitutionalization of International Law* (Oxford, Oxford University Press, 2009) 2.

[96] See, eg, A Orakhelashvili, 'Peremptory Norms in International Law' (2006) Oxford Scholarship Online, available at https://oxford.universitypressscholarship.com/view/10.1093/acprof:oso/9780199546114.001.0001/acprof-9780199546114 (last accessed 16 December 2020).

[97] M Koskenniemi, 'Constitutionalism as a Mindset: Reflections on Kantian Themes about International Law and Globalization' (2007) 8 *Theoretical Inquiries in Law* 9; Klabbers, Peters and Ulfstein (n 95).

[98] E De Wet and J Vidmar, *Hierarchy in International Law: The Place of Human Rights* (Oxford, Oxford University Press, 2012).

[99] CCPR General Comment No 24: Issues Relating to Reservations Made upon Ratification or Accession to the Covenant or the Optional Protocols thereto, or in Relation to Declarations under Article 41 of the Covenant, 4 November 1994, CCPR/C/21/Rev 1/Add 6.

Indeed, the ICJ asserted in the *Barcelona Traction* case that certain basic human rights give rise to international obligations owed by states to all other states, which the Court thus characterised as *erga omnes* obligations.[100] This approach builds its parameters partly with reference to the category of *jus cogens*, also recognised in the VCLT, and partly on the more general assumption that human rights treaties are *special*. The content of *jus cogens* norms when considered in relation to treaty provisions that could be incompatible with such norms is very limited, however, since *jus cogens* comprises only the most basic fundamental rights and freedoms, such as the freedom from torture.[101] If a multilateral treaty contains rules that reproduce norms of *jus cogens*, such norms will take priority. For the most part, however, the special character of human rights treaties rests on the special nature of human rights, as such, which is undeniably different from the content of any other contractual treaties between states. Values enshrined in human rights are considered to be of constitutional importance in most, if not all, states, and the same status should be accorded to the international treaties that embody them. The ECHR can be said to possess these special characteristics, as it imposes obligations on states towards individuals and grants the latter rights of enforcement. Furthermore, as a matter of structure, the ECHR provides its own machinery to interpret and apply ECHR provisions.

A specific example put forward in favour of the argument that human rights treaties are special and different from other treaties concerns their status in the case of state succession. The 1978 Vienna Convention on Succession of States in Respect of Treaties provides for the continuity of obligations in respect of all treaties that were previously binding on the predecessor states. Contrary to this rule, the practice in general international law is that the new state is free to choose whether it will become a party to the treaties adhered to by the predecessor state. Since the rule in the 1978 Vienna Convention does not reflect customary international law, it has been met with little support in the international community. However, this is different for human rights treaties; the new state does not have a choice when it comes to human rights treaties, since the inhabitants of a territory cannot be deprived of rights previously granted to them under a human rights treaty due to succession. Therefore, the continuity of obligations occurs automatically and does not require a formal confirmation by the successor state, which represents an important exception to the general customary rule of non-continuity of treaty obligations.[102] This has been considered as providing strong evidence that human rights treaties not only enjoy superior ranking in comparison

[100] *Barcelona Traction, Light and Power Company Ltd (Belgium v Spain)* [1970] ICJ Rep 3, paras 33–34.

[101] M Scheinin, 'Human Rights Treaties and the Vienna Convention on the Law of Treaties: Conflict or Harmony?' in Venice Commission, *The Status of International Treaties on Human Rights* (Strasbourg, Council of Europe Publishing, 2006) 43, 49.

[102] Other exceptions are treaties providing for territorial regimes. See M Kamminga, 'Human Rights Treaties and State Succession' in *The Status of International Treaties on Human Rights* (Strasbourg, Council of Europe Publishing, 2006). See also Human Rights Committee, General Comment No. 26: Continuity of obligations, 8 September 1997.

to other international treaties, but they are also 'permanent and inalienable'.[103] Nevertheless, in practice, a formal notification that the new state considers itself bound is welcome in order to clarify any ambiguities that may exist. An example of such a practice in the ECHR system would be the dissolution of the Czech and Slovak Federal Republic. The Council of Europe's Committee of Ministers decided that the Czech Republic and the Slovak Republic were to be regarded as having succeeded to the Convention retroactively from their date of independence, and the ECtHR followed suit.

Another distinct characteristic of human rights treaties is the test of the compatibility of reservations employed in relation to such treaties. Since human rights treaties are intended to be subject to the wide participation of the states, the right to make a reservation is an important tool in achieving that, while, at the same time, a reservation cannot be contrary to the object and purpose of the Treaty and its acceptance will depend on specific circumstances.[104]

What can be concluded here is that there is an emerging theory in international law that human rights treaties have a special status in international law, and therefore they take priority over other international treaties. This could be used as an argument to say that obligations under ECHR law should take priority over EU law obligations in the event of a conflict. The same does not necessarily apply to the EU Treaties since, as argued before, there is no obvious reason why, from a general international law point of view, EU Treaties or EU law should have priority. While EU law has certain distinct characteristics, such as primacy and direct effect, this in itself does not mean that it is hierarchically superior to other international treaties. Furthermore, a reference should also be made to the Vienna Convention, in particular its Article 30(2), which refers to conflict clauses found in the treaties themselves. In that context, Article 52(3) of the EU Charter is important, as it can be seen as a conflict clause specifically designed for conflicts between the ECHR and the EU Charter (in light of which EU law has to be interpreted), providing that corresponding Charter and Convention rights shall have the same meaning and scope. This means that EU law should be interpreted and applied in conformity with the ECHR whenever the Charter rights that are at stake correspond to the Convention rights. In practical terms, this means that, in such instances, ECHR law prevails.

VI. Conclusion

This chapter has sought to analyse the ways in which conflicts between EU and ECHR law can be resolved from the point of view of national courts. This has

[103] M Kamminga, 'Human Rights Treaties and State Succession' in Venice Commission, *The Status of International Treaties on Human Rights* (Strasbourg, Council of Europe Publishing, 2006) 31, 41.

[104] Reservations to the Convention on the Prevention and Punishment of the Crime of Genocide, Advisory Opinion [1951] ICJ Rep 24. See also Art 19 VCLT.

required an assessment of the status of EU and ECHR law in the legal systems of EU Member States. Furthermore, the chapter has examined the conflict rules contained in the provisions of the EU Treaties and the ECHR, as interpreted by the CJEU and ECtHR respectively. Last but not least, the chapter has looked at the rules of conflict as they exist in international law. After all, both EU law and the ECHR are international treaties, and international law may become relevant for some national courts.

The first part of the analysis has demonstrated that most constitutions give a special status to both EU and ECHR law and do not offer clear rules as to which one takes priority in the event of a conflict. This is generally true for monist states but also for dualist states, most of which have at some point given a special status to the ECHR in the national legal orders and where national courts do not directly give priority to EU law, even though that may seem logical from the point of view of a dualist approach. This means that the national courts in most countries will have to look beyond the national constitution for a solution.

What we can conclude from looking at the conflict rules in international law is that there is an emerging theory that human rights treaties are *lex specialis* due to their special nature and, as such, should have priority over other international treaties. This is an argument that could be used by national courts to justify giving precedence to the ECHR over EU law, where the higher hierarchical level is not already granted in the constitution. However, an argument could be made that EU law is *lex specialis* too, because of its autonomy and supranational character.[105] The CJEU has repeatedly held that the EU legal order is autonomous and bound by international law only to the extent that EU law itself allows it. While this is not how international law normally works, this view plays an important role in determining the place of EU law in international law as well as the relationship between the two. The argument is thus circular: determining the status of EU law in international law also includes the view of the CJEU that claims that EU law is *special*. As a consequence, arguments can be made for both EU and ECHR law as having a special status in international law, and the latter does not provide conclusive answers in that respect.

Furthermore, national courts could decide to consult the VCLT, which contains some conflict rules. However, even though the Vienna Convention is written in a way that appears to be applicable to all treaty relationships between states, it contains a number of assumptions that do not apply to human rights treaties and other treaties that possess certain characteristics, such as the EU Treaties. Indeed, the VCLT implies or refers to reciprocal treaty relationships between states, where every right by one state corresponds to a duty of another state. This again would not apply to human rights treaties or to the EU Treaties, since they create concrete obligations for states towards individuals and are not based on reciprocity.

[105] Scheinn (n 101).

Nevertheless, the VCLT does offer a way out: Article 30(2) of the Vienna Treaty refers to conflict clauses that can be included in the treaties and later applied in cases of conflicts. Indeed, if there is a conflict clause in the treaties themselves, that clause should be applied to resolve the conflict (unless one of them can be considered *lex superior*). Here again, Article 52(3) of the EU Charter becomes relevant. This provision, as argued before, is meant to regulate the consistency between EU and ECHR law, requiring a consistent interpretation of the corresponding Charter and Convention rights.[106] It is thus suggested that Article 52(3) of the Charter can be used as a specific conflict rule by national courts in order to deal with conflicts between EU law (interpreted in light of the Charter) and ECHR law, by ultimately giving priority to the ECHR. However, given that the CJEU has interpreted Article 52(3) differently and inconsistently in its case law, the way in which a national court will deal with a perceived conflict between EU and ECHR law will depend on the arguments used, and the responses are bound to vary.

[106] See in particular ch 2, section III.A.ii.

6

Scenarios from the Member States

I. Introduction

This book has reviewed the foundations of EU fundamental rights law; reconstructed the relationships between the different components of EU fundamental rights; illustrated when and why these components may clash; and criticised the approach of the Court of Justice in this context. The task of the last part of the book has been to assess how national courts can and should deal with what they perceive to be conflicts between EU law and the ECHR.

The first step has been to examine available conflict rules from the point of view of national courts. This required an assessment of the status of EU and ECHR law in the domestic legal systems of EU Member States. As argued in chapter 5, both EU law and the ECHR have been given a special status in most systems either in the provisions of the constitution, or in the case law of constitutional or other highest courts. Even the traditional dichotomy between the monist and dualist approaches does not affect this conclusion because of the way in which the ECHR is embedded in national legal systems, even in dualist states. Moreover, chapter 5 found that international (treaty) law is inconclusive when it comes to resolving conflicts between the EU Treaties and ECHR law. Since both of them are special from the perspective of general international law (the EU Treaties because of their supranational character and the ECHR because it is a human rights treaty), the 'normal' conflict rules cannot be applied. The only provisions that may offer guidance are thus those provided in the Treaties themselves. The most important in this regard is Article 52(3) of the EU Charter, which could be seen as a rule of conflict: in the event of a divergence in the approach of the two European Courts, such a conflict must be resolved in favour of the approach adopted by the Strasbourg Court. However, the CJEU has interpreted this provision differently and inconsistently over time, thereby not giving a clear instruction regarding the obligations arising from it.

The second step, which is the task of this final chapter, is to investigate how national courts actually deal with what they perceive to be conflicting obligations arising from EU and ECHR law. The chapter develops a scenario analysis of ways to approach the specific conflicts between EU and ECHR law, inspired by some examples from the actual case law of national courts. The aim is to discern and categorise different choices national courts have made when faced with a situation in which complying with EU law leads or may lead to a violation of the ECHR, or when ensuring compliance with the ECHR standards may mean a failure to comply with EU law obligations. The case law of national courts is thus used as an inspiration to illustrate different approaches.

When faced with incompatibility between EU law (or the national implementing act) and the Convention, national courts have to decide on a course of action: to seek conform interpretation (section II); to ensure compliance with the ECHR, even if that means failure to execute an EU law obligation, thus risking that their decision may violate EU law (section III); to examine the cases on the basis of their own constitution and thus reframe the conflict between EU law and the Convention rights as a conflict between EU law and national fundamental rights (section IV); or to make a preliminary reference to the CJEU, asking the Court how the incompatibility should be resolved (section V). Section VI provides an overall assessment and analysis of the findings.

II. Conform Interpretation

The first scenario under analysis is a classic one: national courts seek a conform interpretation of two seemingly conflicting positions without explicitly following one or the other. In 2014, the UK Supreme Court was confronted with a decision of the Court of Appeal that, after having identified an incompatibility between EU law and the ECHR, felt compelled to follow EU law and disregard the ECHR, because 'the decision of CJEU was binding on courts of this country'.[1] The Supreme Court, however, decided to conduct an analysis of the case law of the European courts on its own, and reached what it considered to be a consistent reading of both.[2]

The case arose from the joined appeals of four Iranian and Eritrean asylum seekers against their return to Italy under the Dublin Regulation. The applicants claimed to be at risk of ill-treatment in Italy, their first country of entry according to the Dublin system, for reasons including homelessness and hardship, a risk of rape and a lack of access to psychological treatment. The Home Secretary certified the claims at issue as clearly unfounded on the basis that Italy was not in systemic breach of its international obligations and that there was no other reason to refrain from their removal. The right to appeal could only be permitted if it was shown that Italy was 'in systemic rather than sporadic breach of its international obligations', as required by EU law, which the appellants failed to prove.

The appellants' application for judicial review was refused at first instance but allowed at the Court of Appeal. The Court of Appeal stated at the outset that it was confronted with conflicting decisions of the ECtHR and CJEU in the case at

[1] *EM (Eritrea) v Secretary of State for the Home Department* [2014] UKSC 12 [32].

[2] ibid. For the judgment of the Court of Appeal, see *EM (Eritrea) and Others v Secretary of State for the Home Department* [2012] EWCA Civ 1336.

hand. It referred specifically to paragraphs 81 and 82 of the CJEU's *NS* judgment,[3] in which the Court of Justice had made a distinction between a true systemic deficiency and operational problems, whereby only in the former cases are transfers not allowed. Accordingly, even if the problems would create a substantial risk that asylum seekers would be treated in a manner incompatible with their fundamental rights, they should still be transferred. At the same time, however, the ECtHR requires its Contracting Parties to refrain from transferring in such situations. Interestingly, the Court of Appeal reached this conclusion in reference to *MSS v Belgium and Greece* only (*Tarakhel* was not decided at the time), thus already predicting what would follow later regarding the systemic deficiency requirement in the case law of the two European Courts.[4]

It is evident from the judgment that the Court faced a dilemma in deciding the case, as it was inclined to follow the Strasbourg jurisprudence while at same time being aware of the requirements coming from Luxembourg. Comparing the *MSS* and the *NS* judgments, the Court of Appeal concluded that the requirements appear to be different in Strasbourg and Luxembourg: while proof of individual risk seemed sufficient for the ECtHR to prevent a Dublin II return, such proof of risk, however grave and whether or not arising from operational problems, was deemed insufficient for the Luxembourg Court, without proof of a true systemic deficiency in the state's system. While the Court of Appeal found that the threshold established by the CJEU 'existed nowhere else in refugee law', it ultimately adopted the interpretation consistent with its interpretation of the CJEU's decision in *NS*.[5]

The Supreme Court conducted its own analysis of the relevant cases and reached a different conclusion. The principal issue for the Supreme Court was to determine whether the complainants were required to demonstrate that there were *systemic deficiencies* in the asylum procedure and in the reception conditions of asylum seekers in the country, which amounted to substantial grounds for believing that the asylum seekers would face a real risk of being subjected to inhuman or degrading treatment.[6]

First, the Court stated that there can be little doubt that the existence of a presumption that Member States would comply with their international obligations

[3] Joined Cases C-411/10 and C-493/10 *NS and others*, ECLI:EU:C:2011:865. Paras 81 and 82 read as follows:

> 81. It is not however inconceivable that the system may, in practice, experience major operational problems in a given Member State, meaning that there is a substantial risk that asylum seekers may, when transferred to that Member State, be treated in a manner incompatible with their fundamental rights.
>
> 82. Nevertheless, it cannot be concluded from the above that any infringement of a fundamental right by the Member State responsible will affect the obligations of the other Member States to comply with the provisions of Regulation No 343/2003.

[4] *EM (Eritrea) and Others v Secretary of State for the Home Department* [2012] EWCA Civ 1336 [43]–[48], citing *MSS v Belgium and Greece* App no 30696/09 (ECtHR, 21 January 2011). See later *Tarakhel v Switzerland* App no 29217/12 (ECtHR, 4 November 2014).

[5] ibid [61]. The Court of Appeal referred specifically to paras 81 and 82 of the CJEU's *NS* judgment.

[6] *EM (Eritrea) v Secretary of State for the Home Department* [2014] UKSC 12.

is necessary to produce a workable system, but it is in its nature that it can be rebutted in appropriate circumstances. In the Court's view, an infringement of Article 3 ECHR does not require (or, at least, does not necessarily require) that conditions alleged to constitute inhuman or degrading conditions are the product of systemic shortcomings; it is self-evident that a violation of Article 3 is not dependent on the failure of a system.[7] Furthermore, the Court pointed out that a violation resulting from a systemic failure would in no way be considered as more serious or more deserving of protection.

With respect to the conflicting obligations, the Court pointed out that if the Court of Appeal's interpretation of *NS* were correct, it would give rise to an inevitable tension between the Home Secretary's obligation to abide by EU law, as pronounced by the CJEU, and her duty as a public authority under section 6 of the Human Rights Act 1998. The latter refers to the domestic transposition of the ECHR, which is to be interpreted in accordance with the case law of the Strasbourg Court.

It is interesting to note that all parties to the case, including the appellants, the interveners (United Nations High Commissioner for Refugees) and the respondent, agreed that the Court of Appeal was wrong to hold that the sole ground on which a state is required to exercise its power under Article 3(2) of the Regulation is when the source of risk is a systemic deficiency in the asylum procedure or reception conditions of another state.[8] In other words, they all disagreed with the CJEU's findings and conclusions in the *NS* case (at least, to the extent that the Court of Appeal interpreted the *NS* case correctly, which, in my opinion, it did). The fact that the Supreme Court reached a different conclusion from that of the Court of Appeal as to what the CJEU *meant to say* in the *NS* case is due to its approach in the analysis rather than the literal reading of the case.

The Supreme Court ruled that the systemic deficiency test applied by the Court of Appeal, and derived from EU law, is incorrect. It found that account had to be taken of the practical realities that lie at the heart of the inquiry; evidence of what happens on the ground must be capable of rebutting the presumption, if it can be shown sufficiently clearly that there is a real risk of Article 3 ill-treatment if there is an enforced return. The correct test is therefore the ECtHR's *Soering* test, which, according to the UK Supreme Court, provides that 'the removal of a person from a member state of the Council of Europe to another country is forbidden if it is shown that there is a real risk that the person transferred will suffer treatment contrary to article 3 of ECHR'.[9] What the Supreme Court thus actually did was to conduct an ECHR conform interpretation of the CJEU's case law. The Supreme

[7] ibid [42].

[8] ibid [2].

[9] ibid [58]. In *Soering v United Kingdom*, the Strasbourg Court indeed held that there is an 'inherent obligation not to extradite [that] also extends to cases in which the fugitive would be faced in the receiving State by a real risk of exposure to inhuman or degrading treatment or punishment proscribed by that Article (art 3)'. See *Soering v United Kingdom*, App no 14038/88 (ECtHR, 7 July 1989) para 88. In addition, Judge De Meyer, in a Concurring Opinion (footnote omitted), stated that 'No State Party to the Convention can in that context, even if it has not yet ratified the Sixth Protocol, be allowed to

Court mentioned, at some point, that Article 3 ECHR contains human rights protection in language equivalent to Article 4 of the Charter, and that the UK is also obliged to observe and promote the application of the Charter whenever it is implementing EU law, without however mentioning Article 52(3) of the Charter.[10]

Concerning the conflicting obligations, the Supreme Court explained that the CJEU did not intend to stipulate that a violation of Article 3 can only be established if it is a result of a systemic deficiency in the asylum procedure and reception conditions of the receiving state. If it did, it would mean that the courts should disregard a real risk of Article 3 ill-treatment other than one resulting from a systemic deficiency in the procedure and reception conditions in the receiving state, which, in the Supreme Court's view, would be rather remarkable. Yet this seems to be exactly what the CJEU meant, particularly because it has been confirmed in the subsequent case law. Even if the wording of the *NS* case is uncertain and open to interpretation, the Luxembourg Court confirmed its systemic deficiency test in the *Puid* and *Abdullahi* cases. In those cases, the Court clearly held that

> the only way in which the applicant for asylum can call into question the choice of that criterion is by pleading systemic deficiencies in the asylum procedure and in the conditions for the reception of applicants for asylum in that latter Member State, which provide substantial grounds for believing that the applicant for asylum would face a real risk of being subjected to inhuman or degrading treatment within the meaning of Article 4 of the Charter.[11]

The UK Supreme Court decided not to consider the latter judgments, even though they had already been rendered and, in this way, facilitated a consistent interpretation of the Luxembourg and Strasbourg case law on the matter. In reality, the Supreme Court followed the interpretation of the ECtHR, without making it explicit and without making a reference to the CJEU. The conform interpretation scenario thus ultimately amounted to changing the meaning of EU law as interpreted by the CJEU in order to ensure consistency with the ECHR, and hence avoid conflicts between the two.

III. Giving Priority to the ECHR

The second scenario arises when national courts notice an incompatibility between an EU law obligation and one of the Convention rights, as interpreted by the ECtHR, and decide to ensure compliance with the ECHR, even if that means

extradite any person if that person thereby incurs the risk of being put to death in the requesting State. Extraditing somebody in such circumstances would be repugnant to European standards of justice, and contrary to the public order of Europe.'

[10] In its assessment, the Supreme Court focused on the ECHR and the Human Rights Act 1998, while the Charter stayed in the background and was referred to mainly in the context of the discussion or quoting of the CJEU's judgments.

[11] Case C-4/11 *Puid*, ECLI:EU:C:2013:740, para 30; Case C-394/12 *Abdullahi*, ECLI:EU:C:2013:813, para 60.

that they risk infringing EU law. This scenario differs from the first one, since national courts do not seek conform interpretations of the different parameters of fundamental rights; instead, they openly acknowledge the incompatibility and choose to follow the ECHR and the case law of the ECtHR, without making a reference to the CJEU.[12]

Already in 2010, the Irish courts were faced with difficulties arising from EU law, in particular the European Arrest Warrant (EAW) Framework Decision and the ECHR.[13] The case concerned an EAW issued by Poland requesting the surrender of Mr Rettinger, who had been convicted for burglary. He had spent 203 days in pre-trial detention in Poland before travelling to Ireland, where he was later arrested. The applicant argued that his surrender would result in a violation of Article 3 ECHR, referring to section 37 of the Irish European Arrest Warrant Act 2003, which states, inter alia, that surrender is prohibited if it would be incompatible with Ireland's obligations under the ECHR or its Protocols. The applicant based his claims on his personal experience in Poland during the pre-trial detention, as well as on the ECtHR decision in *Orchowski v Poland*,[14] in which the ECtHR found prison conditions in Poland to be incompatible with Article 3 ECHR. The Irish High Court decided that the surrender would not violate Article 3 of the Convention, since it was not known which Polish prison the applicant would be sent to. The Irish Supreme Court ruled, however, that the High Court did not apply the correct test, and remanded the case back to the High Court. The Supreme Court argued, relying on the ECtHR's judgments in *Soering v United Kingdom* and *Saadi v Italy*,[15] that it is not necessary for a requested person to prove that he or she will suffer inhuman and degrading treatment; it is enough to establish that there is a real risk of such treatment, distinct from a mere possibility. In order to do that, the High Court must conduct a 'rigorous examination' of 'all the materials before it and, if necessary, material sought by its own motion'.[16]

It does not come as a surprise that, in the two comparable cases in 2013 and 2014, the Irish Supreme and High Courts, respectively, decided to refuse surrender on the basis of an EAW (without making a preliminary reference to the CJEU) because 'to do so would be incompatible with this state's obligations under the European Convention on Human Rights'. In the first case, *Minister for Justice and Equality v Kelly aka Nolan*,[17] the Irish Supreme Court ruled that the surrender of the respondent to the UK would constitute a breach of Article 5 ECHR (the right to liberty, contained in Article 6 of the Charter). The respondent had been sentenced in the UK to a determinate period of two and a half years'

[12] *Minister for Justice, Equality and Law Reform v Rettinger* [2010] IR 783, Irish Supreme Court; *Minister for Justice and Equality v Kelly aka Nolan* [2013] IESC 54, Irish Supreme Court; *Minister for Justice and Equality v Rostaş* [2014] EHC 391 (Irish High Court).

[13] Council Framework Decision 2002/584/JHA of 13 June 2002 on the European arrest warrant and the surrender procedure between Member States, [2002] OJ L190/0001. *Rettinger* (n 12) Appeal Nos 165 & 189.

[14] *Orchowski v Poland*, App no 17885/04 (ECtHR, 22 October 2009).

[15] *Soering v United Kingdom* (n 9); *Saadi v Italy* App no 37201/06 (ECtHR, 28 February 2008).

[16] *Rettinger* (n 13) para 30.

[17] *Kelly aka Nolan* (n 12).

imprisonment, to be followed by an indeterminate sentence for the sake of public safety. The latter part of the sentence was a preventative measure and depended on an assessment of future risk. After serving five years and three months, the respondent fled to Ireland while on temporary release, leading to the EAW from the UK requesting his surrender. The Irish Supreme Court found that the UK's practice of indeterminate sentencing was in conflict with Article 5(1) ECHR, as previously held by the ECtHR, and refused to execute the EAW.

The second case, *Minister for Justice and Equality v Rostaş*,[18] concerned an EAW issued by a Romanian court seeking the return of Ms Rostaş for the purpose of the execution of a prison sentence in respect of a single robbery-type offence. The sentence was passed 16 years previously, when the respondent was 18 years of age, and it was already partly completed. Rostaş refused to consent to her surrender to Romania, raising a number of objections based on unfair trial grounds, including discrimination in the trial process based on race. She relied, inter alia, on section 37(1)(a) of the European Arrest Warrant Act 2003.[19] In substantiating the claim, she referred to numerous reports from the European Commission, the European Parliament and several non-governmental organisations, including Amnesty International and Human Rights Watch, which expounded on and referred to an extensive body of information concerning Romania and the discrimination faced by Roma in that relevant period of time. The respondent also referred to the judgments of the ECtHR concerning discrimination against the Roma in Romania.[20]

[18] *Rostaş* (n 12) para 121.

[19] Section 37(1) of the European Arrest Warrant Act 2003 as amended provides:

A person shall not be surrendered under this Act if—

(a) his or her surrender would be incompatible with the State's obligations under—
  (i) the Convention, or
  (ii) the Protocols to the Convention,
(b) his or her surrender would constitute a contravention of any provision of the Constitution (other than for the reason that the offence specified in the European arrest warrant is an offence to which section 38(1)(b) applies),
(c) there are reasonable grounds for believing that—
  (i) the European arrest warrant was issued in respect of the person for the purposes of facilitating his or her prosecution or punishment in the issuing state for reasons connected with his or her sex, race, religion, ethnic origin, nationality, language, political opinion or sexual orientation, or
  (ii) in the prosecution or punishment of the person in the issuing state, he or she will be treated less favourably than a person who—
    (I) is not his or her sex, race, religion, nationality or ethnic origin,
    (II) …
    (III) speaks a different language than he or she does, or
    (IV) …
    or
  (iii) …

[20] eg *Moldovan and others v Romania (No 1)* App nos 41138/98 and 64320/01 (ECtHR, 5 July 2005); *Moldovan and others v Romania (No 2)* App nos 41138/98 and 64320/01 (ECtHR, 12 July 2005); *Carabulea v Romania* App no 45661/99 (ECtHR, 13 July 2010); *Cobzaru v Romania* App no 48254/99 (ECtHR, 26 July, 2007); *Stoica v Romania* App no 42722/02 (ECtHR, 4 March 2008).

Indeed, Romania was found to be in breach of the ECHR multiple times for the discriminatory attitude of the authorities, including the police and the courts, against the Roma in Romania in the 1990s.

Interestingly, the respondent argued that the mutual trust between Member States, which is the basis of the EAW system, could not apply in this case, because the conviction on which the EAW was based dated back to a period of time when Romania was not considered fit to join the EU and more than 10 years before Romania was permitted to join the Union in 2007. The second claim by the respondent concerned the interference with family rights or the right to respect for family life, as guaranteed under the Irish Constitution, under Article 8 ECHR and the Charter of Fundamental Rights.

After a rigorous examination of the evidence provided, the Irish High Court refused the order to execute the warrant on the basis that to do so would be incompatible with the state's obligations under the ECHR, without making a preliminary reference to the CJEU. The High Court considered that there were substantial grounds for believing that the trial, in which the respondent had been convicted 16 years previously, amounted to a flagrant denial of justice.[21] The Court held there was a wide practice of discrimination against Roma in Romania at the time, and therefore there were reasonable grounds to believe that the respondent, who was Roma and illiterate, was discriminated against in the course of her prosecution and conviction in Romania. In other words, Ms Rostaş was being treated less favourably than a person who was not of her ethnic origin would be.

The fact that it is in Ireland that we find such examples is interesting, because Ireland adopts an dualist approach to international law and the conflict between EU law and ECHR is essentially a conflict between EU law and the Irish national law giving effect to the Convention within the national legal system – namely, the European Convention on Human Rights Act 2003. However, the Irish courts tend to focus on the ECHR itself and view the conflict as one between what EU law requires and the ECHR, as interpreted by the Strasbourg Court.

Similarly, in the UK, the Supreme Court refused to surrender a Polish mother of five children, who was to be tried for fraud in Poland.[22] The main question before the Supreme Court was whether extradition would be incompatible with the rights of the applicant's children to respect for private and family life under Article 8 ECHR. The Supreme Court took several aspects into account, such as the gravity of the offence, the amount of time that had passed since the offence occurred and the fact that the applicant had started a new life in the UK with her five children, two of whom were very young, and the Court decided that the protection of private and family life outweighed the legitimate aim pursued by extradition.

[21] *Rostaş* (n 12).
[22] *F-K v Polish Judicial Authority* [2012] UKSC 25.

It should be noted, however, that the ruling in this case is more of an exception than a rule in the UK, since the UK courts tend to give more weight to the importance of international cooperation in extradition cases in their jurisprudence, and seem not to be very sympathetic to violations of Article 8 ECHR in that context.[23]

With respect to alleged violations of Article 3 ECHR, the UK courts are more generous, but they remain pragmatic nonetheless. In *Krolik v Regional Court in Czestochowa, Poland*,[24] the appellants contested their surrender to Poland because of the Polish prison conditions, arguing that the execution of the warrant would put them at risk of 'inhuman and degrading treatment', in violation of Article 3 ECHR. The High Court relied on a double presumption of fundamental rights compliance – the presumption that Poland, as a Member of the Council of Europe, is able and willing to fulfil its obligations under the Convention, and the presumption underlying the common European asylum system – and required 'clear, cogent and compelling evidence' to rebut it, which was not provided in this case.[25]

There are good reasons to believe that some of these judgments played a role in the CJEU's decision to change its approach in *Aranyosi*[26] and subsequent case law, since the decisions made by national courts would have been very problematic from the perspective of EU law had the Court decided otherwise. A different question is to what extend the national courts in the cases discussed actually applied the strict two-step procedure required under EU law. What is clear is that in all these cases, a national court considered the standard of protection in another Member State to have fallen below the common or minimum European standard, and decided not to execute an obligation under EU law. Moreover, the national courts took those decisions prior to *Aranyosi*, which means that they consciously decided not to execute an EU law obligation in order to ensure compliance with the ECHR, without an instruction or permission to do so from Luxembourg. In other words, they chose to follow the ECHR, as interpreted by the ECtHR.

IV. Reframing the Conflict

Another way to check the compatibility between EU and ECHR law, especially for constitutional courts, is through the lens of the national constitution. This scenario is more likely to occur in states with strong protection of fundamental rights in their domestic legal systems and when some of the most fundamental rights may

[23] For instance, in *Norris v US (No 2)* [2010] UKSC 9, [2010] 2 AC 487, the UK Supreme Court rejected an appeal by a retired businessman who argued that his extradition would result in a violation of Art 8 ECHR, suggesting that, for an Art 8 argument to succeed, the facts would have to be 'exceptional'. On this point, see also JR Spencer, 'Extradition, the EAW and human rights' (2013) 72 *CLJ* 2.

[24] *Krolik v Regional Court in Czestochova, Poland* [2012] EWHC 2357.

[25] ibid [5].

[26] Joined Cases C-404/15 and C-659/15 PPU *Aranyosi and Căldăraru*, ECLI:EU:C:2016:198.

be at stake. But it is no longer a scenario of dealing with the conflicts between EU law and the ECHR; rather, it is reframing the conflict into one that is between EU law and the national constitution, where other rules may be applicable. Even though this scenario moves away from the explicit discussion on the conflicts between EU and ECHR law, it remains relevant in this context for states and courts that have robust fundamental rights systems at home, and which tend to translate the ECHR and the Strasbourg case law into their domestic constitutions. A prominent example of such an approach in the fields under examination is the EAW decision of the German Federal Constitutional Court from December 2015.[27]

The case concerned a constitutional complaint to the German Federal Constitutional Court against an extradition decision adopted by the German *Oberlandesgericht* (Higher Regional Court). The applicant in the case was a citizen of the United States of America, who was sentenced in Italy *in absentia* to a custodial sentence of 30 years and was subsequently arrested in Germany on the basis of an extradition request made by Italy.

The Higher Regional Court decided to order the extradition on the basis of the EAW Framework Decision and the additional information, provided by the Italian authorities, that the applicant, after his surrender, would be granted the express right to a retrial in which the charges against him would be fully examined and in which he would, without reservations, be assured of his right to a defence. In this Court's view, such a re-examination of the charges was guaranteed by the relevant Italian legislation in the version communicated to it. The applicant argued, however, that he did not have any knowledge of his conviction and that there was no guarantee under Italian law that, after his extradition, he would be afforded the right to a trial in which the charges against him would be re-examined based on fact and law in his presence. In particular, referring to the German legal doctrine, he stated that reinstating him into a position to lodge an appeal was not equivalent to being granted the right to a trial at first instance, of which he had been deprived. He claimed that because of the courts' limited competence to hear evidence in such cases, the 'late' appeal did not, as a rule, meet the requirements that apply if the right to be heard is granted at a later stage. He contended that generally no new evidence was heard during the main hearing of the appeal. Consequently, the present legal situation in Italy would not provide for the hearing of new evidence in the case of a conviction *in absentia* and, as such, would be in violation of several articles of the German Basic Law, including Article 1, which protects human dignity, as well as Article 6(3) ECHR. As for the assurances provided by the Italian authorities, the applicant argued that they were insufficient, as they did not have the necessary binding effect under international law and, moreover, it was questionable whether these assurances could be trusted with absolute certainty. In order to support the claim, the applicant also referred to the relevant case law

[27] 2 BvR 2735/14, *Mr R v Order of the Oberlandesgericht Düsseldorf*, Order of the Bundesverfassungsgericht (Second Senate) of 15 December 2015, DE:BVerfG:2015:rs20151215.2bvr273514.

of the ECtHR, in which the Strasbourg Court considered the late appeal under Italian law to provide an insufficient possibility for review. The Higher Regional Court rejected the arguments of the applicant as being unfounded, holding that the specific structure and practice of appeal proceedings under German law could not be taken as the standard to be expected when deciding whether an extradition to another EU Member State is permissible.

The *Bundesverfassungsgericht* found the complaint to be admissible and well-founded. It commenced by acknowledging the importance of primacy and uniform application of EU law across the Member States; without these principles, the EU would not be able to continue to exist as a legal community of (then) 28 Member States. The Court also acknowledged the importance of the principle of mutual recognition and the high level of confidence between states on which the EAW mechanism is based. At the same time, however, the Court pointed out that EU law may be given effect only within the framework of the applicable constitutional order. This meant that the core principles of EU law, such as primacy, uniformity and mutual recognition, were limited by the German constitutional identity, which was beyond the reach of both European integration and constitutional amendment.[28]

The second part of the judgment was devoted to the review of the decision of the Higher Regional Court. The *Bundesverfassungsgericht* ruled that German courts are under an obligation to ensure that the minimum guarantees of rights of the accused in criminal proceedings are respected in extradition decisions, where sentences had been rendered *in absentia*. Accordingly, the decision at hand breached Article 1(1) of the German Constitution, since the Higher Regional Court failed to examine sufficiently whether Mr R would be able to present new evidence in a trial in Italy. The Federal Constitutional Court supported its conclusion, referring to, inter alia, the case law of the ECtHR, in which the Strasbourg Court had found deficiencies in the Italian Criminal Code in the context of trials *in absentia*, as well as to cases of other Higher Regional Courts in Germany that had refused surrender in similar cases based on Article 4(a) of the Framework Decision. As for mutual trust, the *Bundesverfassungsgericht* held that, while important, 'mutual trust is shaken if there are indications based on facts that the requirements indispensable for the protection of human dignity would not be complied with in a case of an extradition'.[29] In this respect, the national authority executing the warrant must investigate both the legal situation and the legal practice of the requesting Member State, if the person concerned has submitted evidence suggesting that the requesting state did not comply with the minimum constitutional requirement.

In its last point in the judgment, the *Bundesverfassungsgericht* clarified rather briefly that there was no need to send a request for a preliminary ruling to the CJEU under Article 267 TFEU, since the correct application of EU law was sufficiently

[28] ibid paras 37–50.
[29] ibid para 74.

clear and there was no room for reasonable doubt (*acte clair*). In the Constitutional Court's opinion, the Framework Decision on the EAW does not require German courts and authorities to execute a warrant without reviewing its compliance with the requirements ensuing from Article 1 of the German Basic Law.

The facts of the case appear very similar to those in *Melloni*, where the CJEU ruled that once the EU had adopted a common fundamental rights standard, EU Member States would no longer be entitled to apply their own higher standards, even when provided for in the constitution, because this would undermine the 'primacy, unity and effectiveness' of EU law.[30] Yet there is one crucial difference: the applicant in the present case was not aware of the proceedings against him and the trial and conviction occurred truly in his absence. Mr Melloni, by contrast, had been informed about the trial, voluntarily decided not to be present and appointed two lawyers who represented him throughout the entire criminal proceedings.

There are two main comments that can be made here. The first one is that the position of the German Constitutional Court is not unique; it is a position shared by most supreme and constitutional courts.[31] It is also not new, since the German Constitutional Court already posed limits to European integration in the *Solange* jurisprudence, as well as in its Maastricht and Lisbon decisions.[32] But there are good reasons to think that the decision of the *Bundesverfassungsgericht* was meant to send a message to the CJEU. The German Constitutional Court could have decided this case on the basis of the EAW Framework Decision alone (which provides for the possibility to suspend a warrant in cases of trials *in absentia*), without invoking the constitutional identity review. The facts of the case at hand meet the conditions for refusing surrender spelled out in the EAW Framework Decision, and there was, in principle, no conflict between EU law and the German Constitution. Nevertheless, the *Bundesverfassungsgericht* decided to make it a constitutional identity control case in order to clarify, once again, that there are limits to EU law and its principles when the constitutional core – more specifically core fundamental rights – is at stake.[33] And it seems to have worked, given the CJEU's decision in *Aranyosi and Căldăraru* rendered a few months later.[34] There is, of course, no trace of the decision of the *Bundesverfassungsgericht* in the *Aranyosi and Căldăraru* judgment, but it can be presumed that it had an impact, not only

[30] Case C-399/11 *Melloni*, ECLI:EU:C:2013:107.

[31] The difference is that Germany, in comparison to most other countries, specifically protects the notion of constitutional identity in Art 79 of the German Constitution – comprising one of the values that even constitutional amendment cannot touch.

[32] BverfGE 37, 291, 29 May 1974, *Solange I*; BverfGE 73, 339, 22 October 1986, *Solange II*; BverfGE 89, 155, 12 October 1993, *Maastricht*; BverfGE 123, 267, 30 June 2009, *Lisbon*.

[33] Some commentators have referred to the decision as a *Solange III* decision. See, eg, M Hong, 'Human Dignity and constitutional identity: The Solange-III Decision of the German Constitutional Court', *Verfassungsblog*, 18 February 2016, available at http://verfassungsblog.de/human-dignity-and-constitutional-identity-the-solange-iii-decision-of-the-german-constitutional-court/ (last accessed 16 December 2020).

[34] *Aranyosi and Căldăraru* (n 26).

because the case was construed as an identity control case but also because of the extensive interpretation of EU law provided by the German Constitutional Court. The Constitutional Court took it upon itself to provide extensive interpretations of provisions of the Framework Decision as well as of the EU Charter, and on the basis of its own interpretation it concluded that there was no conflict between EU law and the German Constitution.[35] In addition and importantly, the *Bundesverfassungsgericht* relied heavily on the case law of the ECtHR, which indeed requires Member States to ensure that the remedy provided under Article 6 ECHR is effective. The statement of the Italian authorities, that a new hearing of evidence was 'in any case not impossible' for the criminal proceedings held *in absentia*, simply falls short of the ECHR and the German (minimum) standards, but also EU fundamental rights standards.

Second, and this relates to the previous point, the case is obviously important in the context of the discussion on conflicts, as it shows that national courts (looking to the ECtHR for guidance and support) can pressure the CJEU to rethink its choices. It is also a tool for national (constitutional) courts that have a possibility to conduct a constitutional identity review and investigate compliance with the national fundamental rights. Bringing EU law into conformity with national fundamental rights, interpreted in light of the ECHR, will also mean bringing EU law in line with the ECHR, and this will thus resolve any potential conflicts. Caution is advised, however, in order to prevent the abuse of this position, which should be reserved for exceptional cases where fundamental rights are truly at stake, or, indeed, as a warning when needed.

In December 2017, the *Bundesverfassungsgericht* decided another EAW case, ruling in favour of a claimant who lodged a constitutional complaint against a decision of the Higher Regional Court of Hamburg ordering his surrender to Romania on the basis of an EAW.[36] The German Higher Regional Court had ordered the surrender relying on the assurances provided to it by the Romanian authorities, as required in the existing case law of the CJEU, even though the guarantees provided were not in accordance with the minimum requirements established by the ECtHR in relation to living space available to prisoners. The ECtHR has explicitly stated that the living space of less than $3m^2$ per prisoner in itself constitutes a violation of Article 3 ECHR.[37] In other cases, the ECtHR indicated that even a space of $4m^2$ would result in a violation of Article 3 ECHR when coupled with other relevant conditions of detention that are lacking,

[35] The German Constitutional Court concluded in para 107 that 'the requirements under Union law with regard to the execution of a European arrest warrant are not lower than those that are required by Art 1 sec 1 GG as minimum guarantees of the rights of the accused'.

[36] Order of the *Bundesverfassungsgericht* (Second Senate) of 19 December 2017, 2 BvR 424/17.

[37] See, amongst others, *Lind v Russia* App no 25664/05 (ECtHR, 6 December 2007) para 59; *Kantyrev v Russia* App no 37213/02 (ECtHR, 21 June 2007) paras 50–51; *Andrey Frolov v Russia* App no 205/02 (ECtHR, 29 March 2007) paras 47–49; and *Labzov v Russia* App no 62208/00 (ECtHR, 16 June 2005) para 44.

such as the availability of ventilation, access to natural light or air, adequacy of heating arrangements and the provision of basic sanitary requirements.[38] Moreover, and importantly, the Strasbourg Court had already condemned Romania for violations of the Convention (in particular Article 3) that point to a structural deficiency specific to Romanian prisons.[39]

In the case at hand, the assurances given by the Romanian authorities clearly did not comply with the ECHR minimum standards, since the guaranteed personal space amounted to $3m^2$ in closed quarters and $2m^2$ in semi-open or open quarters (and this calculation also included space for furniture).[40] But the Romanian authorities explained that they had been working and continued to work on improving the detention conditions, which was apparently sufficient for the Higher Regional Court to consider that the assurances provided were in accordance with EU law overall and the CJEU's case law, since it decided to order the surrender. Subsequently, the applicant lodged a constitutional compliant, arguing that his surrender would amount to a violation of human dignity as protected in Article 1(1) of the German Basic Law.

Interestingly, the German Constitutional Court did not examine the case on the basis of Article 1(1) of the Constitution but found that the challenged decision violated the complainant's right to a lawful judge, as protected in Article 101(1) of the Basic Law, because of, inter alia, the strong presumption that the restricted personal space in Romanian prisons was in violation of Article 3 of the Convention, which the domestic court did not sufficiently take into account. Contrary to the Higher Regional Court, the Constitutional Court considered the case law of the CJEU in this context to be incomplete, thus requiring a request for a preliminary ruling in accordance with Article 267(3) TFEU. The case was referred back to the Higher Regional Court, which submitted question(s) for a preliminary ruling to the CJEU. The outcome of this case is the CJEU's *Dorobantu* judgment, discussed in chapter 4.[41]

A similar development can be found in the case law of the Italian Constitutional Court, albeit not in the context of the EAW. With Order no 24/2017,[42] the *Corte Costituzionale* requested a preliminary ruling from the CJEU concerning the applicability of a national law that prevents the imposition of effective penalties, or provides for longer limitation periods, in cases of fraud affecting the financial interests of the EU (ie in the VAT cases). The request was a follow-up to an earlier

[38] *Babushkin v Russia* App no 67253/01 (ECtHR, 18 October 2007); *Ostrovar v Moldova* App no 35207/03 (ECtHR, 13 September 2005); *Peers v Greece* App no 28524/95 (ECtHR, 19 April 2001).

[39] *Rezmiveş and Others v Romania* App nos 61467/12, 39516/13, 48213/13 and 68191/13 (ECtHR, 25 April 2017); *Ali v Romania* App no 30595/09 (ECtHR, 15 January 2014); *Petrea v Romania* App no 4792/03 (ECtHR, 29 April 2008).

[40] Note, however, that, according to the ECtHR, the calculation of the space of detention must be based solely on the actual area to be used by the prisoner, thus not including the area used for the furniture.

[41] Case C-128/18 *Dorobantu*, ECLI:EU:C:2019:857.

[42] Italian Constitutional Court, Order of 23 November 2016 no 24/2017.

judgment of the CJEU (*Taricco I*),[43] in which the Luxembourg Court held that the national rule interfering with effective penalties for serious fraud affecting the EU's financial interest should be disregarded by national courts (the so-called '*Taricco* rule'). In its order, the *Corte Costituzionale* pointed out that disregarding national legislation concerning the maximum limitation period for criminal offences would mean adversely affecting the principle of legality, which is one of the most fundamental principles of the Italian legal order and hence of the Italian constitutional identity. Essentially, the Italian Constitutional Court asked the CJEU to reconsider the *Taricco* rule in light of, inter alia, Article 4(2) TEU, while also threatening to apply the *contralimiti* doctrine if the CJEU were to refuse.[44] In so doing, the *Corte Costituzionale* relied on the ECHR and the ECtHR's case law for support. It stated that a similar concern is 'shared by the Strasbourg Court', and that it is 'necessary' to look into the compatibility of the *Taricco* rule with Article 7 ECHR.[45] Even though the Constitutional Court found that the level of protection provided in the Italian Constitution was higher than the required minimum under the ECHR, the starting point in the analysis was the ECHR and the case law of the ECtHR, which has given additional weight to its arguments. Moreover, towards the end, the Constitutional Court also stated that there might still be questions regarding compatibility with the ECHR, particularly regarding the requirement of the precision of the provision concerning the punishment regime. In *Taricco II*,[46] the CJEU held that the *Taricco* rule does not oblige national courts to disapply the relevant provision of the Criminal Code if it would lead to a violation of fundamental rights, in particular the principle of legality, which is a common constitutional principle protected under EU law.

Although this line of case law is primarily relevant because of its contribution to the discussion on the conflicts between EU law and national constitutional law, and between the CJEU and the national (constitutional) courts, it also shows the role the ECHR and the Strasbourg case law play in those scenarios. Indeed, national (constitutional) courts tend to use the ECHR and the Strasbourg case law to support their arguments when national law (interpreted in light of the ECHR)

[43] Case C-105/14 *Taricco and Others*, ECLI:EU:C:2015:555. For commentary, see M Timmerman, 'Case C-105/14, Criminal proceedings against Ivo Taricco and Others, Judgment of the Court of Justice (Grand Chamber) of 8 September 2016, EU:C:2015:555: Balancing effective criminal sanctions with effective fundamental rights protection in cases of VAT fraud: Taricco' (2016) 53 *CML Rev* 779; M Bonelli, 'The *Taricco* saga and the consolidation of judicial dialogue in the European Union: CJEU, C-105/14 *Ivo Taricco and others*, ECLI:EU:C:2015:555; and C-42/17 *MAS, M.*, ECLI:EU:C:2017:936 Italian Constitutional Court, Order no 24/2017' (2018) 25 *Maastricht Journal of European and Comparative Law* 357.

[44] Italian Constitutional Court, Order of 23 November 2016 no 24/2017.

[45] ibid para 5.

[46] Case C-42/17 *MAS & MB (Taricco II)*, ECLI:EU:C:2017:936. On the constitutional conflict in the *Taricco* cases, see eg J Larik and R Bruggeman, 'The Elusive Contours of Constitutional Identity: Taricco as a Missed Opportunity' (2020) 35 *Utrecht Journal of International and European Law* 20; V Mitsilegas, 'Judical dialogue in three silences: Unpacking Taricco' (2018) 9 *New Journal of European Criminal Law* 38.

appears to be in conflict with EU law, thus also pointing to the fact that there could be a conflict between EU law and the ECHR, and making it more difficult for the CJEU to depart from it.

V. The Preliminary Reference Procedure

The fourth and last scenario concerns situations in which national courts opt for a judicial dialogue with the CJEU as a way of dealing with what they perceive to be a conflict between EU law and the ECHR.[47] This will often be when EU law itself is deemed to be the source of a breach of fundamental rights, thus putting into question the validity of EU law, and when Member States have no discretion. In such a situation, the preliminary reference procedure appears to be the only option for the national court, since the CJEU holds an exclusive monopoly over a review of EU law.[48]

An example that illustrates this type of response by national courts well is the *N* decision.[49] In this case, the request for a preliminary ruling was made by the Dutch *Raad van State* (Council of State) concerning the validity of the recast Reception Conditions Directive (RCD),[50] which lays down standards for the reception of applicants for international protection.

Mr N was a third-country national who entered the Netherlands in 1995 and made his first asylum application. In the years following his entry, Mr N had been convicted on 21 charges, mostly for theft-related offences, with sentences that varied from fines to terms of imprisonment of three months. After the rejection of his third asylum claim in 2014, he was ordered to leave the territory of the EU and a 10-year entry ban was imposed on him, in accordance with Article 11 of the so-called 'Return Directive' of 2008.[51] In January 2015, he was arrested again for theft and for violating the entry ban, and was sentenced to a term of imprisonment, during which he made a fourth asylum claim. After serving his sentence, he was placed in detention. The detention decision was based on a provision implementing Article 8(3)(e) of the recast RCD, which regulates the detention of persons applying for international protection and provides that an applicant may be detained 'when protection of national security or public order so requires'.

[47] There are many forms and patterns of judicial dialogue. In this context, 'judicial dialogue' refers to dialogue between national courts and the CJEU by means of the preliminary reference procedure, which enables national courts to question the Court of Justice on the interpretation or validity of EU law (Art 267 TFEU).

[48] Case C-314/85 *Foto-Frost*, ECLI:EU:C:1987:452.

[49] Case C-601/15 PPU *N*, ECLI:EU:C:2016:84.

[50] Directive 2013/33/EU of the European Parliament and of the Council of 26 June 2013 laying down standards for the reception of applicants for international protection (recast), [2013] OJ L180/96.

[51] Directive 2008/115/EC of the European Parliament and of the Council of 16 December 2008 on common standards and procedures in Member States for returning illegally staying third-country nationals, [2008] OJ L348/98. Its Art 11 regulates the conditions under which an entry ban may be issued, together with a return decision and the duration of the ban.

The applicant brought an action before the court of first instance, challenging the detention decision and claiming damages. The District Court in The Hague dismissed the claim. Mr N appealed, maintaining that his detention was contrary to Article 5(1)(f) second limb of the ECHR, under which the detention of a foreign national may be justified only when action is being taken against him with a view to deportation or extradition; hence, detention of a foreign national when he was lawfully resident in the Netherlands pending a decision on his asylum application was in breach of the said provision. The Dutch Council of State agreed and decided to refer the question for a preliminary ruling to the CJEU concerning the validity of Article 8(3)(e) of the recast RCD in light of Article 6 of the Charter. The referring court pointed out that, according to the Explanations relating to the Charter, the rights provided for in Article 6 thereof correspond to those guaranteed by Article 5 ECHR and have, by virtue of Article 52(3) of the Charter, the same meaning and scope as those laid down by the ECHR. The referring court also explicitly referred to the judgment of the ECtHR in *Nabil v Hungary*,[52] in which the ECtHR ruled that the detention of asylum seekers, with a view to deportation, is allowed only if the deportation is in progress and there is a real prospect of executing it. This would suggest that the Directive is invalid, since it also allows for detention of an asylum seeker when it is not imposed with a view to removal.

The CJEU addressed the relationship between EU law and the ECHR in its preliminary points in the judgment. The Court reiterated that while Article 6(3) TEU confirms that fundamental rights recognised by the ECHR constitute general principles of EU law, and Article 52(3) of the Charter indeed provides that the rights contained in the Charter that correspond to rights guaranteed by the ECHR are to have the same meaning and scope as those laid down by the ECHR, the latter does not constitute a legal instrument that has been formally incorporated into EU law, as long as the EU has not acceded to it. An examination of the validity of Article 8(3)(e) of the recast RCD must therefore be undertaken solely in the light of the fundamental rights guaranteed by the Charter.[53] Nevertheless, the Court also recognised that the rights laid down in Article 6 of the Charter correspond to those guaranteed by Article 5 ECHR, and that the limitations that may legitimately be imposed on the exercise of the former may not exceed those permitted by the ECHR. At the same time, however, the Court added that the Explanations relating to Article 52 of the Charter indicate that paragraph 3 of that article is intended to ensure the necessary consistency between the Charter and the ECHR, 'without thereby adversely affecting the autonomy of Union law and … that of the Court of Justice of the European Union'.[54]

Here, again, we find the same rhetoric relating to the autonomy of EU law that has been used by the CJEU in earlier judgments and opinions. It would appear that the consistency between the Charter and the ECHR must be ensured only

[52] *Nabil and Others v Hungary* App no 62116/12 (ECtHR, 22 September 2015).
[53] *N* (n 49) para 45.
[54] ibid para 47.

to the extent that it does not affect the autonomy of EU law and of the Court itself. The Court also refers to the Explanations relating to the Charter selectively, emphasising the part of the Explanations that states that consistency ought to be achieved without adversely affecting the Court's autonomy and the autonomy of EU law, while giving little weight to the reference to the case law of the ECtHR in the Charter Explanations, which should be taken into account when interpreting Charter rights that correspond to ECHR rights. With respect to this case, the Court of Justice considered that Article 8(3)(e) of the recast RCD was a limitation on the right to liberty guaranteed by Article 6 of the Charter, at the same time pointing to the legitimate interest in detaining certain persons to protect national security and public order, which also contributes to protecting the rights and freedoms of others. The Court concluded that the EU legislature had struck the correct balance between the right to liberty of the applicant and the requirements of protection of national security and public order. The assessment of Article 8(3)(e) of Directive 2013/33 thus disclosed no grounds to affect the validity of that provision in the light of Article 6 and Article 52(1) and (3) of the Charter.

The judgment raises important questions about the relationship between the EU legal order and the ECHR in cases of conflicts between the two. Under EU law, as interpreted by the CJEU, the validity of EU law is to be checked only in relation to the EU Charter. However, the Dutch Court asked about the validity of EU law on the basis of the ECHR, thus assuming that, or at least wondering if, a breach of the ECHR would mean that EU law is invalid. This seems a natural reaction from the national courts, and one that was seen in earlier cases too, since all EU Member States are also Contracting Parties to the ECHR and have to ensure compliance with the Convention rights in all circumstances, thus also when applying EU law. This puts national courts in a difficult position, particularly in cases in which Member States have discretion in the way they apply EU law (and where the *Bosphorus* presumption would thus not be applicable), but where that discretion has been limited in the case law of the CJEU to the extent that it does not allow for simultaneous compliance with both. The question arises, however, whether the Charter itself would not require a compatibility check with the ECHR, by virtue of Article 52(3)? The answer provided in Luxembourg seems to be a negative one.

This scenario is also well illustrated in the preliminary references in the *Aranyosi* and *LM* cases, discussed extensively in chapter 4 of this book.[55] In *Aranyosi*, the referring German court questioned the validity of the EAW Framework Decision on the basis of the possible violation of Article 3 ECHR, which corresponds to Article 4 of the EU Charter. The referring court made a reference to the case law of the ECtHR, where the Strasbourg Court had found Hungary (the requesting country in *Aranyosi*) to be in violation of Article 3 for reasons regarding overcrowding in its prisons. In this case, the CJEU changed its approach and ruled that national courts had to apply a two-step procedure in such cases, assessing whether there

[55] *Aranyosi and Căldăraru* (n 26); Case C-216/18 PPU *LM*, ECLI:EU:C:2018:586.

was (i) a systemic failure to ensure decent prison conditions in those states and (ii) a real risk that the appellant would be subject to such conditions if the EAW were executed. If the national court finds that there is a real risk of an Article 4 violation, the EAW must be postponed and assurances have to be requested from the issuing Member State. Where such a risk cannot be discounted, the national court must decide whether or not to terminate the surrender procedure.

In *LM*, the Irish High Court was asked to surrender a suspect in a drug offence to Poland under the EAW system, amid concern that he would not receive a fair trial in Poland. The Irish judge asked the Court of Justice whether, where the executing judicial authority had found that the common value of the rule of law enshrined in Article 2 TEU had been breached by the issuing Member State and that that systemic breach of the rule of law constituted a fundamental defect in the system of justice, a national judge could refuse to surrender a suspect, without looking into the details of the concrete case. Moreover, and crucially for the discussion in this chapter, the referring court asked whether the applicable test was the 'flagrant denial of justice' test, normally applied by the ECtHR in extradition cases where applicants raise Article 6 claims. It was not a coincidence that the Irish judge asked this question; it is apparent from the preliminary ruling that under Irish law, the executing judicial authority is required not to surrender the individual concerned if there is a real risk that he will be exposed in the issuing Member State to a flagrant denial of justice, in accordance with the ECHR.[56] The CJEU held that Member States must also perform both procedural steps when it is clear that systemic and grave deficiencies exist in a Member State. In other words, the national judge must look into the details of the concrete case and seek information from the issuing judicial authority, even when there is a systematic erosion of the rule of law in Poland. As to the relation with the ECHR, the CJEU remained completely silent. The ruling makes no reference to the flagrant denial of justice test and to the relevant case law of the ECtHR (other than when summarising the argument put forward by the referring court and the applicant). This is regrettable, not only because the national court was then required to interpret the CJEU's silence and make an assessment on its own,[57] but also because of the wider implications. Indeed, as Dupré has put it:

> The ECJ's silence about the – actual and possible – roles of the European Court of Human Rights is particularly disturbing … Considering the especially strict limitation of individual access to the ECJ, it might be recalled that one court – albeit … the ECJ – might not always be enough for safeguarding the rule of law.[58]

Lastly, a few words on the dialogue between national courts and the ECtHR are in order. There is of course no preliminary reference procedure in the Strasbourg

[56] *Minister for Justice and Equality v Artur Celmer (No 5)* [2018] IEHC 639.

[57] ibid, in particular paras 22–25.

[58] C Dupré, 'Individuals and Judges in Defense of the Rule of Law' (2018) *VerfBlog* at https://verfassungsblog.de/individuals-and-judges-in-defense-of-the-rule-of-law/ (last accessed 16 December 2020).

system, but Protocol 16 to the ECHR offers a similar (or competing if you follow the CJEU's logic)[59] avenue for national courts to seek a solution. Nevertheless, the mechanism of Protocol 16 to the ECHR is still very different from the preliminary ruling procedure. It allows the highest courts and tribunals of a State Party that has ratified it to request the ECtHR to give advisory opinions on questions of principle relating to the interpretation or application of the rights and freedoms defined in the Convention or the protocols thereto. Thus, unlike the preliminary ruling procedure, it is available only to the highest courts in the Member States, which may decide to request an opinion completely at their own discretion, and it produces non-binding advisory opinions.[60] The Protocol entered into force on 1 August 2018 and, at present, only two advisory opinions have been issued.[61] It will be interesting to see how the mechanism will be used in the coming years, and whether the courts from EU Member States will take questions of compatibility between their ECHR and EU law obligations to the Strasbourg Court.

VI. National Courts' Approaches to Conflicts between EU and ECHR Law – An Overall Assessment and Conclusions

When applying EU law, domestic courts may find themselves doubting the compatibility of EU law (or national implementing legislation) with fundamental rights, which could be enshrined in a constitution, the Convention or the Charter. If the incompatibility concerns a constitution, national courts might decide to refer the question to their Constitutional Court, if one exists, or otherwise to another judicial body in charge of interpreting the constitution. If the conflict is between EU law and the ECHR, however, national courts will have to make a choice as to the course of action.

Seeking conform interpretation is the first thing national courts will try to do. Some courts will go to great lengths to find that the jurisprudence of the Luxembourg and Strasbourg Courts is consistent and avoid the conflict altogether. However, the first scenario in this chapter has demonstrated the difficulty with

[59] See the position of the CJEU on Protocol No 16 to the ECHR in CJEU Opinion 2/13 on the EU's accession to the ECHR (Opinion 2/13 *Accession of the European Union to the European Convention for the Protection of Human Rights and Fundamental Freedoms*, ECLI:EU:C:2014:48).

[60] For discussion of Protocol No 16 to the ECHR, see J Gerards, 'Advisory Opinions, Preliminary Rulings, and the New Protocol No 16 to the European Convention of Human Rights: a Comparative and Critical Appraisal' (2014) 21 *Maastricht Journal of European and Comparative Law* 4; K Dzehtsiarou and N O'Meara, 'Advisory Jurisdiction of the European Court of Human Rights: A Magic Bullet for Dialogue and Docket-Control?' (2014) 34 *Legal Studies* 3, 444.

[61] ECtHR Advisory Opinion on Matters of Surrogacy requested by the French Court of Cassation, 10 April 2019, Request no P16-2018-001; ECtHR Advisory Opinion relating to Article 300.1 of Armenia's Criminal Code requested by the Armenian Constitutional Court, 29 May 2020, Request no P16-2019-001.

conform interpretation, namely, the fact that national courts present the outcome of the case as a conform interpretation but, in reality, they give priority to one or to the other. The example of the UK Supreme Court in the *Eritrea* case demonstrates this clearly: the Supreme Court stated that the case law of the Luxembourg and Strasbourg Courts was not inconsistent, but it could be said that ultimately it gave an ECHR-conform interpretation of EU law.

When conform interpretation is not possible, and the national court does not have the option of reverting back to the national constitutional court, it is left with two options: to ensure compliance with the ECHR, following the guidance of the Strasbourg Court, and risk breaching EU law; or to refer the questions of (in)compatibility to the CJEU, the outcome of which may or may not also ensure compliance with the ECHR, depending on the interpretation provided by the CJEU. While the latter scenario is the preferred one, there is a critical aspect that must be considered. National courts should not only refer the questions to the CJEU, but they should also actively engage in a dialogue with the Court, questioning the interpretation of EU law as well as the choices the CJEU has made in that regard, where appropriate, and suggesting their own interpretation of the provisions of EU law in light of the Charter (which should then be interpreted in conformity with the ECHR). It is important that the national courts motivate their interpretation by, inter alia, referring to Article 52(3) of the Charter, but also to the Preamble to the Charter and its Article 53, where relevant.

As demonstrated in chapter 2, the CJEU's interpretation of Article 52(3) over the years has been inconsistent. The inconsistencies may be caused by different things: autonomy of EU law that might be at stake, if the referred questions relate to the interpretation or validity of EU law; the expertise of the Court of Justice in a particular area, etc. Yet the clarity and consistency in the Article 52(3) message remains crucial from the point of view of national courts, given the recurring legal uncertainty at the national level regarding the relationship between EU and ECHR law. This uncertainty is exemplified in most cases discussed in this chapter. It should be noted that there are also examples of cases in which national courts raise questions about compatibility between EU and ECHR law, but without referring to Article 52(3) of the Charter or any other provision. It is almost as if national courts intuitively consider that the two should be in harmony. A case in point is *Puškár*, concerning the interpretation of several provisions of Directive 95/46/EC,[62] as well as Articles 7, 8 and 47 of the Charter and Article 4(3) TEU and Article 267 TFEU. In this case, the Slovak Supreme Court inquired, inter alia, whether a national court should follow the case law of the CJEU where this conflicts with the case law of the ECtHR?[63] Interestingly, the context in which

[62] Directive 95/46/EC of the European Parliament and of the Council of 24 October 1995 on the protection of natural persons with regard to the processing of personal data and on the free movement of such data, [1995] OJ L281/31.

[63] Case C-73/16 *Puškár*, ECLI:EU:C:2017:725. The question was phrased as follows (ibid para 32): 'Is the abovementioned right to an effective legal remedy and to a fair hearing (in particular under

the case was referred involved a dispute between the Slovak Constitutional Court and the Slovak Supreme Court, in which the former only referred to the case law of the ECtHR and did not express any views on the relevant case law of the Court of Justice. The Supreme Court was unsure whether the case law of the CJEU was consistent with the case law of the Slovak Constitutional Court, and thereby also with that of the ECtHR and, if not, to what extent this would be problematic from the perspective of EU law. As mentioned above, the referring court did not make a reference to Article 52(3) when asking this question.

The CJEU found the question to be hypothetical and hence inadmissible, but Advocate General Kokott provided an answer that also included an interpretation of Article 52(3) of the Charter. As she explained, the rights in the Charter, which correspond to rights guaranteed by the ECHR, have the same meaning and scope as conferred by the ECHR, which are, pursuant to the Explanatory Notes on this provision, not determined by the wording of the Convention but, inter alia, by the case law of the Strasbourg Court. Consequently,

> EU law permits the Court of Justice to deviate from the case-law of the ECtHR only to the extent that the former ascribes more extensive protection to specific fundamental rights than the latter. This deviation in turn is only permitted provided that it does not also cause another fundamental right in the Charter corresponding to a right in the ECHR to be accorded less protection than in the case-law of the ECtHR.[64]

Therefore, if the national court would come to a conclusion that the case law of the CJEU provides less protection than the case law of the ECtHR in respect of a specific fundamental right provided for in both the Charter and in the ECHR, such a finding would amount to the view that the interpretation of the fundamental right in question by the Court of Justice is not compatible with Article 52(3), in which case the national court may or must (if there is no judicial remedy against the decision of the national courts itself under national law) call on the CJEU to ascertain how EU law is to be interpreted in that situation.

This brings us to the essence of the argument. There is a clear duty in EU law to ensure consistency between the Charter (and secondary EU law, as well as national law implementing EU law interpreted in the light of it)[65] and the ECHR when the rights correspond, which will be in the majority of the cases.[66] National

Article 47 of the Charter) consistent with an approach taken by the referring court whereby, when, in this case, there is case-law from the European Court of Human Rights which differs from the answer obtained from the Court of Justice of the European Union, the referring court, in accordance with the principle of sincere cooperation in Article 4(3) TEU and Article 267 TFEU, gives precedence to the Court of Justice's legal approach?'

[64] AG Kokott, ibid para 123.

[65] See, eg, Case C-400/10 PPU *McB*, ECLI:EU:C:2010:582, para 51 (the Court held that '[it] is called upon to interpret, in the light of the Charter, the law of the European Union within the limits of the powers conferred on it'). More recently, see Case C-152/17 *Consorzio Italian Management e Catania Multiservizi*, ECLI:EU:C:2018:264, para 33; Case C-260/17 *Anodiki Services EPE*, ECLI:EU:C:2018:864, para 38.

[66] Most ECHR rights have been taken over into the Charter and have been identified as 'corresponding rights' in the Explanations to the Charter.

courts could thus use Article 52(3) as a conflict rule: if there is a conflict in the way in which fundamental rights are protected in the case law of the CJEU and the ECtHR, EU law should align with the ECHR.[67] National courts should not feel compelled to make a choice, because they can actually ensure compliance with both by following the current state of the law as clearly and convincingly worded in Article 52(3) of the EU Charter. Nevertheless, instead of unilaterally applying this rule, national courts should engage in a dialogue with the CJEU, and motivate their views by referring to Article 52(3) of the Charter and the need to preserve clarity, consistency and legal certainty in the complex fundamental rights architecture in which they are called upon to operate in the years to come. Judicial dialogue will also be at its most fruitful when this is kept in mind.

[67] For extensive discussion and arguments as to why this is the way Art 52(3) of the Charter should be interpreted, see ch 2, section III.A.ii and ch 5, section IV.A.

Conclusion

The legal architecture of European fundamental rights is not yet completed. It is a work in progress, both in the courts' practices and in scholarly debate. What is still missing is the formal link between the EU and ECHR systems, as well as a clear vision of the role and place of fundamental rights in EU law. Accession of the EU to the ECHR would have created the link between the two and would have introduced a legal avenue to resolve potential conflicts. However, the CJEU's negative Opinion 2/13 has foreclosed any real possibility for accession in the near future, and even though negotiations resumed recently it is difficult to foresee, keeping in mind the objections in Opinion 2/13, when they will deliver desirable results.[1] In the meantime, national courts continue to struggle with the parallel application of the Charter and Convention rights,[2] as divergences in the approach of the two European Courts have become more frequent and apparent in recent years.

An attempt was made from the outset to explain that not all divergences in the protection of fundamental rights by the CJEU and the ECtHR are problematic; on the contrary, they can be a source of mutual influence, enrichment and cross-fertilisation. However, if the EU standard of fundamental rights protection were to fall below the ECHR minimum standard, as interpreted by the case law of the ECtHR, Member States would face conflicting treaty obligations, since they would be required to comply with their EU law obligations and, at the same time, are required to ensure that the ECHR minimum standards, as determined by the ECtHR, are respected. This book has focused on divergences between EU and ECHR law where the level of protection provided by the CJEU could be considered to be below the minimum level required by the ECtHR.

The EU today acts in fields that impact directly on peoples' lives, in areas such as criminal law, asylum law, immigration law and family matters, and therefore the fields in which the jurisdiction of the CJEU and the ECtHR overlaps are only growing. While the two European Courts have different tasks and missions in their respective systems, they are increasingly faced with similar or same fundamental rights questions. The two case studies covered in Part II of this book have illustrated the tensions in the case law of the two European Courts in the fields of asylum and criminal law, particularly in light of the principle of mutual trust and

[1] Opinion 2/13 *Accession of the European Union to the European Convention for the Protection of Human Rights and Fundamental Freedoms*, ECLI:EU:C:2014:48.

[2] Ch 6. See also the national reports and comparative analyses in M Bobek and J Adams-Prassl (eds), *The EU Charter of Fundamental Rights in the Member States* (Oxford, Hart Publishing, 2020).

recognition, which at times have led to real conflicts. At the same time, it has also been shown that, with time, a degree of convergence between the approaches of Luxembourg and Strasbourg has been achieved. The convergence is stronger in the area of asylum law, more specifically the Dublin Regulation, in comparison to the case law regarding the EAW system. This can be due to different factors, such as the pressure on the CJEU resulting from developments in the case law of the ECtHR and national courts, and the role of the EU legislature.[3]

Nevertheless, it seems important not to overlook the fact that convergence – even when established – is a process involving a constructive dialogue between the two European Courts that takes place over time and is based on judicial comity.[4] In the meantime, however, national courts are in the eye of the storm because they have to make decisions in concrete cases. The problem lies not only in the end result, where it may seem that the CJEU has complied with the ECHR or that the ECtHR has decided to be lenient and accommodating towards the EU legal system, but in the approach, and in the messages that the European Courts send to national courts in the process. Additionally, the risk of new divergences continues to exist, as also shown in Part II,[5] and there may be divergences that simply cannot be resolved through dialogue and convergence. As long as there is no clear legal framework in which these courts operate, the risk of national courts' facing conflicting obligations cannot be fully eliminated. This affects the working of the national courts, but also the legal certainty of Europeans whose rights may be at stake.

This book has advanced two main arguments. First, it has argued that the CJEU and the ECtHR have a duty to facilitate the role of national courts, who continue to bear primary responsibility for the judicial protection of fundamental rights in Europe, by removing any legal uncertainty regarding the effects of having parallel rights in the ECHR and the EU Charter.[6] Second, it has suggested that Article 52(3) of the EU Charter could operate as a conflict rule: in the event of a divergence in the approaches of the two European Courts, national courts should provide an ECHR conform interpretation of EU law. The latter argument finds its basis in the clear wording of Article 52(3) and its object and overall purpose, which, according to the Charter Explanations, is to ensure the necessary consistency between the two.[7] However, the national courts should not unilaterally apply this rule; instead, they should engage in a dialogue with the CJEU, and motivate their views by referring to Article 52(3) of the Charter and the need to ensure and

[3] See in particular ch 3.

[4] K Lenaerts, 'The ECHR and the CJEU: Creating Synergies in the Field of Fundamental Rights Protection' (2018) Solemn hearing for the opening of the Judicial Year 26 January 2018, available at www.echr.coe.int/Documents/Speech_20180126_Lenaerts_JY_ENG.pdf (last accessed 16 December 20120).

[5] See in particular ch 4.

[6] For a similar claim, see S O'Leary, 'Courts, charters and conventions: making sense of fundamental rights in the EU' (2016) 56 *Irish Jurist* 4.

[7] See further chs 2, 5 and 6.

preserve clarity, consistency and legal certainty in the complex fundamental rights architecture in which they are called upon to operate.[8]

What is important to realise, in an attempt to create and safeguard common minimum standards in Europe, is that all actors bear their share of responsibilities. For the ECtHR, the challenge will be to maintain *souci de symétrie*[9] between EU and ECHR law. In other words, the Strasbourg Court will have to find ways to preserve the principled character and integrity of the Convention system while staying sensitive to the fundamental characteristics of EU law and without unduly imposing on the CJEU's exclusive role in interpreting it.[10] For the CJEU, it will be to accept its new role as a fundamental rights court and find a better balance between what its role has always been and the new reality of the EU and EU law today. As discussed in chapter 1, the CJEU is not a human rights court by origin or expertise, but the environment in which it operates has changed dramatically in recent years. Even the most sensitive questions concerning fundamental rights come within the purview of the Court today, and its decisions have a direct impact on the rights and lives of millions of Europeans.[11] In that sense, the CJEU is *also* a fundamental rights court, and the challenge for it will be to accept this new reality, which it has been hesitant to do so far. More specifically, it will have to address aspects of EU fundamental rights law that remain tricky from the perspective of national courts (and litigants), including the exact parameters of the relationship between EU law and the ECHR.

In this respect, the book criticised the uneven references to and interpretation of Article 52(3) of the Charter in the CJEU's case law over the years. In the early post-Charter cases, interpretation of Article 52(3) of the Charter appeared straightforward: when Charter and ECHR rights correspond, their meaning and scope must be the same. In one of those cases, the Court even considered that a reference to the case law of the ECtHR 'must be made' when interpreting and applying a Charter right that corresponds to an ECHR right.[12] This interpretation started to change quite quickly, however, and in more recent cases a reference to Article 52(3) includes a reminder that the said provision is intended to ensure the necessary consistency between the Charter and the ECHR, 'without thereby

[8] Ch 6.

[9] As referred to by the President of the ECtHR in his Concurring Opinion in *Romeo Castaño v Belgium* App No 8351/17 (ECtHR, 9 July 2019). For discussion of the judgment, see L Von Danwitz, 'In Rights We Trust. The ECtHR's judgment in Romeo Castaño v Belgium and the relationship between the ECHR and the principle of mutual trust in EU law' (2019) *Verfassungsblog* at https://verfassungsblog.de/in-rights-we-trust/ (last accessed 16 December 2020); M Zamboni, 'Romeo Castaño v Belgium and the Duty to Cooperate under the ECHR' (2019), *EJIL:Talk!* at www.ejiltalk.org/romeo-castano-v-belgium-and-the-duty-to-cooperate-under-the-echr/ (last accessed 16 December 2020).

[10] Concurring Opinion of Judge Spano in *Romeo Castaño v Belgium* (n 9).

[11] In addition to the case law on asylum and criminal law discussed in chs 3 and 4, see eg Case C-426/16 *Liga van Moskeeën en Islamitische Organisaties Provincie Antwerpen and Others*, ECLI:EU:C:2018:335 and Case C-336/19 *Centraal Israëlitisch Consistorie van België and Others*, ECLI:EU:C:2020:1031 on animal welfare and freedom of religion; Case C-157/15 *G4S v Achbita*, ECLI:EU:C:2017:203 and Case C-188/15 *Bougnaoui*, ECLI:EU:C:2017:204 on freedom of religion and non-discrimination.

[12] Case C-334/12 *Jaramillo and Others*, ECLI:EU:C:2013:134, para 43.

adversely affecting the autonomy of Union law and … that of the Court of Justice of the European Union'.[13] In those cases, the CJEU merely takes account of the corresponding Convention right and the relevant case law of the Strasbourg Court. In the *N* case,[14] concerning detention of asylum seekers in the context of their deportation for reasons of public order and safety, the CJEU went as far as to state that compliance of EU secondary law with fundamental rights must be undertaken 'solely in the light of the fundamental rights guaranteed by the Charter'.[15] At the same time, however, many important judgments in Luxembourg feature extensive references to the ECHR and the case law of the ECtHR, as well as the recognition that corresponding Charter and Convention rights have the same meaning and scope.[16]

There may be different reasons for the inconsistencies in the case law over the years: the autonomy of EU law, the question whether interpretation or validity of EU law is being challenged on the basis of its compliance with the ECHR, the particular expertise of the CJEU in a certain area of EU law, etc. Yet in practical terms, clarity and consistency in the interpretation of legal norms is of the utmost importance, particularly in the multi-layered legal architecture where conflicts are inherent in the very functioning of the system. Since the CJEU has not yet clarified the exact consequences of Article 52(3) of the Charter, it is incumbent on the national courts to take notice of and be guided by this important provision.[17]

Finally, in rounding up this project, it is necessary, albeit very briefly, to make some concessions in respect of the arguments put forward in this book. The first one concerns the implications of the hierarchical approach to the European fundamental rights regime for striking fair balances and providing 'more extensive protection' in fundamental rights cases. While following the interpretation of Article 52(3) as suggested in this book will arguably remove the uncertainty about the parallel effect of the Convention and Charter rights in most cases, it may increase the complexity of decision making in Luxembourg, as well as limit the Court's currently existing space for manoeuvre when the balancing of competing rights is at stake. Balancing of rights is a very complex exercise, involving careful weighing and consideration of two competing rights and interests, which may become even more tricky in certain cases, because providing one fundamental right with a higher level of protection inevitably means a lower level of protection

[13] See, eg, Case C-203/15 *Tele2 Sverige* ECLI:EU:C:2016:970, para 129; Case C-336/19 *Centraal Israëlitisch Consistorie van België and Others*, ECLI:EU:C:2020:1031, para 56.

[14] Case C-601/15 PPU, *N*, ECLI:EU:C:2016:84.

[15] ibid para 46.

[16] See in particular case law regarding Dublin transfers such as Joined Cases C-411/10 and C-493/10 *NS and others*, EU:C:2011:865; and Case C-578/16 PPU *CK and others*, ECLI:EU:C:2017:127. See also Joined Cases C-404/15 and C-659/15 PPU *Aranyosi and Căldăraru*, ECLI:EU:C:2016:198.

[17] S O'Leary, 'The EU Charter Ten Years On: A View from Strasbourg' in M Bobek and J Adams-Prassl (eds), *The EU Charter of Fundamental Rights in the Member States* (Oxford, Hart Publishing, 2020).

for the competing right. At the same time, the obligation to comply with the ECHR minimum standards means that the lower standard of protection may never go below the ECHR standard, which in turn necessarily limits the higher level of protection that can be afforded to the other right. In practical terms, determining the levels of the protection and conducting a balancing exercise may thus become more complex and, as pointed out by the CJEU President Lenaerts, the autonomous development of the Charter may not always be possible.[18]

In addition, the second sentence of Article 52(3) of the Charter explicitly states that EU law may provide more extensive protection, thus going beyond the ECHR. This, again, would be limited by the ECHR minimum standards, because it would be permissible only to the extent that providing more extensive protection of one right does not mean going below the minimum level of protection of the other competing right. In other words, the ECHR minimum standards would also be maximum standards in certain cases. While adopting this interpretation of Article 52(3) may add to the complexity of the balancing exercise in some cases, and it may indeed limit autonomous development of the Charter in that respect, it will provide clarity and consistency in the case law when it comes to the parallel application of the Convention and the Charter, and it will enhance legal certainty for EU citizens. Moreover, leaving aside Article 52(3) of the Charter, the question is what the benefit of autonomously developing EU law in a way that is not compliant with the ECHR minimum standards would be, when the Member States can be held accountable for them in Strasbourg.[19]

Second, the book does not engage with the normative aspect of the main argument. Indeed, one might wonder why should it be, as a matter of principle, the Strasbourg Court and not the Luxembourg Court to set the fundamental rights standards for the EU? After all, the Luxembourg Court could be more progressive when it comes to fundamental rights protection, because it operates in a less diverse environment than the ECtHR and it has a stronger enforcement mechanism. In this regard, it should be noted that the argument I have offered is strictly legal: Article 52(3) requires consistency between corresponding Charter and Convention rights, and it can only be interpreted in one way: when there is a divergence, EU law should align with the ECHR. This interpretation should be followed not because of normative reasons pertaining to the ECHR system, but simply because it is the law that all EU Member States have agreed to be bound by, not only when ratifying the Treaty of Lisbon but also when becoming Contracting Parties to the ECHR.

I started this book with a reference to EU values and the strength of fundamental rights protection in the EU and Europe more broadly. The book has aimed to show that, when it comes to fundamental rights, our values are multi-layered,

[18] K Lenaerts, 'The Role of the EU Charter in the Member States' in Bobek and Adams-Prassl (eds) (n 2) 19, 28.

[19] See J Callewaert, 'Do we still need Article 6(2) TEU? Consideration on the absence of EU accession to the ECHR and its consequences' (2018) 55 *CML Rev* 1685, 1706.

consisting of elements of national constitutions, the ECHR and other international human rights treaties, and EU fundamental rights. It is often said that this implies the need for openness for the mutual interaction between the different layers, but in my view, it also points to the indispensable need for clarity and consistency in the way in which fundamental rights are protected in Europe, particularly from the perspective of national courts and litigants. Without the clearly set minimum standards that are always upheld, and in the wake of the political nationalism spreading in some parts of Europe, the multi-layered union of values may become impossible to sustain.

BIBLIOGRAPHY

Adams, M, de Waele, H, Meeusen, J and Straetmans, G (eds), *Judging Europe's Judges: The Legitimacy of the Case Law of the European Court of Justice* (Oxford, Hart Publishing, 2013)

Albers, P, Beauvais, P, Bohnert, J-F, Böse, M, Langbroek, P, Renier, A and Wahl, T, *Final Report – Towards a Common Evaluation Framework to Assess Mutual Trust in the Field of EU Judicial Cooperation in Criminal Matters* (March 2013)

Albi, A, 'From the banana saga to a sugar saga and beyond, could the post- communist Constitutional Courts teach the EU a lesson in the rule of law?' (2010) 47 *CML Rev* 791

—— 'The European Arrest Warrant, constitutional rights and the changing legal thinking. Values once recognised lost in transition to the EU level?' in M Fletcher, E Herlin-Karnell and C Matera (eds), *The European Union as an Area of Freedom, Security and Justice* (London, Routledge, 2016) ch 6

Alston, P and De Schutter, O, *Monitoring Fundamental Rights in the EU, The Contribution of the Fundamental Rights Agency* (Oxford, Hart Publishing, 2005)

Alston, P and Weiler, JHH, 'An Ever Closer Union in Need of a Human Rights Policy' (1988) 9 *European Journal of International Law* 658

—— and Weiler, JHH, 'An "Ever Closer Union" in Need of a Human Rights Policy: The European Union and Human Rights' in P Alston (ed), *The EU and Human Rights* (Oxford, Oxford University Press, 1999) 3

Anagnostaras, G, 'Mutual Confidence is Not Blind Trust! Fundamental Rights Protection and the Execution of the European Arrest Warrant, *Aranyosi and Căldăraru*' (2016) 53 *CML Rev* 165

——, 'The Common European Asylum System: Balancing Mutual Trust Against Fundamental Rights Protection' (2020) 21 *German Law Journal* 1180

Arestis, G, 'Fundamental Rights in the EU, Three years after Lisbon, the Luxembourg Perspective', *Cooperative Research Paper 02/2013*, College of Europe (2013)

Arnardóttir, OM and Buyse, A, *Shifting Centres of Gravity in Human Rights Protection* (London, Routledge, 2016)

Arnull, AM, 'Opinion 2/94 and Its Implications for the Future Constitution of the Union' in University of Cambridge Centre for European Legal Studies, *The Human Rights Opinion of the ECJ and its Constitutional Implications* (1996) CELS Occasional Paper No 1

Aust, A, *Modern Treaty Law and Practice* (Cambridge, Cambridge University Press, 2007)

Avbelj, M and Komarek, J (eds), *Constitutional Pluralism in the European Union and Beyond* (Oxford, Hart Publishing, 2012)

Bache, I, Bulmer, S, George, S and Parker, O, *Politics in the European Union* (Oxford, Oxford University Press, 2011)

Baratta, R, 'Accession of the EU to the ECHR, The Rationale for the ECJ's Prior Involvement Mechanism' (2013) 50 *CML Rev* 1305

Bárd, P and van Ballegooij, W, 'The effect of CJEU case law concerning the rule of law and mutual trust on national systems' in V Mitsilegas, A di Martino and L Mancano (eds), *The Court of Justice and European Criminal Law: Leading Cases in a Contextual Analysis* (Oxford, Hart Publishing, 2019) 455

Besselink, LFM 'The Member States, the national constitutions, and the scope of the Charter' (2001) 8 *Maastricht Journal of European and Comparative Law* 68

——, 'Constitutional Adjudication in the Era of Globalization: The Netherlands in the Comparative Perspective' (2012) 18 *European Public Law* 231

——, 'The Protection of Fundamental Rights post-Lisbon. The Interaction between the EU Charter of Fundamental Rights, the European Convention on Human Rights (ECHR) and National Constitutions' in *Reports of the XXV FIDE Congress Tallinn* (Tartu University Press, 2012) 1

——, 'The Proliferation of Constitutional Law and Constitutional Adjudication, or How American Judicial Review Came to Europe After All' (2013) 9 *Utrecht Law Review* 2
——, 'The parameters of constitutional conflict after Melloni' (2014) 39 *EL Rev* 531.
——, 'The Bite, the Bark and the Howl: Article 7 TEU and the Rule of Law Initiatives' in A Jakab and D Kochenov (eds), *The Enforcement of EU Law and Values* (Oxford, Oxford University Press, 2017) 128
Besson, S, 'European Human Rights, Supranational Judicial Review and Democracy. Thinking outside the judicial box' in P Popelier, C Van de Heyning and P Van Nuffel (eds), *Human Rights Protection in the European Legal Order: The interaction between the European and the national courts* (Antwerp, Intersentia, 2011) 97
——, 'The Reception Process in Ireland and the United Kingdom' in H Keller and A Stone-Sweet (eds), *A Europe of Rights. The Impact of the ECHR on National Legal Systems* (Oxford, Oxford University Press, 2012) 31
——, 'European Human Rights Pluralism: Notion and Justification' in M Maduro, K Tuori and S Sankari (eds), *Transnational Law: Rethinking European Law and Legal Thinking* (Cambridge, Cambridge University Press, 2014) 170
Bianchi, A, 'Human Rights and the Magic of Jus Cogens' (2008) 19 *The European Journal of International Law* 491
Bianco, G and Martinico, G, 'The Poisoned Chalice, An Italian view on the Kamberaj case', *Working Paper on European Law and Regional Integration no 18* (2013)
Bjorge, E, 'National supreme courts and the development of ECHR rights' (2001) 9 *International Journal of Constitutional Law* 5
Bobek, M and Adams-Prassl, J (eds), *The EU Charter of Fundamental Rights in the Member States* (Oxford, Hart Publishing, 2020)
Bonelli, M, 'The Taricco saga and the consolidations of judicial dialogue in the European Union' (2018) 25 *Maastricht Journal of European and Comparative Law* 3
Borelli, S, 'The (Mis)-Use of General Principles of Law, Lex Specialis and the Relationship between International Human Rights Law and the Laws of Armed Conflict' in L Pineschi (ed), *General Principles of Law: The Role of the Judiciary* (Cham, Springer, 2015) 265
Borgen, CJ, 'Resolving Treaty Conflicts' (2005) 37 *George Washington International Law Review* 573
Bossuyt, M, 'The European Union Confronted with an Asylum Crisis in the Mediterranean, Reflections on Refugees and Human Rights Issues' (2015) 5 *European Journal of Human Rights* 581
Brittain, S, 'The Relationship Between the EU Charter of Fundamental Rights and the European Convention on Human Rights: An Originalist Analysis' (2015) 11 *European Constitutional Law Review* 482
Brouwer, E, 'Mutual Trust and the Dublin Regulation, Protection of Fundamental Rights in the EU and the Burden of Proof' (2013) 9 *Utrecht Law Review* 1
Butler, G, 'A Political Decision Disguised as Legal Argument? Opinion 2/13 and European Union Accession to the European Convention on Human Rights' (2015) 31 *Utrecht Journal of International and European Law* 81
——, 'The Ultimate Stumbling Block? The Common Foreign and Security Policy, and Accession of the European Union to the European Convention on Human Rights' (2016) 39 *Dublin University Law Journal* 229
——, 'The Coming Age of the Court's Jurisdiction in the Common Foreign and Security Policy' (2017) 13 *European Constitutional Law Review* 673
Callewaert, J, 'The European Convention on Human Rights and European Union Law, A Long Way to Harmony' (2009) 6 *European Human Rights Law Review* 768
——, *The Accession of the European Union to the European Convention on Human Rights* (Strasbourg, Council of Europe Publishing, 2014)
——, 'Is EU Accession still a good idea?' in Š Imamović, M Claes and B De Witte (eds), 'The EU Fundamental Rights Landscape after Opinion 2/13' *Maastricht Faculty of Law Working Paper 2016/3*
——, 'Do we still need Article 6(2) TEU? Consideration on the absence of EU accession to the ECHR and its consequences' (2018) 55 *CML Rev* 1685

Carrera, S, De Somer, M and Petkova, B, 'The Court of Justice of the European Union as a Fundamental Rights Tribunal: Challenges for the Effective Delivery of Fundamental Rights in the Area of Freedom, Security and Justice', *Justice and Home Affairs Liberty and Security in Europe Papers No 49* (2012)

Cartabia, M, 'Europe and Rights: Taking Dialogue Seriously' (2009) 5 *European Constitutional Law Review* 5

Cassese, A, *International Law* (Oxford, Oxford University Press, 2005)

Claes, M, *The National Courts' Mandate in the European Constitution* (Oxford, Hart Publishing, 2006)

——, 'The Primacy of EU Law in European and National Law' in D Chalmers and A Arnull (eds), *The Oxford Handbook of European Union Law* (Oxford, Oxford University Press, 2015) 178

——, 'The Validity and Primacy of EU Law and the "Cooperative Relationship" between National Constitutional Courts and the Court of Justice of the European Union' (2016) 23 *Maastricht Journal of European and Comparative Law* 1

——, 'Fundamental Rights' in PJ Kuijper, F Amtenbrink, D Curtin, B De Witte, A McDonnell and S van den Bogaert, *The Law of the European Union* (Alphen a/d Rijn, Kluwer Law International, 2018) 97

Claes, M and Imamović, Š, 'National Courts in the New European Fundamental Rights Architecture' in V Kosta, N Skoutaris and V Tzevelekos (eds), *The EU Accession to the ECHR* (Oxford, Hart Publishing, 2013) 159

—— and Imamović, Š, 'Caught in the middle or leading the way? National courts in the new European fundamental rights landscape' (2013) 4 *Journal européen des droits de l'homme/European Journal of Human Rights* 627

Clapham, A, *Human Rights and the European Community, A Critical Overview*, vol I (Baden-Baden, Nomos, 1991)

Cloots, E, 'Germs of Pluralist Judicial Adjudication, Advocaten voor de Wereld and Other References from the Belgian Constitutional Court' (2010) 47 *CML Rev* 645

Closa, C and Kochenov, D (eds), *Reinforcing the Rule of Law Oversight in the European Union* (Cambridge, Cambridge University Press, 2016)

Conforti, B, 'Consistency among Treaty Obligations' in E Cannizzaro (ed), *The Law of Treaties Beyond the Vienna Convention* (Oxford, Oxford University Press, 2011) 189

Coppell, J and O'Neill, A, 'The European Court of Justice, Taking Rights Seriously?' (1992) 29 *CML Rev* 669

Corten, O and Klein, P, *The Vienna Convention on the Law of Treaties, A Commentary* (Oxford, Oxford University Press, 2011)

Costello, C, 'The *Bosphorus* Ruling of the European Court of Human Rights, Fundamental Rights and Blurred Boundaries in Europe' (2006) 6 *Human Rights Law Review* 1

——, 'Courting Access to Asylum in Europe, Recent Supranational Jurisprudence Explored' (2012) 12 *Human Rights Law Review* 287

Costello, C and Mouzourakis, M, 'Reflections on Reading Tarakhel: Is "How Bad Is Bad Enough" Good Enough?' (2014) 10 *Asiel en Migrantenrecht* 404

Craig, P, *The Lisbon Treaty, Law, Politics, and Treaty Reform* (Oxford, Oxford University Press, 2010).

Crawford, J, *Brownlie's Principles of Public International Law* (Oxford, Oxford University Press, 2012)

Dawson, M, *The Governance of EU Fundamental Rights* (Cambridge, Cambridge University Press, 2017)

——, 'Fundamental Rights in European Union Policy-making: The Effects and Advantages of Institutional Diversity' (2020) Human Rights Law Review 20, 50–73

de Búrca, G, 'The Drafting of the European Union Charter of Fundamental Rights' (2001) 26 *EL Rev* 136

——, 'The European Court of Justice and the International Legal Order after *Kadi*' (2010) 51 *Harvard International Law Journal* 1

——, 'The Road Not Taken, The EU as Global Human Rights Actor' (2011) 105 *American Journal of International Law* 649

——, 'The ECJ and the International Legal Order: A Re-evaluation' in G de Búrca and JHH Weiler, *The Worlds of European Constitutionalism* (Cambridge, Cambridge University Press, 2012) 105

——, 'After the EU Charter of Fundamental Rights: the Court of Justice as a human rights adjudicator?' (2013) 20 *Maastricht Journal of European and Comparative Law* 168

——, 'The Domestic Impact of the EU Charter of Fundamental Rights' (2013) 49 *Irish Jurist* 49

De Jesus Butler, I, 'Ensuring compliance with the Charter of Fundamental Rights in legislative drafting, the practice of the European Commission' (2012) 37 *EL Rev* 4

De Vries, S, Bernitz, U and Weatherill, S (eds), *The Protection of Fundamental Rights in the EU After Lisbon* (Oxford, Hart Publishing, 2013)

De Wet, E, 'The Prohibition of Torture as an International Norm of Jus Cogens and Its Implications for National and Customary Law' (2004) 15 *European Journal of International Law* 97

De Wet, E and Vidmar, J, *Hierarchy in International Law, The Place of Human Rights* (Oxford, Oxford University Press, 2012)

De Witte, B, 'Rules of Change in International Law: How Special is the European Community?' (1994) 25 *Netherlands Yearbook of International Law* 299

——, 'The Past and the Future Role of the European Court of Justice in the Protection of Human Rights' in P Alston (ed), *The EU and Human Rights* (Oxford, Oxford University Press, 1999) 859

——, 'Balancing of Economic Law and Human Rights by the European Court of Justice' in PM Dupuy, F Francioni and EU Petersmann (eds), *Human Rights in International Investment Law and Arbitration* (Oxford, Oxford University Press, 2009) 197

——, 'The Use of the ECHR and Convention Case Law by the European Court of Justice' in P Popelier, C Van de Heyning and P Van Nuffel (eds), *Human Rights Protection in the European Legal Order: The interaction between the European and the national courts* (Antwerp, Intersentia, 2011) 17

——, 'The European Union as an International Legal Experiment' in G de Búrca and JHH Weiler (eds), *The Worlds of European Constitutionalism* (Cambridge, Cambridge University Press, 2012) 19

De Witte, B and Imamović, Š, 'Opinion 2/13 on Accession to the ECHR, Defending the EU Legal Order against a Foreign Human Rights Court' (2015) 40 *EL Rev* 683

De Witte, B and Toggenburg, GN, 'Human Rights and Membership of the European Union' in S Peers and A Ward (eds), *The EU Charter of Fundamental Rights* (Oxford, Hart Publishing, 2004) 59

Dedman, M, *The Origins and Development of the European Union 1945–2008* (Abingdon, Routledge, 2010)

Dinan, D, *Europe Recast: A History of European Union* (New York, Palgrave Macmillan, 2004)

——, *Origins and Evolution of the European Union* (Oxford, Oxford University Press, 2006)

Donnelly, J, *Universal Human Rights in Theory and Practice* (Ithaca, NY, Cornell University Press, 2003)

Dörr, O and Schmalenbach, K (eds), *Vienna Convention on the Law of Treaties: A Commentary* (Heidelberg, Springer, 2012)

Dougan, M, 'The Treaty of Lisbon 2007: Winning minds, not hearts' (2008) 45 *CML Rev* 663

Douglas-Scott, S, 'The European Union and Human Rights after the Treaty of Lisbon' (2011) 11 *Human Rights Law Review* 4

Dutheil de la Rochère, J, 'The EU Charter of Fundamental Rights, Not Binding but Influential, the Example of Good Administration' in A Arnull, P Eeckhout and T Tridimas, *Continuity and Change in EU Law, Essays in Honour of Sir Francis Jacobs* (Oxford, Oxford University Press, 2008) 157

Dzehtsiarou, K and O'Meara, N, 'Advisory Jurisdiction of the European Court of Human Rights, A Magic Bullet for Dialogue and Docket-Control?' (2014) 34 *Legal Studies* 3

Edeson, W and Wooldridge, F, 'European Community Law and Fundamental Human Rights: Some Recent Decisions of the European Court and National Courts' (1976) 1 *Legal Issues of European Integration* 44

Eeckhout, P, 'Community Terrorism Listing, Fundamental Rights, and UN Security Council Resolutions: In Search of the Right Fit' (2007) 3 *European Constitutional Law Review* 183

Engel, C, 'The European Charter of Fundamental Rights – A Changed Political Opportunity Structure and its Normative Consequences' (2001) 7 *European Law Journal* 151

Fabbrini, Fedrico and Larik, J, 'Dialoguing for Due Process, Kadi, Nada, and the Accession of The EU to the ECHR', *Leuven Global Governance Working Paper No 125* (2013)

Fabbrini, F, 'The EU Charter of Fundamental Rights and the Rights to Data Privacy, The Court of Justice as a Human Rights Court' in S de Vries, U Bernitz and S Weatherill (eds), *The EU Charter of Fundamental Rights as a Binding Instrument, Five Years Old and Growing* (Oxford, Hart Publishing, 2015) 261

Fichera, M, *The Implementation of the European Arrest Warrant in the European Union: Law, Policy and Practice* (Antwerp, Intersentia, 2011)

Finke, J, 'Regime-collisions, Tensions between treaties (and how to solve them)' in C Tams, A Tzanakopoulos and A Zimmermann (eds), *Research Handbook on the Law of Treaties* (Cheltenham, Edward Elgar Publishing, 2014) 415

Fleuren, J, 'The Application of Public International Law by Dutch Courts' (2010) 57 *Netherlands International Law Review* 245

Frąckowiak-Adamska, A, 'Drawing Red Lines with No (Significant) Bites: Why an Individual Test is not Appropriate in the *LM* Case' in A von Bogdandy, P Bogdanowicz, I Canor, C Grabenwarter, M Taborowski and M Schmidt (eds), *Defending Checks and Balances in EU Member: Taking Stock of Europe's Actions* (Berlin, Springer, 2021) 443

Fratzke, S, 'Not Adding Up: The Fading Promise of Europe's Dublin System', *EU Asylum, Towards 2020 Project* (Migration Policy Institute Europe, 2015)

Gaja, G, 'The Protection of Human Rights under the Maastricht Treaty' in D Curtin, T Heukels and HG Schermers (eds), *Institutional Dynamics of European Integration* (Dordrecht, Nijhoff Publishers, 1994) 549

Gamper, A, 'Austria, Endorsing the Convention System, Endorsing the Constitution' in P Popelier, S Lambrecht and K Lemmens (eds), *Criticism of the European Court of Human Rights, Shifting the Convention System, Counter- Dynamics at the National and EU Level* (Antwerp, Intersentia, 2016) 75

Gáspár-Szilágyi, S, 'Joined Cases Aranyosi and Căldăraru, Converging Human Rights Standards, Mutual Trust and a New Ground for Postponing a European Arrest Warrant' (2016) 24 *European Journal of Crime, Criminal Law and Criminal Justice* 197

Gauci, J-P, Giuffré, M and Tsourdi, E (L) (eds), *Exploring the Boundaries of Refugee Law: Current Protection Challenges* (Leiden, Brill Nijhoff, 2015)

Gerards, J, 'Advisory Opinions, Preliminary Rulings, and the New Protocol No 16 to the European Convention of Human Rights, a Comparative and Critical Appraisal' (2014) 21 *Maastricht Journal of European and Comparative Law* 4

——, 'Who Decides on Fundamental Rights Issues in Europe? Towards a Mechanism to Coordinate the Roles and the National Courts, the ECJ and the ECtHR' in S de Vries, U Bernitz and S Weatherill (eds), *The EU Charter of Fundamental Rights as a Binding Instrument, Five Years Old and Growing* (Oxford, Hart Publishing, 2015) 47

——, 'The Netherlands: Political Dynamics, Institutional Robustness' in P Popelier, S Lambrecht and K Lemmens (eds), *Criticism of the European Court of Human Rights, Shifting the Convention System, Counter-Dynamics at the National and EU Level* (Antwerp, Intersentia, 2016) 327

Gerards, J and Fleuren, J (eds), *Implementation of the ECHR and the Case Law of the European Court of Human Rights in National Case Law. A Comparative Analysis* (Antwerp, Intersentia, 2014)

Gerards, J and Fleuren, J, 'The Netherlands' in J Gerards and J Fleuren (eds), *Implementation of the ECHR and the Case Law of the European Court of Human Rights in National Case Law. A Comparative Analysis* (Antwerp, Intersentia, 2014) 217

Geyer, F, 'European arrest warrant, Court of Justice of the European Communities, judgment of 3rd May 2007, case C-303/05, *Advocaten voor de Wereld VZW v Leden van de Ministerraad*' (2008) 4 *European Constitutional Law Review* 149

Glas, L and Krommendijk, J, 'From Opinion 2/13 to Avotiņš, Recent Developments in the Relationship between the Luxembourg and Strasbourg Court' (2017) 17 *Human Rights Law Review* 2

Gordon, M, 'The UK's Sovereignty Situation, Brexit, Bewilderment and Beyond' (2016) 27 *King's Law Journal* 333

Gragl, P, *The Accession of the European Union to the European Convention on Human Rights* (Oxford, Hart Publishing, 2013)

——, 'The Shortcomings of Dublin II: Strasbourg's M.S.S. Judgment and Its Implications for the European Union's Legal Order' in W Benedek, F Benoit Rohmer, W Karl and M Nowak(eds), European Yearbook on Human Rights (Vienna, Neuer Wissenschaftlicher Verlag, 2012) 123

——, 'A Giant Leap for European Human Rights? The Final Agreement on the European Union's Accession to the European Convention on Human Rights' (2014) 51 *CML Rev* 13

——, 'The Reasonableness of Jealousy, Opinion 2/13 and EU Accession to the ECHR' in W Benedek, F Benoit Rohmer, W Karl and M Nowak (eds), *European Yearbook on Human Rights 2015* (Vienna, Neuer Wissenschaftlicher Verlag, 2015) 27

——, 'An Olive Branch from Strasbourg? Interpreting the European Court of Human Rights' Resurrection of *Bosphorus* and Reaction to *Opinion 2/13* in the *Avotiņš* Case' (2017) 13 *European Constitutional Law Review* 551

Greer, S, *The European Convention on Human Rights* (Cambridge, Cambridge University Press, 2006)

Groussot, X, Arold, L, Nina, L and Petursson, GT, 'The Paradox of Human Rights Protection in Europe: Two Courts, One Goal?' in OM Arnardóttir and A Buyse (eds), *Shifting Centres of Gravity in Human Rights Protection* (London, Routledge 2016) 8

Groussot, X, Pech, L and Petursson, GT, 'The Scope of Applicationlication of Fundamental Rights on Member States' Actions: in Search of Certainty in EU Adjudication', *Eric Stein Working Paper No 1/2011* (2011)

——, Pech, L and Petursson, GT, 'The Reach of EU Fundamental Rights on Member State Action after Lisbon' in S de Vries, U Bernitz and S Weatherill (eds), *The Protection of Fundamental Rights in the EU after Lisbon* (Oxford, Hart Publishing, 2013) 97

Groussot, X and Grill-Pedro, E, 'Old and new human rights in Europe, the scope of EU rights versus that of ECHR rights' in E Brems and J Gerards (eds), *Shaping Rights in the ECHR: The Role of the European Court of Human Rights in Determining the Scope of Human Rights* (Cambridge, Cambridge University Press, 2013) 232

Guild, E (ed), *Constitutional Challenges to the European Arrest Warrant* (Nijmegen, Wolf Legal Publishers, 2006)

Halberstam, D, '"It's the Autonomy, Stupid!" A Modest Defense of Opinion 2/13 on EU Accession to the European Convention on Human Rights' (2015) 16 *German Law Journal* 105

Hale, B, 'Argentoratum Locutum, Is Strasbourg or the Supreme Court Supreme?' (2012) 12 *Human Rights Law Review* 65

Halleskov Storgaard, L, 'EU Law Autonomy versus European Fundamental Rights Protection – On Opinion 2/13 on EU Accession to the ECHR' (2015) 15 *Human Rights Law Review* 485

Harpaz, G, 'Judicial Review by the European Court of Justice of UN "Smart Sanctions" Against Terror in the Kadi Dispute' (2009) 14 *European Foreign Affairs Review* 65

Helfer, LR, 'Redesigning the European Court of Human Rights, Embeddedness as a Deep Structural Principle of the European Human Rights Regime' (2008) 19 *The European Journal of International Law* 1

Heringa, AW, 'Editorial, Europe's Common Bill of Rights' (1996) 3 *Maastricht Journal of European and Comparative Law* 1

Hillion, C, 'A Powerless Court? The European Court of Justice and the Common Foreign and Security Policy' in M Cremona and A Thies (eds), *The European Court of Justice and External Relations Law, Constitutional Challenges* (Oxford, Hart Publishing, 2014) 69

——, 'Overseeing the Rule of Law in the EU Legal Mandate and Means' in C Closa and D Kochenov (eds), *Reinforcing the Rule of Law Oversight in the European Union* (Cambridge, Cambridge University Press, 2016) 59

Hilson, C, 'Rights and Principles in EU Law, A Distinction without Foundation?' (2008) 15 *Maastricht Journal of European and Comparative Law* 2

Huber, PM, 'The Unitary Effect of the Community's Fundamental Rights: The ERT- Doctrine Needs to be Reviewed' (2008) 14 *European Public Law* 323

Imamović, Š, 'The Court of Justice of the EU as a Human Rights Adjudicator in the Area of Freedom, Security and Justice', *Jean Monnet Working Paper 05/2017* (2017)

Imamović, Š and Muir, E, 'The Dublin III System: More Derogations to the Duty to Transfer Individual Asylum Seekers?' (2017) 2 *European Papers* 719

Jacobs, FG, 'Human Rights in the European Union, the Role of the Court of Justice' (2001) 26 *EL Rev* 337

——, 'Judicial dialogue and the cross-fertilization of legal systems, the European Court of Justice' (2003) 38 *Texas International Law Journal* 547

——, 'The European Convention on Human Rights, the EU Charter of Fundamental Rights and the European Court of Justice, The Impact of European Union accession to the European Convention on Human Rights' in I Pernice, J Kokott and C Saunders (eds), *The Future of the European Judicial System in a Comparative Perspective* (Baden-Baden, Nomos Verlag, 2006) 291

Janssens, C, *The Principle of Mutual Recognition in EU Law* (Oxford, Oxford University Press, 2013)

Jenks, W, 'The Conflict of Law-making Treaties' (1953) 30 *British Yearbook of International Law* 401

Jeutner, V, *Irresolvable Norm Conflicts in International Law* (Oxford, Oxford University Press, 2017)

Kamminga, M, 'Human Rights Treaties and State Succession' in Venice Commission: *The Status of International Treaties on Human Rights* (Strasbourg, Council of Europe Publishing, 2006) 31

Keller, H and Stone Sweet, A (eds), *A Europe of Rights: The Impact of the ECHR on National Legal Systems* (Oxford, Oxford University Press, 2009)

Keller, H and Marti, C, 'Reconceptualizing Implementation, The Judicialization of the Execution of the European Court of Human Rights' Judgments' (2015) 26 *European Journal of International Law* 829

Kelsen, H, *General Theory of Norms*, tr M Hartney (Oxford, Oxford University Press, 1991)

Kirsch, N, 'The Open Architecture of European Human Rights Law', *LSE Working Papers 11/2007*

Klabbers, J, *Treaty Conflict and the European Union* (Cambridge, Cambridge University Press, 2009)

——, 'Contending Approaches to international organizations: Between functionalism and constitutionalism' in J Klabbers and Å Wallendahl (eds), *Research Handbook on the Law of International Organizations* (Cheltenham, Edward Elgar, 2011) 3

Klabbers, J, Peters, A and Ulfstein, G, *The Constitutionalization of International Law* (Oxford, Oxford University Press, 2009)

Klein, E, 'Germany' in J Gerards and J Fleuren (eds), *Implementation of the European Convention on Human Rights and of the Judgments of the ECtHR in National Case Law* (Antwerp, Intersentia, 2014) ch 5

Kochenov, D, 'Busting the myths nuclear: A commentary on Article 7 TEU', *EUI Working Paper 2017/10*

Kochenov, D and Pech, L, 'Better Late Than Never? On the European Commission's Rule of Law Framework and its First Activation' (2016) 24 *Journal of Common Market Studies* 1062

Kokott, J and Sobotta, C, 'Protection of Fundamental Rights in the European Union: On the Relationship between EU Fundamental Rights, the European Convention and National Standards of Protection (2015) 34 *Yearbook of European Law* 60

Komárek, J, 'European constitutionalism and the European arrest warrant, In search of the limits of contrapunctual principles' (2007) 44 *CML Rev* 9

Konstadinides, T, 'Judicial independence and the Rule of Law in the context of non-execution of a European Arrest Warrant: *LM*' (2019) 56 *CML Rev* 743

Korenica, F, *The EU Accession to the ECHR: Between Luxembourg's Search for Autonomy and Strasbourg's Credibility on Human Rights Protection* (Heidelberg, Springer, 2015)

Koskenniemi, M, 'Hierarchy in International Law, A Sketch' (1997) 8 *European Journal of International Law* 566

——, 'Constitutionalism as a Mindset, Reflections on Kantian Themes about International Law and Globalization' (2007) 8 *Theoretical Inquiries in Law* 9

Kosta, V, *Fundamental Rights in EU Internal Market Legislation* (Oxford, Hart Publishing, 2015)

Koutrakos, P, *EU International Relations Law* (Oxford, Hart Publishing, 2006)

Krenn, C, 'Autonomy and Effectiveness as Common Concerns, A Path to ECHR Accession after Opinion 2/13' (2015) 16 *German Law Journal* 147

Krisch, N, 'The Open Architecture of European Human Rights Law', *LSE Working Papers 11/2007* (2007)

Krommendijk, J, 'Opinion 2/13 as a Game Changer in the Dialogue Between the European Courts?' in E Bribosia and I Rorive (eds), *Human Rights Tectonics: Global Dynamics of Integration and Fragmentation* (Antwerp, Intersentia, 2018) 243

——, 'Principled silence or mere silence on principles? The role of the EU Charter's principles in the case law of the Court of Justice' (2015) 11 *European Constitutional Law Review* 321

Kuhnert, K, 'Bosphorus – Double standards in European human rights protection?' (2006) 2 *Utrecht Law Review* 2

Kuijer, M, 'The challenging relationship between the European Convention on Human Rights and the EU legal order: consequences of a delayed accession' (2018) 24 *The International Journal of Human Rights* 1

Kuijper, PJ, Amtenbrink, F, Curtin, D, De Witte, B, McDonnell, A and van den Bogaert, S, *The Law of the European Union* (Alphen a/d Rijn, Kluwer Law International, 2018)

Kumm, M and Comella, VF, 'The Primacy Clause of the Constitutional Treaty and the Future of Constitutional Conflict in the European Union', *Jean Monnet Working Paper 5/04*

Ladenburger, C, 'The Principle of Mutual Trust between Member States in the Area of Freedom, Security and Justice' (2020) 3 *Zeitschrift für Europarechtliche Studien* 373

Lambrecht, S and Rauchegger, C, 'European Union, The EU's Attitude to the ECHR' in P Popelier, S Lambrecht and K Lemmens (eds), *Criticism of the European Court of Human Rights. Shifting the Convention System: Counter- Dynamics at the National and EU Level* (Antwerp, Intersentia, 2016) 41

Larik, J and Bruggeman, R, 'The Elusive Contours of Constitutional Identity: Taricco as a Missed Opportunity' (2020) 35 *Utrecht Journal of International and European Law* 20

Lawson, R, 'Confusion and Conflict? Diverging Interpretations of the European Convention on Human Rights in Strasbourg and Luxembourg' in R Lawson and M de Blois (eds), *The Dynamics of the Protection of Human Rights in Europe – Essays in Honour of Professor Henry G Schermers*, vol III (The Hague, Martinus Nijhoff Publishers, 1994) 219

Leconte, C and Muir, E, 'Understanding Resistance to EU Fundamental Rights Policy' (2014) 15 *Human Rights Review* 1

Leczykiewicz, Dorota, 'Effective Judicial Protection of Human Rights after Lisbon' (2010) 35 *EL Rev* 326

Lemmens, K, 'Criticising the European Court of Human Rights or Misunderstanding the Dynamics of Human Rights Protection?' in P Popelier, S Lambrecht and K Lemmens (eds), *Criticism of the European Court of Human Rights, Shifting the Convention System, Counter-Dynamics at the National and EU Level* (Antwerp, Intersentia, 2016) 23

——, 'Protocol No 16 to the ECHR: Managing Backlog through Complex Judicial Dialogue?' (2019) 15 *European Constitutional Law Review* 691

Lenaerts, K, 'Exploring the Limits of the EU Charter of Fundamental Rights' (2012) 8 *European Constitutional Law Review* 375

——, 'The EU Charter of Fundamental Rights, Scope of Application and Methods of Interpretations' in MT D'Alessio, V Kronenberger and V Placco (eds), *De Rome à Lisbonne: les juridictions de l'Union européenne à la croisée des chemins. Mélanges en l'honneur de Paolo Mengozzi* (Brussels, Bruylant, 2013) 107

——, 'The Principle of Mutual Recognition in the Area of Freedom, Security and Justice', The Fourth Annual Sir Jeremy Lever Lecture, All Souls College, University of Oxford, 30 January 2015

——, 'La vie après l'avis: Exploring the principle of mutual (yet not blind) trust' (2017) 54 *CML Rev* 805

——, 'The Role of the EU Charter in the Member States' in M Bobek and J Adams-Prassl (eds), *The EU Charter of Fundamental Rights in the Member States* (Oxford, Hart Publishing, 2020) 19

Lenaerts, K and De Smijter, E, 'The Charter and the role of the European Courts' (2001) 8 *Maastricht Journal of European and Comparative Law* 90

Lenart, J, '"Fortress Europe": Compliance of the Dublin II Regulation with the European Convention for the Protection of Human Rights and Fundamental Freedoms' (2012) 28 *Utrecht Journal of International and European Law* 4

Letsas, G, 'The ECHR as a living instrument, its meaning and legitimacy' in A Føllesdal, B Peters and G Ulfstein, *Constituting Europe, The European Court of Human Rights in a National, European and Global Context* (Cambridge, Cambridge University Press, 2013) 106

Linderfalk, U, 'The Effect of Jus Cogens Norms, Whoever Opened Pandora's Box, Did You Ever Think About the Consequences?' (2007) 18 *European Journal of International Law* 853
Lock, T, *The European Court of Justice and International Courts* (Oxford, Oxford University Press, 2015)
——, 'Rights and Principles in the EU Charter of Fundamental Rights' (2019) 56 CML Rev 1201.
——, 'The Future of EU Human Rights: Is accession to the ECHR still desirable?' (2020) 7 *Journal of International and Comparative Law* 2
Luchtman, M, 'The ECJ's Recent Case Law on Ne Bis In Idem: Implications for Law Enforcement in a Shared Legal Order' (2018) 55 *CML Rev* 1717
Maiani, F and Migliorini, S, 'One Principle to Rule Them All? Anatomy of Mutual Trust in The Law of the Area of Freedom, Security and Justice' (2020) 57 *CML Rev* 7
Mak, E, 'Report on the Netherlands and Luxembourg' in G Martinico and O Pollicino (eds), *The National Judicial Treatment of the ECHR and EU Laws, A Comparative Constitutional Perspective* (Groningen, Europa Law Publishing, 2010)
Mancini, F, 'Safeguarding Human Rights: The role of the Court of Justice of the European Communities' in F Mancini (ed), *Democracy and Constitutionalism in the European Union, Collected Essays* (Oxford, Hart Publishing, 2000) 82
Martinico, G, 'Is the European Convention Going to Be 'Supreme'? A Comparative- Constitutional Overview of ECHR and EU Law before National Courts' (2012) 23 *The European Journal of International Law* 401
Martinico, G and Pollicino, O (eds), *The National Judicial Treatment of the ECHR and EU Laws. A Comparative Constitutional Law Perspective* (Groningen, Europa Law Publishing, 2010)
—— and Pollicino, O, *The Interaction between Europe's Legal Systems Judicial Dialogue and the Creation of Supranational Laws* (Cheltenham, Edward Elgar Publishing, 2012)
Masterman, R, 'The United Kingdom, From Strasbourg Surrogacy Towards a British Bill of Rights?' in P Popelier, S Lambrecht and K Lemmens (eds), *Criticism of the European Court of Human Rights, Shifting the Convention System, Counter-Dynamics at the National and EU Level* (Antwerp, Intersentia, 2016) 449
Mathisen, KL, 'The Impact of the Lisbon Treaty, in particular Article 6 TEU, on Member States' obligations with respect to the protection of fundamental rights', *University of Luxembourg, Law Working Paper Series Paper 2010-01*
McCrudden, C, 'Using Comparative Reasoning in Human Rights Adjudication: The Court of Justice of the European Union and the European Court of Human Rights Compared' (2013) 15 *Cambridge Yearbook of European Legal Studies* 383
Milanović, M, 'Norm Conflict in International Law, Whither Human Rights?' (2009) 20 *Duke Journal of International and Comparative Law* 69
——, 'The Lost Origins of Lex Specialis, Rethinking the Relationship between Human Rights and International Humanitarian Law' in JD Ohlin, *Theoretical Boundaries of Armed Conflict and Human Rights* (Cambridge, Cambridge University Press, 2016) 78
Mitsilegas, V, 'Judical dialogue in three silences: Unpacking Taricco' (2018) 9 *New Journal of European Criminal Law* 38
Mole, N, 'Can *Bosphorus* be maintained?' (2015) 16 *ERA Forum* 467.
Morano-Foadi, S and Vickers, L (eds), *Fundamental Rights in the EU* (Oxford, Hart Publishing, 2015)
Moriarty, B, 'Human Rights in EC/EU law' in B Moriarty and E Massa, *Human Rights Law* (Oxford, Oxford University Press, 2012) ch 8.
Morijn, J, 'Judicial Reference to the EU Fundamental Rights Charter, First Experiences and Possible Prospects' Coimbra Human Rights Centre Working Paper (2002)
——, 'The EU Fundamental Rights Charter, the European Commission and the Council of Ministers, checking the "Charter checklist" Part 1 and 2 (2011)
——, 'After Opinion 2/13, How to Move on in Strasbourg and Brussels?' *EUtopia law* (5 January 2015)
Mus, JB, *Verdragsconflicten voor de Nederlandse rechter* (Zwolle, WEJ Tjeenk Willink, 1996)
O'Leary, S 'Courts, charters and conventions: making sense of fundamental rights in the EU' (2016) 56 *Irish Jurist* 4

——, 'The EU Charter Ten Years On: A View from Strasbourg' in M Bobek and J Adams-Prassl (eds), *The EU Charter of Fundamental Rights in the Member States* (Oxford, Hart Publishing, 2020) 37

Orakhelashvili, A, 'Peremptory Norms in International Law' (2006) Oxford Scholarship Online, available at https://oxford.universitypressscholarship.com/view/10.1093/acprof:oso/9780199546114.001.0001/acprof-9780199546114

Paasivirta, E and Kuijper, PJ, 'Does One Size Fit All? The European Community and the Responsibility of International Organizations' (2005) 26 *Netherlands Yearbook of International Law* 169

Pabel, K, 'Germany: The Long Way of Integrating the Strasbourg Perspective into the Proteciton of Fundamental Rights' in P Popelier, S Lambrecht and K Lemmens (eds), *Criticism of the European Court of Human Rights, Shifting the Convention System, Counter-Dynamics at the National and EU Level* (Antwerp, Intersentia, 2016) 155

Pauwelyn, J, *Conflict of Norms in Public International Law, How WTO Law Relates to Other Rules of International Law* (Cambridge, Cambridge University Press, 2003)

Pech, L, 'Between Judicial Minimalism and Avoidance: The Court of Justice's Sidestepping of Fundamental Constitutional Issues in Römer and Dominguez' (2012) 49 *CML Rev* 40

Peers, S, 'Bosphorus. European Court of Human Rights. Limited Responsibility of European Union Member States for Actions within the Scope of Community Law. Judgment of 30 June 2005, *Bosphorus Airways v Ireland*, Application No 45036/98' 2 (2006) *European Constitutional Law Review* 443

——, 'The EU's Accession to the ECHR, The Dream Becomes a Nightmare' (2015) 16 *German Law Journal* 213

Pergantis, V, 'The "Sovereignty Clause" of the Dublin Regulations in the Case-Law of the ECtHR and the CJEU: The Mirage of a Jurisprudential Convergence?' in GC Bruno, FM Palombino and A Di Stefano (eds), *Migration Issues before International Courts and Tribunals* (Rome, CNR Edizioni, 2019) 409

Pernice, I, 'The Treaty of Lisbon and Fundamental Rights' in S Griller and J Ziller (eds), *The Lisbon Treaty. EU Constitutionalism without a Constitutional Treaty?* (Heidelberg, Springer, 2008) 235

Polakiewicz, J, 'EU Law and the ECHR: Will EU Accession to the European Convention on Human Rights Square the Circle?' (2013) 13 *European Human Rights Law Review* 592

Popelier P 'Report on Belgium' in G Martinico and O Pollicino (eds), *The National Judicial Treatment of the ECHR and EU Laws* (Groningen, Europa Law Publishers, 2010) 81

——, 'Belgium, Faithful, Obedient, and Just a Little Irritated' in P Popelier, S Lambrecht and K Lemmens (eds), *Criticism of the European Court of Human Rights, Shifting the Convention System, Counter-Dynamics at the National and EU Level* (Antwerp, Intersentia, 2016) 119

Popelier, P, Van de Heyning, C and van Nuffel, P (eds), Human Rights Protection in the European Legal Order: The interaction between the European and the national courts (Antwerp, Intersentia, 2011)

——, Lambrecht, S and Lemmens, K (eds), *Criticism of the European Court of Human Rights, Shifting the Convention System, Counter-Dynamics at the National and EU Level* (Antwerp, Intersentia, 2016)

Prechal, S, de Vries, S and van Eijken, H, 'The Principle of Attributed Powers and the "Scope of EU Law"' in LFM Besselink, F Penning and S Prechal (eds), *The Eclipse of the Legality Principle in the European Union* (Alphen aan den Rijn, Kluwer Law International, 2011) 213

Ravasi, E, *Human Rights Protection by the ECtHR and the ECJ* (Leiden, Brill Nijhoff, 2017)

Rosas, A, 'The European Union and Fundamental Rights/Human Rights' in C Krause and M Scheinin (eds), *International Protection of Human Rights, A Textbook* (Institute for Human Rights, Abo Academy University, 2009) 7

——, 'Is the EU a Human Rights Organisation?', *Cleer Working Papers 2011/1*

——, 'The Status in EU Law of International Agreements Concluded by EU Member States' (2011) 34 *Fordham International Law Journal* 1304

——, 'When is the EU Charter of Fundamental Rights Applicable at National Level?' (2012) 19 *Jurisprudence* 4

——, 'Five Years of Charter Case Law, Some Observations' in S de Vries, U Bernitz and S Weatherill (eds), *The EU Charter of Fundamental Rights as a Binding Instrument, Five Years Old and Growing* (Oxford, Hart Publishing, 2015) 11

Rosas, A and Armati, L, *EU Constitutional Law, An Introduction* (Oxford, Hart Publishing, 2018)
Ruggieri Laderchi, FP, 'Report on Italy' in A-M Slaughter, A Stone Sweet and JHH Weiler (eds), *The European Courts and National Courts* (Oxford, Hart Publishing, 1998) 147
Ryngaert, C, 'Oscillating between embracing and avoiding Bosphorus: the European Court of Human Rights on Member State responsibility for acts of international organisations and the case of the EU' (2015) 39 *EL Rev* 2
Sadat-Akhavi, A, *Methods of Resolving Conflicts between Treaties* (Leiden, Brill, 2003)
Sadurski, W, 'Accession's Democracy Dividend, The Impact of the EU Enlargement upon Democracy in the New Member States of Central and Eastern Europe' (2004) 10 *European Law Journal* 4
——, 'EU Enlargement and Democracy in New Member States' in W Sadurski, A Czarnota and M Krygier (eds), *Spreading Democracy and the Rule of Law?* (Dordrecht, Springer, 2006) 27
——, 'Adding Bite to a Bark: The Story of Article 7, EU Enlargement, and Jörg Haider' (2010) 16 *Columbia Journal of European Law* 385
——, *Constitutionalism and the Enlargement of Europe* (Oxford, Oxford University Press, 2012)
Sarmiento, D, 'European Union: the European arrest warrant and the quest for constitutional coherence' (2008) 6 *International Journal of Constitutional Law* 171
Scheeck, L, 'Competition, Conflict and Cooperation between European Courts and the Diplomacy of Supranational Judicial Networks', *Garnet Working Paper 23/07* (2007)
Scheinin, M, 'Human Rights Treaties and the Vienna Convention on the Law of Treaties: Conflict or Harmony?' in Venice Commission, *The Status of International Treaties on Human Rights* (Strasbourg, Council of Europe Publishing, 2006) 43
Schermers, HG, 'Matthews v United Kingdom, Judgment of 18 February 1999' (1999) 36 *CML Rev* 673
Schwarz, M, 'Let's talk about trust, baby: Theorizing trust and mutual recognition in the EU's area of freedom, security and justice' (2018) 24 *European Law Journal* 124
Shaw, J, *International Law* (Cambridge, Cambridge University Press, 2014)
Shelton, D, 'Normative Hierarchy in International Law' (2006) 100 *American Journal of International Law* 291
Simma, B and Pulkowski, D, 'Of Planets and the Universe, Self-Contained Regimes in International Law' (2006) 17 *European Journal of International Law* 483
Soo, A, 'Divergence of European Union and Strasbourg Standards on Defence Rights in Criminal Proceedings? Ibrahim and the others v the UK (13th of September 2016)' (2017) 25 *European Journal of Crime, Criminal Law and Criminal Justice* 4
Spano, R, 'The rule of law as the lodestar of the European Convention on Human Rights: The Strasbourg Court and the independence of the judiciary' [2021] *European Law Journal* 1
Spaventa, E, 'A Very Fearful Court? The Protection of Fundamental Rights in the European Union after Opinion 2/13' (2015) 22 *Maastricht Journal of European and Comparative Law* 35
Spencer, JR, 'Extradition, the EAW and human rights' (2013) 72 *CLJ* 2
Spielmann, D, 'Human Rights Case Law in the Strasbourg and Luxembourg Courts: Conflicts, Inconsistencies, and Complementarities' in P Alston, MR Bustelo and J Heenan (eds), *The EU and Human Rights* (Oxford, Oxford University Press, 1999) 757
Stirk, PMR, *A History of European Integration since 1914* (London, Pinter, 1996)
Stone Sweet, A and Mathews, J, 'Proportionality Balancing and Global Constitutionalism', *47 Faculty Scholarship Series Paper 1296* (2008)
Temple Lang, J, 'The Sphere in Which Member States are Obliged to Comply with the General Principles of Community Fundamental Rights Principles' (1991) 2 *Legal Issues of European Integration* 23
Timmerman, M, 'Case C-105/14, Criminal proceedings against Ivo Taricco and Others, Judgment of the Court of Justice (Grand Chamber) of 8 September 2016, EU:C:2015:555: Balancing effective criminal sanctions with effective fundamental rights protection in cases of VAT fraud: Taricco' (2016) 53 *CML Rev* 779
Timmermans, C, 'The Relationship between the European Court of Justice and the European Court of Human Rights' in A Arnull, C Barnard, M Dougan and E Spaventa (eds), *A Constitutional Order of States? Essays in EU Law in Honour of Alan Dashwood* (Oxford, Hart Publishing, 2011) 151

Tinsley, A, 'The Reference in Case C-396/11 Radu: When does the Protection of Fundamental Rights Require Non-execution of a European Arrest Warrant?' (2012) 2 *European Criminal Law Review* 3

Tizzano, A, 'The Role of the ECJ in the Protection of Fundamental Rights' in A Arnull, P Eeckhout and T Tridimas (eds), *Continuity and Change in EU Law: Essays in Honour of Francis Jacobs* (Oxford, Oxford University Press, 2008) 125

Torres Pérez, A, *Conflicts of Rights in the European Union, A Theory of Supranational Adjudication* (Oxford, Oxford University Press, 2009).

——, '*Melloni* in Three Acts, From Dialogue to Monologue' (2014) 10 *European Constitutional Law Review* 308

——, 'A predicament for domestic courts, caught between the European Arrest Warrant and fundamental rights' in B De Witte, JA Mayoral, U Jaremba, M Wind and K Podstawa (eds), *National Court and EU Law: New Issues, Theories and Methods* (Cheltenham, Edward Elgar, 2016) 191

Tridimas, T, 'Fundamental Rights, General Principles of EU Law, and the Charter' (2014) 16 *Cambridge Yearbook of European Legal Studies* 361

Van de Heyning, C, 'PO Kokkelvisserij vs The Netherlands, Applicationlication no 13645/05, 20 January 2009' (2009) 46 *CML Rev* 2125

——, 'No Place Like Home: Discretionary Space for the Domestic Protection of Fundamental Rights' in P Popelier, C Van de Heyning and P Van Nuffel (eds), *Human Rights Protection in the European Legal Order, The Interaction between the European and the National Courts* (Antwerp, Intersentia, 2011) 65

Van de Heyning, C and Lawson, R, 'EU law and the European Court of Justice case law as inspiration and challenge to the European Court of Human Rights jurisprudence' in P Popelier, C Van de Heyning and P Van Nuffel (eds) *Human Rights Protection in the European Legal Order, The Interaction between the European and the National Courts* (Antwerp, Intersentia, 2011) 35

Verrijdt, W, 'Belgium' in S Griller (ed), *National Constitutions and EU Integration* (Oxford, Hart Publishing, forthcoming)

Vesterdorf, B, 'A Constitutional Court for the EU?' (2006) 4 *International Journal of Constitutional Law* 607

Vidmar, J, 'Norm Conflicts and Hierarchy in International Law: Towards a Vertical International Legal System?' in E de Wet and J Vidmar (eds), *Hierarchy in International Law, The Place of Human Rights* (Oxford, Oxford University Press, 2012) 13

Von Bogdandy, A, 'The European Union as a Human Rights Organization? Human Rights and the core of the European Union' (2000) 37 *CML Rev* 1307

Von Bogdandy, A and Schill, S, 'Overcoming Absolute Primacy, Respect for National Identity under the Lisbon Treaty' (2011) 48 *CML Rev* 1417

Vranes, E, 'The Definition of 'Norm Conflict' in International Law and Legal Theory' (2006) 17 *European Journal of International Law* 395

Walker, N, 'The Idea of Constitutional Pluralism' (2002) 65 *MLR* 317

Wassenberg, B, *History of the Council of Europe* (Strasbourg, Council of Europe Publishing, 2013)

Weiler, JHH, 'Eurocracy and Distrust. Some Questions concerning the Role of the European Court of Justice in the Protection of Fundamental Human Rights within the Legal Order of the European Communities' (1986) 612 *Washington Law Review* 1112

——, 'The Transformation of Europe' (1992) 100 *Yale Law Journal* 2403

——, 'Fundamental Rights and Fundamental Boundaries: On the Conflict of Standards and Values in the Protection of Human Rights in the European Legal Space' in JHH Weiler, *The Constitution of Europe* (Cambridge, Cambridge University Press, 1999) 102

——, 'Editorial, Does the European Union Truly Need a Charter of Rights?' (2000) 6 *European Law Journal* 96

——, 'On the Values, Virtues (and Vices) of the European Construct: What we can learn from Aristotle, Aquinas and Maimonides', presentation at the Hertie School of Governance (13 March 2012)

Weiß, W, 'Human Rights in the EU, Rethinking the Role of the European Convention on Human Rights After Lisbon' (2011) 7 *European Constitutional Law Review* 1

Willems, A, 'Mutual Trust as a Term of Art in EU Criminal Law: Revealing its Hybrid Character' (2016) 9 *European Journal of Legal Studies* 211

Williams, A, *EU Human Rights Policies: A Study In Irony* (Oxford, Oxford University Press, 2004)

——, 'Fundamental Rights in the New European Union' in C Barnard (ed), *The Fundamentals of EU Law Revisited, Assessing the Impact of the Constitutional Debate* (Oxford, Oxford University Press, 2007) 71

Wolfrum, R and Matz, N, *Conflicts in International Environmental Law* (Berlin/London, Springer, 2003)

Wouters, J and Verhoeven, S, 'The Prohibition of Genocide as a Norm of Ius Cogens and Its Implications for the Enforcement of the Law of Genocide' (2005) 5 *International Criminal Law Review* 401

Xanthopoulou, E, *Fundamental Rights and Mutual Trust in the Area of Freedom, Security and Justice: A Role for Proportionality?* (Oxford, Hart Publishing, 2020)

Yowell, P, 'The Justiciability of the Charter of Fundamental Rights in the Domestic Law of Member States' in PM Huber and K Ziegler (eds), *The EU and National Constitutional Law* (Munich, Richard Boorberg Verlag, 2012) 107

Ziegler, KS, Wicks, E and Hodson, L (eds), *The UK and European Human Rights, A Strained Relationship?* (Oxford, Hart Publishing, 2015)

Reports

Albers, P, Beauvais, P, Bohnert, J-F, Böse, M, Langbroek, P, Renier, A and Wahl, T, *Towards a Common Evaluation Framework to Assess Mutual Trust in the Field of EU Judicial Cooperation in Criminal Matters* (March 2013)

Besselink, LFM, Claes, M, Imamović, Š and Reestman, J-H, *National Constitutional Avenues for Further EU Integration*, Report for the European Parliament's Committees on Legal Affairs and on Constitutional Affairs No PE 493.046, Brussels: European Union (2014)

Human Rights Watch World Report 2014

International Law Commission (ILC), 'Report of the International Law Commission on the Fragmentation of International Law, Difficulties arising from the diversification and expansion of International Law' (13 April 2006) A/CN.4/L.663/Rev.1 (ILC Fragmentation Study)

Koskenniemi, M, 'Fragmentation of International Law, Difficulties Arising from the Diversification and Expansion of International Law' (13 April 2006) UN Doc A/CN.4/L.682

International Commission of Jurists, 'Workshop on Migration and Human Rights in Europe' (2011)

Meijers Committee, *The Principle of Mutual Trust in European Asylum, Immigration and Criminal Law, Reconciling Trust and Fundamental Rights* (2011)

Venice Commission, *Are There Differentiations Among Human Rights? Jus Cogens, Core Human Rights, Obligations Erga Omnes and Non-Derogability*, CDL-UD(2005)020rep-e

——, 'Opinion on the amendments to the Act of 25 June 2015 on the Constitutional Tribunal of Poland' CDL-AD(2016)001

Blogs

Callewaert, J, 'Manifest deficiency in the execution of a European arrest warrant – judgment of the European Court of Human Rights in the case Bivolaru and Moldovan v. France' Portal of Prof. Dr. iur. Johan Callewaert

Dupré, C, 'Individuals and Judges in Defense of the Rule of Law' *Verfassungsblog*, 28 July 2018

Frąckowiak-Adamska, A. 'Mutual trust and independence of the judiciary after the CJEU judgment in LM – new era or business as usual?' EU Law Analysis 15 August 2018

Hong, M, 'Human Dignity and constitutional identity: The Solange-III Decision of the German Constitutional Court', Verfassungsblog, 18 February 2016

Peers, S, 'Human Rights and the European Arrest Warrant: Has the ECJ turned from poacher to gamekeeper?' EU Law Analysis 12 November 2016

Von Danwitz, L, 'In Rights We Trust. The ECtHR's judgment in Romeo Castaño v Belgium and the relationship between the ECHR and the principle of mutual trust in EU law' *Verfassungsblog*, 21 August 2019

Zamboni, M, 'Romeo Castaño v Belgium and the Duty to Cooperate under the ECHR' *Blog of the European Journal of International Law*, 19 August 2019

Speeches

Churchill, Winston, speech delivered at the University of Zurich, 19 September 1946

Lenaerts, Koen, 'The ECHR and the CJEU: Creating Synergies in the Field of Fundamental Rights Protection', 26 January 2018

Polakiewicz, Jorg, 'Speech: The Future of Fundamental Rights Protection without Accession', 26 June 2006

Perez de los Cobos, Francisco, Solemn hearing on the occasion of the opening of the judicial year of the European Court of Human Rights, 30 January 2015

Spielmann, Dean, Solemn hearing for the opening of the judicial year of the European Court of Human Rights, 30 January 2015

Spielmann, Dean, 'The Judicial Dialogue between the European Court of Justice and the European Court of Human Rights or How to Remain Good Neighbours After the Opinion 2/13', delivered at FRAME, 27 March 2017

INDEX

A v B and Others 86
Abdida 66
Abdullahi 67, 100–101, 105, 179
Accession of the EU to the ECHR
Opinion 2/94 35
Opinion 2/13 2, 6, 37, 42, 46, 53, 65–74, 124, 198
Advocaten voor de Wereld 117–119
Åkerberg Fransson 26, 56, 58, 64
AMS 25
Aranyosi and Căldăraru 10, 119, 123–127, 131–132, 136–138, 183, 186–187, 192–193
Area of Freedom, Security and Justice (AFSJ)
case law 7, 93
case law divergences 9, 91
Cassis de Dijon 93
CJEU cases 91, 94–95
Common European Asylum System 91
Dublin system *See* Dublin system
European Arrest Warrant 10
principles of mutual trust and recognition 7, 9, 73, 91–95, 121, 124
Treaty of Amsterdam 93
Ástráðsson 133
asylum law
CJEU cases 2, 92
Common European Asylum System 9–10, 91
Dublin system *See* Dublin system
ECtHR and 92
EU law 5
fundamental rights and 92
migrants' rights, EU policy 40, 41
mutual trust principle 10, 91–95
non-refoulement principle 97
Reception Conditions Directive 190–192
Return Directive 190
Austria
dualist legal system 81
ECHR, status 81, 152
international human rights treaties 151–152
national courts 86
Avotiņš v Latvia 52–54, 73–74, 128–129

Belgium
EU law and ECHR, primacy over national legislation 76, 80–81, 82, 85
international human rights treaties 151–152
Bingham LJ 83
Bivolaru and Moldovan v France 74, 128–130
Bogdandy, A von 39–40
Bosphorus v Ireland
conflict rule, as 159–160
Dublin system and 98
presumption of equivalent protection 48–55, 60, 73–74, 87, 159–160
Bot AG 122–123, 125–126
Brügge 94
Bulgaria
international human rights treaties 151

Cassis de Dijon 93
Charter of Fundamental Rights
Article 4 100–101, 103–106, 107, 109, 110, 124–128, 130, 132, 179
Article 6 191–192
Article 7 32
Article 8 32
Article 23 25
Article 25 25
Article 26 25
Article 27 25
Article 33 25
Article 34 25
Article 34(1) 25
Article 35 25
Article 36 25
Article 37 25
Article 38 25
Article 47 122
Article 48 122
Article 51 33, 157–158
Article 51(1) 26

Article 52(3) 2, 4, 11–12, 33, 56, 58–62, 65, 66, 87, 111, 134, 156–157, 174, 175, 179, 195, 197, 199–202
Article 52(4) 33–34
Article 52(5) 25
Article 52(7) 33, 59
Article 53 34, 56, 66, 122–123, 157, 191, 195
binding nature 2, 24, 27, 28, 40, 43, 45, 63, 67
Charter Strategy 28
CJEU and 2, 5–6, 25–26, 31–32, 58–62, 63–65
CJEU case law 24–25, 60–62
conflict avoidance 156–157
'constitutional traditions common to Member States' 33–34
content 24–25
Council of Ministers proposals, compatibility 29–30
declaration 22–23
Dublin system and 97, 99–101, 103–106, 107, 109, 110
ECHR and 1, 2, 5, 6, 9, 11, 33, 56, 63, 87, 155–158, 168, 191–192, 196–197, 198, 200
ECtHR references to 65
enforcement 25
ESC rights 25
EU accession to ECHR 23, 35, 43, 45, 65, 87
EU integration and 44
EU law and legislative process 2, 27–31, 85–87
European Arrest Warrant and 120–121, 122–123, 124–128, 132, 134, 137
European Commission proposals, compatibility 27–29
European Parliament proposals, compatibility 30–31
external EU relations 24
Explanations relating to the Charter 25–26, 33, 59, 157, 191–192, 199
legal basis 24
legal status 23, 24
national constitutional rights and 33–35
national courts and 86–87
national judiciaries, role 84–85
objective 23, 24
Poland, application to 38
primacy doctrine 34, 85–86
primary EU law, as 24
principles and rights distinguished 25–26
scope 24, 26–27, 41
Solidarity 25
'third generation' rights 25
Treaty on European Union 23
Treaty of Lisbon 2, 23, 24
UK, application to 38

Churchill, Winston 16–17

CK and others 103–106, 110

Committee on Civil Liberties, Justice and Home Affairs (LIBE) 31

Committee of Ministers
enforcement of ECtHR judgments 79

Common European Asylum System (CEAS)
AFSJ *See* Area of Freedom, Security and Justice
Dublin system *See* Dublin system
generally 91

Common Foreign and Security Policy (CFSP) 24

conflict rules
balancing (proportionality balancing) 144
Bosphorus doctrine 159–160
Charter of Fundamental Rights 156–157, 175, 197, 199
conflict clauses, generally 153, 165, 174
conflict clauses in ECHR 158–160
conflict clauses in EU treaties 153–158
conform interpretation 144, 176–179, 195, 199–200
dates of conflicting treaties 154, 165–166
domestic effect of international law 146
erga omnes obligations and 170–171
EU law and ECHR 4, 5, 11, 47, 143–174
fundamental rights, conflict with ECHR 34–35
fundamental rights treaties, status 149–153, 155–156, 170–174, 175
international law 143, 161–174
jus cogens norms 161–163, 165, 167, 169, 171
Levy case 155
lex posterior derogat legi priori 165–166, 167
lex specialis derogat legi generali 167–172, 173
lex superior derogat legi inferiori 164–165, 167
multilateral treaties 161
national constitutions 145–146
national courts 143, 152–153
national legislation and EU law 4, 5, 11, 19–20, 146–149

pacta sunt servanda 154
primacy doctrine *See* primacy doctrine
treaty conflicts 143, 144–146, 153, 161
treaty divergences or inconsistencies 145
VCLT *See* Vienna Convention on the Law of Treaties
Connolly 54–55, 87
constitutional pluralism 6
Constitutional Treaty, EU 147, 148
Costa v ENEL 84
Council of Europe (CoE)
creation 15, 16–17
European Union and 15–16, 44
fundamental rights protection, generally 15–16, 17, 44
membership 1, 17
purpose 15, 17
Council of Ministers' proposals
Charter compatibility 29–30
Court of Justice of the European Union (CJEU)
A v B and Others 86
Abdida 66
Abdullahi 67, 100–101, 105, 179
Advocaten voor de Wereld 117–119
Åkerberg Fransson 26, 56, 58, 64
AMS 25
Aranyosi and Căldăraru 10, 119, 123–127, 131–132, 136–138, 183, 186–187, 192–193
Area of Freedom, Security and Justice 91
Article 344 TFEU and 69–70
asylum cases 2, 92, 95, 97
Brügge 94
Cassis de Dijon 93
Charter rights and principles 25–26, 31–32, 58–62, 63–65
CK and others 103–106, 110
Connolly 54–55, 87
Costa v ENEL 84
development of EU fundamental rights 19–21, 22, 24, 32, 200
Digital Rights Ireland 29, 30, 32
direct effect doctrine 84–85, 88
divergences between EU and ECHR law 4, 9, 91
Dorobantu 127–128, 136, 188
Draft Accession Agreement, rejection 2, 6, 37, 65–72
Dublin system 95, 97, 99–101, 103–106, 107–111
ECHR and 20–21, 34, 46, 56–62, 63, 87–88
ECtHR and 2, 4, 9, 36, 45–46, 54–55, 63–74, 87–88, 134–139, 198–200
ECtHR case law and 134–135, 156, 196
ECtHR compared 45–46
ECtHR interpretations, incompatible 33, 63, 92, 127–130, 176–179
enforcement of judgments 85
ERT line of cases 21
EU Charter and 2, 5–6, 24–25, 63–65
European Arrest Warrant decisions 10, 112–113, 120–127, 130, 136–138
expanding scope of EU law 2, 5, 19–21, 22, 24, 87
fundamental rights cases 2, 6, 7, 18, 20–21, 22, 24, 30, 31–32, 41–42, 63–65
fundamental rights court, as 40, 41–42, 43, 46, 63–65, 202
fundamental rights as general principles of EU law 38–39, 43, 56–58
Geitling and Sgarlata 18–19
generally 2, 45–46, 200
Glatzel 25
Google Spain 64
Gözütok 94
Hauer 20
Ibrahim and others 108
Iida 26–27
Internationale Handelsgesellschaf 84
Jaramillo 60
Jawo 107, 110
jurisdiction 22
Kamberaj 25, 57–58
Kücükdeveci 32, 38
legal parochialism 65
LM case 10, 113, 130–132, 134, 136, 137, 138, 192–193
MA and others 108–109
McB v LE 60
M'Bodj 66
Melloni 34–35, 67, 119, 122–123, 136, 137, 157, 186
Menci 4–5
ML case 127, 136
mutual recognition principle 9, 10, 66–69, 93, 94–95, 138
mutual trust principle 10, 66–69, 94–95, 113, 119, 139
N and others 61
national courts and 11–12, 84–88, 149–153
national measures derogating from EU law 20

national measures implementing or applying EU law 20
new rights, integration into EU system 38
Nold 20
NS case 10, 67, 99–100, 101, 103, 105, 110, 126, 177–179
Opinion 2/13 2, 6, 37, 42, 45, 46, 53, 55, 65–72, 87, 124, 157, 198
Opinion 2/94 35
Piotrowski 128, 137
preliminary references to 176, 185–186, 190–194, 195
preliminary rulings 12, 34, 50–51, 53, 122–123, 188–189
primacy doctrine 84–85
Puid 100–101, 179
Radu 119, 120–121, 122, 134, 136, 137
rights developed in case law 24–25, 63–65
Rutili 20
Simmenthal 84
Sky Österreich 64
Stauder 19
Stork 18
Taricco rule 189
Treaty of Amsterdam 22
Volker and Schecke 32
Wachauf line of cases 21
Zoran Spasic 64
courts
Brighton Declaration 3
CJEU *See* Court of Justice of the European Union
ECtHR *See* European Court of Human Rights
legal certainty diminished by multi-level system 3–4
national *See* national courts
criminal law
CJEU cases 2
criminal proceedings *See also* **European Arrest Warrant**
legality principle 118, 189
rights of suspects 40
Croatia
international human rights treaties 151
transfer of powers to EU 148
Cruz Villalón AG 45, 121
Czech Republic
international human rights treaties 150, 172
transfer of powers to EU 148
data protection
CJEU cases 2
EU policy, generally 40
Data Retention Directive 29, 32
de Búrca, G 63
democracy
CoE mission to protect 15, 17
EU Action Plan on Human Rights and Democracy 41
Treaty on European Union 18
Denmark
dualist legal system 74
transfer of powers to EU 148
Digital Rights Ireland 29, 30, 32
discrimination
EEC treaty 18
European Arrest Warrant and 118, 182
vertical application of Charter rights 38
Donnelly J 134
Dorobantu 127–128, 136, 188
Draft Accession Agreement (DAA)
Article 344 TFEU and 65–66, 69–70
co-respondent mechanism 65–66, 70–71
common foreign and security policy 66, 72
mutual trust and recognition principle 66–69
prior-involvement procedure 66, 71–72
rejection by CJEU 2, 6, 37, 65–72
dualist legal systems
European Convention on Human Rights 74–77, 81, 84, 149, 175
international treaties 146
national and international law 74–77
Dublin system
Abdullahi 67, 100–101, 105, 179
aim 9, 95–97
application 96
Area of Freedom, Security and Justice 91–92
Bosphorus presumption and 98
Charter rights and 97, 99–101, 103–106, 107, 109, 110
CJEU decisions 95, 97, 99–101, 103–106, 107–111
CK and others 103–106, 110
discretion, margin of 98
Dublin II 95, 98
Dublin III 92, 96, 103–106, 110–111
Dublin IV, proposed 96
EAW mechanism, comparability 126–127, 130

ECHR, compliance with 51–52, 97, 98–99, 102–103, 107, 109, 110–111
ECtHR cases 95, 98–99, 102–103, 109–111
EM (Eritrea) v Secretary of State for the Home Department 176–179, 195
EURODAC 96
'first point of entry' 96
fundamental rights in participating states 97
generally 9–10, 91–92, 95–97
Geneva Convention rights and 97
Ibrahim and others 108
inhuman and degrading treatment, prohibition 98–101, 102, 103–108, 110, 176–179, 180–181
Jawo 107, 110
MA and others 108–109
MSS v Belgium and Greece 51–52, 92, 98–99, 100, 110, 177
mutual trust principle 10, 68, 91–92, 96–97, 105, 106, 107–110
non-EU countries 96
non-refoulement principle 97, 98–99
NS and others 10, 67, 99–100, 101, 103, 105, 110, 126, 177–179
Puid 100–101, 179
Recital 32 10, 105, 110, 111
sovereignty clause 98, 103, 110
systemic deficiency test 100–101, 102, 103–110, 177–179
Tarakhel v Switzerland 68, 92, 100, 102–103, 105, 106, 110
Dupré, C 193

economic, social and cultural (ESC) rights
Charter of Fundamental Rights 25
EM (Eritrea) v Secretary of State for the Home Department 176–179, 195
equality
EU policy, generally 40
European Arrest Warrant and 118
Levy case 155
Treaty on European Union 18
***erga omnes* obligations** 170–172
Barcelona Traction 171
***ERT* line of cases** 21
EURODAC
Dublin system and 96
European Arrest Warrant (EAW)
adoption 112
advantages 114
Advocaten voor de Wereld case 117–119
Aranyosi and Căldăraru 10, 119, 123–127, 131–132, 136–138, 183, 186–187, 192–193
Avotiņš v Latvia 128–129
Bivolaru and Moldovan v France 128–130
Charter rights 120–121, 122–123, 124–128, 130, 132, 134
CJEU judgments 10, 112–113, 120–127, 130, 134–138
constitutional challenges 117
convictions *in absentia* 121, 124–127, 184–186
criticisms of 114–115
detention conditions in issuing state 127–128, 136, 180–181, 183, 187–188
Dorobantu 127–128, 136, 188
double criminality requirement 114–115, 118–119
Dublin Regulation, comparability 126–127, 130
ECtHR decisions 113, 116, 128–130, 134–135
equality principle 118
European Convention rights 120–121, 122–123, 128, 129, 130, 134–135
F-K case 182–183
fair trial, right to 112, 115, 119, 120–123, 132–133, 136, 137, 193
family life, right to 182–183
flagrant denial of justice test 133–135, 182, 193
Framework Decision, regulation by 10, 91, 117–118
fundamental rights infringements in issuing state 112–113, 116–117, 119–129, 136
fundamental rights obligations 114–117, 135, 136
generally 9, 112–114
human dignity, violation 188
incompatible ECtHR and CJEU judgments 127–130
inhuman and degrading treatment, prohibition 115, 116, 119, 123–130, 136, 180–181
issue, conditions to be met 114
judicial independence and 130–135, 237
Kelly aka Nolan 180–181
Krolik 183
legality principle 118, 189
LM case 10, 113, 130–132, 134, 136, 137, 138, 192–193

Melloni 34–35, 67, 119, 121–123, 136, 137, 157, 186
ML case 127, 136
Mr R case 184–187
mutual recognition principle 10, 112–113, 114, 116–119, 121, 124, 128, 136, 137, 185
mutual trust principle 112–113, 116–117, 119–130, 132–133, 135, 136–138, 182, 185
national constitutional law and 184–187
national courts 135–138
non-discrimination principle 118
non-execution, grounds for 112, 115–116, 138
Piotrowski 128, 137
pre-Charter period 117–119
presumption of equivalent protection 112, 121, 129
primacy doctrine and 34, 123, 136, 186
Radu 119, 120–121, 122, 134, 136, 137
Rettinger 180–181
Rostaş 181–182
rule of law principle, risk of breach 130–131, 193
TEU fundamental rights principles 116, 125, 132, 137
treaty amendments 147
two-step procedure 113, 125, 130, 133–139, 183, 192–193
European Atomic Energy Community (EURATOM) 18
European Coal and Steel Community (ECSC) 17, 18
European Commission
Better Regulation Guidelines 29
Charter Strategy 28
impact assessments 28–29
proposals, Charter compatibility 27–29
European Community
creation 16–19
objective 18
European Convention on Human Rights (ECHR)
acts of another Member State 52–54
acts of EU institutions 50–51
Article 1 79, 159–160
Article 3 47, 98–99, 102–103, 109, 122, 128, 130, 134, 158–159, 178–179, 180–181, 183
Article 5 180–181, 191
Article 6 50, 52, 55, 122, 133, 134–135, 184, 187
Article 7 189
Article 8 102, 159, 182, 183
Article 13 77–78, 99
Article 32 59
Article 34 134
Article 35(1) 78
Article 50 37
Article 53 4, 67, 78, 158
Article 59(2) 36
Bosphorus presumption of equivalent protection 48–55, 60, 73–74, 87, 98, 159–160
Charter of Fundamental Rights and 1, 2, 5–6, 9, 11, 33, 56, 63, 87, 155–158, 168, 191–192, 196–197, 198, 200–202
CJEU and 20–21, 46, 56–62, 63, 87–88
conflict clauses 158–160
conflicts with EU law 47, 143–174, 175–197
conflicts with other treaties 143–144, 158
domestic remedies to be exhausted first 5
Draft Accession Agreement (DAA) 2, 6, 37, 65–66, 68–72
dualist legal systems 74–77, 81, 84, 149, 175
Dublin system and 51–52, 97, 98–99, 102–103, 107, 109, 110–111
EAW mechanism and 120–121, 122–123, 128, 129, 134
ECtHR case law 30, 33, 59–60, 64, 87, 98–99
enforcement mechanisms 17
establishment 17
EU accession 16, 23, 35–37, 40, 42, 43, 45, 56, 65–72, 87, 191, 198
EU institutions 36, 50–51, 54–55
EU law and 1, 2, 3–4, 6–7, 11–12, 15, 16, 37–39, 46–62, 87–88, 149, 155–157, 191, 198, 200
EU Member States 36, 46–55
evolution of rights under 60
individual complaint mechanism 80
integration into EU 18
international treaty founding and governing 143–144
James and Others v United Kingdom 77–78
meaning and scope of rights under 11, 59–60
monist legal systems 74–76, 80–81, 84
MSS v Belgium and Greece 98–99, 100, 177
mutual trust principle 66–69, 92
national courts, role 3, 5, 9, 77–84, 149–153

national legislation and 4, 5, 45, 74–84, 149–153
non-EU Member States 49
non-refoulement principle 98–99
protection gap 54–55
Protocol 1 20
Protocol 14 79
Protocol 16 3, 66, 69, 78–79, 194
signatories 1, 20, 23
status in EU law 56–62
status in international treaty law 174, 175
supranational character 11
Tarakhel v Switzerland 102–103
Taricco rule and 189
Treaty on European Union 157
Treaty of Lisbon 2
violation, ECtHR hearings 1
Wagner and JMWL v Luxembourg 78
European Council 22–23
Joint Declaration on Human Rights 21
mutual recognition principle 93–94
European Court of Human Rights (ECtHR)
admissible cases 54–55, 87
advisory opinions 3
Ástráðsson 133
asylum cases 95
Avotiņš v Latvia 52–54, 73–74, 128
Bivolaru and Moldovan v France 74, 128–130
Bosphorus presumption of equivalent protection 48–55, 60, 73–74, 87, 98, 138, 159–160
case law 7, 30, 33, 45, 59–60, 63–65, 87
Charter of Fundamental Rights, references to 65
CJEU and 2, 4, 9, 36, 45–46, 54–55, 63–74, 87–88, 134–139, 156, 196, 198–200
CJEU compared 45–46
CJEU interpretations, incompatible 33, 63, 92, 127–130, 176–179
Committee of Ministers, role 79
compliance with judgments 78–80
Connolly 54–55, 87
development of EU fundamental rights 16, 33, 45, 60, 63
divergences between EU and ECHR law 4, 6–7, 9, 91
Dublin system 95, 98–99, 102–103, 109–111
enforcement of judgments 78–80
ergo omnes effect of judgments, implied 80
EU law and 16, 46–55, 200
European Arrest Warrant decisions 113, 116, 128–130
extraterritoriality 133
generally 2, 45
individual complaints 1
James and Others v United Kingdom 77–78
Kokkelvisserij v The Netherlands 50–51
legitimacy, challenges to 2
Matthews v United Kingdom 47
meaning and scope of ECHR rights, determination 59
Michaud v France 52
MSS v Belgium and Greece 51–52, 92, 98–99, 100, 110, 177
mutual recognition principle 9, 113
mutual trust principle 10
Nabil v Hungary 191
national courts and 2–3, 11–12, 69, 77–84, 88, 149, 189–190, 193–194
non-execution of judgments 2
Orchowski v Poland 180–181
overburdened 2
Paposhvili v Belgium 105
pilot judgments 79
protection gap 54–55, 87
reference to 78–79, 80
res interpretata 45
Soering v United Kingdom 133, 158–159, 178, 180
supranational jurisdiction 149
Tarakhel v Switzerland 68, 92, 100, 102–103, 105, 106, 110
Xero Flor w Polsce sp. z o.o. v Poland 133
European Defence Community Treaty (EDC Treaty) 17
European Economic Community (EEC)
establishment 18, 43
purpose 18, 43
Single European Act 22
European Parliament
Impact Assessment unit 31
legislative proposals, Charter compatibility 30–31
European Political Community Treaty (EPC Treaty) 17–18
European Social Charter 24
European Union (EU)
Brussels I Regulation 53
centralising effect of fundamental rights policy 39
Charter *See* Charter of Fundamental Rights
common foreign and security policy 66, 72

conflict clauses in EU treaties 153–158
conflicts with international treaties 143–144
Constitutional Treaty 147, 148
Council of Europe and 15–16, 44
creation 15, 16–19, 43
EAW *See* European Arrest Warrant
ECHR, accession to 16, 23, 35–37, 40, 42, 43, 45, 56, 65–72, 87, 191, 198
ECHR integration 18
establishment 143–144, 146
EU integration, generally 44
external relations 24, 41
founding principles 68–69
fundamental rights protection, generally 15–16, 18, 39–43, 68–69
international character 146–148
international law, Members bound by 163
international treaties, Members' right to enter 153
Istanbul Convention 40
law *See* European Union law
limits to European integration 185–187
Lisbon Treaty *See* Lisbon Treaty
Maastricht Treaty 22
Member States' transfer of power to 147–148
mutual recognition principle *See* mutual recognition principle
mutual trust principle *See* mutual trust principle
national constitutions and 147–148, 185–187
no explicit fundamental rights competence 40, 41, 42–43
policy-making process, generally 27
primacy doctrine, generally 144
responsibility for acts of another Member State 52–54
TEU *See* Treaty on European Union
treaties founding and governing 143–144, 146–147, 175

European Union (EU) institutions
ECHR and 36, 50–51
responsibility for acts of 50–51

European Union law
Bosphorus presumption of equivalent protection 48–55, 60, 73–74, 87, 98, 138, 159–160
CJEU *See* Court of Justice of the European Union
Commission Better Regulation Guidelines 29
Commission impact assessments 28–29
compatibility with Charter 27–31
compatibility with national law 19–20
conflict clauses in EU treaties 153–160
conflicts with ECHR 47, 143–174, 175–197
Council Regulation (EEC) 990/93 48–50
development by ECtHR 16, 33, 45, 60, 63, 87
development of fundamental rights protection 1–2, 8, 15–16, 19–45, 60, 63–65
direct effect doctrine 84–85, 88, 169
Direct Elections Act 1976 47
Directive 78/2000 38
ECHR and 1, 2, 3–4, 6–7, 11–12, 15, 16, 46–62, 87–88, 143–144, 149, 155–157, 191, 197, 202
ECtHR and 16, 46–55
EU Charter, generally 2, 11, 24
EU Treaties and 147
expanding scope 2, 5
founding principles 95
fundamental rights, role 39–43, 198
fundamental rights 'checklist' 28
fundamental rights culture 1–2, 8, 15–16, 19–45, 60, 63–65
fundamental rights as general principles of 37–39, 41–42, 43, 56–58, 68–69, 191
Habitats Directive 50–51
Interinstitutional Agreement on Better Law Making 29
international law, qualification as 146–147
international treaty law 147
Kokkelvisserij v The Netherlands 50–51
Matthews v United Kingdom 47
mutual recognition principle 91
mutual trust principle 91–92
national judiciaries and 84–85
national legislation and 45, 74, 77, 84–88, 145–149, 194–197
primacy doctrine *See* primacy doctrine
primary law 47, 153, 155–156
Reception Conditions Directive 190–192
Return Directive 190
review, preliminary reference procedure 190–194, 195
secondary legislation 40, 48
supranational character 11, 175
validity 147

extradition *See also* **European Arrest Warrant**
double criminality requirement 114–115, 118–119

Soering v United Kingdom 133, 158–159, 178, 180
extraterritoriality
ECtHR cases 133

fair trial, right to
European Arrest Warrant and 112, 115, 119, 120–123, 132–133, 137, 193
flagrant denial of justice test 133–135, 182, 193
Finland
transfer of powers to EU 148
Framework Decision EAW *See* **European Arrest Warrant**
France
ECHR, status 80, 81, 82
Levy case 155
monist legal system 75, 80
free movement of goods
Cassis de Dijon 93
freedom
Treaty on European Union 18
Frontini 20
fundamental rights
asylum law and 92
breach 22, 23–24
centralising effect of EU policy 39
Charter of *See* Charter of Fundamental Rights
checklist for legislative proposals 28
Citizenship and Free Movement of Persons (FREMP Working Party) 30
CJEU as human rights court 40, 43, 63–65, 202–203
conflicts between 34–35
'constitutional traditions common to Member States' 33–34
Council of Europe 15–16, 17, 44
development of EU law, generally 15–16, 19–45, 60, 63–65
ECHR *See* European Convention on Human Rights
ECtHR *See* European Court of Human Rights
enforcement 1, 22
erga omnes obligations 170–172
EU Action Plan on Human Rights and Democracy 41
EU compliance with 42–43
EU founding principle, as 68–69
EU law, generally 8, 37–43, 56, 68–69, 198
EU Member States, varying records 112
European Arrest Warrant *See* European Arrest Warrant
external EU relations 41
general principles of EU law, ECHR and 37–39, 41–42, 43, 56–58
hierarchy of systems 6–7, 9, 36
impact assessments and 28–29
international treaties *See* international treaties
Lisbon Treaty 16
mutual trust principle *See* mutual trust principle
national (constitutional) legislation 1
new, integration into EU system 38
primacy doctrine and 85, 186
principles and rights distinguished 25
protection within EU, generally 1–2
Treaty on European Union 18, 23, 116
vertical application 38
Fundamental Rights Agency (FRA) 30–31, 41

Geitling and Sgarlata 18–19
Geneva Convention
Dublin system and 97
Gerards, J and Fleuren, J 84
Germany
dualist legal system 74, 77, 81
ECHR, status 77, 81–82
Görgülü 81–82
international human rights treaties 151
limits to European integration 185–187
Mr R case 184–187
primacy doctrine and 85
Solange jurisprudence 19, 186–187
transfer of powers to EU 148
Glatzel 25
Google Spain 64
Görgülü 81–82
Gözütok 94
Greece
international human rights treaties 151

Hauer 20
human dignity
Treaty on European Union 18
human rights *See* **fundamental rights**

***IB* case** 121
Ibrahim and others 108
Iceland
Dublin system 96
Iida 26–27

Impact Assessment Board
fundamental rights and 28–29
inhuman and degrading treatment, prohibition
Dublin system and 98–101, 102, 103–108, 110, 176–179, 180–181
European Arrest Warrant and 115, 116, 119, 123–129, 136
Interinstitutional Agreement on Better Law Making 29
internal market
mutual trust and recognition principle 93
international law
conflict rules *See* conflict rules
customary 144, 161, 163
EU law as 146–148
EU Member States 163
jus cogens 161–163, 165, 167, 169, 171
lex specialis derogat legi generali 167–172, 173
national legislation 74–78, 146
pacta sunt servanda 154
international treaties
balancing (proportionality balancing) 144
conflict clauses 153–174
conflicts between 143, 144–145, 161 *see also* conflict rules
conform interpretation 144, 176–179
dates of conflicting treaties 154, 165–166
divergences or inconsistencies 145
dualist legal systems 146
EU Member States 153
human rights treaties, status 149–153, 155–156, 170–174, 175
lex posterior derogat legi priori 165–166, 167
lex specialis derogat legi generali 167–172, 173
lex superior derogat legi inferiori 164–165, 167
monist legal systems 146
multilateral 161
national legislation and 1, 11, 74–76, 149–153
pacta sunt servanda 154
primacy 151–152, 163, 169
VCLT *See* Vienna Convention on the Law of Treaties
Internationale Handelsgesellschaf 84
Ireland
Charter of Fundamental Rights 86
dualist legal system 74, 75, 76
ECHR, status 76, 82
Kelly aka Nolan 180–181
primacy doctrine and 85
Rettinger 180–181
Rostaş 181–182
Istanbul Convention 40
Italy
dualist legal system 74, 77, 81
ECHR, status 75, 77, 81
international human rights treaties 150
primacy doctrine and 85
status of EU law 75

Jacobs AG 19, 60
James and Others v United Kingdom 77–78
Jaramillo 60
Jawo 107, 110
Joint Declaration on Human Rights 21
judicial cooperation in EU
mutual recognition and trust principles 138
judicial independence
Ástráðsson 133
European Arrest Warrant and 130–135, 137
LM case 130–132
Xero Flor w Polsce sp. z o.o. v Poland 133
***jus cogens* norms**
Kadi 162–163
Nicaragua 162
Vienna Convention 161–163, 165, 169, 171

Kadi 162–163
Kamberaj 25, 57–58
Kelly aka Nolan 180
Kokkelvisserij v The Netherlands 50–51
Kokott AG 69, 196
Kücükdeveci 32, 38

Lagrange AG 154
Lambrecht, S and Rauchegger, C 64
legal certainty
multi-level court system and 3–4
Lenaerts, K 44, 202
lex posterior derogat legi priori 165–166, 167
lex specialis derogat legi generali
conflict rules 167–172, 173
self-contained regimes 169–172
lex superior derogat legi inferiori 164–165, 167
Liechtenstein
Dublin system 96
***LM* case** 10, 113, 130–132, 134, 136, 137, 138, 192–193

MA and others 108–109
Maastricht Treaty 22, 56
McB v LE 60
Mance LJ 83
Martinico, G 149
Matthews v United Kingdom 47
Melloni 34–35, 67, 119, 121–123, 136, 137, 157, 186
Menci 4–5
Michaud v France 52
migrants' rights *See* **asylum law; Dublin system**
minority rights
  Treaty on European Union 18
***ML* case** 127, 136
monist legal systems
  European Convention on Human Rights 74–76, 80–81, 84
  international treaties 146
  national and international law 74–75
Monnet, Jean 17
***Mr R* case** 184–187
MSS v Belgium and Greece 51–52, 92, 98–99, 100, 110, 177
mutual recognition principle
  Area of Freedom, Security and Justice 7, 9, 73, 91–95, 121, 124
  Avotiņš v Latvia 52–54, 73–74
  Brügge 94
  Brussels I Regulation 53
  Cassis de Dijon 93
  CJEU approach to 10, 94–95, 138
  CJEU Opinion 2/13 66–69, 124
  constitutional ranking 67–68
  ECtHR and CJEU 9, 113
  EU law, generally 91, 124, 138, 199
  European Arrest Warrant 10, 112–113, 114, 116–119, 121, 124–127, 129, 136, 137, 185
  fundamental rights protection and 92
  Görgülü 94
  judicial cooperation in EU 138
  meaning 94
  mutual trust principle and 94–95
  national criminal law and 136
  origins 93–95
  scope 95
  Treaty of Lisbon 94
mutual trust principle
  Area of Freedom, Security and Justice 7, 9, 73, 91–95, 124
  Avotiņš v Latvia 54, 73–74
  CJEU approach to 10, 94–95, 113, 116–117, 119
  CJEU Opinion 2/13 66–69, 124
  constitutional ranking 67–68
  Dublin system 10, 68, 91–92, 96–97, 105, 106, 107–110
  ECHR and 66–69, 92
  EU law, generally 91–92, 124, 199
  European Arrest Warrant and 112–113, 116–117, 119–130, 132–133, 135, 136–138, 182, 185
  fundamental rights protection and 7, 9, 92, 96–97
  judicial cooperation in EU 138
  meaning 94
  mutual recognition principle and 94–95
  national criminal law and 136
  NS case 10, 110
  origins 93–95
  presumption of fundamental rights compliance 96–97, 177–178

***N* case** 61, 190–192
national constitutions
  conflicting treaty obligations 145–146, 198
  EU Member States 147–148
  EU/ECHR conflicts and 183–197
  limits to European integration 185–187
national courts
  A v B and Others 86
  Austria 86
  case law 7, 74
  Charter of Fundamental Rights and 86–87
  CJEU and 11–12, 84–88
  as common courts of EU law 85–86, 88
  conflict rules *See* conflict rules
  conform interpretation, seeking 176–179, 195, 199–200
  direct effect doctrine 84–85, 88
  ECHR and 3, 5, 9, 69, 74, 77–84, 149–153, 189–194
  ECHR given priority over EU law 176, 179–183, 195
  ECtHR and 2–3, 11–12, 69, 77–84, 88, 149–153, 193–194
  ECtHR case law 189–190
  EU fundamental rights and 3
  EU law and 3, 84–88
  EU/ECHR conflicts, case law 175–197, 198–200
  European Arrest Warrant and 135–138
  Frontini 20

preliminary references to the CJEU 176, 185–186, 190–194, 195
primacy doctrine 84–85, 88
reframing EU/ECHR conflicts 176, 183–190
role 2, 3, 5
Solange jurisprudence 19, 186–187
Taricco rule 189
Treaty of Lisbon 84–86
national legislation
A v B and Others 86
conflicts between value systems or institutions 34–35
conflicts with ECHR *See* conflict rules
conflicts with EU law *See* conflict rules
derogating from EU law 20
dualist systems 74–77, 146
ECHR and, generally 4, 5, 45, 74–84, 149–153
EU law and 45, 74, 77, 84–88, 145–149, 194–197
fundamental rights as a core principle 69
implementing or applying EU law 20
international law and 74–77, 146
international treaties and 1, 11, 74–76, 149–153
monist systems 74–75, 146
mutual recognition principle and 136
mutual trust principle and 136
***ne bis in idem* principle** 4–5, 26
Netherlands
EU law and ECHR primacy 75–76, 80, 82, 85, 151
transfer of powers to EU 148
Nicaragua 162
Nold 20
Norway
Dublin system 96
NS and others 10, 67, 99–100, 101, 103, 105, 110, 126, 177–179

Paposhvili v Belgium 105
Pauwelyn, J 167
Phillips LJ 83
pilot judgments
European Court of Human Rights 79
Piotrowski 128, 137
Poland
Charter of Fundamental Rights 38
international human rights treaties 151
LM case 130–132, 136, 192–193
transfer of powers to EU 148
Portugal
Charter of Fundamental Rights 86
international human rights treaties 75, 150
Prigge 38
primacy doctrine
Belgium 76, 85
Charter of Fundamental Rights and 85–86
Charter and national constitutional rights 34–35
CJEU approach 85–86
Costa v ENEL 84
EU law, generally 77, 84–87, 123, 144, 186, 190
European Arrest Warrant and 123, 136
European Union, generally 144
fundamental rights legislation 85, 186
Germany 85
international treaties 151–152, 163, 169
Internationale Handelsgesellschaf 84
Ireland 85
Italy 85
national courts and 85–86, 88
Netherlands 76, 85
resistance to 84
Simmenthal 84
United Kingdom 85
protection gap
Connolly 54–55, 87
Puid 100–101, 179
Puškár 195–196

R (Ullah) v Special Adjudicator 83
Radu 119, 120–121, 122, 134, 136, 137
Ress J 50
Rettinger 180–181
Roadmap for strengthening procedural rights of suspected or accused persons in criminal proceedings 117
Romania
international human rights treaties 75, 149–150
prison conditions in, and EAW mechanism 187–188
Rome Treaty 18
Rostaş 181–182
rule of law
CoE mission to protect 15, 17
LM case 130–132, 136, 193
Treaty on European Union 18
Rutili 20

Saadi v Italy 180
Schuman, Robert 17
Sharpston AG 120–121, 134
Simmenthal 84
Single European Act 22
Sky Österreich 64
Slivenko and others v Latvia 159
Slovak Federal Republic
international human rights treaties 150, 172
Puškár 195–196
Soering v United Kingdom 133, 158–159, 178, 180
***Solange* jurisprudence** 19, 186–187
Spain
Charter of Fundamental Rights 86
international human rights treaties 75, 150
transfer of powers to EU 148
Spano, Róbert Ragnar 133
Spielmann, Dean 72–73
Stauder 19
Stork 18
subsidiarity
Charter of Fundamental Rights 26
Sweden
dualist legal system 74
Switzerland
Dublin system 96

Tanchev AG 105, 134
Tarakhel v Switzerland 68, 92, 100, 102–103, 105, 106, 110
***Taricco* rule** 189
'third generation' rights 25
transparency
Better Regulation Guidelines 29
Charter of Fundamental Rights 25
Treaty of Amsterdam 22
Area of Freedom, Security and Justice 93
sanctions, political mechanism for 22
Treaty on European Union (TEU)
accession of EU to ECHR 35–37
Article 2 18, 24, 95, 112, 137
Article 6 23, 38–39, 87, 112, 116, 137, 191
Article 6(1) 24
Article 6(2) 22, 35, 65, 66, 118
Article 6(3) 37–38, 56–58, 157
Article 7 22, 23
Article 19 85
Article 34(2) 118, 153
Article 48 147
Article 218 37
Charter of Fundamental Rights 23
European Arrest Warrant and 116, 125, 132
external EU policies 41
international treaties, Member States' right to enter 153
serious and persistent breach of fundamental rights 23–24
Treaty on the Functioning of the European Union (TFEU)
Article 165(3) 153
Article 166(3) 153
Article 167(3) 153
Article 168(3) 153
Article 267 85, 86
Article 344 65–66, 69–70
Article 351 153–154, 155
Treaty of Lisbon
accession of EU to ECHR 35–37, 43, 45
Article 1 146
Charter of Fundamental Rights 2, 23, 24, 32, 43
declaration 23
generally 7, 16, 45, 146, 203
international character of EU 146
mutual recognition principle 94
national courts, role 84–86
primacy doctrine 84–86
Vienna Convention 146–147

United Kingdom
Charter of Fundamental Rights 38
declaration of incompatibility 83
dualist legal system 74, 75, 76
ECHR, status 76, 77–78, 82–83
EM (Eritrea) v Secretary of State for the Home Department 176–179, 195
F-K case 182–183
national courts 82–83
parliamentary sovereignty doctrine 76, 85
primacy doctrine and 85
R (Ullah) v Special Adjudicator 83

Vienna Convention on the Law of Treaties (VCLT)
application 166–167, 169
Article 30 161, 163–167, 172, 174
conflict clauses 153, 165, 174
customary international law 161
generally 143, 145, 161–162, 173–174
inter se agreements 161
jus cogens 161–163, 165, 167, 169, 171
lex posterior derogat legi priori 165–166, 167
lex specialis derogat legi generali 167–172, 173

lex superior derogat legi inferiori 164–165, 167
multilateral treaties 161
status 161
subject matter of conflicting treaties 166–167
Treaty of Lisbon 146–147

***Wachauf* line of cases** 21
Weiler, J 61–62
Weiler, J and Alston, P 39

Xero Flor w Polsce sp. z o.o. v Poland 133

Zoran Spasic 64

www.ingramcontent.com/pod-product-compliance
Lightning Source LLC
Chambersburg PA
CBHW071258180926
51613CB00001B/72
9781509940585